D0889742

Praise for Richard Elliott Friedman's Other Ground-Breaking Works

For *The Hidden Face of God:*

"An exhilarating book. A work of biblical scholarship and metaphysical speculation that is also entertaining, reader-friendly and surprisingly passionate."—*Washington Post*

"A fascinating and dazzling piece of detective work."—*Publishers Weekly*

"This is a book that confronts momentous issues. Friedman, building out from his commanding knowledge of the biblical texts, proposes a striking evolution in the Western consciousness of God from the early iron age to the era of astrophysics."
—Robert Alter, author of *The Art of Biblical Narrative*

"Friedman captures and holds one's interest, pours out fresh ideas in a torrent, and thoroughly intrigues."—Frank Moore Cross, Hancock professor emeritus, Harvard University

"Lively and engaging, grounded in solid scholarship and passionately argued. Friedman raises some important questions and answers them persuasively."—Harold Kushner, author of *When Bad Things Happen to Good People*

For *Who Wrote the Bible?:*

"Friedman has gone much further than other scholars in analyzing the identity of the Biblical authors. Provocative. Promises to rekindle heated debate about the Good Book's origins."—*U.S. News & World Report*

"There is no other book quite like this one. It may well be unique. . . . brilliantly presented . . ."—*Los Angeles Times*

". . . intriguing . . . thought provoking . . . enjoyable . . . If you have ever thought biblical scholarship as dry as dust, then join detective Friedman as he tracks down his elusive authors. He has an eye for clues the average reader passes over unnoticed, and a lively style illumined by apt contemporary allusions."—*New York Times*

"Controversial. Now the documentary theory is entering the public arena. That's because of Mr. Friedman's book."—*The Wall Street Journal*

"An outstanding cultural contribution. Friedman brings this material to life with a keen instinct for holding off the disclosure of each discovery until exactly the right moment. This book could make Sunday School as exciting as Saturday night."—*Kirkus Reviews*

For *The Hidden Book in the Bible:*

"Richard Elliott Friedman is that rare biblical scholar who is both able to address a broad audience and willing to raise large speculative issues about the Bible. Now, in his new book, he proposes that we can detect in the Bible . . . the earliest long prose masterwork in world literature. Friedman can be impressively resourceful in seeing connections. Friedman has devised a challenging, exhilarating theory that will force biblical scholars to rethink some basic assumptions. A bold thesis that should give everyone pause."
—*New York Times*, Robert Alter

"[It] may be a brilliant piece of scholarly detective work and is surely a virtuoso piece of narrative construction. Provocative and engaging, Friedman's book blows like a fresh breeze through the halls of biblical studies."—*Publishers Weekly*

"Exciting, provocative, ambitious yet reverent, Friedman's latest book is as usual grounded in impeccable scholarship."—Donal Spoto, author of *The Hidden Jesus*

"Impressive new translations and interpretations of Hebrew scripture . . ."
—*San Francisco Chronicle*

For *Commentary on the Torah:*

"This is a culminating work by a remarkable scholar. Friedman has had a place in the company of the great scholars of the recent past; now we find him another place of equal value and importance among an older generation of legendary commentators on the Hebrew Scriptures: Kimhi and Abarbanel, Rashbam and Nachmanides, and that perennial master of the written Word, Rashi. We will leave the comparison at that point, in order to emphasize the remarkable scope and depth, the brilliance and winsomeness of this new but constant Companion to the Holy Scriptures."—David Noel Freedman

"Like the prototypical commentator, Rashi, Richard Friedman conveys a vast amount of learning with a light touch. His translations are fresh and vibrant. His masterful commentary blends scholarly precision, literary sensitivity and spiritual reflection."
—Daniel Matt, author of *The Essential Kabbalah*

"This is the way to study Torah! Friedman has produced a commentary that is both traditional and modern, drawing on the best of medieval commentaries and modern scholarship but adding his own perspective as well. He probes the theological and moral questions that make the Torah the ever-challenging text that it is. He models for us the most intelligent—and traditional—way to make the Torah live in our own lives."—Rabbi Elliot N. Dorff, Ph.D., rector and distinguished professor of philosophy, University of Judaism

"Friedman's reading is close and keen—able to dig out half-hidden details and problems in the text and offer convincing explanations of them. And yet none of what he writes is remote and obscure; it is rather in easily accessible prose, which brings out the continuing vitality and power of the Biblical text in a compelling way."—Peter Machinist, Hancock professor of Hebrew and other oriental languages, Harvard University

"Friedman has written a commentary that is both learned and engaging, consistently reaching out to the reader in order to make the Biblical text relevant to contemporary spiritual and ethical perplexity. Lucid, judicious, provocative; a major achievement."
—Arnold Eisen, professor of religious studies, Stanford University

THE
BIBLE

with Sources Revealed

Also by Richard Elliott Friedman:

Who Wrote the Bible?

The Hidden Book in the Bible

The Hidden Face of God
(originally published as *The Disappearance of God*)

Commentary on the Torah

The Exile and Biblical Narrative

The Creation of Sacred Literature, editor

The Poet and the Historian, editor

The Future of Biblical Studies: The Hebrew Scriptures, co-editor

THE

BIBLE

with Sources Revealed

A NEW VIEW INTO
THE FIVE BOOKS OF MOSES

Richard Elliott Friedman

HarperSanFrancisco

A Division of HarperCollins*Publishers*

HarperCollins books may be purchased for educational, business, or sales promotional use. For information please write: Special Markets Department, HarperCollins Publishers, Inc., 10 East 53rd Street, New York, NY 10022.

HarperCollins Web site: http://www.harpercollins.com
HarperCollins®, ▆®, and HarperSanFrancisco™
are trademarks of HarperCollins Publishers, Inc.

FIRST EDITION
Designed by Joseph Rutt

Library of Congress Cataloging-in-Publication Data
is available on request.

ISBN 0–06–053069–3

04 05 06 07 RRD(H) 10 9 8 7 6 5 4 3 2

This book is dedicated to
Michael Robinowitz
for the fiftieth anniversary of our friendship

CONTENTS

THE

BIBLE

with Sources Revealed

INTRODUCTION

For centuries, scholars from many backgrounds have worked on discovering how the Bible came to be. They were religious and nonreligious, Christians and Jews. Their task was not to prove whether the Bible's words were divinely revealed to the authors. That is a question of faith, not scholarship. Rather, they were trying to learn the history of those authors: what they wrote, when they wrote, and why they wrote. The solution that has been the most persuasive for over a century is known as the Documentary Hypothesis. The idea of this hypothesis is that the Bible's first books were formed through a long process. Ancient writers produced documents of poetry, prose, and law over many hundreds of years. And then editors used these documents as sources. Those editors fashioned from these sources the Bible that people have read for some two thousand years.

Those who disagreed with this hypothesis came from two opposite ends of the spectrum: the most traditional and the most radical. The most traditional scholars—mainly fundamentalist Christians and Orthodox Jews—adhered to the ancient answers to these questions: the first five books of the Bible were written down by Moses personally, the book of Joshua was written down by Joshua himself, and so on. The most radical scholars argued that the Bible's books were written later and later—and that they were less and less true.

One problem was that these groups of scholars only rarely engaged each other. Both traditional and radical scholars (and laypersons who followed them) have claimed that the hypothesis has been overthrown, that "hardly anybody believes that anymore," but, it must be said, neither group has ever responded to the classic and current arguments that made the Documentary Hypothesis the central model of the field. The hypothesis that, supposedly, no one believes anymore continues to be the model in which most scholars work. It continues to be taught in courses in major universities and seminaries. And it continues to be outlined in introductory textbooks on biblical studies. The primary arguments for it continue to go undebated—and frequently unmentioned.

This lack of engagement was unfortunate. I can testify to this from my personal experience. On one side, I have engaged in discussion and debates with my more radical colleagues at professional meetings and in print. And, on the other side, I have sat at the same table with Orthodox rabbis and with fundamentalist Christian scholars. And when I have presented this subject in university classes, I have tried to be as sensitive to the feelings of my fundamentalist and orthodox students as possible. The goal was not to shake them up or produce faith crises. Rather, I urged them to discuss these matters with their clergy, friends, family, or whomever they trusted to be helpful to them. I hope that we have all learned that we can sit down with people with whom we disagree and learn together. And so it is a shame that traditional and radical scholars so rarely engage the scholarship with which they disagree.

This should not come down to humorous disdain for the positions of others. It must come down to evidence. The collection of evidence in this book is meant to be the largest tabulation of evidence in one place to date. And it is hard data. "Style" is not included here, for example, since style is not usually a satisfactory criterion for distinguishing sources because it often involves subjective judgments. The exception is when we can observe an element of style that is definable and quantifiable. As an example of such an element, punning (paronomasia) occurs frequently in some of the sources but is rare in others.[1]

The straightforward tabulation of evidence appears in the pages that follow this introduction. The heart and soul of this book, though, are to be found in the text of the Bible itself, which follows that tabulation. In this book you will find the text of the first five books of the Bible: Genesis, Exodus, Leviticus, Numbers, and Deuteronomy. These books are known collectively by several names: as the Torah (from the Hebrew word meaning "instruction"), as the Humash (from the Hebrew word meaning "five"), as the Pentateuch (from the Greek, meaning "five scrolls"), and as the Five Books of Moses (reflecting the tradition that Moses first wrote them down). The sources of these five books are distinguished from one another by means of differing type font styles and colors. The most persuasive thing is to read the text itself with the sources distinguished. One can choose any of several ways to do this. One can read the component texts individually all the way through, one at a time. Or the reader can take several biblical stories and read each of them with an eye on the component stories coming

---

[1] Punning occurs frequently, for example, in the texts known in scholarship as the sources J and E, but it is rare in the texts known as the sources P and D.

together. Or the reader may choose to do what I did myself when I worked on this text: When I did my translation, I did not start at Genesis 1:1 and proceed in order. Rather, I translated the work in the order in which it was written.[2] I thus experienced, in a way, the formation of the Torah from its sources into what became the first five books of the Bible. It was an inspiring and instructive experience indeed, and now everyone who wishes is able to experience the formation of these books as well.

The purposes of this book, therefore, are:

1. To present the largest collection of evidence ever assembled in one place concerning this hypothesis.

2. To make it possible to read each of the source texts individually, to see their artistry, their views of God, Israel, and humankind, and their connection to their moment in history.

3. To make it possible to see the steps in the Bible's formation out of these sources.

4. To help readers appreciate that the whole is more than the sum of its parts. The Bible is a rich, complex, beautiful work as a result of the extraordinary way in which it was created.

The basic hypothesis is: These biblical books were assembled from sources. The historical context in which these sources were written and then edited together was as follows:

For two centuries (from 922 to 722 BCE) the biblical promised land was divided into two kingdoms: the kingdom of Israel in the north and the kingdom of Judah in the south. A text known as **J** was composed during this period. It is called J because, from its very first sentence, it refers to God by the proper name of YHWH (Jahwe in German, which was the language of many of the founding works in this field). It includes the famous biblical stories of the garden of Eden, Cain and Abel, the flood, the tower of Babylon ("Babel"), plus stories of the patriarchs Abraham, Isaac, and Jacob, as well as stories of Joseph and then of Moses, the exodus from Egypt, the revelation at Mount Sinai, and Israel's travels through the wilderness to the promised land. J was composed by an author living in the southern kingdom of Judah.

---

[2] I first translated J, then E. Then I pursued the editing of J and E together by the redactor known as RJE. Then I translated P, then D (in its stages). Then I translated the remaining small texts (such as Genesis 14). And then I pursued the editing of all these together by the redactor known as R.

A second text, known as **E**, was composed during this same period. E was composed by a priest living in the northern kingdom of Israel. It is called E because it refers to the deity simply as God, which in the original Hebrew is Elohim, or by the divine name El in its stories until the time of Moses. That is, unlike J, the E text developed the idea that the proper name of God, YHWH, was not known on earth until God chose to reveal it to Moses. E does not include any stories of the earth's early history, such as creation or the flood. Its first part appears to be missing. It begins in the middle of the story of Abraham. It then includes stories of Isaac, Jacob, Joseph, Moses, the plagues and exodus, the revelation at the mountain, and the wilderness travels. Some of these stories have parallels in the J stories, and some of them are different. For example, E includes the stories of the near sacrifice of Isaac and of the golden calf, which do not appear in J. J includes the story of Sodom and Gomorrah, which does not appear in E. And both J and E have the story of Joseph's being sold into slavery, but the details of how it happened differ. E also includes a law code (Exodus 21–23), which has no parallel in J.

In the year 722 BCE, the Assyrian empire destroyed the northern kingdom of Israel. J and E were then no longer separated by a border. These two versions of the people's history now existed side by side in the kingdom of Judah. In the years that followed, someone assembled a history that used both J and E as sources. The editor/historian who combined J and E into a single work is known as the Redactor of JE, or **RJE** for short.

The third main source is known as **P** because one of its central concerns is the priesthood. In critical scholarship, there are two main views of when it was composed. One view is that P was the latest of the sources, composed in the sixth or fifth century BCE. The other view is that P was composed not long after J and E were combined—specifically, that it was produced by the Jerusalem priesthood as an alternative to the history told in JE. Linguistic evidence now supports the latter view and virtually rules out the late date for P.[3] P, like E, involves both stories and laws. The P laws and instructions take up half of the books of Exodus and Numbers and practically all of the book of Leviticus. The P stories parallel the JE stories to a large extent in both content and order, including stories of creation, the flood, the divine covenant with Abraham, accounts of Isaac and Jacob, the enslavement, exodus, Sinai, and wilderness. Also like E, the P stories

---

[3]This is discussed below. I have also brought evidence for the earlier date for P in *The Exile and Biblical Narrative*, in *Who Wrote the Bible?*, and in "Torah" in *The Anchor Bible Dictionary* (New York: Doubleday, 1992), vol. 6, pp. 605–622.

follow the idea that the divine name YHWH was not known until the time of Moses.

The final main source is known as **D** because it takes up most of the book of Deuteronomy. More specifically, Deuteronomy comprises: (1) a law code that takes up chapters 12–26, known as **Dtn**; (2) an introductory text that precedes this law code and casts the book as the farewell speech of Moses before his death, taking up chapters 1–11, and then a continuation of this text following the law code, taking up chapters 27–30; (3) two old poems that are included as a parting message from Moses for the future (chapters 32 and 33); and (4) reports of the last acts of Moses, bringing together portions from all the sources (J, E, P, and D). D is part of a longer work, known as the Deuteronomistic History (**Dtr**), which includes the books of Deuteronomy, Joshua, Judges, 1 and 2 Samuel, and 1 and 2 Kings. Dtr contains sources that are as old as J and E or possibly even older, but the formation of the work took place in the reign of King Josiah of Judah, circa 622 BCE. It was later extended into a slightly longer second edition; this took place during the exile that followed the destruction of the southern kingdom of Judah by Babylon in 587 BCE. The original, Josianic edition of the Deuteronomistic history is called **Dtr1**; and the second, exilic edition is called **Dtr2**.

All these sources and editions were put together by an editor into the final five-book work. This final editor is known as the Redactor, or for short: **R.**

The next section of this book is a collection of evidence, containing the seven main bodies of evidence in support of this hypothesis. After that section comes the text of the first five books of the Bible in English translation. The sources and editing are identified in that text by distinctly styled and colored fonts.

Identification of the sources was attempted in books as long as a hundred years ago. One work, called "The Polychrome Bible" (1903), used colors. Another used lines and columns in the text (Carpenter and Hartford-Battersby, 1902). These were not successful. I do not know all of the reasons, but I can readily imagine the problems of printing and cost involved in those days. But advances in technology in our generation have now made it possible for everyone to have a Bible with this information.

In order to make the sources easy to identify at a glance, we found that it was best to use a variety of tools available for printing: various fonts, bold and italic typefaces. We were also able to use two colors to aid identification, and we used background screens to show where redactors had added to the text. A key to the sources appears on page 32. A brief version of the key appears at the top of each right-hand page as an additional aid.

ADDITIONAL NOTES

The English translation here is my own. For those who are interested, my explanation of the standards of my translation may be found in my *Commentary on the Torah*, pp. xiii–xvi.[4]

Some of these sources and editorial work extend beyond Deuteronomy. I have presented evidence elsewhere that J continues into a narrative that is distributed through the books of Joshua, Judges, 1 and 2 Samuel, and the first two chapters of 1 Kings.[5] P also appears to me clearly to continue into the latter half of the book of Joshua. And Dtr1 and Dtr2 encompass the books of Deuteronomy through 2 Kings. But these go beyond the scope of this book, which is meant to cover the five books of the Torah.

The process of identifying the sources is a continuing task. Some of the source identifications of verses here are different from those I made in *Who Wrote the Bible?*, which first appeared fifteen years ago, and which were modified in a second edition. Where these differences occur, readers should regard the identifications in this book as representing my more recent thinking.

I have assembled evidence in other books and articles to show the flaws in recent attacks on the Documentary Hypothesis from the radical and traditional ends of the spectrum. The present book is more concerned with the positive presentation of the evidence on which the hypothesis stands. For those who wish to see the evidence against those recent attacks, see the Appendix in *The Hidden Book in the Bible* (pp. 350–378); and my articles "Solomon and the Great Histories," in *Jerusalem in Bible and Archaeology— The First Temple Period*, ed. Ann Killebrew and Andrew Vaughn (Atlanta: Society of Biblical Literature, 2002); "An Essay on Method," in *Le-David Maskil*, ed. Richard Elliott Friedman and William Henry Propp (Biblical and Judaic Studies from the University of California, San Diego; Winona Lake, IN: Eisenbrauns, 2003); "Some Recent Non-arguments Concerning the Documentary Hypothesis," in *Texts, Temples, and Traditions: A Tribute to Menahem Haran*, ed. Michael Fox et al. (Winona Lake, IN: Eisenbrauns, 1996), pp. 87–101; and "Late for a Very Important Date," *Bible Review* 9:6 (1993): 12–16.

---

[4]One difference: italics for emphasis in the *Commentary on the Torah* are eliminated here because they might be misunderstood to be a source marker.

[5]R. E. Friedman, *The Hidden Book in the Bible* (San Francisco: HarperSanFrancisco, 1998).

COLLECTION
OF EVIDENCE

The Seven Main Arguments

The process of identifying the biblical sources took centuries. The process of refining our identifications of these sources has been ongoing, and it continues to the present day. Initially, it was a tentative division based on simple factors: where the name of God appeared in the texts, similar stories appearing twice in the texts, contradictions of fact between one text and another. Accounts of this early identifying and refining may be found in many introductions to this subject and in my *Who Wrote the Bible?* The collection of evidence here is not a review of that history of the subject. It is a tabulation of the evidence that has emerged that establishes the hypothesis. It is grouped here in seven categories, which form the seven main arguments for the hypothesis in my judgment.

1. LINGUISTIC

When we separate the texts that have been identified with the various sources, we find that they reflect the Hebrew language of several distinct periods.

The development of Hebrew that we observe through these successive periods indicates that:

+ The Hebrew of J and E comes from the earliest stage of biblical Hebrew.

+ The Hebrew of P comes from a later stage of the language.

+ The Hebrew of the Deuteronomistic texts comes from a still later stage of the language.

+ P comes from an earlier stage of Hebrew than the Hebrew of the book of Ezekiel (which comes from the time of the Babylonian exile).

✦ All of these main sources come from a stage of Hebrew known as Classical Biblical Hebrew, which is earlier than the Hebrew of the postexilic, Persian period (known as Late Biblical Hebrew).

This chronology of the language of the sources is confirmed by Hebrew texts outside the Bible. The characteristics of Classical Biblical Hebrew are confirmed through comparison with inscriptions that have been discovered through archaeology, which come from the period before the Babylonian exile (587 BCE). The characteristics of Late Biblical Hebrew are confirmed through comparison with the Hebrew of later sources such as the Dead Sea Scrolls.[1]

Despite the power of this evidence, it is practically never mentioned by those who oppose the hypothesis.

2. TERMINOLOGY

Certain words and phrases occur disproportionately—or even entirely—in one source but not in others. The quantity of such terms that consistently belong to a particular source is considerable. Thus:

The mountain that is called Sinai in J and P (twenty times) is called Horeb or "the Mountain of God" in E and D (fourteen times). In thirty-four occurrences of these names, there is no exception to this distinction.

The phrase "in that very day" (*bě'eṣem hayyôm hazzeh*) occurs eleven times in the Torah. Ten of the eleven are in P. (And the eleventh is in R, in a passage that R modeled on P; Deut 32:48.)

The phrase "the place where YHWH sets his name" or "the place where YHWH tents his name" occurs ten times in D but never in J, E, or P.

---

[1]Robert Polzin, *Late Biblical Hebrew: Toward an Historical Typology of Biblical Hebrew Prose* (Atlanta: Scholars Press, 1976); Gary Rendsburg, "Late Biblical Hebrew and the Date of P," *Journal of the Ancient Near Eastern Society* 12 (1980): 65–80; Ziony Zevit, "Converging Lines of Evidence Bearing on the Date of P," *Zeitschrift für die alttestamentliche Wissenschaft* 94 (1982): 502–509; Jacob Milgrom, *Leviticus 1–16*, Anchor Bible 3 (New York: Doubleday, 1991), pp. 3–13; Milgrom, "Numbers, Book of," *Anchor Bible Dictionary*, vol. 4, pp. 1148–1149; Avi Hurvitz, "The Evidence of Language in Dating the Priestly Code," *Revue Biblique* 81 (1974): 24–56; Hurvitz, *A Linguistic Study of the Relationship Between the Priestly Source and the Book of Ezekiel* (Paris: Gabalda, 1982); Hurvitz, בין לשון ללשון (Jerusalem: Bialik Institute, 1972); Hurvitz, "Continuity and Innovation in Biblical Hebrew—The Case of 'Semantic Change' in Post-Exilic Writings," *Abr-Naharaim* Supp. 4 (1995), pp. 1–10; Hurvitz, "The Usage of שש and בוץ in the Bible and Its Implication for the Date of P," *Harvard Theological Review* 60 (1967): 117–121; Ronald Hendel, "'Begetting' and 'Being Born' in the Pentateuch: Notes on Historical Linguistics and Source Criticism," *Vetus Testamentum* 50 (2000): 38–46.

The phrase "gathered to his people" as a euphemism for death occurs eleven times, and all eleven are in P.

The phrase "fire came out from before YHWH" occurs three times, all in P.

The phrase "and he [or they] fell on his face" occurs eight times, all in P.

The phrase "be fruitful and multiply" occurs twelve times, all in P.

The phrase "YHWH's glory" (*kĕbōd yhwh*) occurs thirteen times, and twelve are in P.

The word "plague" (*ngp*) occurs fifteen times; fourteen are in P.

The word "possession" (*'ăhuzzāh*) occurs thirty-five times in the Torah, and thirty-three are in P. (The thirty-fourth is an R passage repeating a verse from P, and the thirty-fifth is uncertain.)

The word "chieftain" (*nāśî'*) occurs sixty-nine times in the Torah. Sixty-seven are in P. (The other two are in J and E.)

The word "congregation" (*'ēdāh*) occurs more than one hundred times in the Torah, all in P, without a single exception.

The root *'dp* occurs eight times in the Torah, and they are all in P.

The word "property" (*rĕkûš*) occurs in the anomalous source in Genesis 14 (four times) and once in the words of the Redactor. It occurs eight times in the four main sources, and all eight are in P, never in J, E, or D.

The word "complain" (Hebrew *lwn* and *tĕlûnôt*) occurs twenty-three times in the Torah, and twenty-two are in P.

The word "cubit" occurs fifty-nine times in the Torah, and fifty-six are in P.

The term "to expire" (*gw'*) occurs eleven times in P but never in J, E, or D.

The phrase "lengthen your days in the land" occurs twelve times, and eleven are in D.

The phrase "with all your heart and with all your soul" occurs nine times, and all are in D.

The phrases "to go after other gods" and "to turn to other gods" and "to worship other gods" occur thirteen times, all in D.

The phrase "listen to the voice of YHWH" (*šm' bqwl yhwh*) occurs twelve times, all in D.

The term "to lie with" as a euphemism for sex (*škb*) occurs thirteen times in the Torah, and eleven are in J. (The other two occur in a single passage in E; Gen 30:15–16.)

The term "to know" as a euphemism for sex (*yd'*) occurs five times in J but never in the other sources.

The term "Sheol," identifying the place where the dead go, occurs six times in J but never in the other sources.

The term "to suffer" (*'ṣb*) occurs seven times, and all seven are in J.[2]

3. CONSISTENT CONTENT

a) *The Revelation of God's Name*

This line of evidence is frequently described as a matter of terminology: namely, that different sources use different names for God. But that is not correct. The point is not that sources have different names of God. The point is that the different sources have a different idea of when the name YHWH was first revealed to humans. According to J, the name was known since the earliest generations of humans. Referring to a generation before the flood, J says explicitly, "Then it was begun to invoke the name YHWH" (Gen 4:26). The use of the name by humans may go back even earlier in J, because Eve uses it when she names Cain (Gen 4:1). But in E and P it is stated just as explicitly that YHWH does not reveal this name until the generation of Moses. In Genesis YHWH instead tells Abraham that His name is El Shadday, thus:

> YHWH appeared to Abram and said to him, "I am El Shadday."
> (Gen 17:1)

And then when YHWH speaks to Moses in Exodus, the text says:

> And God spoke to Moses and said to him, "I am YHWH. And I appeared to Abraham, to Isaac, and to Jacob as El Shadday, and I was not known to them by my name, YHWH.
> (Exod 6:2–3)

The sources in the text are then nearly 100 percent consistent on this matter. The E and P sources identify God as El or simply as "God" (Hebrew: Elohim) until the name is revealed to Moses. After that, they use the name YHWH as well. The J source meanwhile uses the name YHWH from the beginning.

I added one more element to this picture. The J source never uses the word God (Elohim) in narration. When individual persons in the story are

---

[2] I have limited the cases here to terminology within the Torah itself. For fifty cases of terms that occur disproportionately or entirely in J or in texts related to J that are found in Joshua, Judges, Samuel, and Kings, see R. E. Friedman, *The Hidden Book in the Bible*, Appendix 4, pp. 379–389.

quoted, they may use this word; but the J *narrator* never uses the word, without a single exception in the Masoretic Text.

For the entire Torah, the picture is as follows: the names YHWH and El and the word God (Elohim) occur more than two thousand times, and the number of exceptions to this picture is three. Despite this phenomenal fact, we still find writers on this subject asserting that "the names of God" do not prove anything.

b) The Sacred Objects: Tabernacle, Ark, Cherubs, Urim and Tummim, Moses' Staff and Aaron's Staff

The Tabernacle is mentioned more than two hundred times in P. It receives more attention than any other subject. It is the only permitted site of sacrifice. It is the place where major ceremonies and laws must be carried out. It is the place where all revelation takes place after Sinai. But it is never so much as mentioned in J or D. It is mentioned three times in E.

The ark is identified as being crucial to Israel's travels and military success in J (Num 10:33–36; 14:44), but it is never mentioned in E.

Golden cherubs spread their wings over the ark in P. And cherubs guard the way to the garden of Eden in J. But they are not mentioned in E or D.

In P, the Urim and Tummim are kept in the High Priest's breastplate and are used in apparent divine consultation in judgment. But they are never mentioned in J, E, or D.[3]

In E, miracles are performed with Moses' staff (Exod 4:2–5,17, 20; 7:15–17,20b; 9:23; 10:13; 17:5–6,8). But in P, it is Aaron's staff that is used for performing miracles (Exod 7:9–12,19; 8:1–2,12–13; Num 17:16–26; 20:8).[4]

c) Priestly Leadership

In the P source, access to the divine is limited to Aaronid priests. In all the stories in P, there are no mentions of dreams, of angels, or talking animals, though these things occur in J, E, and D. As for human leaders: the words "prophet" and "prophesy" occur thirteen times in E and D, but not in P (or J). The single exceptional occurrence of the word "prophet" in P

---

[3]In the Torah, outside of P, they are mentioned only in the old poem "The Blessing of Moses" in Deut 33:8.

[4]The sole possible exception is the P episode of the Red Sea, in which Moses holds his staff as he raises his hand (the same hand or the other one?) over the sea as it splits.

(Exod 7:1) uses the word figuratively, and it refers to the High Priest Aaron himself! Judges, too, are never mentioned in P (as opposed to D, which says: go to the priest *and the judges* in matters of law). In P, only the Aaronid priests have access to the Urim and Tummim. In P, all other, non-Aaronid Levites are not priests. In P, atonement for sin is to be achieved only by means of sacrifices that are brought to the Aaronid priests. It is not achieved by mere repentance or through divine mercy. Indeed, in P the words "mercy," "grace," "repentance," and "kindness" (*hesed*) never occur.

This is more than a point of terminology. P not only lacks the terms that express divine mercy; its stories as well convey the merciful side of God far less than the other sources' stories do. For example, in the story of the scouts whom Moses sends into the land, in the J version God says He will destroy the people and start over with a new nation descended from Moses; but Moses intercedes, God relents, and the divine sentence is commuted to forty years in the wilderness instead. But in P there is no such entreaty and relenting; God simply declares the forty-year sentence, and that is that. In both terminology and narrative, P characterizes God as acting according to justice more than as acting according to mercy. If one wishes to be forgiven for an offense, one cannot simply be sorry; one must bring a sacrifice to the priest. As with the absence of angels and prophets, in P the priesthood is the only sanctioned path to God.

In D, on the other hand, all Levites are priests. P regularly refers to "the priests *and* the Levites" (that is, as two separate groups) while D just as regularly refers to "the Levitical priests" (that is, as a single group).

Further conveying the idea in P that priests are the only channel to God, there are no blatant anthropomorphisms in P. In J, God walks in the garden of Eden, personally makes Adam's and Eve's first clothing, personally closes Noah's ark and smells Noah's sacrifice. In E, God wrestles with Jacob and stands on the crag at Meribah as Moses strikes it and water comes out. And in E and perhaps J as well, Moses actually sees the form of God at Sinai/Horeb. In P there is nothing so direct and physical as this. In P such things are metaphorical, as when the Egyptian magicians say that a plague is "the finger of God," or they are mysterious, as when humans are said to be created "in the image of God," which may or may not mean something physical.

d) Numbers

Ages, dates, measurements, numbers, order, and precise instructions are an obvious, major concern in P. There is nothing even nearly comparable in degree in J, E, or D.

4. CONTINUITY OF TEXTS (NARRATIVE FLOW)

One of the most compelling arguments for the existence of the source documents is the fact that, when the sources are separated from one another, we can read each source as a flowing, sensible text. That is, the story continues without a break. One of the primary purposes of this book is to demonstrate this fact. One can read the texts and see that, when we separate the two flood stories and read each of them (J and P, Genesis 6–9), for example, each reads as a complete, continuous story. And we can observe this kind of continuity through at least 90 percent of the text from Genesis to Deuteronomy.

Specifically, the combined JE text that was assembled by RJE reads as a flowing narrative, with only an occasional gap. When interrupted by material from P or other sources, it picks up after the interruption where it had left off. The P text likewise is a flowing narrative, with only an occasional lacuna. Within JE, each of its source texts, J and E, flows sensibly much of the time as well, but not always. It appears that RJE was willing to make cuts in his received texts (J and E) to a far greater degree than was R in his received texts (JE, P, D, and other, smaller texts).

This high degree of narrative continuity in P also weighs against supplementary versions of the hypothesis, in which some scholars propose that P was never an independent document. They argue that P was rather composed around the JE text as a supplement to it. The narrative flow of P is entirely contrary to these models.[5]

One might object that the scholar has simply divided the text in such a way as to produce this result. But that is not possible. So much of the text flows smoothly in this way that it is not possible that any scholar could have constructed it to do so while keeping all the evidence consistently within sources. The scholar would still have to keep all the sources' similar versions of common stories (known as "doublets") separated. The scholar would still have to keep all the characteristic terminology of each source within the passages attributed to that particular source. The scholar would still have to keep all the linguistic evidence for the stages of Hebrew intact, all the occurrences of the divine name consistent within sources, and all the other lines of evidence intact—all of this while producing stories that flow smoothly. I submit that no such phenomenally consistent results would be possible to construct.

---

[5]See William H. C. Propp, "The Priestly Source Recovered Intact?" *Vetus Testamentum* 46 (1996): 458–478, for bibliography and treatment of the arguments on this matter. To my mind, Propp's arguments and evidence weigh definitively against supplementary hypotheses.

5. CONNECTIONS WITH OTHER PARTS OF THE BIBLE

When distinguished from one another, the individual sources each have specific affinities with particular portions of the Bible. D has well-known parallels of wording with the book of Jeremiah. P has such parallels with the book of Ezekiel. J and E are particularly connected with the book of Hosea. This is not simply a matter of a coincidence of subject matter in these parallel texts. It is a proper connection of language and views between particular sources and particular prophetic works.

a) Jeremiah and D

In treating the book of Jeremiah, it is customary to distinguish the poetic portions of the book from the prose. When we do so, we find that D has marked connections to both the poetry and the prose of the book of Jeremiah.[6] In the poetry, there are at least forty-five occurrences of terms or phrases that are characteristic of D and/or the Deuteronomistic history. For example:

✦ from the smallest to the biggest

✦ stubborn and rebellious

✦ early rain and late rain in its time

✦ grain, wine, oil, herd, flock

✦ they left me

✦ go after Baal (or: other gods)

✦ [*dōmen*] on the face of the field

✦ circumcise your heart[7]

✦ they went after emptiness and became empty

---

[6]For discussion, history of scholarship, and bibliography on the relationship between Jeremiah and the Deuteronomistic history, see Jack R. Lundbom, "Jeremiah, Book of," *Anchor Bible Dictionary*, vol. 3, pp. 706–721; R. E. Friedman, "The Deuteronomistic School," in *Fortunate the Eyes That See: Essays in Honor of David Noel Freedman in Celebration of His Seventieth Birthday*, ed. A. Beck et al. (Grand Rapids, MI: Eerdmans, 1995), pp. 70–80; L. G. Perdue and B. W. Kovacs, eds., *A Prophet to the Nations: Essays in Jeremiah Studies* (Winona Lake, IN: Eisenbrauns, 1984); Louis Stulman, *The Prose Sermons of the Book of Jeremiah* (Atlanta: Scholars Press, 1986); S. Mowinckel, *Zur Komposition des Buches Jeremia* (Oslo, 1914); and Mowinckel, *Prophecy and Tradition* (Oslo,1946).

[7]For a lengthier treatment of these texts, even limiting the cases to language that occurs only in Jeremiah and Dtr and nowhere else in the Hebrew Bible, and further limiting these cases strictly to occurrences of such language that are integral to their poetic contexts and not suspect of having been added secondarily, see Friedman, "The Deuteronomistic School," pp. 76–78.

When we examine the prose of Jeremiah, we find an even more pervasive array of parallels with the language of D and the Deuteronomistic history. Thirty chapters of prose in Jeremiah have terms and phrases that are characteristic of Dtr. For example:

+ with all my heart and all my soul
+ brought them out from the land of Egypt, from the iron furnace
+ all the array of the skies
+ and it will be, if you *listen* to YHWH
+ they left me and burnt incense to other gods
+ on every high hill and under every attractive tree
+ obstinacy of heart
+ an alien, an orphan, or a widow
+ [God's] name is called on this house
+ cast them out from before His face
+ your carcass will become food for every bird of the skies and for the animals of the earth, with no one making them afraid
+ I call witness
+ here, I'm bringing a bad thing
+ everyone who hears it: his two ears will ring
+ fire has ignited in my anger

b) Ezekiel and P

Parallels between P and the book of Ezekiel are at least as noticeable and striking as those between D and Jeremiah. For example:

+ The P list of blessings and curses in Leviticus 26 promises blessings "if you will go by my laws, and if you will observe my commandments, and you will do them" (26:3), and it promises curses "if you will reject my laws, and if your souls will scorn my judgments so as not to do all my commandments" (26:14). Ezekiel indicts the people, drawing on those words: "You did not go by my laws, and you did not do my judgments" (5:7).
+ The P curses include "you will eat your sons' flesh" (26:29). Ezekiel threatens, "fathers will eat sons" (5:10).
+ Ezekiel's warnings in that verse also use the word *zrh* for scattering, which likewise occurs in the P curse passage (Lev 26:33); and

Ezekiel uses the word šʾr for a remnant in that verse, which occurs in the P context as well (Lev 26:36,39).

✦ P threatens: "and I shall let loose the wild animal among you, and it will bereave you . . . and I shall bring a sword over you . . . and I shall let an epidemic go among you" (Lev 26:22,25). And Ezekiel says: "I shall let loose hunger and wild animal, and they will bereave you, and epidemic and blood will pass through you, and I shall bring a sword over you" (5:17).

✦ In the P version of the exodus from Egypt, YHWH says to Moses, "I shall bring you to the land that I raised my hand to give to Abraham, to Isaac, and to Jacob, and I shall give it to you" (Exod 6:8). In the book of Ezekiel, YHWH says to Ezekiel, "I brought them to the land that I raised my hand to give to them" (Ezek 20:28; see also 20:6,42).

✦ There are other matching elements between these two passages, Exodus 6 and Ezekiel 20. Both have references to YHWH's making Himself known (in the Niphal form of the root *ydʿ*—Exod 6:3; Ezek 20:5). Both have references to God's outstretched arm (Exod 6:6; Ezek 20:33–34).

✦ In P, God charges the priests "to distinguish between the holy and the secular, and between the impure and the pure" (Lev 10:10). In Ezekiel, God criticizes the priests because they "have not distinguished between holy and secular and have not made known [the difference] between the impure and the pure" (Ezek 22:26).

For more examples, see Exod 6:6–7 and cf. Ezek 20:6,9; see Lev 26:21 and cf. Ezek 20:8; and see Lev 26:43 and cf. Ezek 20:13,16,24.

Especially noteworthy is the recent demonstration by William Propp that a passage in Ezekiel quotes a passage from P that is divided as it stands in the combined text of the Torah.[8]

c) Hosea and J and E

Hosea, meanwhile, when speaking about Jacob and Esau, cites only J and E, but nothing of the P version of those events:

In the womb he "heeled" his brother,
and by his might he fought with God,
and he fought with an angel and was able;

---

[8]See note 5.

he cried, and he was gracious to him.
He found him at Beth-El,
and there He spoke with him.
(Hos 12:4–5)

The connection between the womb and the grabbing of his brother's heel is well known from J (Gen 25:24–26). The fighting with God[9] and being "able" connects to an equally well known passage from E (Gen 32:25–31). The reference to finding him at Beth-El and especially referring to speaking "with" (Hebrew *'im*) him calls to mind the J version of the story of the revelation to Jacob (Gen 28:13–16,19).[10]

Hosea also refers to the Israelites' heresy at Baal Peor (Hos 9:10). This event is known from J (Num 25:1–5). Only J refers to it as "Baal Peor." The P version of this event speaks of "the matter of Peor" (Num 25:18 [twice]; 31:16) but never uses the name Baal Peor.

d) J and the Court History

A vast series of connections exists between J and the Court History of David, which takes up nearly all of the book of 2 Samuel. This has been observed by many scholars during the past century. They have offered a variety of explanations for it, including that the two texts were written by the same author, or that one text imitated the other or was influenced by the other. I have presented the evidence that J and the Court History, as well as some texts in Joshua, Judges, and 1 Samuel, were written by the same author. I refer those who are interested in the broader treatment of this matter, with bibliography and the evidence and arguments for the common

---

[9]The poetic parallel between its being a fight with God and, at the same time, with an angel corresponds to the E text in Genesis, in which Jacob fights with "a man," but then is named Israel, which is explained as meaning "fights with God." And Jacob names the place Peni-El, which is explained as meaning "face of God," because, he says, "I've seen God face-to-face." The hypostasis of God through the form of a man is an angel. See my *Commentary on the Torah*, pp. 63 and 112; and *The Hidden Face of God*, pp. 9–13.

[10]Alan Jenks argues that this passage in Hosea does not refer specifically to J or E, but rather to common epic traditions behind those two sources. Jenks, *The Elohist and North Israelite Traditions* (Atlanta: Scholars Press, 1977), p. 133. He bases this argument on differences of detail: he says that Jacob "heeled" his brother outside the womb, not *"in the womb"* in J; and the mention of crying has no referent in the J story. In the first place, in J Jacob does in fact come out of the womb already holding Esau's heel—that is, he was already grasping it from "in" the womb. But more to the point, the text in Hosea is poetry, and we cannot read it with the specificity of the prose accounts in Genesis. A poet's images need not be restricted to the prose text that is their source. Nonetheless, the details that are included in this text do point to J and E as being its sources, and they do not point to P or D.

authorship of J and the Court History, to my *The Hidden Book in the Bible.*[11] For the purpose of this present collection of evidence, I simply note the fact that it is possible to observe a singular connection between the Court History and J, whereas there is no such connection with E, P, or D. This is further strong evidence that J was originally an independent source.

6. RELATIONSHIPS AMONG THE SOURCES: TO EACH OTHER AND TO HISTORY

The sources each have connections to specific circumstances in history. And they have identifiable relationships with each other.

a) J and E and the Kingdoms of Judah and Israel

From 922 to 722, Israel was divided into two kingdoms: the kingdom of Israel in the north and the kingdom of Judah in the south. J has numerous elements that connect it with Judah, and E has numerous elements that connect it with Israel:

In J Abraham lives in Hebron/Mamre (Gen 13:18; 18:1). Hebron was Judah's capital.

In J the scouts whom Moses sends see only Hebron and other locations in Judah; they see nothing of what became the northern kingdom of Israel (Num 17–20,22–24).

In that story, the sole scout who has a positive view is Caleb. The Calebite territory was located in Judah and included Hebron.

In J—and only in J—Judah is a significant figure. There is a narrative about him, the story of Judah and Tamar (Genesis 38). It ends with the birth of Peres, ancestor of the clan from which the kings of Judah were traced. Jacob's deathbed blessing favors Judah and promises his descendants the scepter. Judah's wife is *bat šûa'* (daughter of Shua), paralleling the name of the wife of David (*bat šeba'*—Bathsheba) and mother of all the kings of Judah through her son Solomon.[12] In J Judah is the brother who saves Joseph from their other brothers' plans to kill him (Gen 37:26–27; 42:22); it is Judah who assures Jacob that he will see that Benjamin will safely go to and return from Egypt (Gen 43:8–9), and it is Judah who speaks for his brothers and defends Benjamin to Joseph in Egypt (44:18–34).

---

[11]A chart in part 4 of the Appendix lists twenty words and phrases that occur only in these texts and nowhere else in the Hebrew Bible, plus over twenty more that occur disproportionately in these texts; pp. 379–387.

[12]*bat šûa'* and *bat šeba'* are so similar that the two names are confused with each other in 1 Chr 3:5.

Other elements in J connect with the monarchy of Judah. In J God promises Abraham the land "from the river of Egypt to the great river, the river Euphrates" (Gen 15:18). This matches the borders attributed to David, first king of Judah. In J the root of the name Rehoboam (*rḥb*) occurs six times. (It never occurs in E.) Rehoboam was the first king of Judah as a separate kingdom from the northern kingdom of Israel.

Other elements in J relate to the twelve brothers who become the eponymous ancestors of the twelve tribes of Israel. In J the stories of the births and namings of the brothers cover only the first four: Reuben, Simeon, Levi, and Judah. That is, it reaches only as far as Judah! Moreover, only Judah, out of these four, actually survived as a community with a land of its own. Also, in J there is a report that Reuben has sex with his father Jacob's concubine; and in J there is a story in which Simeon and Levi massacre the men of Shechem. These acts are singled out in Jacob's deathbed blessings when he bypasses these three oldest brothers and promises the monarchy to Judah.

The J story of the massacre at Shechem also casts a negative light on the acquisition of the city of Shechem. Shechem was the capital of the northern kingdom of Israel, built by Jeroboam I, the king who had rebelled against Judah.

In J there is more about Jacob and Esau than in other sources. And in J Esau is identified as the ancestor of Edom. In J there is also a list of the kings of Edom (Genesis 36). And J alone has an account of Israel's encounter with Edom during the journey from Egypt to the promised land (Num 20:14–20). Judah bordered Edom; Israel did not. And it is reported in Samuel and Kings that David conquered Edom and that it remained subjugated to Judah until the reign of Jehoram.

In J the ark is important (Num 10:33–36; 14:41–44), but in E it is never mentioned. The ark was located in Judah, not in Israel.

According to 1 Kings, the symbols of God's presence in Judah were golden cherubs placed over the ark, whereas the symbols of that presence in Israel were two golden calves, erected by Jeroboam I. Cherubs are mentioned in J but not in E. And in J, in the Ten Commandments, the commandment against idols is stated as forbidding molten gods (Exod 34:17). The golden calves of Israel were molten and are thus forbidden; but the golden cherubs of Judah were not molten. (They were carved from wood and then gold plated.)

In E, meanwhile, the connections are disproportionately with the northern kingdom of Israel. And, more specifically, they relate to the Levites of the priesthood of Shiloh. Thus:

In E Israel acquires its territory at the city of Shechem, the future capital of Israel, by a purchase rather than by violence (Gen 33:18–19).

In E the stories of the births and namings of the brothers do not include Judah (or Reuben, Simeon, and Levi), but they do include all the tribes that were part of the northern kingdom of Israel: Dan, Naphtali, Gad, Asher, Issachar, Zebulun, Ephraim, Manasseh, and Benjamin. And in E the birthright is awarded to Joseph—and since the birthright is a double portion, this results in two tribes being created from Joseph: Ephraim and Manasseh, which were the two largest tribes of the kingdom of Israel. Further, in E Ephraim is favored over Manasseh (Gen 48:13–20); Ephraim was Jeroboam's tribe and frequently the dominant tribe of Israel, so much so that Ephraim is sometimes used in the Hebrew Bible as a euphemism for the entire northern kingdom. Shechem, which was built by Jeroboam, was in the hills of Ephraim. And in E there is a pun: when Joseph is awarded the double portion, it is referred to as "one shoulder over your brothers" (Gen 48:22), and the word for shoulder there is *sekem* (i.e. Shechem).

Shechem is identified in the book of Joshua (24:32) as the traditional burial site of Joseph, and it is in E that the story appears in which Joseph asks to be buried back in Canaan, not in Egypt. E then contains the notice in the exodus story that the people take Joseph's bones with them when they leave Egypt.

Northern Israel's first king, Jeroboam I, is associated with another city, Penuel, which he is reported to have built (1 Kgs 12:25). E contains the story of Jacob's fight with God, which concludes in the naming of the place where it happens: Penuel (Gen 32:31).

In E Reuben is the one who saves Joseph from their other brothers' plans to kill him (Gen 37:22), and it is Reuben who assures Jacob that he will see that Benjamin will safely go to and return from Egypt (Gen 42:37).

Whereas J is favorable to Judah's royal family of David, Solomon, and Rehoboam, E contains elements that are implicitly critical of them. Solomon established work-companies (Hebrew *missîm*), a policy of required labor for the king, which so offended the northern tribes that it is identified in the book of Kings as a reason for their break with Judah and formation of the northern kingdom of Israel when Rehoboam came to the throne: their first act of rebellion is to stone the head of the work-companies (1 Kgs 12:18). E reflects this pointedly, as it describes the Egyptians' enslavement of Israel in the words "they set commanders of work-companies (*missîm*) over it" (Exod 1:11).

Joshua, whether historical or legendary, was understood to have come from the tribe of Ephraim. And E develops the special standing of Joshua as Moses' successor (Exod 17:9–14; 24:13; 32:17; 33:11; Num 11:28; Deut 31:14–15, 23), while J never mentions him.

E contains a corpus of law, the Covenant Code (Exodus 21–23). This suggests that E comes from priests since law codes in the Hebrew Bible otherwise come exclusively from priests (D, P, and Ezekiel).

Other elements of E confirm this priestly connection and point to a particular northern priestly group. The priests of Shiloh have a specific relationship with the northern kingdom of Israel and with E. Their place in the Jerusalem priesthood in Judah suffered when King Solomon expelled their chief priest, Abiathar, and gave the chief priesthood solely to an Aaronid priest. The prophet Ahijah from Shiloh instigated Jeroboam's rebellion and formation of the northern kingdom (1 Kgs 11:29–39). Later, however, Jeroboam failed to make these excluded Levites the sole priests of his new kingdom. Following Jeroboam's establishment of the golden calves, Ahijah of Shiloh condemned his dynasty (1 Kgs 14). The E story of the golden calf corresponds to these events: by saying that Aaron made the golden calf at Horeb, it denigrates both the Aaronid religious establishment of Jerusalem and the golden-calf religious establishment of northern Israel. It is the Levites in this E story, however, who are zealous to destroy the golden-calf heresy.

While J forbids molten gods, which can throw the golden calves into question, E forbids "gods of silver and gods of gold" (Exod 20:23), which likewise may apply to both the northern and southern religious establishments.

And in E, when Moses sees the golden calf he shatters the tablets that he had brought down from the mountain, and there is no report of his getting a second set of tablets. This would question whether there are actually authentic tablets in the ark in Judah.

In E there is also another story in which Aaron is demeaned. Aaron and Miriam speak against Moses regarding his Cushite wife, but God personally sides with Moses against Aaron and declares that Moses' experience of God is superior to that of Aaron or any other prophet. In both the golden-calf story and the Cushite wife story, Aaron acknowledges Moses' superior standing by addressing him as "my lord."

b) P and the Period Following the Fall of the Kingdom of Israel

P has elements that connect it to the time of Hezekiah, king of Judah (715–687 BCE):

P makes distinctions between Aaronid priests and all other Levites. This distinction is of tremendous importance in P. It comes up repeatedly in the P narrative and law codes. Only the Aaronids may serve as priests; all other Levites serve as lesser clergy. The book of Chronicles reports that this distinction was a development of the reign of Hezekiah (2 Chr 31:2). Moreover, this distinction appears in a source of the book of Chronicles that was composed during the reign of Hezekiah, which argues especially for its accuracy.[13] From the time of Wellhausen, this innovation was widely held in scholarship to derive from the prophet Ezekiel (especially Ezekiel 44), but this was not correct. Ezekiel does not distinguish Aaronid priests from the other Levites. He specifically distinguishes one particular group of priests, the Zadokites, not Aaronids. Moreover, since it has now been shown linguistically that the Hebrew of P precedes that of the book of Ezekiel, it is no longer possible to argue that this central innovation in P is based on that prophetic book.[14] The separation of Aaronid priests from the Levites is a Hezekian event.

This is complemented by the other major mark of P: centralization of worship. In J and E, people sacrifice at various locations. But in P, one is permitted to sacrifice only at the Tabernacle and nowhere else on earth. This, too, was a Hezekian policy, eliminating all places of sacrificial worship outside the Temple in Jerusalem. Kings and Chronicles coalesce on this point: there was no centralization before Hezekiah. The merger of centralization with the divisions of priesthood within the Levites is associated with only one king of Israel or Judah, and that is Hezekiah. (D has centralization but does not have the divisions of the priesthood; and, in any case, other well-known aspects of D connect it to the reign of Josiah, Hezekiah's great-grandson.)

Only in P is the law of centralization expressed in terms of the Tabernacle. P devotes more space and attention to the Tabernacle (also called the Tent of Meeting) than to any other subject. The construction of the Taber-

---

[13]See Baruch Halpern, "Sacred History and Ideology: Chronicles' Thematic Structure—Indications of an Earlier Source," in *The Creation of Sacred Literature*, ed. R. E. Friedman (Berkeley: Univ. of California Press, 1981), pp. 35–54; H. G. M. Williamson, *Israel in the Books of Chronicles* (Cambridge, England, 1977), pp. 120–125.

[14]See note 1 above, especially Hurvitz, "Evidence of Language in Dating the Priestly Code,") pp. 24–56; Hurvitz, *Linguistic Study of the Relationship Between the Priestly Source and the Book of Ezekiel*. For additional evidence that P had to precede Ezekiel, see Propp, "The Priestly Source Recovered Intact?" in which he shows that a passage in Ezekiel quotes a passage from P that is divided in the combined text of the Torah; Risa Levitt-Kohn, "A Prophet Like Moses? Rethinking Ezekiel's Relationship to the Torah," *Zeitschrift für die alttestamentliche Wissenschaft* 114 (2002): 236–254, showing that the parallels of terms and phrases in P and Ezekiel reflect Ezekiel's dependence on P and not the reverse; R. E. Friedman, *The Exile and Biblical Narrative* (Atlanta: Scholars Press, 1981), pp. 61–64; Friedman, *Who Wrote the Bible?* pp. 168–270.

nacle and related objects takes up two very large sections of P (Exodus 25–31 and 35–39). After its dedication in the last chapter of Exodus, all revelation takes place there. Sacrifice and various other practices can be performed there and nowhere else (Lev 1:3,5; 3:2,8,13; 4:5–7,14–18; 6:9,19,23; 14:11; 16:1–34; 17:1–9; Num 5:17; 6:10; 19:4). And P says more than a dozen times: *the performance of these commandments at the Tabernacle is the law forever* (Exod 27:21; 28:43; 30:21; Lev 3:17; 6:11; 10:9; 16:29,34; 17:7; 24:3,8; Num 18:23; 19:10). This view in P of the necessity of the Tabernacle's presence forever further supports the linguistic and historical connections of P to the era in which the first Temple was standing in Jerusalem. Scholars in the nineteenth century thought that the Tabernacle was a fiction, but in the twentieth century and in the present century archaeological evidence and internal biblical evidence mutually pointed to the historicity of the Tabernacle in ancient Israel.[15] I assembled evidence that further supported this conclusion and that indicated that the Tabernacle was located in the first Temple in Jerusalem.[16] This, in turn, agreed with all the other evidence and arguments that P was composed in the first Temple period. It made no sense at all to picture P being composed in the postexilic, second Temple period, because P required all sacrifices and the other ceremonies to be performed only at the Tabernacle, *forever*—but the Tabernacle no longer existed in that period!

---

[15]Frank Moore Cross, "The Priestly Tabernacle," *Biblical Archaeologist* 10 (1947): 45–68; Cross, *Canaanite Myth and Hebrew Epic* (Cambridge: Harvard Univ. Press, 1973); Cross, *From Epic to Canon* (Baltimore: Johns Hopkins Univ. Press, 1998), pp. 84–95; Y. Aharoni, "The Solomonic Temple, the Tabernacle, and the Arad Sanctuary," in *Orient and Occident: Essays Presented to Cyrus H. Gordon on the Occasion of His Sixty-fifth Birthday*, ed. H. A. Hoffner Jr. (Neukirchen: Neukirchener, 1973); Menahem Haran, "Shiloh and Jerusalem: The Origin of the Priestly Tradition in the Pentateuch," *Journal of Biblical Literature* 81 (1962): 14–24; Haran, "The Priestly Image of the Tabernacle," *Hebrew Union College Annual* 36 (1965): 191–226; Haran, *Temples and Temple Service in Ancient Israel* (New York: Oxford Univ. Press, 1978); Michael M. Homan, *To Your Tents, O Israel!* (Leiden: Brill, 2002); and see the citations in the note that follows this one.

[16]This evidence, argumentation, and bibliography appear in R. E. Friedman, "The Tabernacle in the Temple," *Biblical Archaeologist* 43 (1980): 241–248; *The Exile and Biblical Narrative* (Atlanta: Scholars Press, 1981), pp. 48–61; *Who Wrote the Bible?*, 2d ed. (San Francisco: HarperSanFrancisco, 1996), pp. 174–187; "Tabernacle," *Anchor Bible Dictionary* (New York: Doubleday, 1992), vol. 6, pp. 292–300. The only challenge to this position as of this date has come from Victor Hurowitz, "The Form and Fate of the Tabernacle: Reflections on a Recent Proposal," *Jewish Quarterly Review* 86 (1995): 127–151. Hurowitz's arguments (which, unfortunately, were marred by some immature discourtesy) have been criticized by Michael M. Homan, *To Your Tents, O Israel!* pp. 167–173. See also my comment on one of Hurowitz's methodological errors in R. E. Friedman, "An Essay on Method," in *Le-David Maskil*, ed. R. E. Friedman and William Henry Propp (Winona Lake, IN: Eisenbrauns, 2003).

The same may be said of the ark, tablets, cherubs, and Urim and Thummim. They are all prominent in P but were associated only with the first Jerusalem Temple, never with the second, postexilic Temple.

c) D and the Period of Josiah

D has elements that connect it to the reign of Josiah, king of Judah (640–609 BCE).

Deuteronomy is part of a seven-book work that tells the history of Israel from Moses to the exile in Babylon (Deuteronomy, Joshua, Judges, 1 and 2 Samuel, 1 and 2 Kings). This work is called the Deuteronomistic history because it constructs the fate of Israel in each period by the standards of Deuteronomy: did the people and their kings follow the commandments in Deuteronomy or not? The story that begins with Moses culminates in King Josiah in a number of ways:

In D it is said about Moses, "a prophet did not rise again in Israel like Moses." In Kings it is said about Josiah, "after him none rose like him" (2 Kgs 23:25). This expression, "none rose like him," is applied to no one else in the Hebrew Bible.[17]

In D, Moses says, "love YHWH, your God, with all your heart and with all your soul and with all your might" (Deut 6:5). In Kings, it is said about Josiah that he alone turned to YHWH "with all his heart and with all his soul and with all his might" (2 Kgs 23:25). This threefold expression occurs nowhere else in the Hebrew Bible.[18]

In D, Moses instructs that, if a matter of law is too difficult, one should inquire (*drš*) what to do via a priest or judge at the chosen place (Deut 17:8–12). Only one king in the Deuteronomistic history is ever pictured as doing this: Josiah. He inquires via the priest Hilkiah at Jerusalem (2 Kgs 22:13,18).

D also contains the Law of the King. Both the command about inquiring and the Law of the King require that one do exactly as one is instructed and "not turn from the commandment, right or left" (Deut 17:11,20). This admonition against turning right or left occurs in two other places in D and two more places early in Deuteronomistic literature (Josh 1:7; 23:6). Only

---

[17]A text describing Hezekiah as being likewise without parallel uses a different phrase: "there was none like him" (2 Kgs 18:5). As Moshe Weinfeld has pointed out, Hezekiah is described in terms related to P while Josiah is described in terms related to D. Weinfeld, *Deuteronomy 1–11*, Anchor Bible (New York: Doubleday, 1991), p. 65.

[18]I learned this from Baruch Halpern.

one person in the Hebrew Bible is described as having done this: Josiah (2 Kgs 22:2).

At the end of D, Moses writes a "scroll of instruction" (*sēper hattôrāh*) and instructs the Levites to set it at the side of the ark so it will be there as a witness in future days (Deut 31:24–29). The scroll of Torah then is rarely mentioned[19] and plays no part in the history until it is found by the priest Hilkiah in the Temple in Josiah's time (2 Kgs 22:8). The discovery of that scroll is a turning point for Josiah and for Israel.

In D, Moses says to gather all the people and "in the place that He will choose, you shall read this instruction in front of all Israel in their ears" (Deut 31:11). Josiah summons all the people of Judah to the divinely chosen place (Jerusalem), and "he read in their ears" the scroll of instruction (2 Kgs 23:2). (The idiom "to read in their ears" occurs in only one other place in the Deuteronomistic history.)[20]

Josiah's religious reforms following the reading of the scroll of the Torah have connections to D as well. According to D, Moses burns the golden calf and grinds it "thin as dust" (Deut 9:21). According to the Deuteronomistic history, at the site of Jeroboam's golden calf Josiah burns the high place "and made it thin as dust" (2 Kgs 23:15). In the Hebrew Bible, the phrase "thin as dust" occurs only in the Moses and Josiah contexts. Moreover, when the Deuteronomistic history tells the story of Jeroboam's setting up the golden calf, it says that a man of God comes and proclaims that a king descended from David will some day ruin that altar, and it adds: "Josiah is his name!" (1 Kgs 13:2).

D says, "you shall demolish (*ntṣ*) their altars . . . and burn (*śrp*) their Asherahs" (Deut 12:3). Josiah demolishes (*ntṣ*) altars and burns (*śrp*) the Asherah at Jerusalem (2 Kgs 23:6,12).

D prohibits making a statue ("graven image," Hebrew *pesel*) five times (Deut 4:16,23,25; 5:8; 27:15) and instructs the people to "burn the statues of their gods in fire" (7:25). The word "statue" occurs rarely after that (only in one story in Judges 17–18 and in one verse about statues among the Samaritans, 2 Kgs 17:41). Then King Manasseh puts a statue of Asherah at the Temple. And it is Josiah who takes that statue out and burns it as commanded in Deuteronomy (2 Kgs 23:6).

---

[19]It is mentioned only in Josh 1:8; 8:31,34; 23:6. Two of these are the same passages that refer to turning to right or left.

[20]Judg 7:3. Here it derives from a source, not from the Deuteronomistic historian himself, and the idiom has a different meaning from the passages in D and Kings.

Josiah, like Hezekiah, establishes exclusive centralization of sacrifice in Jerusalem. The difference is that Josiah's centralization is described in the terms and context of the full Deuteronomistic history that has preceded it, as we have just seen. Hezekiah's reforms are told in a completely different set of terms.[21]

Josiah's reforms are connected to instructions that are found in D; the narrative of Josiah's making those reforms is told in terms and phrases that are typically found in D; and Josiah's reforms are traced to the promulgation of a particular scroll, which is identified by the same words as the scroll that Moses writes in D. This interlocking chain of connections led to the extremely widely held view in scholarship that the scroll that was read in Josiah's day was D. There have been a variety of conceptions: It may have been just the law code that appears in Deuteronomy (chapters 12–26). It may have been the law code and some of the material that precedes and follows it. It may have been written at the time of Josiah. It may have been written earlier and then made public and authoritative in Josiah's time. But there is little room for doubt that D is linked in some integral way to the reign of Josiah.

d) P Follows JE

The P narrative follows the JE narrative in content and in the order of episodes: creation, flood, Abraham's migration, Abraham's parting from his nephew Lot, the Abrahamic covenant, Hagar and Ishmael, the destruction of Sodom and Gomorrah, the birth of Isaac, Isaac's marriage to Rebekah, Abraham's death, Jacob and Esau, Jacob's journey to Aram, Jacob's offspring, Jacob's return to Canaan, the change of Jacob's name to Israel, Esau's offspring, Joseph in Egypt, Jacob's journey to Egypt, the enslavement of Israel in Egypt, God's summoning of Moses, the plagues, the exodus, the Red Sea, manna, the theophany at Sinai/Horeb, the giving of law at Sinai/Horeb, the departure from Sinai/Horeb, the spies, rebellion in the wilderness, the heresy at Peor, and Moses' death.

This following of the JE sequence of events is not simply a matter of the Redactor's having arranged the P episodes to match those of JE. We can know this because P, when read on its own, still flows as a continuous text. If it were just a collection of rearranged sections, we would not expect it to flow in this way.

---

[21]The account of Hezekiah's reign in fact comes from a separate source that the Deuteronomistic historian used, not from the historian himself. This source covers the kings of Judah from Solomon to Hezekiah. See note 13.

Where P does have a change from what is in JE, we can see the reason for the change in almost every case in terms of the consistent views of the author of P. For example, P, without exception, has no sacrifices until the Tabernacle is established in Exodus 40. P therefore has no story to parallel the J story of Cain and Abel, which involves a sacrifice; P has no sacrifice at the end of the flood story, though J does; P has no sacrifice in the Abrahamic covenant (Genesis 17), though J does (Genesis 15); P has no parallel to the E story of the near-sacrifice of Isaac (and sacrifice of a ram). Also, as noted above, P has no channels to God outside the priesthood, so it never includes angels, dreams, or talking animals, and rarely has a blatant anthropomorphism. P therefore has no parallel to the J story of the garden of Eden, with God walking in the garden and making the humans' clothes, and with a talking snake. Nor does P have the JE Balaam story with the talking ass. P does not have a story of the three angelic visitors to Abraham like that in J. It does not have the story of Jacob wrestling with God or an angel at Peni-El as in E, nor does it have a parallel to the J story of the angel in the burning bush. P does not have the stories of the dreams of Joseph, the drink steward, the baker, and the pharaoh in its account of Joseph.

P does not have the stories of the golden calf or of Moses' Cushite wife, both of which detract from Aaron, the ancestor of the priesthood according to P.

P, on the other hand, has an account of Abraham's purchase of the burial cave of Machpelah at Hebron, while J and E do not; and this fits with the fact that Hebron was a priestly, Aaronid city (Josh 21:13). This story claims a legal holding at Hebron.

Observing this consistent relationship between P and the prior sources is a valuable support for the hypothesis in general, and it helps us to identify the steps by which the sources were formed and the contexts of the sources in history. It reveals that P was composed later than JE, that it was composed by someone who was familiar with J and E in their combined form, and it indicates that P was composed as an alternative to that JE version of Israel's story. It was a retelling of the story in terms that were more suitable to the Aaronid priesthood.

7. CONVERGENCE

Above all, *the strongest evidence establishing the Documentary Hypothesis is that several different lines of evidence converge.* There are more than thirty cases of doublets: stories or laws that are repeated in the Torah, sometimes identically, more often with some differences of detail. The existence of so many overlapping texts is noteworthy itself. But their mere existence is not the strongest argument. One could respond, after all, that this is just a matter of style or narrative strategy. Similarly, there are hundreds of apparent contradictions in the text, but one could respond that we can take them one by one and find some explanation for each contradiction. And, similarly, there is the matter of the texts that consistently call the deity God while other texts consistently call God by the name YHWH, to which one could respond that this is simply like calling someone sometimes by his name and sometimes by his title. The powerful argument is not any one of these matters. It is that all these matters *converge*. When we separate the doublets, this also results in the resolution of nearly all the contradictions. And when we separate the doublets, the name of God divides consistently in all but three out of more than two thousand occurrences. And when we separate the doublets, the terminology of each source remains consistent within that source. (I listed twenty-four examples of such terms, which are consistent through nearly four hundred occurrences, above, in the Terminology section.) And when we separate the sources, this produces continuous narratives that flow with only a rare break. And when we separate the sources, this fits with the linguistic evidence, where the Hebrew of each source fits consistently with what we know of the Hebrew in each period. And so on for each of the six categories that precede this section. The name of God and the doublets were the starting-points of the investigation into the formation of the Bible. But they were not, and are not, major arguments or evidence in themselves. The most compelling argument for the hypothesis is that this hypothesis best accounts for the fact that all this evidence of so many kinds comes together so consistently. To this day, no one known to me who challenged the hypothesis has ever addressed this fact.

Thus, I did not list the doublets as one of the primary arguments for the hypothesis above. The primary argument is rather that so many double stories could line up with so many other categories of evidence, composed of hundreds of points of data. With that larger argument in mind, we can now take account of the doublets and add them to the picture in this collection of evidence:

1. Creation. Gen 1:1–2:3 (P) and Gen 2:4b–25 (J).

2. Genealogy from Adam. Gen 4:17–26 (J) and 5:1–28,30–32 (Book of Records).

3. The flood. Gen 6:5–8; 7:1–5,7,10,12,16b–20,22–23; 8:2b–3a,6,8–12,13b,20–22 (J) and 6:9–22; 7:8–9,11,13–16a,21,24; 8:1–2a,3b–5,7,13a,14–19; 9:1–17 (P).

4. Genealogy from Shem. Gen 10:21–31 (J and P) and 11:10–26 (Book of Records).

5. Abraham's migration. Gen 12:1–4a (J) and 12:4b–5 (P).

6. Wife/sister. Gen 12:10–20 (J) and 20:1–18 (E) and 26:6–14 (J). (Triplet)

7. Abraham and Lot separate. Gen 13:5,7–11a,12b–14 (J) and 13:6,11b–12a (P).

8. The Abrahamic covenant. Genesis 15 (J, E, and R) and 17 (P).

9. Hagar and Ishmael. Gen 16:1–2,4–14 (J) and 16:3,15–16 (P) and 21:8–19 (E). (Triplet)

10. Prophecy of Isaac's birth. Gen 17:16–19 (P) and 18:10–14 (J).

11. Naming of Beer-sheba. Gen 21:22–31 (E) and 26:15–33 (J).

12. Jacob, Esau, and the departure to the east. Gen 26:34–35; 27:46; 28:1–9 (P) and 27:1–45; 28:10 (J).

13. Jacob at Beth-El. Gen 28:10,11a,13–16,19 (J) and 28:11b–12, 17–18,20–22 (E) and 35:9–15 (P). (Triplet)

14. Jacob's twelve sons. Gen 29:32–35; 30:1–24; 35:16–20 (JE) and Gen 35:23–26 (P).

15. Jacob's name changed to Israel. Gen 32:25–33 (E) and 35:9–10 (P).

16. Joseph sold into Egypt. Gen 37:2b,3b,5–11,19–20,23,25b–27, 28b,31–35; 39:1 (J) and 37:3a,4,12–18,21–22,24,25a,28a,29–30 (E).

17. YHWH commissions Moses. Exod 3:2–4a,5,7–8,19–22; 4:19–20a (J) and 3:1,4b,6,9–18; 4:1–18,20b–21a,22–23 (E) and 6:2–12 (P). (Triplet)

18. Moses, Pharaoh, and the plagues. Exod 5:3–6:1; 7:14–18,20b–21, 23–29; 8:3b–11a,16–28; 9:1–7,13–34; 10:1–19,21–26,28–29; 11:1–8 (E) and 7:6–13,19–20a,22; 8:1–3a,12–15; 9:8–12 (P).

19. The Passover. Exod 12:1–20,28,40–50 (P) and 12:21–27,29–36, 37b–39 (E).

20. The Red Sea. Exod 13:21–22; 14:5a,6,9a,10b,13–14,19b,20b, 21b,24,27b,30–31 (J) and 14:1–4,8,9b,10a,10c,15–18,21a,21c, 22–23,26–27a, 28–29 (P).

21. Manna and quail in the wilderness. Exod 16:2–3,6–35a (P) and Num 11:4–34 (E).

22. Water from a rock at Meribah. Exod 17:2–7 (E) and Num 20:2–13 (P).

23. Theophany at Sinai/Horeb. Exod 19:1; 24:15b–18a (P) and 19:2b–9,16b–17,19; 20:18–21 (E) and 19:10–16a,18,20–25 (J). (Triplet)

24. The Ten Commandments. Exod 20:1–17 (R) and 34:10–28 (J) and Deut 5:6–18 (D). (Triplet)

25. Kid in mother's milk. Exod 23:19 (Covenant Code) and 34:26 (J) and Deut 14:21 (D). (Triplet)

26. Forbidden animals. Leviticus 11 (P) and Deuteronomy 14 (D).

27. Centralization of sacrifice. Leviticus 17 and Deuteronomy 12.

28. Holidays. Leviticus 23 (P) and Numbers 28–29 (R) and Deut 16:1–17 (D). (Triplet)

29. The spies. Num 13:1–16,21,25–26,32; 14:1a,2–3,5–10,26–29 (P) and 13:17–20,22–24,27–31,33; 14:1b,4,11–25,39–45 (J).

30. Heresy at Peor. Num 25:1–5 (J) and 25:6–19 (P).

31. Appointment of Joshua. Num 27:12–23 (P) and Deut 31:14–15,23 (E).

I have seen it claimed that such doublets are a common phenomenon in ancient Near Eastern literature. That is false. No such phenomenon exists. Doublets are not common in Near Eastern prose because there is *no* Near Eastern prose, in the form of either history-writing or long fiction, prior to these biblical texts. It is not even common in Near Eastern poetry. The poetic text that comes closest to the qualities of the biblical text that we are discussing here is the *Epic of Gilgamesh*, and the *Epic of Gilgamesh* is a composite of several sources. It is a *demonstration* of composition by combining sources in the ancient Near East, not a refutation of it![22]

I have also seen the claim that the scholar just chooses the evidence to fit his or her arrangement: for example, that the scholar assigns every verse that has the word "congregation" in it to P and then says that the recurrence of this word in P is proof of the hypothesis. This argument should be seen to be false in the light of all the evidence presented here.

---

[22]Jeffrey H. Tigay, ed., *Empirical Models for Biblical Criticism* (Philadelphia: Univ. of Pennsylvania Press, 1985); R. E. Friedman, "Some Recent Non-arguments Concerning the Documentary Hypothesis," in *Texts, Temples, and Traditions: A Tribute to Menahem Haran*, ed. Michael Fox et al. (Winona Lake, IN: Eisenbrauns, 1996), pp. 87–101.

No scholar is clever enough to make all of these terms line up within the sources—and to make it all come out consistent with the other signs of the sources. In the text of the Torah that appears in the next section of this book, one can observe each of the doublets with the sources identified. One can then observe all the characteristic terms, the resolution of the contradictions, the separation of the words that are used to identify the deity, the continuity of each story within the doublet, and all the other categories of evidence. The combined weight of the evidence that one will observe there, together with the evidence that is collected here in this section, should make it clear why this explanation of the biblical origins has been so compelling for more than a century. And, whether one agrees with this explanation, questions it, or challenges it, one will have in front of him or her the evidence to address. It is amazing that at this point, when such a mass of evidence is available, some writers still discuss this at so low a level as, for example, arguing about whether "different names of God" constitutes proof or not, or whether doublets prove multiple authorship, or whether a beautiful literary structure (for example, a chiasm) is evidence for a single author. Or some just say that "the hypothesis was disproved long ago" or "nobody accepts it anymore."

Here, rather, is the evidence, for anyone to see, evaluate, acknowledge, or refute.

KEY TO SOURCES

J	Green
E	**Green Sans Bold**
P	**Blue Sans**
RJE	Green with background screen
R	Blue with background screen
Other Independent Texts	*Blue Italic*
Genesis 14	*Green Italic*
Dtn	*Green Sans Italic*
Dtr1	Blue
Dtr2	**Blue Bold**

GENESIS

1 ¹In the beginning of God's creating the skies and the earth— ²when the earth had been shapeless and formless,* and darkness was on the face of the deep, and God's spirit was hovering on the face of the water— ³God** said, "Let there be light." And there was light. ⁴And God saw the light, that it was good, and God separated between the light and the darkness. ⁵And God called the light "day" and called the darkness "night." And there was evening, and there was morning: one day.

⁶And God said, "Let there be a space within the water, and let it separate between water and water." ⁷And God made the space, and it separated between the water that was under the space and the water that was above the space. And it was so. ⁸And God called the space "skies." And there was evening, and there was morning: a second day.

⁹And God said, "Let the waters be concentrated under the skies into one place, and let the land appear." And it was so. ¹⁰And God called the land "earth," and called the concentration of the waters "seas." And God saw that it was good. ¹¹And God said, "Let the earth generate plants, vegetation that produces seed, fruit trees, each making fruit of its own kind, which has its

---

*This is one of the passages in P that is reversed in the book of Jeremiah. Jeremiah says, "I looked at the earth, and here it was shapeless and formless, and to the skies, and their light was gone" (Jer 4:23). He is not simply quoting P; he is playing on it and reversing it. In this case he uses its language of creation to describe a vision of the creation being undone: the earth goes back to be an unformed mass, and the light of day goes out. (See *Who Wrote the Bible?* p. 167.) This is one small part of the evidence that P was written by the time of Jeremiah. It is also part of the evidence for establishing the relationship between P and the Deuteronomistic literature (which is associated with the book of Jeremiah; see the Collection of Evidence, pp. 14–15).

**The deity is mentioned thirty-five times in the creation account and in every case is called "God" (Hebrew: Elohim), never by the name YHWH.

seed in it, on the earth." And it was so: ¹²The earth brought out plants, vegetation that produces seeds of its own kind, and trees that make fruit that each has seeds of its own kind in it. And God saw that it was good. ¹³And there was evening, and there was morning: a third day.

¹⁴And God said, "Let there be lights in the space of the skies to distinguish between the day and the night, and they will be for signs and for appointed times and for days and years. ¹⁵And they will be for lights in the space of the skies to shed light on the earth." And it was so. ¹⁶And God made the two big lights—the bigger light for the regulation of the day and the smaller light for the regulation of the night—and the stars. ¹⁷And God set them in the space of the skies to shed light on the earth ¹⁸and to regulate the day and the night and to distinguish between the light and the darkness. And God saw that it was good. ¹⁹And there was evening, and there was morning: a fourth day.

²⁰And God said, "Let the water swarm with a swarm of living beings, and let birds fly over the earth on the face of the space of the skies." ²¹And God created the big sea serpents and all the living beings that creep, with which the water swarmed, by their kinds, and every winged bird by its kind. And God saw that it was good. ²²And God blessed them, saying, "Be fruitful and multiply and fill the water in the seas, and let the birds multiply in the earth." ²³And there was evening and there was morning, a fifth day.

²⁴And God said, "Let the earth bring out living beings by their kind, domestic animal and creeping thing and wild animals of the earth by their kind." And it was so. ²⁵And God made the wild animals of the earth by their kind and the domestic animals by their kind and every creeping thing of the ground by their kind. And God saw that it was good.

²⁶And God said, "Let us make a human, in our image, according to our likeness, and let them dominate the fish of the sea and the birds of the skies and the domestic animals and all the earth and all the creeping things that creep on the earth." ²⁷And God created the human in His image. He created it in the image of God; He created them male and female. ²⁸And God blessed them, and God said to them, "Be fruitful and multiply and fill the earth and subdue it and dominate the fish of the sea and the birds of the skies and every animal that creeps on the earth." ²⁹And God said, "Here, I have placed all the vegetation that produces seed that is on the face of all the earth for you and every tree, which has in it the fruit of a tree producing seed. It will be food for you ³⁰and for all the wild animals of the earth and for all the birds of the skies and for all the creeping things on the earth, everything in which there is a living being: every plant of vegetation, for food." And it was so.

³¹And God saw everything that He had made, and, here, it was very good. And there was evening and there was morning, the sixth day.

2

¹And the skies and the earth and all their array were finished. ²And in the seventh day God finished His work that He had done and ceased in the seventh day from all His work that He had done. ³And God blessed the seventh day and made it holy because He ceased in it from doing all His work, which God had created.

⁴These are the records of the skies and the earth when they were created:*

In the day that YHWH God** made earth and skies‡— ⁵when all produce of the field had not yet been in the earth, and all vegetation of the field had not yet grown, for YHWH God had not rained on the earth, and there had been no human to work the ground, ⁶and a river had come up from the earth and watered the whole face of the ground— ⁷YHWH God fashioned a human, dust from the ground, and blew into his nostrils the breath of life, and the human became a living being.

---

*Gen 2:4a is the first of ten uses of the phrase "These are the records of . . ." They introduce both narratives and lists; and they introduce texts that come from several different sources. They are the work of the Redactor as a way of editing the source texts of Genesis into a continuous story. The Redactor derived the formula from a text that was originally an independent work, The Book of Records (*tôlĕdōt*), which begins at Gen 5:1.

**The text now changes, always referring to the deity by the proper name: YHWH, eleven times. In Genesis 2 and 3 the word "God" appears each time after the name YHWH. But this double identification, "YHWH God," occurs only in these introductory chapters and nowhere else in the Pentateuch. It therefore appears to be an effort by the Redactor (R) to soften the transition from the P creation, which uses only "God" (thirty-five times), to the coming J stories, which will use only the name YHWH.

‡The P creation story begins with "the skies and the earth" (1:1) whereas the J story begins here with "earth and skies," reversing the order. This is not a proof of anything, but it is notable because, from their very first words, the sources each reflect their perspectives. P is more heaven-centered, almost a picture from the sky looking down, while J is more human-centered (and certainly more anthropomorphic), more like a picture from the earth looking up.

This is also an example of the way in which the combining of the sources produced a work that is greater than the sum of its parts. The more transcendent conception of God in P merges with the more personal conception in J, and the result is: the Five Books of Moses in its final form now conveys a picture of God who is both the cosmic God and the "God of your father." And that combined conception of the deity who is both transcendent and personal has been a central element of Judaism and Christianity ever since.

⁸And YHWH God planted a garden in Eden at the east, and He set the human whom He had fashioned there. ⁹And YHWH God caused every tree that was pleasant to the sight and good for eating to grow from the ground, and the tree of life within the garden, and the tree of knowledge of good and bad.

¹⁰And a river was going out from Eden to water the garden, and it was dispersed from there and became four heads. ¹¹The name of one was Pishon; that is the one that circles all the land of Havilah where there is gold. ¹²And that land's gold is good; bdellium and onyx stone are there. ¹³And the name of the second river is Gihon; that is the one that circles all the land of Cush. ¹⁴And the name of the third river is Tigris; that is the one that goes east of Assyria. And the fourth river: that is Euphrates.*

¹⁵And YHWH God took the human and put him in the garden of Eden to work it and to watch over it. ¹⁶And YHWH God commanded the human, saying, "You may eat from every tree of the garden. ¹⁷But from the tree of knowledge of good and bad: you shall not eat from it, because in the day you eat from it: you'll die!"

¹⁸And YHWH God said, "It's not good for the human to be by himself. I'll make for him a strength corresponding to him." ¹⁹And YHWH God fashioned from the ground every animal of the field and every bird of the skies and brought it to the human to see what he would call it. And whatever the human would call it, each living being, that would be its name. ²⁰And the human gave names to every domestic animal and bird of the skies and every animal of the field. But He did not find for the human a strength corresponding to him.

²¹And YHWH God caused a slumber to descend on the human, and he slept. And He took one of his ribs and closed flesh in its place. ²²And YHWH God built the rib that He had taken from the human into a woman

---

*All of the sources reflect literary artistry, but the specific nature of their respective artistry differs. In J, the art of wordplay is particularly characteristic. Here there is punning on the names of all four rivers that flow out of Eden. One is Gihon, and in J the snake receives a curse that it will go on its belly (Gen 3:14); "belly" in Hebrew is *gĕḥōn*. Another river is Pishon, and in J the human becomes "a living being" (2:7), Hebrew *nephesh*, which has the same root letters as Pishon reversed. (Hebrew is written with only consonants, no vowels, so a root reversal, known as methasis, is particularly visible.) Another river is Euphrates, written in Hebrew as *prt*, which occurs in J in the same verse as *gĕḥōn* in the meeting of two words '*pr t'kl* ("you shall eat dust," 3:14). The other river is Tigris, called in Hebrew *ḥdql*, which also occurs in a metathesis of two words in the J story: *ydw wlqḥ* ("his hand and take," 3:22). In other wordplay in this J text, the human in Hebrew is *'ādām*, and he is taken from the ground (Hebrew *'ădāmāh*). The woman is called *Eve*, Hebrew *ḥawwāh*, a Semitic root that can also mean snake. And the snake is the most "sly," Hebrew *'ārûm*, of animals, and later the human is naked, Hebrew *'êrōm*.

and brought her to the human. ²³And the human said, "This time is it: bone from my bones and flesh from my flesh. This will be called 'woman,' for this one was taken from 'man.'"*

²⁴On account of this a man leaves his father and his mother and clings to his woman, and they become one flesh.

²⁵And the two of them were naked, the human and his woman, and they were not embarrassed.

3

¹And the snake was slier than every animal of the field that YHWH God had made, and he said to the woman, "Has God indeed said you may not eat from any tree of the garden?"

²And the woman said to the snake, "We may eat from the fruit of the trees of the garden. ³But from the fruit of the tree that is within the garden God has said, "You shall not eat from it, and you shall not touch it, or else you'll die."

⁴And the snake said to the woman, "You won't die! ⁵Because God knows that in the day you eat from it your eyes will be opened, and you'll be like God**—knowing good and bad." ⁶And the woman saw that the tree was good for eating and that it was an attraction to the eyes, and the tree was desirable to bring about understanding, and she took some of its fruit, and she ate, and gave to her man with her as well, and he ate. ⁷And the eyes of the two of them were opened, and they knew that they were naked. And they picked fig leaves and made loincloths for themselves.

⁸And they heard the sound of YHWH God walking in the garden in the wind of the day, and the human and his woman hid from YHWH God among the garden's trees. ⁹And YHWH God called the human and said to him, "Where are you?"

---

*The order of creation in Gen 1–2:3 (P) is first plants, then animals, then man and woman; but in the creation account in Gen 2:4b–24 (J) the order is man, then plants, then animals, then woman.

**This is a superb example of how the joining of the sources often produced something greater than the sum of the parts, something that perhaps neither of the authors of the sources (in this case J and P) envisioned. In the P creation story, God creates the humans "in the image of God." Whether that means something physical or spiritual, it means at the very least that humans are pictured as participating in the divine in some way that an animal does not. Humans have a connection to the divine. Now, in the Eden story, which is part of J, the snake tempts the humans precisely with the idea that "you'll be like God." This is presumably not an argument that would have worked on an animal, but the humans, who are now understood in the combined text to be connected to the divine image, are attracted by it. P, J, and R all contribute to forming one of the major theological and psychological points of the Bible.

¹⁰And he said, "I heard the sound of you in the garden and was afraid because I was naked, and I hid."

¹¹And He said, "Who told you that you were naked? Have you eaten from the tree from which I commanded you not to eat?"

¹²And the human said, "The woman, whom you placed with me, she gave me from the tree, and I ate."

¹³And YHWH God said to the woman, "What is this that you've done?" And the woman said, "The snake tricked me, and I ate."

¹⁴And YHWH God said to the snake, "Because you did this, you are cursed out of every domestic animal and every animal of the field, you'll go on your belly, and you'll eat dust all the days of your life. ¹⁵And I'll put enmity between you and the woman and between your seed and her seed. He'll strike you at the head, and you'll strike him at the heel."

¹⁶To the woman He said, "I'll make your suffering and your labor pain great. You'll have children in pain. And your desire will be for your man, and he'll dominate you."

¹⁷And to the human He said, "Because you listened to your woman's voice and ate from the tree about which I commanded you saying, 'You shall not eat from it,' the ground is cursed on your account. You'll eat from it with suffering all the days of your life. ¹⁸And it will grow thorn and thistle at you, and you'll eat the field's vegetation. ¹⁹By the sweat of your nostrils you'll eat bread until you go back to the ground, because you were taken from it; because you are dust and you'll go back to dust."

²⁰And the human called his woman "Eve," because she was mother of all living.

²¹And YHWH God made skin garments for the human and his woman and dressed them.

²²And YHWH God said, "Here, the human has become like one of us, to know good and bad. And now, in case he'll put out his hand and take from the tree of life as well, and eat and live forever": ²³And YHWH God put him out of the garden of Eden, to work the ground from which he was taken. ²⁴And He expelled the human, and He had the cherubs and the flame of a revolving sword reside at the east of the garden of Eden to watch over the way to the tree of life.

4

¹And the human had known Eve, his woman, and she became pregnant and gave birth to Cain and said, "I've created a man with YHWH." ²And she went on to give birth to his brother, Abel. And Abel was a shepherd of flocks, and Cain was a worker of ground. ³And it was at the end of

some days, and Cain brought an offering to YHWH from the fruit of the ground. ⁴And Abel brought, as well, from the firstborn of his flock and their fat. And YHWH paid attention to Abel and his offering ⁵and did not pay attention to Cain and his offering. And Cain was very upset, and his face was fallen.

⁶And YHWH said to Cain, "Why are you upset, and why has your face fallen? ⁷Is it not that if you do well you'll be raised, and if you don't do well then sin crouches at the threshold? And its desire will be for you. And you'll dominate it."

⁸And Cain said to his brother Abel. And it was while they were in the field, and Cain rose against Abel his brother and killed him.

⁹And YHWH said to Cain, "Where is Abel your brother?"

And he said, "I don't know. Am I my brother's watchman?"

¹⁰And He said, "What have you done? The sound! Your brother's blood is crying to me from the ground! ¹¹And now you're cursed from the ground that opened its mouth to take your brother's blood from your hand. ¹²When you work the ground it won't continue to give its potency to you. You'll be a roamer and rover in the earth."

¹³And Cain said to YHWH, "My crime is greater than I can bear. ¹⁴Here, you've expelled me from the face of the ground today, and I'll be hidden from your presence, and I'll be a roamer and rover in the earth, and anyone who finds me will kill me."

¹⁵And YHWH said to him, "Therefore: anyone who kills Cain, he'll be avenged sevenfold." And YHWH set a sign for Cain so that anyone who finds him would not strike him. ¹⁶And Cain went out from YHWH's presence and lived in the land of roving, east of Eden.

¹⁷And Cain knew his wife, and she became pregnant and gave birth to Enoch. And he was a builder of a city, and he called the name of the city like the name of his son: Enoch. ¹⁸And Irad was born to Enoch, and Irad fathered Mehuya-el, and Mehuya-el fathered Metusha-el, and Metusha-el fathered Lamech. ¹⁹And Lamech took two wives. The one's name was Adah, and the second's name was Zillah. ²⁰And Adah gave birth to Yabal. He was father of tent-dweller and cattleman. ²¹And his brother's name was Yubal. He was father of every player of lyre and pipe. ²²And Zillah, too, gave birth to Tubal-Cain, forger of every implement of bronze and iron. And Tubal-Cain's sister was Naamah. ²³And Lamech said to his wives:

> Adah and Zillah, listen to my voice,
> Wives of Lamech, hear what I say.
> For I've killed a man for a wound to me

And a boy for a hurt to me,

24   For Cain will be avenged sevenfold
And Lamech seventy-seven.

²⁵And Adam knew his wife again, and she gave birth to a son, and she called his name Seth "because God put another seed for me in place of Abel because Cain killed him." ²⁶And a son was born to Seth, him as well, and he called his name Enosh.*

Then it was begun to invoke the name YHWH.**

5

¹*This is the Book of Records‡ of the Human. In the day of God's creating a human, He made it in the likeness of God. ²He created them male and female, and He blessed them and called their name "Human" in the day of their being created. ³And the human lived a hundred thirty years, and he fathered in his likeness—like his image—and called his name Seth. ⁴And the human's days after his fathering Seth were eight hundred years, and he fathered sons and daughters. ⁵And all of the human's days that he lived were nine hundred years and thirty years. And he died.*

⁶And Seth lived five years and a hundred years, and he fathered Enosh.‡‡ ⁷And Seth lived after his fathering Enosh seven years and eight hundred years,

---

*The J genealogy traces Adam's line through Cain alone and mentions no other surviving children. The Book of Records genealogy traces Adam's line through Seth and never mentions Cain or Abel. The Redactor added this line explaining that Seth was born to Adam and Eve as a replacement for Abel, thus rconciling the two sources.

**Here the J narrative declares unequivocally that invoking the divine name YHWH began in this early generation of humans on earth. According to E and P, this does not begin until the time of Moses.

‡The "Book of Records (or: Generations)" is a separate document, used by the Redactor to form a logical framework for the combined sources in Genesis. Within that framework, the stories of J, E, and P now flow through a chronology of the generations from the first humans to the generation of Jacob's twelve sons.

‡‡The two genealogical lists, one from J and one from the Book of Records, have some names that are the same or similar and others that are different, perhaps indicating a common, more ancient source, thus:

Cain	Seth
Enoch	Enosh
Irad	Cainan
Mehuya-el	Mahalalel
Metusha-el	Jared
Lamech	Enoch
	Methuselah
	Lamech

and he fathered sons and daughters. *⁸And all of Seth's days were twelve years and nine hundred years. And he died.*

⁹And Enosh lived ninety years, and he fathered Cainan. ¹⁰And Enosh lived after his fathering Cainan fifteen years and eight hundred years, and he fathered sons and daughters. ¹¹And all of Enosh's days were five years and nine hundred years. And he died.

¹²And Cainan lived seventy years, and he fathered Mahalalel. ¹³And Cainan lived after his fathering Mahalalel forty years and eight hundred years, and he fathered sons and daughters. ¹⁴And all of Cainan's days were ten years and nine hundred years. And he died.

¹⁵And Mahalalel lived five years and sixty years, and he fathered Jared. ¹⁶And Mahalalel lived after his fathering Jared thirty years and eight hundred years, and he fathered sons and daughters. ¹⁷And all of Mahalalel's days were ninety-five years and eight hundred years. And he died.

¹⁸And Jared lived sixty-two years and a hundred years, and he fathered Enoch. ¹⁹And Jared lived after his fathering Enoch eight hundred years, and he fathered sons and daughters. ²⁰And all of Jared's days were sixty-two years and nine hundred years. And he died.

²¹And Enoch lived sixty-five years, and he fathered Methuselah. ²²And Enoch walked with God after his fathering Methuselah three hundred years, and he fathered sons and daughters. ²³And all of Enoch's days were sixty-five years and three hundred years. ²⁴And Enoch walked with God, and he was not, because God took him.

²⁵And Methuselah lived eighty-seven years and a hundred years, and he fathered Lamech. ²⁶And Methuselah lived after his fathering Lamech eighty-two years and seven hundred years, and he fathered sons and daughters. ²⁷And all of Methuselah's days were sixty-nine years and nine hundred years. And he died.

²⁸And Lamech lived eighty-two years and a hundred years, and he fathered a son ²⁹and called his name Noah, saying, "This one will console us from our labor and from our hands' suffering from the ground, which YHWH has cursed."* ³⁰And Lamech lived after his fathering Noah ninety-five years and five hundred years, and he fathered sons and daughters. ³¹And all of Lamech's days were seventy-seven years and seven hundred years. And he died.

---

*This verse appears to have been added to this Book of Records list. This source's pattern does not include giving origins of names anywhere else; like P, it never calls the deity by the name YHWH but only uses Elohim in Genesis; and the cursing of the ground comes from J. Either this verse came from J and was moved to this spot by the Redactor, or else it was written by the Redactor as part of the uniting of the sources in the flood story.

³²*And Noah was five hundred years old, and Noah fathered Shem, Ham, and Yaphet.*

6 ¹And it was when humankind began to multiply on the face of the ground and daughters were born to them: ²and the sons of God* saw the daughters of humankind, that they were attractive, and they took women, from all they chose. ³And YHWH said, "My spirit won't stay in humankind forever, since they're also flesh; and their days shall be a hundred twenty years."** ⁴The Nephilim were in the earth in those days and after that as well, when the sons of God came to the daughters of humankind, and they gave birth by them. They were the heroes who were of old, people of renown.

⁵And YHWH‡ saw that human bad was multiplied in the earth, and every inclination of their heart's thoughts was only bad all the day. ⁶And YHWH regretted that He had made humankind in the earth.

And He was grieved to His heart.

⁷And YHWH said, "I'll wipe out the human whom I've created from the face of the earth, from human to animal to creeping thing, and to the bird of the skies, because I regret that I made them." ⁸But Noah found favor in YHWH's eyes.

⁹These are the records of Noah:‡‡

Noah was a virtuous man. He was unblemished in his generations. Noah walked with God. ¹⁰And Noah fathered three sons: Shem, Ham, and Yaphet. ¹¹And the earth was corrupted before God, and the earth was filled with violence. ¹²And God saw the earth; and, here, it was corrupted, because all

---

*This is the only occurrence of the word God in narration in all of J in the Masoretic Text. It is not part of the issue of the name of God distinction because it is not independent but is rather part of a fixed phrase, *bĕnê 'ĕlōhîm*, which can mean either "sons of God" or "sons of the gods" (plural), meaning divine beings of some sort.

**YHWH sets the maximum age of humans at 120 here in J; but many persons live longer than this (9:29; 11:10–26,32—which come from a separate source, the Book of Records). In J, no one lives longer than 120 years, and it culminates with the report that Moses lives to the maximum of 120 (Deut 34:7).

‡The deity is always referred to by name in the J flood story, ten times; and is always referred to as "God" in the P flood story, sixteen times.

‡‡The Redactor uses the formula "These are the records of . . ." here and in subsequent passages to introduce sections of the story. His use of these words, which recall the opening words of the Book of Records, contributes to the chronology that provides the continuity of the combined narrative in Genesis. (See the notes on Gen 2:4 and 5:1.)

flesh had corrupted its way on the earth. ¹³And God said to Noah, "The end of all flesh has come before me, because the earth is filled with violence because of them. And here: I'm destroying them with the earth. ¹⁴Make yourself an ark of gopher wood, make rooms with the ark, and pitch it outside and inside with pitch. ¹⁵And this is how you shall make it: three hundred cubits the length of the ark, fifty cubits its width, and thirty cubits its height. ¹⁶You shall make a window for the ark, and you shall finish it to a cubit from the top, and you shall make the ark's entrance in its side. You shall make lower, second, and third stories for it. ¹⁷And I, here: I'm bringing the flood, water on the earth, to destroy all flesh in which is the breath of life from under the skies. Everything that is in the earth will expire. ¹⁸And I shall establish my covenant with you. And you'll come to the ark, you and your sons and your wife and your sons' wives with you. ¹⁹And of all the living, of all flesh, you shall bring two of each* to the ark to keep alive with you. They shall be male and female. ²⁰Of the birds by their kind and of the domestic animals by their kind, of all the creeping things of the ground by their kind, two of each will come to you to keep alive. ²¹And you, take some of every food that will be eaten and gather it to you, and it will be for you and for them for food." ²²And Noah did it. According to everything that God commanded him, he did so.

7 ¹And YHWH said to Noah, "Come, you and all your household, into an ark, for I've seen you as virtuous in front of me in this generation. ²Of all the pure animals, take seven pairs, man and his woman; and of the animals that are not pure, two, man and his woman. ³Also of the birds of the skies seven pairs, male and female, to keep seed alive on the face of the earth. ⁴Because in seven more days I'll rain on the earth, forty days and forty nights, and I'll wipe out all the substance that I've made from on the face of the earth."

⁵And Noah did according to all that YHWH had commanded him. ⁶*And Noah was six hundred years old when the flood was, water on the earth.*

---

*The number of animals on the ark is seven pairs of pure and one pair of impure in Gen 7:2,3 (J); but it is only one pair of each, whether pure or impure, in 6:19–20; 7:8,9,15 (P). This fits with the fact that in J Noah will offer sacrifices at the end of the flood, so he needs more than two of each animal—or else his sacrifice would end a species. But in P, there are no sacrifices in the story until the establishment of the Tabernacle in Exodus 40, so two of each animal are sufficient.

⁷And Noah and his sons and his wife and his sons' wives with him came to the ark from before the waters of the flood. **⁸Of the animals that were pure and of the animals that were not pure, and of the birds and everyone that creeps on the ground, ⁹they came by twos to Noah, to the ark, male and female, as God had commanded Noah. ¹⁰And seven days later the waters of the flood were on the earth. ¹¹In the six hundredth year of Noah's life, in the second month, in the seventeenth day of the month, on this day all the fountains of the great deep were split open, and the apertures of the skies were opened.* ¹²And there was rain on the earth, forty days and forty nights. ¹³In this very day Noah came, and Shem and Ham and Yaphet, Noah's sons, and Noah's wife and his sons' three wives with them to the ark, ¹⁴they and all the wild animals by their kind and all the domestic animals by their kind and all the creeping animals that creep on the earth by their kind and all the birds by their kind, all fowl, all winged things. ¹⁵And they came to Noah, to the ark, by twos of all flesh in which was the breath of life, ¹⁶and those that came were male and female; some from all flesh came, as God had commanded him.** And YHWH closed it for him. ¹⁷And the flood was on the earth for forty days, and the waters multiplied and raised the ark, and it was lifted from the earth. ¹⁸And the waters grew strong and multiplied very much on the earth, and the ark went on the face of the waters. ¹⁹And the waters had grown very, very strong on the earth, so they covered all the high mountains that are under all the skies. ²⁰Fifteen cubits above, the waters grew stronger, and they covered the mountains. **²¹And all flesh that creep on the earth—of the birds and of the domestic animals and of the wild animals and of all the swarming creatures that swarm on the earth, and all the humans— expired.**** ²²Everything that had the breathing spirit of life in its nostrils, everything that was on the ground, died. ²³And He wiped out all the substance that was on the face of the earth, from human to animal to creeping thing and to bird of the skies, and they were wiped out from the earth, and just Noah and those who were with him in the ark were left. **²⁴And the water grew strong on the earth a hundred fifty days.**

---

*In the P creation story, God creates a space (firmament) that separates waters that are above it from waters below. The universe in that story is thus a habitable bubble surrounded by water. This same conception is assumed in the P flood story, in which the "apertures of the skies" and the "fountains of the great deep" are broken up so that the waters flow in. The J creation account has no such conception, and in the J flood story it just rains.

**P uses the term "expired." J uses the term "died." This is consistent with the rest of P, which uses the term "expired" eleven times, whereas it never occurs in J, E, or D.

8

¹And God remembered Noah and all the wild animals and all the domestic animals that were with him in the ark, and God passed a wind over the earth, and the water decreased. ²And the fountains of the deep and the apertures of the skies were shut, And the rain was restrained from the skies. ³And the waters went back from on the earth, going back continually, and the water receded at the end of a hundred fifty days. ⁴And the ark rested in the seventh month, in the seventeenth day of the month, on the mountains of Ararat. ⁵And the water went on receding until the tenth month. In the tenth month, in the first of the month, the tops of the mountains appeared. ⁶And it was at the end of forty days, and Noah opened the window of the ark that he had made. ⁷And he let a raven go,* and it went back and forth until the water dried up from the earth. ⁸And he let a dove go from him to see whether the waters had eased from the face of the earth. ⁹And the dove did not find a resting place for its foot, and it came back to him to the ark, for waters were on the face of the earth, and he put out his hand and took it and brought it to him to the ark. ¹⁰And he waited still another seven days, and he again let a dove go from the ark. ¹¹And the dove came to him at evening time, and here was an olive leaf torn off in its mouth, and Noah knew that the waters had eased from the earth. ¹²And he waited still another seven days, and he let a dove go, and it did not come back to him ever again. ¹³And it was in the six hundred and first year, in the first month, in the first of the month: the water dried from on the earth. And Noah turned back the covering of the ark and looked, and here the face of the earth had dried. ¹⁴And in the second month, in the twenty-seventh day of the month, the earth dried up.**

¹⁵And God spoke to Noah, saying, ¹⁶"Go out from the ark, you and your wife and your sons and your sons' wives with you. ¹⁷Bring out with you all the living things that are with you, of all flesh, of the birds and of the domestic animals and of all the creeping animals that creep on the earth, and they will swarm in the earth and be fruitful and multiply on the earth."

¹⁸And Noah went out, and his sons and his wife and his sons' wives with him. ¹⁹All the living things, all the creeping animals and all the birds, all that creep on the earth went out from the ark by their families.

---

*In P Noah sends out a raven. In J he sends out a dove (three times). (In the Epic of Gilgamesh, the hero of the flood sends out a raven, a dove, and a swallow.)

**In P the flood lasts a year (or a year and ten days). In J it is the more familiar forty days and nights.

²⁰And Noah built an altar to YHWH, and he took some of each of the pure animals and of each of the pure birds, and he offered sacrifices on the altar.* ²¹And YHWH smelled the pleasant smell, and YHWH said to his heart, "I won't curse the ground on account of humankind again, because the inclination of the human heart is bad from their youth, and I won't strike all the living again as I have done. ²²All the rest of the earth's days, seed and harvest, and cold and heat, and summer and winter, and day and night will not cease."

9 ¹And God blessed Noah and his sons and said to them, "Be fruitful and multiply and fill the earth. ²And fear of you and dread of you will be on every living thing of the earth and on every bird of the skies, in every one that will creep on the earth and in all the fish of the sea. They are given into your hand. ³Every creeping animal that is alive will be yours for food; I've given every one to you like a plant of vegetation, ⁴except you shall not eat flesh in its life, its blood, ⁵and except I shall inquire for your blood, for your lives. I shall inquire for it from the hand of every animal and from the hand of a human. I shall inquire for a human's life from the hand of each man for his brother. ⁶One who sheds a human's blood: by a human his blood will be shed, because He made the human in the image of God. ⁷And you, be fruitful and multiply, swarm in the earth and multiply in it."

⁸And God said to Noah and to his sons with him, saying, ⁹"And I: here, I'm establishing my covenant with you and with your seed after you ¹⁰and with every living being that is with you, of the birds, of the domestic animals, and of all the wild animals of the earth with you, from all those coming out of the ark to every living thing of the earth. ¹¹And I shall establish my covenant with you, and all flesh will not be cut off again by the floodwaters, and there will not be a flood again to destroy the earth." ¹²And God said, "This is the sign of the covenant that I'm giving between me and you and every living being that is with you for eternal generations: ¹³I've put my rainbow in the clouds, and it will become a covenant sign between me and the earth. ¹⁴And it will be when I bring a cloud over the earth, and the rainbow

---

*Noah had seven pairs of each of the pure (sacrificeable) animals, so now he is able to sacrifice some. P has no stories involving sacrifices until the establishment of the priesthood and the Tabernacle (Exodus 40), and so the P flood story requires only two of each animal. This explains the distinction in the note on Gen 6:19 above.

will appear in the cloud, ¹⁵and I'll remember my covenant that is between me and you and every living being of all flesh, and the waters will not become a flood to destroy all flesh again. ¹⁶And the rainbow will be in the cloud, and I'll see it, to remember an eternal covenant between God and every living being of all flesh that is on the earth." ¹⁷And God said to Noah, "This is the sign of the covenant that I've established between me and all flesh that is on the earth."

¹⁸And Noah's sons who went out from the ark were Shem and Ham and Yaphet. And Ham: he was the father of Canaan. ¹⁹These three were Noah's sons, and all the earth expanded from these. ²⁰And Noah began to be a man of the ground, and he planted a vineyard. ²¹And he drank from the wine and was drunk. And he was exposed inside his tent. ²²And Ham, the father of Canaan, saw his father's nakedness and told his two brothers outside. ²³And Shem and Yaphet took a garment and put it on both their shoulders and went backwards and covered their father's nakedness. And they faced backwards and did not see their father's nakedness. ²⁴And Noah woke up from his wine, and he knew what his youngest son had done to him. ²⁵And he said, "Canaan is cursed. He'll be a servant of servants to his brothers." ²⁶And he said, "Blessed is YHWH, God of Shem, and may Canaan be a servant to them." ²⁷May God enlarge Yaphet, and may he dwell in the tents of Shem, and may Canaan be a servant to them."

²⁸And Noah lived after the flood three hundred years and fifty years, ²⁹and all of Noah's days were nine hundred years and fifty years. And he died.

10

¹And these are the records of Noah's sons, Shem, Ham, and Yaphet: And children were born to them after the flood. ²Yaphet's children were Gomer and Magog and Madai and Yawan and Tubal and Meshech and Tiras. ³And Gomer's children were Ashkenaz and Riphath and Togarmah. ⁴And Yawan's children were Elisha and Tarshish, Kittim and Dodanim. ⁵The islands of the nations in their lands were dispersed out from these, each by its language, by their families within their nations.

⁶And Ham's children were Cush and Egypt and Put and Canaan. ⁷And Cush's children were Seba and Havilah and Sabtah and Raamah and Sabteca. And Raamah's children were Sheba and Dedan. ⁸And Cush fathered Nimrod. He began being a man of power in the earth. ⁹He was a powerful hunter before YHWH. On account of this it is said: "A powerful

hunter before YHWH like Nimrod!" [10]And the beginning of his kingdom was Babylon and Erech and Akkad and Calneh in the land of Shinar. [11]Asshur came out of that land and built Nineveh and Rehovoth-Ir and Calah, [12]and Resen between Nineveh and Calah. It is the big city. [13]And Egypt fathered Ludim and Anamim and Lehabim and Naphtuhim [14]and Pathrusim and Casluhim, from which the Philistines came out, and Caphtorim. [15]And Canaan fathered Sidon, his firstborn, and Heth [16]and the Jebusite and the Amorite and the Girgashite [17]and the Hivite and the Arkite and the Sinite [18]and the Arvadite and the Zemarite and the Hamathite. And later the families of the Canaanites were dispersed. [19]And the Canaanite border was from Sidon, as you come to Gerar, up to Gaza, as you come to Sodom and Gomorrah and Admah and Zeboim, up to Lasha. **[20]These are Ham's children, by their families, by their languages, in their lands, within their nations.**

[21]Children were born to Shem, him as well, father of all of Eber's children, older brother of Yaphet. **[22]Shem's children were Elam and Asshur and Arpachshad and Lud and Aram. [23]And Aram's children were Uz and Hul and Gether and Mash.** [24]And Arpachshad fathered Shelah, and Shelah fathered Eber. [25]And two sons were born to Eber. The name of one was Peleg, because in his days the earth was divided, and his brother's name was Joktan. [26]And Joktan fathered Almodad and Sheleph and Hazarmaveth and Jerah [27]and Hadoram and Uzal and Diklah [28]and Obal and Abimael and Sheba [29]and Ophir and Havilah and Jobab. All these are Joktan's children. [30]And their home was from Mesha, as you come to Sephar, to the mountain of the east. **[31]These are Shem's children, by their families, by their languages, in their lands, by their nations.**

[32]These are the families of Noah's children by their records in their nations, and the nations were dispersed from these in the earth after the flood.

11

[1]And it was: all the earth was one language and the same words. [2]And it was when they were traveling from the east: and they found a valley in the land of Shinar and lived there. [3]And they said to one another, "Come on, let's make bricks and fire them." And they had brick for stone, and they had bitumen for mortar. [4]And they said, "Come on, let's build ourselves a city and a tower, and its top will be in the skies, and we'll make ourselves a name, or else we'll scatter over the face of all the earth."

⁵And YHWH went down to see the city and the tower that the children of humankind had built. ⁶And YHWH said, "Here, they're one people, and they all have one language, and this is what they've begun to do. And now nothing that they'll scheme to do will be precluded from them. ⁷Come on, let's go down and babble their language there so that one won't understand another's language." ⁸And YHWH scattered them from there over the face of all the earth, and they stopped building the city. ⁹On account of this its name was called Babylon, because YHWH babbled the language of all the earth there, and YHWH scattered them from there over the face of all the earth.

¹⁰These are the records of Shem: *Shem was a hundred years old, and he fathered Arpachshad, two years after the flood. ¹¹And Shem lived after his fathering Arpachshad five hundred years, and he fathered sons and daughters. ¹²And Arpachshad lived thirty-five years, and he fathered Shelah. ¹³And Arpachshad lived after his fathering Shelah three years and four hundred years, and he fathered sons and daughters. ¹⁴And Shelah lived thirty years, and he fathered Eber. ¹⁵And Shelah lived after his fathering Eber three years and four hundred years, and he fathered sons and daughters. ¹⁶And Eber lived forty-three years, and he fathered Peleg. ¹⁷And Eber lived after his fathering Peleg thirty years and four hundred years, and he fathered sons and daughters. ¹⁸And Peleg lived thirty years, and he fathered Reu. ¹⁹And Peleg lived after his fathering Reu nine years and two hundred years, and he fathered sons and daughters. ²⁰And Reu lived thirty-two years, and he fathered Serug. ²¹And Reu lived after his fathering Serug seven years and two hundred years, and he fathered sons and daughters. ²²And Serug lived thirty years, and he fathered Nahor. ²³And Serug lived after his fathering Nahor two hundred years, and he fathered sons and daughters. ²⁴And Nahor lived twenty-nine years, and he fathered Terah. ²⁵And Nahor lived after his fathering Terah nineteen years and a hundred years, and he fathered sons and daughters. ²⁶And Terah lived seventy years, and he fathered Abram, Nahor, and Haran.*

²⁷And these are the records of Terah: Terah had fathered Abram, Nahor, and Haran, and Haran had fathered Lot. ²⁸And Haran died in the lifetime of Terah, his father, in the land of his birthplace, in Ur of the Chaldees. ²⁹And Abram and Nahor took wives. Abram's wife's name was Sarai, and Nahor's wife's name was Milcah, daughter of Haran—father of Milcah and father of Iscah. ³⁰And Sarai was infertile. She did not have a child. ³¹And Terah took Abram, his son, and Lot, son of Haran, his grandson, and Sarai, his daughter-in-law, the wife of Abram, his son; and they went with them from Ur of the Chaldees to go to the land of Canaan. And they came as far as Haran, and

they stayed there.* *³²And Terah's days were five years and two hundred years. And Terah died in Haran.*

12

¹And YHWH said to Abram,** "Go from your land and from your birthplace and from your father's house to the land that I'll show you. ²And I'll make you into a big nation, and I'll bless you and make your name great. And be a blessing! ³And I'll bless those who bless you, and those who affront you I'll curse. And all the families of the earth will be blessed through you." ⁴And Abram went as YHWH had spoken to him, and Lot went with him. **And Abram was seventy-five years old when he went out from Haran. ⁵And Abram took Sarai, his wife, and Lot, his brother's son, and all their property that they had accumulated and the persons whom they had gotten in Haran; and they went out to go to the land of Canaan.**

And they came to the land of Canaan. ⁶And Abram passed through the land as far as the place of Shechem, as far as the oak of Moreh. And the Canaanite was in the land then.

⁷And YHWH appeared to Abram and said, "I'll give this land to your seed." And he built an altar there to YHWH who had appeared to him. ⁸And he moved on from there to the hill country east of Beth-El and pitched his tent—Beth-El to the west and and Ai to the east—and he built an altar there to YHWH and invoked the name YHWH. ⁹And Abram traveled on, going to the Negeb.

---

*R had to solve the problem that in P Abram comes from Ur while in J he comes from Haran. R's solution was to have the family start out in Ur and then stop in Haran for a while. The solution works in this passage, but it leaves a contradiction below: In 12:1 (J) God tells Abram in Haran to leave his land and birthplace, but in the redacted text Abram has already left his land and birthplace, which are back in Ur! And later Abram will tell his servant to "go to my land and my birthplace and take a wife for my son, for Isaac," and the servant goes to Haran, not Ur. Prior to the formation of the Documentary Hypothesis, commentators proposed complicated geographical solutions to deal with this contradiction.

**Abram's name is changed to Abraham only in P (Gen 17:5), and Sarai's name is changed to Sarah (17:15). There is no mention of these changes of names in J or E. It may be that their reference to it was eliminated by the Redactor because it was a particularly blatant duplication, or, more probably, the Redactor changed the names Abraham and Sarah to Abram and Sarai wherever they occurred in J and E prior to Gen 17:5 in order to keep the names consistent in the combined narrative.

¹⁰And there was a famine in the land, and Abram went down to Egypt to reside there because the famine was heavy in the land. ¹¹And it was when he was close to coming to Egypt: and he said to Sarai, his wife, "Here, I know that you're a beautiful woman. ¹²And it will be when the Egyptians see you that they'll say, 'This is his wife,' and they'll kill me and keep you alive. ¹³Say you're my sister so it will be good for me on your account and I'll stay alive because of you."* ¹⁴And it was as Abram came to Egypt, and the Egyptians saw the woman, that she was very beautiful. ¹⁵And Pharaoh's officers saw her and praised her to Pharaoh, and the woman was taken to Pharaoh's house. ¹⁶And he was good to Abram on her account, and he had a flock and oxen and he-asses and servants and maids and she-asses and camels. ¹⁷And YHWH plagued Pharaoh and his house, big plagues, over the matter of Sarai, Abram's wife.

¹⁸And Pharaoh called Abram and said, "What is this you've done to me? Why didn't you tell me that she was your wife? ¹⁹Why did you say, 'She's my sister,' so I took her for a wife for myself! And now, here's your wife. Take her and go." ²⁰And Pharaoh commanded people over him, and they let him and his wife and all he had go.

13

¹And Abram went up from Egypt, he and his wife and all he had and Lot with him, to the Negeb. ²And Abram was very heavy with livestock and silver and gold. ³And he went on his travels from the Negeb as far as Beth-El, as far as the place where his tent was at the start, between Beth-El and Ai, ⁴to the place of the altar that he had made there at the beginning. And Abram invoked the name YHWH there.

⁵And Lot, who was going with Abram, also had a flock and oxen and tents. **⁶And the land did not suffice them to live together, because their property was great, and they were not able to live together.** ⁷And there was a quarrel between those who herded Abram's livestock and those who herded

---

*There are three stories in Genesis in which a patriarch's wife is represented to be his sister, a king learns that she is actually the patriarch's wife, and then the husband and wife leave and prosper: Gen 12:10–20 (J); 20:1–18 (E); and 26:6–14 (J). The first and third are both J. They do not overlap characters: the first story is about Abraham-Sarah-Pharaoh; the second is about Isaac-Rebekah-Abimelek. The second story combines characters from each of the other two: Abraham-Sarah-Abimelek. The first and third stories use the name YHWH. The second story just says "God."

Lot's livestock. And the Canaanite and the Perizzite lived in the land then. ⁸And Abram said to Lot, "Let there be no quarreling between me and you and between my herders and your herders, because we're brothers. ⁹Isn't the whole land before you? Separate from me: if left then I'll go right, and if right then I'll go left." ¹⁰And Lot raised his eyes and saw all the plain of the Jordan, that all of it was well-watered (before YHWH's destroying Sodom and Gomorrah) like YHWH's garden, like the land of Egypt, as you come to Zoar. ¹¹And Lot chose all the plain of the Jordan for himself, and Lot traveled east. **And they separated, each from his brother. ¹²Abram lived in the land of Canaan, and Lot lived in the cities of the plain.** And he tented as far as Sodom. ¹³And the people of Sodom were very bad and sinful to YHWH.

¹⁴And YHWH said to Abram after Lot's separation from him, "Lift your eyes and see from the place where you are to the north and south and east and west. ¹⁵For all the land that you see, I'll give it to you and to your seed forever. ¹⁶And I'll make your seed like the dust of the earth, so that if a man could count the dust of the earth then your seed also could be counted. ¹⁷Get up, go around in the land to its length and its width, because I'm giving it to you." ¹⁸And Abram took up his tent and came and lived among the oaks of Mamre which are in Hebron, and he built an altar to YHWH there.

14

¹*And it was in the days of Amraphel, king of Shinar, Arioch, king of Ellasar, Chedorlaomer, king of Elam, and Tidal, king of Goiim:** ²*They made war with Bera, king of Sodom, and Birsha, king of Gomorrah, Shinab, king of Admah, and Shemeber, king of Zeboiim, and the king of Bela. (That is Zoar).* ³*All these were allied at the Siddim Valley. (That is the Dead Sea.)* ⁴*Twelve years they served Chedorlaomer, and the thirteenth year they revolted,* ⁵*and in the fourteenth year Chedorlaomer and the kings who were with him came, and they struck the Rephaim in Ashteroth Karnaim and the Zuzum in Ham and the Emim in Shaveh Kiriataim* ⁶*and the Horites in their mountain Seir to El Paran, which is by the wilderness.* ⁷*And they came back and came to En Mishpat (that is Kadesh) and struck the area of the Amalekites and also the Amorites who live in Hazazon Tamar.* ⁸*And the king of Sodom and the king of Gomorrah and the*

---

*This story comes from a separate narrative source. It does not have any of the characteristic signs of J, E, or P.

king of Admah and the king of Zeboiim and the king of Bela (that is Zoar) went out and aligned with them for war in the Siddim Valley, ⁹*with Chedorlaomer, king of Elam, and Tidal, king of Goiim, and Amraphel, king of Shinar, and Arioch, king of Ellasar—four kings with five.* ¹⁰*And Siddim Valley was pits, pits of bitumen, and the kings of Sodom and Gomorrah fled, and they fell there; and those who were left fled to the mountain.* ¹¹*And they took all the property of Sodom and Gomorrah and all their food, and they went.* ¹²*And they took Lot, Abram's brother's son, and his property when they went. And he had been living in Sodom.* ¹³*And an escapee came and told Abram the Hebrew, and he was tenting among the oaks of Mamre the Amorite, brother of Eshcol and brother of Aner; and they were covenant partners of Abram.* ¹⁴*And Abram heard that his brother had been taken prisoner, and he had his trained men, born in his house, unsheathe: three hundred eighteen. And he pursued as far as Dan.* ¹⁵*And he divided against them by night, he and his servants, and he struck them and pursued them as far as Hobah, which is at the left of Damascus.* ¹⁶*And he brought back all the property, and he also brought back Lot, his brother, and his property, and also the women and the people.* ¹⁷*And the king of Sodom came out to him after he came back from striking Chedorlaomer and the kings who were with him at the Shaveh Valley. (That is the valley of the king.)*

¹⁸*And Melchizedek, king of Salem, had brought out bread and wine. And he was a priest of El the Highest.* ¹⁹*And he blessed him and said, "Blessed is Abram to El the Highest, creator of skies and earth.* ²⁰*And blessed is El the Highest, who delivered your foes into your hand." And he gave him a tithe from everything.*

²¹*And the king of Sodom said to Abram, "Give the persons to me, and take the property for you."*

²²*And Abram said to the king of Sodom, "I've lifted my hand to YHWH, El the Highest, creator of skies and earth,* ²³*that, from a thread to a shoelace, I won't take anything that is yours, so you won't say, 'I made Abram rich.'* ²⁴*Except only what the boys have eaten and the share of the people who went with me: Aner, Eshcol, and Mamre. They shall take their share."*

15

¹After these things YHWH's word came to Abram in a vision, saying, "Don't fear, Abram. I'm a shield for you. Your reward is very much."

²And Abram said, "My Lord, YHWH, what would you give me when I go childless and my household is an acquired person!" (That is Damascus

Eliezer.) ³And Abram said, "Here, you haven't given me seed. And, here, a member of my household is taking possession of what is mine."

⁴And, here, YHWH's word came to him, saying, "This one won't take possession from you, but rather one who will come out of your insides: he will take possession from you." ⁵And He brought him outside and said, "Look at the skies and count the stars—if you'll be able to count them." And He said to him, "That is how your seed will be."

⁶And he trusted in YHWH, and He considered it for him as virtue. ⁷And He said to him, "I am YHWH, who brought you out of Ur of the Chaldees* to give you this land, to possess it."

⁸And he said, "My Lord YHWH, how will I know that I'll possess it?"

⁹And He said to him, "Take a three-year-old heifer and a three-year-old she-goat and a three-year-old ram and a dove and a pigeon for me."

¹⁰And he took all of these for Him and split them up the middle and set each half opposite its other half, but he did not split the birds. ¹¹And birds of prey came down on the carcasses, and Abram retrieved them. ¹²And the sun was about to set, and a slumber had come over Abram; and, here, a big, dark terror was coming over him.

¹³And He said to Abram, "You shall know that your seed will be an alien in a land that is not theirs, and they will serve them, and they will degrade them four hundred years. ¹⁴But I'll judge the nation whom they'll serve as well, and after that they'll go out with much property. ¹⁵And you: you'll come to your fathers in peace. You'll be buried at a good old age. ¹⁶And a fourth generation will come back here, because the Amorite's crime is not yet complete."

¹⁷And the sun was setting,** and there was darkness, and here was an oven of smoke and a flame of fire that went between these pieces. ¹⁸In that day YHWH made a covenant with Abram, saying, "I've given this land to your seed, from the river of Egypt to the big river, the river Euphrates: ¹⁹the

---

*If this portion of the text is J, then the text would have said originally "brought you out of Haran." R would have changed Haran to Ur here to make this consistent with the combined text in Gen 11:31–12:4. See the note on Gen 11:31.

**15:13–17 appears to be an addition to this story because (1) it is enclosed by a resumptive repetition: the sun is about to set in v. 12 and then is reported to set in v. 17; (2) the prediction of the future that God gives Abram has nothing to do with the covenant ceremony that is taking place; and (3) these lines merge terms that are characteristic of each of the sources: the phrase "alien in a land" is reminiscent of J (Exod 2:22), the phrase "will degrade them" is reminiscent of E (Exod 1:11–12), and the word for "property" otherwise occurs only in P (and once in the separate source of Genesis 14). The reference to four hundred years of slavery in Egypt may relate to the "thirty years and four hundred years" in P (Exod 12:40).

Cainites and the Kenizzites and the Kadmonites ²⁰and the Hittites and the Perizzites and the Rephaim ²¹and the Amorites and the Canaanites and the Girgashites and the Jebusites."

16

¹And Abram's wife Sarai had not given birth by him. And she had an Egyptian maid, and her name was Hagar. ²And Sarai said to Abram, "Here, YHWH has held me back from giving birth. Come to my maid. Maybe I'll get 'childed' through her." And Abram listened to Sarai's voice. **³And Sarai, Abram's wife, took Hagar, the Egyptian, her maid, at the end of ten years of Abram's living in the land of Canaan, and gave her to Abram, her husband, as a wife to him.** ⁴And he came to Hagar, and she became pregnant. And she saw that she had become pregnant, and her mistress was lowered in her eyes.

⁵And Sarai said to Abram, "My injury is on you. I, I placed my maid in your bosom, and she saw that she had become pregnant, and I was lowered in her eyes. Let YHWH judge between me and you."

⁶And Abram said to Sarai, "Here, your maid is in your hand. Do to her whatever is good in your eyes." And Sarai degraded her, and she fled from her.

⁷And an angel of YHWH found her at a spring of water in the wilderness, by the spring on the way to Shur, ⁸and said, "Hagar, Sarai's maid, from where have you come, and where will you go?"

And she said, "I'm fleeing from Sarai, my mistress."

⁹And the angel of YHWH said to her, "Go back to your mistress, and suffer the degradation under her hands." ¹⁰And the angel of YHWH said, "I'll multiply your seed, and it won't be countable because of its great number." ¹¹And the angel of YHWH said to her, "Here, you're pregnant and will give birth to a son, and you shall call his name Ishmael, for YHWH has listened to your suffering. ¹²And he'll be a wild ass of a man, his hand against everyone, and everyone's hand against him, and he'll tent among all his brothers."

¹³And she called the name of YHWH who spoke to her "You are El-roi," for she said, "Have I also seen after the one who sees me here?" ¹⁴On account of this the well was called "the well Lahai-roi." Here it is between Kadesh and Bered.

¹⁵And Hagar gave birth to a son for Abram, and Abram called the name of his son whom Hagar had borne Ishmael. ¹⁶And Abram was eighty years and six years old when Hagar gave birth to Ishmael for Abram.

17

¹And Abram was ninety years and nine years old, and YHWH appeared to Abram and said to him, "I am El Shadday.* Walk before me and be unblemished, ²and let me place my covenant between me and you, and I'll make you very, very numerous." ³And Abram fell on his face, and God spoke with him, saying, ⁴"I: here, my covenant is with you, and you'll become a father of a mass of nations. ⁵And your name will not be called Abram anymore, but your name will be Abraham,** because I've set you to be a father of a mass of nations. ⁶And I'll make you very, very fruitful and make you into nations. And kings will come out of you. ⁷And I'll establish my covenant between me and you and your seed after you for their generations as an eternal covenant, to become God to you and to your seed after you. ⁸And I'll give you and your seed after you the land where you're residing, all the land of Canaan, as an eternal possession, and I'll become a God to them." ⁹And God said to Abraham, "And you: you shall observe my covenant, you and your seed after you through their generations. ¹⁰This is my covenant that you shall observe between me and you and your seed after you: every male is to be circumcised among you. ¹¹And you shall be circumcised at the flesh of your foreskin, and it will become a sign of a covenant between me and you. ¹²And at eight days old every male shall be circumcised among you through your generations: homeborn or purchased with money from any foreigner who is not from your seed. ¹³Your homeborn and the one purchased with your money will be circumcised. And my covenant will become an eternal covenant in your flesh. ¹⁴And an uncircumcised—a male the flesh of whose foreskin will not be circumcised—that person will be cut off from his people. He has broken my covenant."

---

*This entire chapter is P, the Priestly version of the Abrahamic covenant. Those who misunderstand the matter of the name of God in the sources mistakenly think that the mention of God's name, YHWH, in v. 1 is an exception to the hypothesis. On the contrary, this verse is precisely the point. The issue is not that the sources use different names for God. It is that the sources have different ideas of when God's name was *revealed* to human beings. In J it is known from the early generations of human beings. In E and P it is not revealed until the generation of Moses. So in P God says to Moses, "I appeared to Abraham, to Isaac, and to Jacob as El Shadday, and I was not known to them by my name, YHWH" (Exod 6:3). And, completely consistent with that, P says here that "YHWH appeared to Abram and said to him, 'I am El Shadday.'" That is not an exception to the rule. That *is* the rule!

**Abram's name is changed to Abraham here in P, and Sarai's name is changed to Sarah (v. 15). There is no mention of these changes of names in the other sources, but the Redactor has most probably made the change consistent for the rest of the narrative. From here on, all sources will use Abraham and Sarah, not Abram and Sarai.

¹⁵And God said to Abraham, "Sarai, your wife: you shall not call her name Sarai, because her name is Sarah. ¹⁶And I'll bless her, and I'll also give you a son from her. And I'll bless her, and she'll become nations. Kings of peoples will be from her."

¹⁷And Abraham fell on his face and laughed and said in his heart, "Will he be born to someone who's a hundred years old?! And will Sarah, who's ninety years old, give birth?!" ¹⁸And Abraham said to God, "If only Ishmael will live before you."

¹⁹And God said, "But Sarah, your wife, is giving birth to a son for you. And you shall call his name Isaac. And I'll establish my covenant with him as an eternal covenant for his seed after him. ²⁰And I've listened to you about Ishmael. Here, I've blessed him, and I'll make him fruitful and make him very, very numerous. He'll father twelve chieftains, and I'll make him into a big nation. ²¹But I'll establish my covenant with Isaac, whom Sarah will bear for you at this appointed time in the next year." ²²And He finished speaking with him, and God went up from Abraham.

²³And Abraham took Ishmael, his son, and all his homeborn and everyone purchased with his money, every male among the men of Abraham's house, and he circumcised the flesh of their foreskin in that very day, as God had spoken with him. ²⁴And Abraham was ninety-nine years old when he was circumcised, the flesh of his foreskin, ²⁵and Ishmael, his son, was thirteen years old when he was circumcised at the flesh of his foreskin. ²⁶In that very day Abraham was circumcised, and Ishmael, his son; ²⁷and all the men of his house, homeborn and purchased with money from a foreigner, were circumcised with him.

18

¹And YHWH appeared to him at the oaks of Mamre. And he was sitting at the tent entrance in the heat of the day, ²and he raised his eyes and saw, and here were three people standing over him. And he saw and ran toward them from the tent entrance and bowed to the ground. ³And he said, "My Lord, if I've found favor in your eyes don't pass on from your servant. ⁴Let a little water be gotten, and wash your feet and relax under a tree, ⁵and let me get a bit of bread, and satisfy your heart. Afterward you'll pass on, for that's why you've passed by your servant."

And they said, "Do that, as you've spoken."

⁶And Abraham hurried to the tent, to Sarah, and said, "Hurry, three measures of fine flour. Knead it and make cakes." ⁷And Abraham ran to the herd and took a calf, tender and good, and he gave it to a servant, and he

hurried to prepare it. [8]And he took curds and milk and the calf that he had prepared and placed them in front of them, and he was standing over them under the tree, and they ate.

[9]And they said to him, "Where is Sarah, your wife?"

And he said, "Here in the tent."

[10]And He said, "I shall come back to you at the time of life, and, here, Sarah, your wife, will have a son."

And Sarah was listening at the tent entrance, which was behind him. [11]And Abraham and Sarah were old, well along in days; Sarah had stopped having the way of women. [12]And Sarah laughed inside her and said, "After I've become worn out am I to have pleasure?! And my lord is old!"

[13]And YHWH said to Abraham, "Why is this? Sarah laughed, saying, 'Shall I indeed give birth? And I am old!' Is anything too wondrous for YHWH? [14]At the appointed time I'll come back to you, at the time of life, and Sarah will have a son."

[15]And Sarah lied, saying, "I didn't laugh," because she was afraid.

And He said, "No, but you did laugh."

[16]And the people got up from there and gazed at the sight of Sodom, and Abraham was going with them to send them off. [17]And YHWH had said, "Shall I conceal what I'm doing from Abraham, [18]since Abraham will become a big and powerful nation, and all the nations of the earth will be blessed through him? [19]For I've known him for the purpose that he'll command his children and his house after him, and they'll observe YHWH's way, to do virtue and judgment, and for the purpose of YHWH's bringing upon Abraham what He spoke about him."

[20]And YHWH said, "The cry of Sodom and Gomorrah: how great it is. And their sin: how very heavy it is. [21]Let me go down, and I'll see if they've done, all told, like the cry that has come to me. And if not, let me know." [22]And the people turned from there and went to Sodom.

And Abraham was still standing before YHWH, [23]and Abraham came over and said, "Will you also annihilate the virtuous with the wicked? [24]Maybe there are fifty virtuous people within the city. Will you also annihilate and not sustain the place for the fifty virtuous who are in it? [25]Far be it from you to do a thing like this, to kill virtuous with wicked—and it will be the same for the virtuous and the wicked—far be it from you. Will the judge of all the earth not do justice?"

[26]And YHWH said, "If I find in Sodom fifty virtuous people within the city, then I'll sustain the whole place for their sake."

[27]And Abraham answered, and he said, "Here I've undertaken to speak to my Lord, and I'm dust and ashes. [28]Maybe the fifty virtuous people will be short by five. Will you destroy the whole city for the five?"

And He said, "I won't destroy if I find forty-five there."

²⁹And he went on again to speak to Him and said, "Maybe forty will be found there."

And He said, "I won't do it for the sake of the forty."

³⁰And he said, "May my Lord not be angry, and let me speak. Maybe thirty will be found there."

And He said, "I won't do it if I find thirty there."

³¹And he said, "Here I've undertaken to speak to my Lord. Maybe twenty will be found there."

And He said, "I won't destroy for the sake of the twenty."

³²And he said, "May my Lord not be angry, and let me speak just this one time. Maybe ten will be found there."

And He said there, "I won't destroy for the sake of the ten."

³³And YHWH went when He had finished speaking to Abraham, and Abraham went back to his place.

19

¹And the two angels came to Sodom in the evening, and Lot was sitting at Sodom's gate, and Lot saw and got up toward them, and he bowed, nose to the ground. ²And he said, "Here, my lords, turn to your servant's house and spend the night and wash your feet, and you'll get up early and go your way."

And they said, "No, we'll spend the night in the square." ³And he pressed them very much, and they turned to him and came to his house, and he made a feast and baked unleavened bread for them, and they ate.

⁴They had not yet lain down, and the people of the city, the people of Sodom, surrounded the house, from youth to old man, all the people, from the farthest reaches. ⁵And they called to Lot and said to him, "Where are the people who came to you tonight? Bring them out to us, and let's know them!"

⁶And Lot went out to them at the entrance and closed the door behind him, ⁷and he said, "Don't do bad, my brothers." ⁸Here I have two daughters who haven't known a man. Let me bring them out to you, and do to them as is good in your eyes. Only don't do anything to these people, because that is why they came under the shadow of my roof."

⁹And they said, "Come over here," and they said, "This one comes to live, and then he judges! Now we'll be worse to you than to them." And they pressed the man, Lot, very much and came over to break down the door. ¹⁰And the people reached their hand out and brought Lot in to them in the

house, and they closed the door. ¹¹And they struck the people who were at the house's entrance with blindness, from smallest to biggest, and they wearied themselves with finding the entrance.

¹²And the people said to Lot, "Who else do you have here—son-in-law and your sons and your daughters and all that you have in the city—take them out from the place, ¹³because we're destroying this place, because its cry has grown big before YHWH's face, and YHWH has sent us to destroy it."

¹⁴And Lot went out and spoke to his sons-in-law, who had married his daughters, and said, "Get up, get out of this place, for YHWH is destroying the city." And he was like a joker in his sons-in-law's eyes.

¹⁵And as the dawn rose the angels urged Lot, saying, "Get up, take your wife and your two daughters who are present, or else you'll be annihilated for the city's crime." ¹⁶And he delayed. And the people took hold of his hand and his wife's hand and his two daughters' hands because of YHWH's compassion for him, and they brought him out and set him outside the city.

¹⁷And it was as they were bringing them outside, and He said, "Escape for your life. Don't look behind you and don't stop in all of the plain. Escape to the mountain or else you'll be annihilated."

¹⁸And Lot said to them, "Let it not be, my Lord. ¹⁹Here, your servant has found favor in your eyes, and you've magnified your kindness that you've done for me, keeping my soul alive, and I'm not able to escape to the mountain, in case the bad thing will cling to me and I'll die. ²⁰Here, this city is close to flee there, and it's small. Let me escape there—isn't it small?—and my soul will live."

²¹And He said to him, "Here, I've granted you this thing, too, that I won't overturn the city of which you spoke. ²²Quickly, escape there, because I can't do a thing until you get there."

On account of this the city's name was called Zoar.

²³The sun rose on the earth, and Lot came to Zoar. ²⁴And YHWH rained brimstone and fire on Sodom and on Gomorrah, from YHWH out of the skies. ²⁵And He overturned these cities and all of the plain and all of the residents of the cities and all the growth of the ground. ²⁶And his wife looked behind him, and she was a pillar of salt!

²⁷And Abraham got up early in the morning to the place where he had stood in YHWH's presence, ²⁸and he gazed at the sight of Sodom and Gomorrah and at the sight of all the land of the plain. And he saw: and, here, the smoke of the land went up like the smoke of a furnace.

²⁹**And it was, when God destroyed the cities of the plain, that God remembered Abraham and let Lot go from inside the overthrow: at the over-throwing of the cities in which Lot lived.**

³⁰And Lot went up from Zoar and lived in the mountain, and his two daughters with him, because he feared to live in Zoar, and he lived in a cave, he and his two daughters. ³¹And the firstborn said to the younger one, "Our father is old, and there's no man in the earth to come to us in the way of all the earth. ³²Come on, let's make our father drink wine, and let's lie with him and make seed live from our father." ³³And they made their father drink wine in that night, and the firstborn came and lay with her father. And he did not know of her lying down and her getting up. ³⁴And it was on the next day, and the firstborn said to the younger one, "Here, I lay with my father last night. Let's make him drink wine tonight as well, and you come and lie with him, and we'll make seed live from our father." ³⁵And they made their father drink wine in that night as well, and the younger one got up and lay with him, and he did not know of her lying down and her getting up. ³⁶And Lot's two daughters became pregnant by their father. ³⁷And the firstborn gave birth to a son and called his name Moab. He is the father of Moab to this day. ³⁸And the younger one, she, too, gave birth to a son and called his name ben-Ammi. He is the father of the children of Ammon to this day.

20

¹And Abraham traveled from there to the Negeb country, **and he lived between Kadesh and Shur and resided in Gerar.* ²And Abraham said of Sarah, his wife, "She's my sister." And Abimelek, king of Gerar, sent and took Sarah.**

³**And God came to Abimelek in a night dream and said to him, "Here, you're dead over the woman whom you took, for she's a man's wife!" ⁴And Abimelek had not come close to her, and he said, "My Lord, will you kill a vir-tuous nation as well? ⁵Didn't he say to me, 'She's my sister'? And she—she, too—said, 'He's my brother.' I did this in my heart's innocence and in my hands' cleanness."**

---

*This is the first occurrence of a text from the source E. It certainly does not appear to be the beginning of the source, as Abraham and Sarah come out of nowhere. It appears that RJE favored J for the opening part of the story. We therefore cannot know what origi-nally preceded this in E, and so we do not know if E included a story of creation, flood, genealogy, and so on.

⁶And God said to him in the dream, "I, too, knew that you did this in your heart's innocence; and I, too, held you back from sinning against me. On account of this, I didn't let you touch her. ⁷And now, give the man's wife back, because he's a prophet, and he'll pray for you. And live! And if you don't give back, know that you will die, you and all that you have."

⁸And Abimelek got up in the morning and called to all his servants and spoke all these things in their ears, and the people were very afraid. ⁹And Abimelek called Abraham and said to him, "What have you done to us, and how did I sin against you, that you brought a big sin over me and over my kingdom? You've done things with me that are not done!" ¹⁰And Abimelek said to Abraham, "What did you see, that you did this thing?"

¹¹And Abraham said, "Because I said, 'There just isn't the fear of God in this place, and they'll kill me on account of my wife.' ¹²And also she is, in fact, my sister, my father's daughter but not my mother's daughter, and she became a wife to me. ¹³And it was when God had me roam from my father's house, and I said to her, 'This will be your kindness that you'll do with me: to every place where we come, say about me, "He's my brother."'"

¹⁴And Abimelek took sheep and oxen and servants and maids, and he gave them to Abraham, and he gave Sarah, his wife, back to him. ¹⁵And Abimelek said, "Here's my land in front of you. Live wherever it's good in your eyes." ¹⁶And to Sarah he said, "Here, I've given a thousand weights of silver to your brother. Here, it's a covering of eyes for you with everyone with you, and you're justified with everyone."

¹⁷And Abraham prayed to God, and God healed Abimelek and his wife and his maids, and they gave birth, ¹⁸because YHWH had held back every womb of Abimelek's house on account of Sarah, Abraham's wife!

21

¹And YHWH had taken account of Sarah as He had said, **and YHWH did to Sarah as He had spoken.** * ²And Sarah became pregnant and gave birth to a son for Abraham in his old age **at the appointed time that God had spoken.** ³**And Abraham called the name of his son who was born to him, to whom Sarah had given birth for him: Isaac. ⁴And Abraham circum-**

---

*This must be recognized as one of the rare instances in which the name YHWH occurs in a passage that is identified as P. It is probably a result of the editing process, in which the two halves of verse 1 had extremely similar content and structure to one another. The fact that the Redactor chose to retain both of them is further confirmation that he was trying to retain both of his main sources (P and JE) in their entirety whenever it was possible.

cised Isaac, his son, at eight days old, as God had commanded him. ⁵And Abraham was a hundred years old when Isaac, his son, was born to him.

⁶And Sarah said, "God has made laughter for me. Everyone who hears will laugh for me." ⁷And she said, "Who would have said to Abraham, 'Sarah has nursed children'? Yet I've given birth to a son in his old age."

⁸And the boy grew and was weaned. And Abraham made a big feast in the day that Isaac was weaned. ⁹And Sarah saw the son of Hagar, the Egyptian, whom she had borne to Abraham, fooling around. ¹⁰And she said to Abraham, "Drive this maid out—and her son, because the son of this maid will not inherit with my son, with Isaac."

¹¹And the thing was very bad in Abraham's eyes in regard to his son. ¹²And God said to Abraham, "Let it not be bad in your eyes about the boy and about your maid. Everything that Sarah tells you: listen to her voice; because seed for you will be called by Isaac. ¹³And I'll make the maid's son into a nation as well, because he's your seed."

¹⁴And Abraham got up early in the morning and took bread and a bottle of water and gave to Hagar—he put them on her shoulder—and the boy, and he sent her off. And she went and strayed in the Beer-sheba wilderness. ¹⁵And the water was finished from the bottle, and she thrust the boy under one of the shrubs, ¹⁶and she went and sat opposite, going as far as a bow-shot, because she said, "Let me not see the boy's death." And she sat opposite and raised her voice and wept.

¹⁷And God heard the boy's voice. And an angel of God called to Hagar from the heavens and said to her, "What trouble do you have, Hagar? Don't be afraid. Because God has heard the boy's voice where he is. ¹⁸Get up. Carry the boy and hold him up in your hand, because I shall make him into a big nation." ¹⁹And God opened her eyes, and she saw a water well, and she went and filled the bottle with water and had the boy drink.

²⁰And God was with the boy, and he grew, and he lived in the wilderness and was a bowman. ²¹And he lived in the Paran wilderness, and his mother took him a wife from the land of Egypt.

²²And it was at that time, and Abimelek and Phichol, the commander of his army, said to Abraham, saying, "God is with you in everything that you do. ²³And now, swear to me here by God that you won't act falsely to me and to my offspring and to my posterity. Like the kindness that I've done with you, you'll do with me and with the land in which you've resided."

²⁴And Abraham said, "I'll swear," ²⁵and Abraham criticized Abimelek about a water well that Abimelek's servants had seized.

²⁶And Abimelek said, "I don't know who did this thing; and also, you didn't tell me; and also, I didn't hear of it except for today." ²⁷And Abraham

took sheep and oxen and gave to Abimelek, and the two of them made a covenant. ²⁸And Abraham stood seven ewes of the sheep by themselves. ²⁹And Abimelek said to Abraham, "What are these seven ewes that you've stood by themselves?"

³⁰And he said, "Because you'll take these seven ewes from my hand so that it will be evidence for me that I dug this well." ³¹On account of this he called that place Beer-sheba, because the two of them swore there ³²and made a covenant in Beer-sheba. And Abimelek and Phichol, the commander of his army, got up and went to the land of the Philistines.

³³And he planted a tamarisk in Beer-sheba and he called the name of YHWH El Olam. ³⁴And Abraham resided in the land of the Philistines many days.

22

¹And it was after these things, and God tested Abraham.

And He said to him, "Abraham."

And he said, "I'm here."

²And He said, "Take your son, your only one, whom you love, Isaac, and go to the land of Moriah and make him a burnt offering there on one of the mountains that I'll say to you."

³And Abraham got up early in the morning and harnessed his ass and took his two boys with him and Isaac, his son. And he cut the wood for the burnt offering, and he got up and went to the place that God had said to him. ⁴On the third day: and Abraham raised his eyes and saw the place from a distance. ⁵And Abraham said to his boys, "Sit here with the ass; and I and the boy: we'll go over there, and we'll bow, and we'll come back to you." ⁶And Abraham took the wood for the burnt offering and put it on Isaac, his son, and took the fire and the knife in his hand.

And the two of them went together.

⁷And Isaac said to Abraham, his father; and he said, "My father."

And he said, "I'm here, my son."

And he said, "Here are the fire and the wood, but where is the sheep for the burnt offering?"

⁸And Abraham said, "God will see to the sheep for the burnt offering, my son."

And the two of them went together.

⁹And they came to the place that God had said to him. And Abraham built the altar there and arranged the wood, and he bound Isaac, his son, and put him on the altar on top of the wood. ¹⁰And Abraham put out his hand and took the knife to slaughter his son.

¹¹And an angel of YHWH called to him from the skies and said, "Abraham! Abraham!"

And he said, "I'm here."

¹²And he said, "Don't put your hand out toward the boy, and don't do anything to him, because now I know that you fear God, and you didn't withhold your son, your only one, from me." ¹³And Abraham raised his eyes and saw, and here was a ram behind, caught in the thicket by its horns. And Abraham went and took the ram and made it a burnt offering instead of his son. ¹⁴And Abraham called the name of that place "YHWH Yir'eh," as is said today: "In YHWH's mountain it will be seen."

¹⁵And an angel of YHWH called to Abraham a second time from the skies.* **¹⁶And He**** said, "I swear by me—word of YHWH—that because you did this thing and didn't withhold your son, your only one, ¹⁷that I'll bless you and multiply your seed like the stars of the skies and like the sand that's on the seashore, and your seed will possess its enemies' gate. ¹⁸And all the nations of the earth will be blessed through your seed because you listened to my voice."**

¹⁹And Abraham went back to his boys, and they got up and went together to Beer-sheba, and Abraham lived in Beer-sheba.

²⁰And it was after these things, and it was told to Abraham, saying, "Here Milcah has given birth, she also, to sons for your brother Nahor: ²¹Uz, his firstborn, and Buz his brother, and Kemuel, the father of Aram,

---

*It is possible that in the original old E story, Abraham actually carries out the sacrifice of Isaac. The evidence that vv. 11–14, in which the sacrifice is stopped, were added by RJE is as follows: (1) This is an E text, referring to the deity as God (Elohim) in narration three times (vv. 1,3,9), but suddenly, as Abraham takes the knife in his hand, the text switches to an angel of *YHWH*. (2) Verses 11–15, which describe the angel's instructions to Abraham not to sacrifice his son after all, are enclosed in a resumptive repetition in which the angel calls out two times. (3) Following this resumptive repetition, the angel (or God) says, "because you *did* this thing and *didn't* withhold your son." (4) The story concludes, "And Abraham went back to his boys." Isaac is not mentioned—even though Abraham had explicitly told the boys, "*We'll* come back to you." (5) Isaac never again appears in E after this. (6) In the E story of a revelation at Mount Horeb in Exodus 24, there is a chain of eighteen parallels of language with this story of Isaac, but not one of those parallels comes solely from these verses (11–15). See the note on Exod 24:1. (7) There is a group of midrashic sources that say that Isaac was in fact sacrificed.

In light of these factors, it is possible that in the E story Abraham sacrifices Isaac, but that later this idea of a human sacrifice was repugnant, and so RJE added the lines in which Isaac is spared and a ram is substituted. It is not possible to say how the original E version accounted for the introduction of Jacob. Notably, though, it is in E (in the very next passage that is traced to E) that Abraham later has another wife, Keturah, and has more children. (See *Who Wrote the Bible?* pp. 256–257.)

**In the original E text it is *God* who speaks; but, as the text is edited by RJE, it now appears to be the angel who says this.

²²and Chesed and Hazo and Pildash and Jidlaph and Bethuel. ²³And Bethuel fathered Rebekah." Milcah gave birth to these eight for Nahor, Abraham's brother. ²⁴And his concubine, whose name was Reumah, she too gave birth, to Tebah and Gaham and Tahash and Maacah.

23

¹And Sarah's life was a hundred years and twenty years and seven years: the years of Sarah's life. ²And Sarah died in Kiriath Arba—it is Hebron—in the land of Canaan. And Abraham came to grieve for Sarah and to weep for her. ³And Abraham got up from in front of his dead, and he spoke to the children of Heth, saying, ⁴"I'm an alien and a visitor with you. Give me a possession for a tomb with you so I may bury my dead from in front of me."

⁵And the children of Heth answered Abraham, saying to him, ⁶"Listen to us, my lord. You're a chieftain of God among us. Bury your dead in the choice of our tombs. Not a man of us will hold back his tomb from you, from burying your dead."

⁷And Abraham got up and bowed to the people of the land, to the children of Heth, ⁸and he spoke with them, saying, "If it's acceptable to you to bury my dead from in front of me, listen to me, and intercede for me with Ephron, son of Zohar, ⁹that he'll give me the cave of Machpelah which he has, that is at the edge of his field. For full price let him give it to me among you as a possession for a tomb."

¹⁰And Ephron was sitting among the children of Heth, and Ephron, the Hittite, answered Abraham in the ears of the children of Heth, for all who were coming to his city's gate, saying, ¹¹"No, sir. Listen to me: I've given the field to you, and I've given the cave that's in it to you. I've given it to you before the eyes of the children of my people. Bury your dead."

¹²And Abraham bowed in front of the people of the land, ¹³and he spoke to Ephron in the ears of the people of the land, saying, "Just if you'll listen to me: I've given the money for the field. Take it from me so I may bury my dead there."

¹⁴And Ephron answered Abraham, saying to him, ¹⁵"Sir, listen to me. Land worth four hundred shekels of silver: what's that between me and you?! And bury your dead."

¹⁶And Abraham listened to Ephron, and Abraham weighed out to Ephron the money that he had spoken in the ears of the children of Heth: four hundred shekels of silver, at the merchant's current rate. ¹⁷And Ephron's field

that was in Machpelah, which faces Mamre, the field and the cave that was in it and every tree that was in the field, that was in all of its border all around, was established ¹⁸for Abraham as a purchase in the eyes of the children of Heth, among all who were coming to his city's gate.

¹⁹And after that Abraham buried Sarah, his wife, at the cave of the field of Machpelah, facing Mamre—it is Hebron—in the land of Canaan. ²⁰And the field and the cave that was in it were established for Abraham as a possession for a tomb from the children of Heth.

24

¹And Abraham was old, well along in days, and YHWH had blessed Abraham in everything. ²And Abraham said to his servant, the elder of his house, who was in charge of all that he had, "Place your hand under my thigh, ³and I'll have you swear by YHWH, God of the skies and God of the earth, that you won't take a wife for my son from the daughters of the Canaanite among whom I live, ⁴but you'll go to my land and my birthplace and take a wife for my son, for Isaac."

⁵And the servant said to him, "Maybe the woman won't be willing to follow me to this land. Shall I take back your son to the land you came from?"

⁶And Abraham said to him, "Watch yourself, that you don't take my son back there. ⁷YHWH, God of the skies, who took me from my father's house and from the land of my birth and who spoke to me and who swore to me, saying, 'I'll give this land to your seed,' He'll send His angel ahead of you, and you shall take a wife for my son from there. ⁸And if the woman won't be willing to go after you then you'll be freed from this oath of mine. Only you are not to take my son back there."

⁹And the servant placed his hand under his lord Abraham's thigh and swore to him about this thing. ¹⁰And the servant took ten camels of his lord's camels and went, and all of his lord's best things were in his hand. And he got up and went to Aram Naharaim, to the city of Nahor, ¹¹and he had the camels kneel outside the city at the water well at evening time, the time that the women went out to draw water. ¹²And he said, "YHWH, God of my lord Abraham, make something happen in front of me today and show kindness to my lord Abraham: ¹³Here I am, standing over the spring of water, and the daughters of the people of the city are going out to draw water. ¹⁴And let it be that the girl to whom I'll say, 'Tip your jar so I may drink,' and she'll say, 'Drink, and I'll water your camels, too,' she'll be the

one you've pointed out for your servant, for Isaac, and I'll know by this that you've shown kindness to my lord."

[15]And he had not even finished speaking, and here was Rebekah—who was born to Bethuel son of Milcah, wife of Nahor, Abraham's brother—coming out, and her jar was on her shoulder. [16]And the girl was very good looking, a virgin, and no man had known her. And she went down to the spring and filled her jar and went up. [17]And the servant ran toward her and said, "Give me a little water from your jar."

[18]And she said, "Drink, my lord," and she hurried and lowered her jar on her arm and let him drink.

[19]And she finished letting him drink, and she said, "I'll draw water for your camels, too, until they finish drinking." [20]And she hurried and emptied her jar into the trough and ran again to the well to draw water, and she drew water for all his camels. [21]And the man, astonished at her, was keeping quiet so as to know if YHWH had made his trip successful or not.

[22]And it was when the camels finished drinking: and the man took a gold ring—its weight was a beqa—and two bracelets for her arms—their weight was ten of gold. [23]And he said, "Tell me, whose daughter are you? Is there a place at your father's house for us to spend the night?"

[24]And she said to him, "I'm a daughter of Bethuel, Milcah's son whom she bore to Nahor." [25]And she said to him, "We also have plenty of both straw and fodder, also a place to spend the night."

[26]And the man knelt and bowed to YHWH [27]and said, "Blessed is YHWH, God of my lord Abraham, whose kindness and faithfulness have not left my lord. I: YHWH has led me to the house of my lord's brother."

[28]And the girl ran and told her mother's household about these things. [29]And Rebekah had a brother, and his name was Laban, and Laban ran outside to the man, at the spring. [30]And it was when he saw the ring and the bracelets on his sister's hands and when he heard his sister Rebekah's words, saying, "The man spoke like this to me." And he came to the man, and here he was standing by the camels at the spring. [31]And he said, "Come, blessed one of YHWH. Why do you stand outside when I've prepared the house and a place for the camels!" [32]And the man came to the house and unloaded the camels and gave straw and fodder to the camels and water to wash his feet and the feet of the people who were with him. [33]And [bread] was set in front of him to eat.

And he said, "I won't eat until I've said what I have to say."

And he said, "Speak."

[34]And he said, "I am Abraham's servant. [35]And YHWH has blessed my lord very much, and he has become great. And He has given him a flock

and oxen and silver and gold and male and female servants and camels and asses. ³⁶And my lord's wife Sarah gave birth to a son by my lord in her old age, and he has given him everything that he has. ³⁷And my lord had me swear, saying, 'You shall not take a wife for my son from the daughters of the Canaanite in whose land I live, ³⁸but you shall go to my father's house and to my family and take a wife for my son.' ³⁹And I said to my lord, 'Maybe the woman won't follow me.' ⁴⁰And he said to me, 'YHWH, before whom I have walked, will send His angel with you and make your trip successful, and you shall take a wife for my son from my family and from my father's house. ⁴¹Then you'll be freed from my oath: when you'll come to my family, and if they won't give her to you, then you'll be free from my oath.' ⁴²And I came to the spring today, and I said, 'YHWH, God of my lord Abraham, if you're making my trip on which I'm going successful, ⁴³here I am, standing at the spring of water, and let it be that the young woman who goes to draw water and I say to her, "Let me drink a little water from your jar," ⁴⁴and she says to me, "Both drink yourself and I'll draw water for your camels, too," she will be the woman whom YHWH has designated for my lord's son.' ⁴⁵I hadn't even finished speaking in my heart, and here was Rebekah coming out, and her jar was on her shoulder, and she went down to the spring and drew water. And I said to her, 'Give me a drink.' ⁴⁶And she hurried and lowered her jar from on her and said, 'Drink, and I'll water your camels, too.' And I drank, and she watered the camels, too. ⁴⁷And I asked her and said, 'Whose daughter are you?' And she said, 'The daughter of Bethuel son of Nahor, whom Milcah bore for him.' And I put the ring on her nose and the bracelets on her hands, ⁴⁸and I knelt and bowed to YHWH and blessed YHWH, my lord Abraham's God, who had led me in a faithful way to take a daughter of my lord's brother for his son. ⁴⁹And now, if you're exercising kindness and faithfulness with my lord, tell me; and if not, tell me; so I'll turn to right or to left."

⁵⁰And Laban and Bethuel answered, and they said, "The thing has come from YHWH. We can't speak bad or good to you. ⁵¹Here is Rebekah before you. Take her and go, and let her be a wife to your lord's son as YHWH has spoken." ⁵²And it was, when Abraham's servant heard their words, that he bowed to the ground to YHWH. ⁵³And the servant brought out silver articles and gold articles and garments and gave them to Rebekah and gave precious things to her brother and to her mother. ⁵⁴And they ate and drank, he and the people who were with him, and spent the night.

And they got up in the morning, and he said, "Send me back to my lord."

⁵⁵And her brother and her mother said, "Let the girl stay with us a few days—or ten. After that, she'll go."

⁵⁶And he said to them, "Don't hold me back, since YHWH has made my trip successful. Send me away, so I may go to my lord."

⁵⁷And they said, "We'll call the girl and ask her from her own mouth." ⁵⁸And they called Rebekah and said to her, "Will you go with this man?"

And she said, "I'll go."

⁵⁹And they sent their sister Rebekah and her nurse and Abraham's servant and his people. ⁶⁰And they blessed Rebekah and said to her, "You're our sister. Become thousands of ten-thousands. And may your seed possess the gate of those who hate him." ⁶¹And Rebekah and her maids got up and rode on the camels and followed the man, and the servant took Rebekah and went.

⁶²And Isaac was coming from the area of the well Lahai-roi, and he was living in the territory of the Negeb, ⁶³and Isaac went to meditate in a field toward evening, and he raised his eyes and saw, and here were camels coming. ⁶⁴And Rebekah raised her eyes and saw Isaac, and she fell from the camel. ⁶⁵And she said to the servant, "Who is that man who's walking in the field toward us?"

And the servant said, "He's my lord." And she took a veil and covered herself.

⁶⁶And the servant told Isaac all the things that he had done. ⁶⁷And Isaac brought her to his mother Sarah's tent. And he took Rebekah, and she became his wife, and he loved her.

And Isaac was consoled after his mother.

25

¹**And Abraham went on and took a wife, and her name was Keturah, ²and she gave birth to Zimran and Jokshan and Medan and Midian and Ishbak and Shuah for him. ³And Jokshan fathered Sheba and Dedan. And the children of Dedan were Ashurim and Letushim and Leummim. ⁴And the children of Midian: Ephah and Epher and Hanoch and Abida and Eldaah. All these were children of Keturah.*** ⁵And Abraham gave everything that he had to Isaac. ⁶And Abraham gave gifts to the children of the concubines that Abraham had, and he sent them away from Isaac, his son, while he was still living: east, to the land of the East.

---

*Here the Midianites and Medanites are introduced in E. It is in E that they will figure later, in the story of Joseph. See the note on Gen 37:28.

⁷And these are the days of the years of Abraham's life that he lived: a hundred years and seventy years and five years. ⁸And he expired. And Abraham died at a good old age, old and full, and was gathered to his people. ⁹And Isaac and Ishmael, his sons, buried him at the cave of Machpelah at the field of Ephron, son of Zohar, the Hittite, facing Mamre, ¹⁰the field that Abraham bought from the children of Heth. Abraham was buried there—and Sarah, his wife.

¹¹And it was after Abraham's death, and God blessed Isaac, his son. And Isaac lived at the well Lahai-roi.

¹²And these are the records of Ishmael, son of Abraham, to whom Hagar, the Egyptian, Sarah's maid, gave birth for Abraham: ¹³And these are the names of Ishmael's sons, by their names, according to their records: Ishmael's firstborn was Nebaioth, and Kedar and Adbeel and Mibsam ¹⁴and Mishma and Dumah and Massa, ¹⁵Hadar and Tema, Jetur, Naphish and Kedmah. ¹⁶These are they, Ishmael's sons, and these are their names in their settlements and in their encampments, twelve chieftains by their clans. ¹⁷And these are the years of Ishmael's life: a hundred years and thirty years and seven years. And he expired and died and was gathered to his people. ¹⁸And they tented from Havilah to Shur, which faces Egypt, as you come toward Asshur. He fell facing all of his brothers.

¹⁹And these are the records of Isaac, son of Abraham: Abraham had fathered Isaac. ²⁰And Isaac was forty years old when he took Rebekah, daughter of Bethuel, the Aramean, from Paddan Aram, sister of Laban, the Aramean, to him as a wife.* ²¹And Isaac prayed to YHWH for his wife because she was infertile, and YHWH was prevailed upon by him, and his wife Rebekah became pregnant. ²²And the children struggled inside her, and she said, "If it's like this, why do I exist?" And she went to inquire of YHWH.

²³And YHWH said to her,

> Two nations are in your womb,
> and two peoples will be dispersed from your insides,
> and one people will be mightier than the other people,
> and the older the younger will serve.

²⁴And her days to give birth were completed, and here were twins in her womb. ²⁵And the first came out all ruddy, like a hairy robe, and they called

---

*P has no report of the births of Jacob and Esau. P jumps from the report of Isaac's marriage to Rebekah here to the report of Esau's marriages below (26:34f.) This is one of the very few gaps in P, which otherwise generally flows as an unbroken narrative when it is read separately from J, E, and D.

his name Esau. ²⁶And after that his brother came out, and his hand was holding Esau's heel, and he called his name Jacob. And Isaac was sixty years old at their birth.

²⁷And the boys grew up, and Esau was a man who knew hunting, a man of the field, and Jacob was a simple man, living in tents. ²⁸And Isaac loved Esau because he put game meat in his mouth, and Rebekah loved Jacob.

²⁹And Jacob made a stew, and Esau came from the field, and he was exhausted. ³⁰And Esau said to Jacob, "Will you feed me some of the red stuff, this red stuff, because I'm exhausted." (On account of this he called his name "Edom.")

³¹And Jacob said, "Sell your birthright to me, today."

³²And Esau said, "Here I'm going to die, and what use is this, that I have a birthright?"

³³And Jacob said, "Swear to me, today."

And he swore to him and sold his birthright to Jacob. And Jacob gave bread and lentil stew to Esau. And he ate and drank and got up and went. And Esau disdained the birthright.

26

¹And there was a famine in the land (other than the first famine, which was in Abraham's days), and Isaac went to Abimelek, king of the Philistines, at Gerar. ²And YHWH appeared to him and said, "Don't go down to Egypt. Reside in the land that I say to you. ³Stay on in this land, and I'll be with you and bless you, for I'll give all these lands to you and your seed, and I'll uphold the oath that I swore to Abraham your father, ⁴and I'll multiply your seed like the stars of the skies and give to your seed all these lands, and all the nations of the earth will be blessed through your seed ⁵because Abraham listened to my voice and kept my watch, my commandments, my laws, and my instructions." ⁶And so Isaac lived in Gerar.

⁷And the people of the place asked about his wife, and he said, "She's my sister," because he was afraid to say, "My wife," or else "the people of the place will kill me for Rebekah, because she's good looking." ⁸And it was when his days extended there: and Abimelek, king of the Philistines, gazed through the window, and he saw: and here was Isaac "fooling around" with Rebekah his wife!

⁹And Abimelek called Isaac and said, "But, here, she's your wife! And how could you say, 'She's my sister'?"

And Isaac said to him, "Because I said, 'Or else I'll die over her.'"

¹⁰And Abimelek said, "What is this you've done to us? One of the people nearly could have lain with your wife, and you would have brought guilt on us." ¹¹And Abimelek commanded all the people saying, "He who touches this man or his wife will be put to death!"

¹²And Isaac planted seed in that land, and he harvested a hundredfold in that year. And YHWH blessed him, ¹³and the man became great, and he went on getting greater until he was very great ¹⁴and had livestock of flocks and livestock of herds and a large number of servants. And the Philistines envied him. ¹⁵And the Philistines stopped up all the wells that his father's servants had dug in his father Abraham's days, and they filled them with dirt. ¹⁶And Abimelek said to Isaac, "Go from among us, because you've become much mightier than we are." ¹⁷And Isaac went from there and camped in the wadi of Gerar and lived there. ¹⁸And Isaac went back and dug the water wells that they had dug in the days of his father Abraham and that the Philistines had stopped up after Abraham's death, and he called them by names, like the names that his father had called them. ¹⁹And Isaac's servants dug in the wadi and found a well of fresh water there. ²⁰And the shepherds of Gerar quarreled with Isaac's shepherds, saying, "The water is ours." And he called the name of the well Esek because they tangled with him. ²¹And they dug another well, and they quarreled over it also, and he called its name Sitnah. ²²And he moved on from there and dug another well, and they did not quarrel over it, and he called its name Rehovot and said, "Because now YHWH has widened for us, and we've been fruitful in the land."

²³And he went up from there to Beer-sheba. ²⁴And YHWH appeared to him that night and said, "I'm your father Abraham's God. Don't be afraid, because I'm with you, and I'll bless you and multiply your seed on account of Abraham, my servant." ²⁵And he built an altar there and invoked the name YHWH. And he pitched his tent there, and Isaac's servants dug a well there.

²⁶And Abimelek and Ahuzat, his companion, and Phihchol, the commander of his army, went to him from Gerar. ²⁷And Isaac said to them, "Why have you come to me, since you hated me and sent me away from you?"

²⁸And they said, "We've seen that YHWH has been with you; and we say, 'Let there be an oath between us, between us and you, and let us make a covenant with you ²⁹that you won't do bad toward us as we haven't touched you and as we've done only good toward you and sent you away in peace. You are now blessed by YHWH.'" ³⁰And he made a feast for them, and they ate and drank. ³¹And they got up early in the morning and swore,

each man to his brother, and Isaac sent them away, and they went from him in peace. ³²And it was in that day, and Isaac's servants came and told him about the well that they had dug and said to him, "We found water." ³³And he called it Seven. On account of this the name of the city is Beer-sheba to this day.

³⁴And Esau was forty years old, and he took a wife: Judith, daughter of Beeri, the Hittite, and Basemath, daughter of Elon, the Hittite. ³⁵And they were a bitterness of spirit to Isaac and to Rebekah.

27

¹And it was when Isaac was old and his eyes were too dim for seeing: and he called Esau, his older son, and said to him, "My son."

And he said to him, "I'm here."

²And he said, "Here, I've become old. I don't know the day of my death. ³And now, take up your implements: your quiver and your bow, and go out to the field and hunt me some game ⁴and make me the kind of delicacies that I love and bring them to me and let me eat, so my soul will bless you before I die."

⁵And Rebekah was listening as Isaac was speaking to Esau, his son. And Esau went to the field to hunt game to bring. ⁶And Rebekah said to Jacob, her son, saying, "Here I've heard your father speaking to Esau, your brother, saying, ⁷'Bring me game and make me delicacies so I may eat, and I'll bless you in the presence of YHWH before my death.' ⁸And now, my son, listen to my voice, to what I'm commanding you. ⁹Go to the flock and take two good goat kids for me from there, and I'll make them the kind of delicacies that your father loves. ¹⁰And bring them to your father, and he'll eat, so he'll bless you before his death."

¹¹And Jacob said to Rebekah, his mother, "Here, Esau, my brother, is a hairy man and I'm a smooth man. ¹²Maybe my father will feel me, and I'll be like a trickster in his eyes, and I'll bring a curse on me and not a blessing."

¹³And his mother said to him, "Let your curse be on me, my son; just listen to my voice and go take them for me." ¹⁴And he went and took and brought them to his mother, and his mother made the kind of delicacies that his father loved. ¹⁵And Rebekah took the finest clothes of Esau, her older son, that were with her in the house and put them on Jacob, her younger son, ¹⁶and put the skins of the goat kids on his hands and on the smooth part of his neck. ¹⁷And she put the delicacies and the bread that she'd made in the hand of Jacob, her son. ¹⁸And he came to his father.

And he said, "My father."

And he said, "I'm here. Who are you, my son?"

¹⁹And Jacob said to his father, "I'm Esau, your firstborn. I did as you spoke to me. Get up, sit, and eat some of my game so your soul will bless me."

²⁰And Isaac said to his son, "What's this? You were quick to find it, my son."

And he said, "Because YHWH your God made it happen for me."

²¹And Isaac said to Jacob, "Come over, and I'll feel you, my son: is this you, my son Esau, or not?" ²²And Jacob came over to Isaac, his father, and he felt him. And he said, "The voice is the voice of Jacob, and the hands are the hands of Esau." ²³And he did not recognize him because his hands were hairy like the hands of Esau, his brother, and he blessed him. ²⁴And he said, "Is this you, my son Esau?"

And he said, "I am."

²⁵And he said, "Bring it over to me and let me eat some of my son's game so that my soul will bless you. And he brought it over to him, and he ate; and he brought him wine, and he drank. ²⁶And Isaac, his father, said to him, "Come over and kiss me, my son." ²⁷And he came over and kissed him, and he smelled the aroma of his clothes and blessed him and said, "See, my son's aroma is like the aroma of a field that YHWH has blessed. ²⁸And may God give you from the dew of the skies and from the fat of the earth and much grain and wine. ²⁹May peoples serve you and nations bow to you. Be your brothers' superior, and may your mother's sons bow to you. May those who curse you be cursed and those who bless you be blessed."

³⁰And it was as Isaac finished blessing Jacob, and it was: Jacob had just gone out from the presence of Isaac, his father!—and Esau, his brother, came from his hunting. ³¹And he, too, had made delicacies and brought them to his father. And he said to his father, "Let my father get up and eat some of his son's game so you yourself will bless me."

³²And Isaac, his father, said to him, "Who are you?"

And he said, "I'm your son, your firstborn, Esau."

³³And Isaac trembled—a very big trembling. And he said, "Who then is the one who hunted game and brought it to me, and I ate some of it all before you came, and I blessed him? He will in fact be blessed."

³⁴When Esau heard his father's words he cried—a very big and bitter cry. And he said to his father, "Bless me, also me, my father."

³⁵And he said, "Your brother came with deception, and he took your blessing."

³⁶And he said, "Was his name really called Jacob! And he's usurped me two times now. He's taken my birthright, and, here, now he's taken my blessing." And he said, "Haven't you saved a blessing for me?"

³⁷And Isaac answered, and he said to Esau, "Here I've made him your superior, and I've given all his brothers as servants, and I've endowed him with grain and wine. And for you: where, what, will I do, my son?"

³⁸And Esau said to his father, "Is it one blessing that you have, my father? Bless me, also me, my father." And Esau raised his voice and wept.

³⁹And Isaac, his father, answered, and he said to him, "Here, away from the fat of the earth will be your home, and from the dew of the skies from above. ⁴⁰And you'll live by your sword. And you'll serve your brother. And it will be that when you get dominion you'll break his yoke from your neck."

⁴¹And Esau despised Jacob because of the blessing with which his father blessed him, and Esau said in his heart, "The days of mourning for my father will be soon, and then I'll kill Jacob, my brother."

⁴²And the words of Esau, her older son, were told to Rebekah, and she sent and called to Jacob, her younger son, and said to him, "Here, Esau, your brother, consoles himself regarding you with the idea of killing you. ⁴³And now, my son, listen to my voice and get up, flee to Laban, my brother, at Haran ⁴⁴and live with him for a number of days until your brother's fury will turn back, ⁴⁵until your brother's anger turns back from you and he forgets what you did to him. And I'll send and take you from there. Why should I be bereaved of the two of you as well in one day?"

⁴⁶And Rebekah said to Isaac, "I'm disgusted with my life because of the daughters of Heth! If Jacob takes a wife from the daughters of Heth like these daughters of the land, why do I have a life!"

28

¹And Isaac called Jacob, and he blessed him and commanded him, and he said to him, "You shall not take a wife from the daughters of Canaan. ²Get up. Go to Paddan Aram, to the house of Bethuel, your mother's father, and take a wife from there, from the daughters of Laban, your mother's brother. ³And may El Shadday bless you and make you fruitful and multiply you, so you'll become a community of peoples, ⁴and may He give you the blessing of Abraham, to you and to your seed with you, for you to possess the land of your residences, which God gave to Abraham." ⁵And Isaac sent Jacob, and he went to Paddan Aram, to Laban, son of Bethuel, the Aramean, brother of Rebekah, mother of Jacob and Esau.

⁶And Esau saw that Isaac had blessed Jacob and sent him to Paddan Aram to take a wife for himself from there when he blessed him, and he had commanded him, saying, "You shall not take a wife from the daughters of

Canaan," ⁷and Jacob had listened to his father and to his mother and had gone to Paddan Aram. ⁸And Esau saw that the daughters of Canaan were bad in his father Isaac's eyes. ⁹And Esau went to Ishmael and took Mahalath, daughter of Ishmael, son of Abraham, sister of Nebaioth, in addition to his wives as a wife for him.

¹⁰And Jacob left Beer-sheba and went to Haran. ¹¹And he happened upon a place and stayed the night there because the sun was setting. **And he took from the stones of the place and set it as his headrest and lay down in that place. ¹²And he dreamed. And here was a ladder, set up on the earth, and its top reaching to the skies. And here were angels of God, going up and going down by it.** ¹³And here was YHWH standing over him, and He said, "I am YHWH, your father Abraham's God and Isaac's God. The land on which you're lying: I'll give it to you and to your seed. ¹⁴And your seed will be like the dust of the earth, and you'll expand to the west and east and north and south, and all the families on the earth will be blessed through you and through your seed. ¹⁵And here I am with you, and I'll watch over you everywhere that you'll go, and I'll bring you back to this land, for I won't leave you until I've done what I've spoken to you."

¹⁶And Jacob woke from his sleep and said, "YHWH is actually in this place, and I didn't know!" **¹⁷And he was afraid, and he said, "How awesome this place is! This is none other than God's house, and this is the gate of the skies!" ¹⁸And Jacob got up early in the morning and took the stone that he had set as his headrest and set it as a pillar and poured oil on its top.** ¹⁹And he called that place's name Beth-El, though in fact Luz was the name of the city at first. **²⁰And Jacob made a vow, saying, "If God will be with me and watch over me in this way that I'm going and give me bread to eat and clothing to wear, ²¹and I come back in peace to my father's house, then YHWH* will become my God, ²²and this stone that I set as a pillar will be God's house, and everything that you'll give me I'll tithe to you."**

29

¹And Jacob lifted his feet and went to the land of the people of the east. ²And he looked, and here was a well in the field, and here were three flocks of sheep lying by it, because they watered the flocks from that well, and the stone on the mouth of the well was big, ³and all the flocks

---

*This is one of only three occurrences in the Torah in which the name of God appears in a source other than J prior to the revelation of the name to Moses in Exodus.

would be gathered there, and they would roll the stone from the mouth of the well and would water the sheep and then would put the stone back in its place on the mouth of the well. ⁴And Jacob said to them, "My brothers, where are you from?"

And they said, "We're from Haran."

⁵And he said to them, "Do you know Laban, son of Nahor?"

And they said, "We know."

⁶And he said to them, "Is he well?"

And they said, "Well. And here's Rachel, his daughter, coming with the sheep."

⁷And he said, "Here, it will still be daytime for a long time, not the time for gathering the livestock. Water the sheep and go, pasture them."

⁸And they said, "We can't until all the flocks will be gathered and they'll roll the stone from the mouth of the well, and then we'll water the sheep."

⁹He was still speaking with them, and Rachel came with her father's sheep, because she was a shepherdess. ¹⁰And it was when Jacob saw Rachel, daughter of Laban, his mother's brother, and the sheep of Laban, his mother's brother: and he went over and rolled the stone from the mouth of the well and watered the sheep of Laban, his mother's brother. ¹¹And Jacob kissed Rachel and raised his voice and wept. ¹²And Jacob told Rachel that he was her father's kin and that he was Rebekah's son, and she ran and told her father. ¹³And it was, when Laban heard the news of Jacob, his sister's son, that he ran to him and embraced him and kissed him and brought him to his house. And he told Laban all these things. ¹⁴And Laban said to him, "You are indeed my bone and my flesh." And he stayed with him a month. ¹⁵And Laban said to Jacob, "Is it right because you're my brother that you should work for me for free? Tell me what your pay should be." ¹⁶And Laban had two daughters. The older one's name was Leah, and the younger one's name was Rachel. ¹⁷And Leah's eyes were tender, and Rachel had an attractive figure and was beautiful. ¹⁸And Jacob loved Rachel.

And he said, "I'll work for you seven years for Rachel, your younger daughter."

¹⁹And Laban said, "Better for me to give her to you than for me to give her to another man. Live with me."

²⁰And Jacob worked seven years for Rachel, and they were like a few days in his eyes because of his loving her. ²¹And Jacob said to Laban, "Give me my wife, because my days have been completed, and let me come to her." ²²And Laban gathered all the people of the place and made a feast.

²³And it was in the evening, and he took Leah, his daughter, and brought her to him. And he came to her.

²⁴And Laban gave her his maid Zilpah—to Leah, his daughter, as a maid.

²⁵And it was in the morning, and here she was: Leah! And he said to Laban, "What is this you've done to me? Didn't I work with you for Rachel? And why have you deceived me?"

²⁶And Laban said, "It's not done like that in our place, to give the younger one before the firstborn. ²⁷Complete this week, and this one will be given to you as well—for the work that you'll do with me: another seven years."

²⁸And Jacob did so; and he completed this week, and he gave him Rachel, his daughter, for a wife. ²⁹And Laban gave his maid Bilhah to Rachel, his daughter—to her as a maid. ³⁰And he also came to Rachel. And he also loved Rachel more than Leah. And he worked with him another seven years.

³¹And YHWH saw that Leah was hated, and He opened her womb, and Rachel was infertile. ³²And Leah became pregnant and gave birth to a son and called his name Reuben because she said, "Because YHWH looked at my suffering, so that now my man will love me." ³³And she became pregnant again and gave birth to a son and said, "Because YHWH listened because I was hated and gave me this one, too." And she called his name Simeon. ³⁴And she became pregnant again and gave birth to a son, and she said, "Now, this time my man will become bound to me because I've given birth to three sons for him." On account of this his name was called Levi. ³⁵And she became pregnant again and gave birth to a son and said, "This time I'll praise YHWH." On account of this she called his name Judah. And she stopped giving birth.

30

¹And Rachel saw that she had not given birth for Jacob. **And Rachel was jealous of her sister, and she said to Jacob, "Give me children. And if not I'm dying!"**

²And Jacob's anger flared at Rachel, and he said, "Am I in place of God, who has held back the fruit of the womb from you?!"

³And she said, "Here's my maid, Bilhah. Come to her, and she'll give birth on my knees, and I too will get a child through her." ⁴And she gave him

Bilhah, her maid, as a wife. **And Jacob came to her. ⁵And Bilhah became pregnant and gave birth to a son for Jacob. ⁶And Rachel said, "God has judged me and heard my prayer as well and has given me a son." On account of this she called his name Dan. ⁷And Bilhah, Rachel's maid, became pregnant again and gave birth to a second son for Jacob. ⁸And Rachel said, "I've had Godlike struggles with my sister. I've also prevailed." And she called his name Naphtali.**

⁹And Leah saw that she had stopped giving birth, and she took Zilpah, her maid, and gave her to Jacob as a wife. ¹⁰And Zilpah, Leah's maid, gave birth to a son for Jacob. ¹¹And Leah said, "With fortune!" and called his name Gad. ¹²And Zilpah, Leah's maid, gave birth to a second son for Jacob. ¹³And Leah said, "With my happiness!—because daughters will wish me happiness," and called his name Asher.

¹⁴And in the days of wheat harvest Reuben went and found mandrakes in the field and brought them to Leah, his mother. And Rachel said to Leah, "Give me some of your son's mandrakes."

¹⁵And she said to her, "Is your taking my man a small thing? And you're taking my son's mandrakes, too?!"

And Rachel said, "Then let him lie with you tonight in return for your son's mandrakes."

¹⁶And Jacob came from the field in the evening, and Leah went out to him and said, "You are to come to me, because I've hired you with my son's mandrakes." And he lay with her that night. ¹⁷And God listened to Leah, and she became pregnant and gave birth to a fifth son for Jacob. ¹⁸And Leah said, "God has given my hire because I gave my maid to my man," and she called his name Issachar. ¹⁹And Leah became pregnant again and gave birth to a sixth son for Jacob. ²⁰And Leah said, "God has given me a good gift. This time my man will value me highly, because I've given birth to six sons for him," and she called his name Zebulun. ²¹And after that she gave birth to a daughter and called her name Dinah.

²²And God remembered Rachel, and God listened to her and opened her womb, ²³and she became pregnant and gave birth to a son. And she said, "God has taken away my humiliation" ²⁴and called his name Joseph, saying, "May YHWH add another son to me."* ²⁵And it was when Rachel had given birth to Joseph: and Jacob said to Laban, "Send me away so I may go to my

---

*J and E each give an etymology of the name Joseph. In E it is based on the root *'sp*, meaning "taken away," but in J it is based on the similar root *ysp*, meaning "add." RJE united the two by adding the word "saying" between them.

place and my land. ²⁶Give me my wives and my children for whom I've worked for you and let me go; because you know my work that I've done for you."

²⁷And Laban said to him, "If I've found favor in your eyes, I've divined that YHWH has blessed me because of you," ²⁸and he said, "Designate your pay for me, and I'll give it."

²⁹And he said to him, "You know how I've worked for you and how your cattle have become with me, ³⁰that a little that you had before me expanded into a lot, and YHWH blessed you wherever I set foot. And now, when shall I also take care of my house?"

³¹And he said, "What shall I give you?"

And Jacob said, "You won't give me anything—if you'll do this thing for me: Let me go back; I'll tend and watch over your flock. ³²I'll pass among all your flock today removing from there every speckled and spotted lamb and every brown lamb among the sheep and every spotted and speckled one among the goats—and that will be my pay. ³³And my virtue will answer for me in a future day: when you'll come upon my pay, it will be in front of you. Any one that isn't speckled and spotted among the goats and brown among the sheep, it's stolen with me."

³⁴And Laban said, "Here, let it be according to your word." ³⁵And in that day he removed the he-goats that were streaked and spotted and the she-goats that were speckled and spotted, every one that had white in it, and every brown one among the sheep, and set them in his sons' hand ³⁶and put three days' distance between him and Jacob. And Jacob was tending Laban's remaining sheep.

³⁷And Jacob took a rod of fresh poplar and one of almond tree and one of plane tree, and he peeled white stripes in them, exposing the white that was on the rods. ³⁸And he set up the rods that he had peeled in the channels in the watering troughs at which the flock came to drink, facing the flock. And they copulated when they came to drink. ³⁹And the flock mated at the rods, and the flock gave birth to streaked, speckled, and spotted ones. ⁴⁰And Jacob separated the sheep and had the flock face the streaked and every brown one among Laban's flock, and he set his own droves apart and did not set them by Laban's flock. ⁴¹And it was that whenever the fittest sheep would copulate Jacob would put the rods in the channels before the sheep's eyes so that they would copulate by the rods, ⁴²and when the sheep were feebler he would not put them, so the feeble ones became Laban's and the fitter ones became Jacob's. ⁴³And the man expanded very, very much, and he had many sheep and female and male servants and camels and asses.

31

¹And he heard Laban's sons' words, saying, "Jacob has taken everything that was our father's, and he has made all this wealth from what was our father's." ²And Jacob saw Laban's face; and, here, he was not like the day before yesterday with him. ³And YHWH said to Jacob, "Go back to your fathers' land and to your birthplace, and I'll be with you." ⁴And Jacob sent and called Rachel and Leah to the field, to his flock, ⁵and said to them, "I see your father's face, that he's not like the day before yesterday to me. And my father's God has been with me, ⁶and you know that I served your father with all my might, ⁷and your father has toyed with me and changed my pay ten times, and God hasn't let him do bad with me. ⁸If he would say this: 'The speckled will be your pay,' then all the flock gave birth to speckled. And if he would say this: 'The streaked will be your pay,' then all the flock gave birth to streaked. ⁹And God has delivered your father's livestock and given them to me. ¹⁰And it was at the time of the flock's being in heat, and I raised my eyes and saw in a dream: and here were the he-goats that were going up on the flock: streaked, speckled, and spotted.

¹¹"And an angel of God said to me in the dream, 'Jacob.'

"And I said, 'I'm here.'

¹²"And he said, 'Raise your eyes and see all the he-goats that are going up on the flock: streaked, speckled, and spotted. Because I've seen everything that Laban is doing to you. ¹³I am the God at Beth-El, where you anointed a pillar, where you made a vow to me. Now get up, go from this land, and go back to the land of your birth.'"

¹⁴And Rachel and Leah answered, and they said to him, "Do we still have a portion and legacy in our father's house? ¹⁵Aren't we thought of as foreigners by him, because he sold us and has eaten up our money as well?! ¹⁶Because all the wealth that God has delivered from our father: it's ours and our children's. And now, do everything that God has said to you." ¹⁷And Jacob got up and carried his children and his wives on the camels. ¹⁸And he drove all his cattle and all his property that he had acquired, the cattle that were in his possession that he had acquired in Paddan Aram, to come to Isaac, his father, at the land of Canaan.

¹⁹And Laban had gone to shear his flock. And Rachel stole the teraphim that her father had. ²⁰And Jacob stole the heart of Laban, the Aramean, by not telling him that he was fleeing. ²¹And he fled, he and everyone he had, and he got up and crossed the river and set his face toward the mountain of

Gilead. ²²And it was told to Laban on the third day that Jacob had fled. ²³And he took his brothers with him and pursued him seven days' journey and caught up to him in the mountain of Gilead. ²⁴And God came to Laban, the Aramean, in a night dream and said to him, "Watch yourself in case you speak with Jacob: from good to bad."

²⁵And Laban caught up to Jacob, and Jacob had set up his tent in the mountain, and Laban set up with his brothers in the mountain of Gilead. ²⁶And Laban said to Jacob, "What have you done, that you've stolen my heart and driven off my daughters like prisoners by the sword? ²⁷Why did you hide so as to flee, and you stole from me, and you didn't tell me? And I would have sent you off with happiness and with songs and with a drum and with a lyre. ²⁸And you didn't permit me to kiss my sons and my daughters. Now you've been foolish to do this. ²⁹The god at my hand has the means to do bad to you. But your father's God said to me yesterday, saying, 'Watch yourself from speaking with Jacob: from good to bad.' ³⁰And now, you went, because you longed for your father's house. Why did you steal my gods?"

³¹And Jacob answered, and he said to Laban, "Because I was afraid. Because I said, 'In case you'll seize your daughters from me.' ³²Let the one with whom you'll find your gods not live. In front of our brothers, recognize and take what of yours is with me." And Jacob did not know that Rachel had stolen them.

³³And Laban came in Jacob's tent and Leah's tent and the two maids' tent, and he did not find them. And he came out from Leah's tent and came in Rachel's tent. ³⁴And Rachel had taken the teraphim and put them in the camel's saddle and sat on them. And Laban felt around the whole tent and did not find them. ³⁵And she said to her father, "Let it not offend in my lord's eyes that I'm not able to get up before you, because I have the way of women." And he searched and did not find the teraphim.

³⁶And Jacob was angered, and he quarreled with Laban, and Jacob answered, and he said to Laban, "What is my offense? What is my sin, that you blazed after me, ³⁷that you felt around all my belongings? What did you find out of all of your house's belongings? Set it here, in front of my brothers and your brothers, and let them judge between the two of us. ³⁸This twenty years I've been with you, your ewes and your she-goats haven't lost their off-spring, and I haven't eaten your flock's rams. ³⁹I haven't brought you one torn up. I would miss it: you would ask it from my hand, be it stolen by day or stolen by night. ⁴⁰I was . . . In the daytime heat ate me up, and ice in the night. And my sleep fled from my eyes. ⁴¹This twenty years I've had in your house: I worked for you fourteen years for your two daughters and six years

for your flock, and you changed my pay ten times. ⁴²If I hadn't had my father's God, the God of Abraham and Awe of Isaac, by now you would have sent me away empty-handed. God saw my degradation and my hands' exhaustion, and He pointed it out last night."

⁴³And Laban answered, and he said to Jacob, "The daughters are my daughters, and the sons are my sons, and the flock is my flock, and everything that you see: it's mine. But what shall I do to my daughters, to these, today, or to their children to whom they've given birth? ⁴⁴So now, come and let's make a covenant, I and you, and let it be a witness between me and you."

⁴⁵And Jacob took a stone and set it up as a pillar, ⁴⁶and Jacob said to his brothers, "Collect stones." And they took stones and made a pile and ate there at the pile. ⁴⁷And Laban called it yĕgar sahădûta', and Jacob called it gal-'ēd.

⁴⁸And Laban said, "This pile is a witness between me and you today." On account of this he called its name Gal-Ed. (⁴⁹And Mizpah, because he said, "May YHWH observe between me and you when one is hidden from the other.") ⁵⁰"If you degrade my daughters and if you take wives in addition to my daughters, no man is with us. See: God is witness between me and you." ⁵¹And Laban said to Jacob, "Here is this pile, and here is the pillar that I've cast between me and you. ⁵²This pile is a witness, and the pillar is a witness that I won't cross this pile to you and you won't cross this pile and this pillar to me for bad. ⁵³Let Abraham's God and Nahor's gods, their father's gods, judge between us."

And Jacob swore by the Awe of his father, Isaac. ⁵⁴And Jacob made a sacrifice in the mountain and called his brothers to eat bread, and they ate bread and spent the night in the mountain.

32

¹And Laban got up early in the morning and kissed his sons and his daughters and blessed them and went. And Laban went back to his place, ²and Jacob went his way. And angels of God came upon him. ³And Jacob said when he saw them, "This is a camp of God," and he called that place's name Mahanaim.

⁴And Jacob sent messengers ahead of him to Esau, his brother, to the land of Seir, the territory of Edom, ⁵and commanded them saying, "You shall say this: 'To my lord, to Esau, your servant Jacob said this, "I've stayed with Laban and delayed until now, ⁶and ox and ass and sheep and male and

female servant have become mine. And I'm sending to tell my lord so as to find favor in your eyes.'"'"

⁷And the messengers came back to Jacob saying, "We came to your brother, to Esau, and also he's coming to you—and four hundred men with him." ⁸And Jacob was very afraid, and he had anguish. And he divided the people who were with him and the sheep and the oxen and the camels into two camps. ⁹And he said, "If Esau will come to one camp and strike it, then the camp that is left will survive."

¹⁰And Jacob said, "God of my father Abraham and God of my father Isaac, YHWH, who said to me, 'Go back to your land and to your birthplace, and I'll deal well with you,' ¹¹I'm not worthy of all the kindnesses and all the faithfulness that you've done with your servant, because I crossed this Jordan with just my rod, and now I've become two camps. ¹²Save me from my brother's hand, from Esau's hand, because I fear him, in case he'll come and strike me, mother with children. ¹³And you've said, 'I'll do well with you, and I'll make your seed like the sand of the sea, that it won't be countable because of its great number.'"

¹⁴And he spent that night there.

And he took an offering for Esau, his brother, from what had come into his hand: ¹⁵two hundred she-goats and twenty he-goats, two hundred ewes and twenty rams, ¹⁶thirty nursing camels and their offspring, forty cows and ten bulls, twenty she-asses and ten he-asses. ¹⁷And he placed them in his servants' hands, each herd by itself, and he said to his servants, "Pass on in front of me, and keep a distance between each herd and the next." ¹⁸And he commanded the first, saying, "When my brother, Esau, meets you and asks you, saying, 'To whom do you belong, and where are you going, and to whom do these in front of you belong?' ¹⁹then you'll say, 'To your servant, to Jacob. It's an offering sent to my lord, to Esau. And here he is behind us as well.'" ²⁰And he also commanded the second, also the third, also all of those who were going behind the herds, saying, "You'll speak this way to Esau when you find him, ²¹and you'll say, 'Here is your servant, Jacob, behind us as well.'" Because he said, "Let me appease his face with the offering that's going in front of me, and after that I'll see his face; maybe he'll raise my face." ²²And the offering passed ahead of him. And he had spent that night in the camp.

²³And he got up in that night and took his two wives and his two maids and his eleven boys and crossed the Jabbok ford. ²⁴And he took them and had them cross the wadi, and he had everything that was his cross. ²⁵And Jacob was left by himself.

And a man wrestled with him until the dawn's rising. ²⁶And he saw that he was not able against him, and he touched the inside of his thigh, and the inside of Jacob's thigh was dislocated during his wrestling with him.

²⁷And he said, "Let me go, because the dawn has risen."

And he said, "I won't let you go unless you bless me."

²⁸And he said to him, "What is your name?"

And he said, "Jacob."

²⁹And he said, "Your name won't be said 'Jacob' anymore but 'Israel,' because you've struggled with God and with people and were able."

³⁰And Jacob asked, and he said, "Tell your name."

And he said, "Why is this that you ask my name?" And he blessed him there.

³¹And Jacob called the place's name Peni-El "because I've seen God face-to-face, and my life has been delivered."

³²And the sun rose on him as he passed Penuel, and he was faltering on his thigh. ³³On account of this the children of Israel to this day will not eat the tendon of the vein that is on the inside of the thigh, because he touched the inside of Jacob's thigh, the tendon of the vein.

33

¹And Jacob raised his eyes and looked, and here was Esau coming, and four hundred men with him.* And he divided the children among Leah and Rachel and the two maids; ²and he placed the maids and their children first, and Leah and her children following, and Rachel and Joseph following, ³and he passed in front of them. And he bowed to the ground seven times until he came up to his brother. ⁴And Esau ran to him and embraced him and fell on his neck and kissed him. And they wept. ⁵And he raised his eyes and saw the women and the children, and he said, "Who are these whom you have?"

---

*Genesis 32 and 33 offer some of the most difficult problems for distinguishing between J and E. Gen 33:1–17 could be J or E or a combination of both that is now perhaps impossible to separate. When Jacob tells Esau to "Take my blessing" (33:11), it seems to be Jacob's recompense for having appropriated Esau's blessing, which happened in J (Genesis 27). But when Jacob tells Esau that seeing Esau's face is "like seeing God's face" (33:10), it seems to be a reference back to his having said that "I've seen God face-to-face," which happened in E (32:31). My identifications of J and E in this section are tentative.

And he said, "The children with whom God has graced your servant."

⁶And the maids came over, they and their children, and bowed. ⁷And Leah and her children, too, came over, and they bowed. And then Joseph and Rachel came over, and they bowed.

⁸And he said, "Who is all this camp of yours that I met?"

And he said, "To find favor in my lord's eyes."

⁹And Esau said, "I have a great deal, my brother. Let what's yours be yours."

¹⁰And Jacob said, "Don't. If I've found favor in your eyes, then you'll take my offering from my hand, because on account of this I've seen your face— like seeing God's face!—and you've accepted me. ¹¹Take my blessing that's been brought to you, because God has been gracious to me and because I have everything." And he pressed him, and he took it.

¹²And he said, "Let's travel, and let's go. And let me go alongside you."

¹³And he said to him, "My lord knows that the children are weak and the nursing sheep and oxen are with me, and they'll drive them one day and all the sheep will die. ¹⁴Let my lord pass on in front of his servant; and I, let me move along at my pace required by the task that's before me and required by the children until I come to my lord at Seir."

¹⁵And Esau said, "Let me set with you some of the people who are with me."

And he said, "Why have I found favor in my lord's eyes?"

¹⁶And Esau went back on his way to Seir that day, ¹⁷and Jacob traveled to Sukkot. And he built a house for himself and made booths for his cattle. On account of this he called the place's name Sukkot. ¹⁸And Jacob came, safe, to the city of Shechem, which was in the land of Canaan, when he was coming from Paddan Aram,* and camped in front of the city. ¹⁹And he bought the section of field in which he pitched his tent from the hand of the sons of Hamor, father of Shechem, for a hundred qesita. ²⁰And he set up an altar there and called it "El, God of Israel."

---

*Paddan Aram is used only in P for the place in which Jacob had spent the years with Laban, but it comes here in the middle of the JE story of Jacob's return. Also, the phrase in which it occurs ("which was in the land of Canaan, when he was coming from Paddan Aram") is unnecessary in the JE story. This phrase is therefore likely to have been added by the Redactor. The reason for the addition may be that the combination of the sources now made it seem that Jacob's return to his father, Isaac, was taking an excessive amount of time. P had said that Jacob had set out on his way back in Gen 31:18, but he does not arrive until the P notice in 35:27. This addition identifies his stay at Shechem as just a stop on the way.

34

¹And Dinah, Leah's daughter, whom she had borne to Jacob, went out to see the daughters of the land. ²And Shechem, son of Hamor, the Hivite, the chieftain of the land, saw her. And he took her and lay with her and degraded her. ³And his soul clung to Dinah, Jacob's daughter, and he loved the girl and spoke on the girl's heart. ⁴And Shechem said to Hamor, his father, "Get me this girl for a wife."

⁵And Jacob heard that he had defiled Dinah, his daughter; and his sons were with his cattle in the field, and Jacob kept quiet until they came. ⁶And Hamor, Shechem's father, went out to Jacob to speak with him. ⁷And Jacob's sons came from the field when they heard, and the men were pained, and they were very furious, for he had done a foolhardy thing among Israel, to lie with Jacob's daughter, and such a thing is not done. ⁸And Hamor spoke with them, saying, "Shechem—my son—his soul longs for your daughter. Give her to him as a wife, ⁹and marry with us; give your daughters to us and take our daughters to you, ¹⁰and live with us; and the land will be before you: live and go around in it and take possession in it."

¹¹And Shechem said to her father and to her brothers, "Let me find favor in your eyes, and I'll give whatever you say to me. ¹²Make a bride-price and gift on me very great, and let me give whatever you say to me, and give me the girl as a wife."

¹³And Jacob's sons answered Shechem and Hamor, his father, with deception as they spoke because he had defiled Dinah, their sister. ¹⁴And they said to them, "We aren't able to do this thing, to give our sister to a man who has a foreskin, because that's a disgrace to us. ¹⁵Only this way will we consent to you: if you'll be like us, every male among you to be circumcised. ¹⁶And we'll give our daughters to you and take your daughters to us, and we'll live with you, and we'll become one people. ¹⁷And if you won't listen to us, to be circumcised, then we'll take our daughter and go."

¹⁸And their words were good in Hamor's eyes and in Hamor's son Shechem's eyes. ¹⁹And the boy did not delay to do the thing, for he desired Jacob's daughter. And he was more respected than all his father's house. ²⁰And Hamor and his son Shechem came to the gate of their city and spoke to the people of their city, saying, ²¹"These people are peaceable with us, and they'll live in the land and go around in it, and the land, here, has enough breadth for them. Let's take their daughters for us as wives and give our daughters to them. ²²Only in this way will these people consent to us to live with us, to be one people: if every male among us is circumcised as they are circumcised. ²³Their cattle and possessions and all their animals: won't they be ours? Only let's consent to them, and they'll live with us." ²⁴And every-

one who went out of the gate of his city listened to Hamor and to his son Shechem; and every male, everyone who went out of the gate of his city, was circumcised.

²⁵And it was on the third day, when they were hurting, and two of Jacob's sons, Simeon and Levi, Dinah's brothers, each took his sword, and they came upon the city stealthily, and they killed every male. ²⁶And they killed Hamor and his son Shechem by the sword and took Dinah from Shechem's house and went out. ²⁷Jacob's sons had come upon the corpses and despoiled the city because they had defiled their sister. ²⁸They took their sheep and their oxen and their asses and what was in the city and what was in the field. ²⁹And they captured and despoiled all their wealth and all their infants and their wives and everything that was in the house. ³⁰And Jacob said to Simeon and to Levi, "You've caused me anguish, making me odious to those who live in the land, to the Canaanite and to the Perizzite, and I'm few in number, and they'll be gathered against me and strike me, and I'll be destroyed, I and my house."

³¹And they said, "Shall he treat our sister like a prostitute?"

35

¹And God said to Jacob, "Get up. Go up to Beth-El and live there and make an altar there to God, who appeared to you when you were fleeing from Esau, your brother."

²And Jacob said to his house and to everyone who was with him, "Put away the foreign gods that are among you and be purified and change your clothes; ³and let's get up and go up to Beth-El, and I'll make an altar there to God, who answered me in a day of my trouble, and He was with me in the way that I went." ⁴And they gave all the foreign gods that were in their hand and the rings that were in their ears to Jacob, and Jacob stashed them under the oak that was by Shechem. ⁵And they traveled, and God's terror was on the cities that were arround them, and they did not pursue the children of Jacob. ⁶And Jacob came to Luz, which is in the land of Canaan—it is Beth-El—he and all the people who were with him. ⁷And he built an altar there and called the place El of Beth-El because God was revealed to him there when he was fleeing from his brother.

⁸And Deborah, Rebekah's nurse, died and was buried beneath Beth-El, beneath an oak, and he called its name Oak of Weeping.

⁹And God appeared to Jacob again when he was coming from Paddan Aram, and He blessed him. ¹⁰And God said to him, "Your name is Jacob. Your name will not be called Jacob anymore, but rather Israel will be your name."

And He called his name Israel. ¹¹And God said to him, "I am El Shadday. Be fruitful and multiply. A nation and a community of nations will be from you, and kings will come out from your hips. ¹²And the land that I gave to Abraham and to Isaac: I'll give it to you, and I'll give the land to your seed after you." ¹³And God went up from on him in the place where He had spoken with him. ¹⁴And Jacob set up a pillar in the place where He had spoken with him, a stone pillar, and he poured a libation on it and spilled oil on it. ¹⁵And Jacob called the name of the place where God had spoken to him there Beth-El.

¹⁶And they traveled from Beth-El, **and there was still the span of the land to come to Ephrat, and Rachel gave birth, and she had difficulty in her labor. ¹⁷And it was when she was having difficulty in her labor, and the midwife said to her, "Don't be afraid, because this, too, is a son for you." ¹⁸And it was as her soul was going out—because she died—and she called his name Ben-oni. And his father called him Benjamin. ¹⁹And Rachel died. And she was buried on the road to Ephrat. It is Bethlehem. ²⁰And Jacob set up a pillar on her grave. It is the pillar of Rachel's grave to this day.**

²¹And Israel traveled and pitched his tent past Migdal-Eder. ²²And it was when Israel was tenting in that land: and Reuben went and lay with Bilhah, his father's concubine. And Israel heard.

And Jacob's sons were twelve. ²³The sons of Leah were Jacob's firstborn, Reuben, and Simeon and Levi and Judah and Issachar and Zebulun. ²⁴The sons of Rachel were Joseph and Benjamin. ²⁵And the sons of Bilhah, Rachel's maid, were Dan and Naphtali. ²⁶And the sons of Zilpah, Leah's maid, were Gad and Asher. These were Jacob's sons, who were born to him in Paddan Aram.*

²⁷And Jacob came to Isaac, his father, at Mamre, at Kiriath Arba—it is Hebron—where Abraham and Isaac had resided.

²⁸And Isaac's days were a hundred years and eighty years, ²⁹and Isaac expired. And he died and was gathered to his people, old and full of days. And Esau and Jacob, his sons, buried him.

36

¹And these are the records of Esau: He is Edom. ²**Esau had taken his wives from the daughters of Canaan: Adah, daughter of Elon, the**

---

*Here it says that Benjamin is born in Paddan Aram (P); but according to Gen 35:16–19 (E) he is born in Canaan, near Bethlehem.

Hittite, and Aholibamah, daughter of Anah, daughter of Zibeon, the Hivite, ³and Basemath, daughter of Ishmael, sister of Nebaioth.* ⁴And Adah gave birth for Esau to Eliphaz, and Basemath gave birth to Reuel, ⁵and Aholibamah gave birth to Jeush and Jalam and Korah. These are Esau's sons, who were born to him in the land of Canaan. ⁶And Esau took his wives and his sons and his daughters and all the persons of his household and his cattle and all of his animals and all of his possessions that he had acquired in the land of Canaan, and he went to a land, from the presence of Jacob, his brother, ⁷because their property was too great for them to live together, and the land of their residences was not able to suffice them because of their cattle. ⁸And Esau lived in Mount Seir. Esau: he is Edom.

⁹And these are the records of Esau, father of Edom, in Mount Seir. ¹⁰These are the names of Esau's sons: Eliphaz, son of Adah, Esau's wife; Reuel, son of Basemath, Esau's wife. ¹¹And Eliphaz's sons were Teman, Omar, Zepho, and Gatam and Kenaz. ¹²And Timna had been a concubine of Eliphaz, son of Esau, and she gave birth to Amalek for Eliphaz. These are the sons of Adah, Esau's wife. ¹³And these are the sons of Reuel: Nahath and Zerah, Shammah and Mizzeh. These were the sons of Basemath, Esau's wife. ¹⁴And these were the sons of Aholibamah, daughter of Anah, daughter of Zibeon, Esau's wife: and she gave birth for Esau to Jeush and Jalam and Korah.

¹⁵These are the chiefs of the children of Esau:** the sons of Eliphaz, Esau's firstborn: chief Teman, chief Omar, chief Zepho, chief Kenaz, ¹⁶chief Korah, chief Gatam, chief Amalek. These are the chiefs of Eliphaz in the land of Edom. These are the sons of Adah. ¹⁷And these are the sons of Reuel, son of Esau: chief Nahath, chief Zerah, chief Shammah, chief Mizzah. These are the chiefs of Reuel in the land of Edom. These are the sons of Basemath, Esau's wife. ¹⁸And these are the sons of Aholibamah, Esau's wife: chief Jeush, chief Jaalam, chief Korah. These were the chiefs of Aholibamah, daughter of Anah, Esau's wife. ¹⁹These are the sons of Esau, and these are their chiefs. That is Edom.

²⁰These are the sons of Seir the Horite, who live in the land: Lotan and Shobal and Zibeon and Anah ²¹and Dishon and Ezer and Dishan. These are the chiefs of the Horites, the children of Seir, in the land of Edom. ²²And the children of Lotan are Hori and Hemam, and Lotan's sister is Timna. ²³And

---

*There are discrepancies between the names of Esau's wives here and in Gen 26:34–35; 28:9. The differences may be scribal, or there may be a source other than P in this list.

**The sources of the Esau genealogical lists in 36:15–30 are difficult to identify. Grouping them here with the P lists is tentative.

these are the children of Shobal: Alvan and Manahath and Ebal, Shepho and Onam. ²⁴And these are the children of Zibeon: Ajah and Anah—that is Anah who found the water in the wilderness when he tended the asses of Zibeon, his father. ²⁵And these are the children of Anah: Dishon and Aholibamah, daughter of Anah. ²⁶And these are the children of Dishon: Hemdan and Eshban and Ithran and Cheran. ²⁷These are the children of Ezer: Bilhan and Zaavan and Akan. ²⁸These are the children of Dishan: Uz and Aran. ²⁹These are the chiefs of the Horites: chief Lotan, chief Shobal, chief Zibeon, chief Anah, ³⁰chief Dishon, chief Ezer, chief Dishan. These are the chiefs of the Horites by their chiefdoms in the land of Seir.

³¹And these are the kings who ruled in the land of Edom before a king ruled the children of Israel.* ³²And Bela son of Beor ruled in Edom, and the name of his city was Dinhabah. ³³And Bela died, and Jobab son of Zerah from Bozrah ruled in his place. ³⁴And Jobab died, and Husham of the land of Temani ruled in his place. ³⁵And Husham died, and Hadad son of Bedad, who struck Midian in the field of Moab, ruled in his place, and the name of his city was Avith. ³⁶And Hadad died, and Samlah of Masrekah ruled in his place. ³⁷And Samlah died, and Saul of Rehoboth on the river ruled in his place. ³⁸And Saul died, and Baal-hanan son of Achbor ruled in his place. ³⁹And Baal-hanan son of Achbor died, and Hadar ruled in his place, and the name of his city was Pau; and his wife's name was Mehetabel daughter of Matred daughter of Mezahab.

⁴⁰And these are the names of the chiefs of Esau by their families, by their places, by their names: chief Timnah, chief Alvah, chief Jetheth, ⁴¹chief Aholibamah, chief Elah, chief Pinon, ⁴²chief Kenaz, chief Teman, chief Mibzar, ⁴³chief Magdiel, chief Iram.

These are the chiefs of Edom by their homes in the land of their possession. That is Esau, father of Edom.

37

¹And Jacob lived in the land of his father's residences, in the land of Canaan. ²These are the records of Jacob: Joseph, at seventeen years old, had been tending the sheep with his brothers, and he was a boy with the sons of Bilhah and the sons of Zilpah, his father's wives; and Joseph

---

*As early as the eleventh century CE it was pointed out that the Edomite king list in this chapter was made up of names of persons who would have reigned long after Moses had died. It was one of the earliest passages that scholars said must have been written by someone other than Moses.

brought a bad report of them to their father. **³And Israel had loved Joseph most of all his children because he was a son of old age to him.** And he made him a coat of many colors. **⁴And his brothers saw that their father loved him most of all his brothers. And they hated him. And they were not able to speak a greeting to him.**

⁵And Joseph had a dream and told it to his brothers, and they went on to hate him more. ⁶And he said to them, "Listen to this dream that I had: ⁷and here we were binding sheaves in the field; and here was my sheaf rising and standing up, too; and, here, your sheaves surrounded and bowed to my sheaf."

⁸And his brothers said to him, "Will you rule over us?! Will you dominate us?!" And they went on to hate him more because of his dreams and because of his words.

⁹And he had yet another dream and told it to his brothers. And he said, "Here, I've had another dream, and here were the sun and the moon and eleven stars bowing to me." ¹⁰And he told it to his father and to his brothers.

And his father was annoyed at him and said to him, "What is this dream that you've had? Shall we come, I and your mother and your brothers, to bow to you to the ground?!" ¹¹And his brothers were jealous of him, and his father took note of the thing.

¹²And his brothers went to feed their father's sheep in Shechem. ¹³And Israel said to Joseph, "Aren't your brothers feeding in Shechem? Come on and I'll send you to them."

And he said to him, "I'm here."

¹⁴And he said to him, "Go, see how your brothers are and how the sheep are and bring me back word." And he sent him from the valley of Hebron.

And he came to Shechem. ¹⁵And a man found him, and here he was straying in a field. And the man asked him, saying, "What are you looking for?"

¹⁶And he said, "I'm looking for my brothers. Tell me, where are they feeding?"

¹⁷And the man said, "They traveled on from here. Because I heard them saying, 'Let's go to Dothan.'"

And Joseph went after his brothers and found them in Dothan. ¹⁸And they saw him from a distance, and before he came close to them they conspired against him: to kill him. ¹⁹And the brothers said to one another, "Here comes the dream-master, that one there! ²⁰And now, come on and let's kill him and throw him in one of the pits, and we'll say a wild animal ate him, and we'll see what his dreams will be!" **²¹And Reuben heard, and he saved him from their hand. And he said, "Let's not take his life." ²²And Reuben said to them, "Don't spill blood. Throw him into this pit that's in**

the wilderness, and don't put out a hand against him"—in order to save him from their hand, to bring him back to his father. ²³And it was when Joseph came to his brothers: and they took off Joseph's coat, the coat of many colors, which he had on. **²⁴And they took him and threw him into the pit. And the pit was empty; there was no water in it. ²⁵And they sat down to eat bread.**

And they raised their eyes and saw, and here was a caravan of Ishmaelites coming from Gilead, and their camels were carrying spices and balsam and myrrh, going to bring them down to Egypt. ²⁶And Judah said to his brothers, "What profit is there if we kill our brother and cover his blood? ²⁷Come on and let's sell him to the Ishmaelites, and let our hand not be on him, because he's our brother, our flesh." And his brothers listened.* **²⁸And Midianite people, merchants, passed, and they pulled and lifted Joseph from the pit.** And they sold Joseph to the Ishmaelites for twenty weights of silver. And they brought Joseph to Egypt.** **²⁹And Reuben came back to the pit, and here: Joseph was not in the pit. And he tore his clothes. ³⁰And he went back to his brothers and said, "The boy's gone! And I, where can I go?"**

³¹And they took Joseph's coat and slaughtered a he-goat and dipped the coat in the blood. ³²And they sent the coat of many colors and brought it to their father and said, "We found this. Recognize: is it your son's coat or not?"‡

---

*In vv. 21–22 (E) it is Reuben who saves Joseph from the brothers' plan to kill him, but in vv. 26–27 (J), it is Judah who saves him from death. This fits with the concentration on and favoritism toward Judah in J in general.

**In J the Ishmaelites bring Joseph to Egypt and sell him to Potiphar; in E it is the Midianites. (They are also referred to as Medanites below. Note that the births of both Midian and Medan come from E, Gen 25:2,4.) RJE combined these by making it appear that the Midianites sell him to the Ishmaelites, who then sell him in Egypt. But this still leaves a contradiction, because v. 36 (E) still says that the Midianites (or Medanites) sell him to Potiphar, but 39:1 (J) says that "Potiphar . . . bought him from the hand of the Ishmaelites who had brought him down there."

‡In J, in order to get the blessing intended for Esau, Jacob deceives their father by using his brother's cloak and the meat and hide of a goat. Now, in the same source, the brothers deceive their father by using their brother's coat dipped in the blood of a goat. This is one of a series of paybacks for deception that form a chain in the J narrative.

Second, the brothers here say, "Recognize," which is what Tamar says to Judah in the next chapter when she shows him the evidence that he is receiving a payback for having deceived her (38:25).

Third, in J the brothers (not the Midianites) sell Joseph for *twenty* weights of silver. Later, Joseph will arrange to have *twenty* portions of silver returned to their grain sacks (nine portions on the first return, eleven portions on the second return), again hinting at the ironic payback to the brothers' deception.

Many scholars still refer to a Joseph "novella," which they regard as a united work coming from a distinct source. However, the fact that J and E can be identified and

³³And he recognized it and said, "My son's coat. A wild animal ate him. Joseph is torn up!" ³⁴And Jacob ripped his clothes and wore sackcloth on his hips and mourned over his son many days. ³⁵And all his sons and all his daughters got up to console him, and he refused to be consoled, and he said, "Because I'll go down mourning to my son at Sheol," and his father wept for him.

³⁶And the Medanites sold him to Egypt, to Potiphar, an official of Pharaoh, chief of the guards.

38

¹And it was at that time, and Judah went down from his brothers and turned to an Adullamite man, and his name was Hirah. ²And Judah saw a daughter of a Canaanite man there, and his name was Shua. And he took her and came to her. ³And she became pregnant and gave birth to a son, and he called his name Er. ⁴And she became pregnant again and gave birth to a son, and she called his name Onan. ⁵And she proceeded again to give birth to a son, and she called his name Shelah. (And he was at Chezib when she gave birth to him.) ⁶And Judah took a wife for Er, his firstborn, and her name was Tamar. ⁷And Er, Judah's firstborn, was bad in YHWH's eyes, and YHWH killed him. ⁸And Judah said to Onan, "Come to your brother's wife and couple as a brother-in-law with her and raise seed for your brother." ⁹And Onan knew that the seed would not be his. And it was when he came to his brother's wife: and he spent on the ground so as not to give seed for his brother. ¹⁰And what he did was bad in YHWH's eyes, and He killed him, too.

¹¹And Judah said to Tamar, his daughter-in-law, "Live as a widow at your father's house until my son Shelah grows up" (because he said, "Or else he, too, will die like his brothers"). And Tamar went and lived at her father's house.

¹²And the days were many, and Judah's wife, the daughter of Shua, died. And Judah was consoled. And he went up to his sheepshearers, he and his friend Hirah, the Adullamite, to Timnah.

¹³And it was told to Tamar, saying, "Here, your father-in-law is going up to Timnah to shear his sheep." ¹⁴And she took off her widowhood clothes

---

distinguished in the Joseph story show this "novella" view to be wrong. The connections between the Jacob and Joseph stories in J, i.e. the chain of paybacks for deceptions, also show that the Joseph story is not independent; it is intricately linked to its context in J. (See *The Hidden Book in the Bible*, pp. 36–45.)

from on her and covered herself with a veil and wrapped herself and sat in a visible place that was on the road to Timnah, because she saw that Shelah had grown up and she had not been given to him as a wife. ¹⁵And Judah saw her and thought her to be a prostitute because she had covered her face. ¹⁶And he turned to her by the road.

And he said, "Come on. Let me come to you," because he did not know that she was his daughter-in-law.

And she said, "What will you give me when you come to me?"

¹⁷And he said, "I'll have a goat kid sent from the flock."

And she said, "If you'll give a pledge until you send it."

¹⁸And he said, "What is the pledge that I'll give you?"

And she said, "Your seal and your cord and your staff that's in your hand." And he gave them to her, and he came to her, and she became pregnant by him.

¹⁹And she got up and went and took off her veil from on her and put on her widowhood clothes. ²⁰And Judah sent the goat kid by the hand of his friend the Adullamite to take back the pledge from the woman's hand, and he did not find her. ²¹And he asked the people of her place, saying, "Where is the sacred prostitute? She was visibly by the road."

And they said, "There was no sacred prostitute here."

²²And he came back to Judah and said, "I didn't find her, and also the people of the place said 'There was no sacred prostitute here.'"

²³And Judah said, "Let her take them or else we'll be a disgrace. Here, I've sent this goat kid, and you didn't find her."

²⁴And it was about three months, and it was told to Judah, saying, "Your daughter-in-law Tamar has whored, and, here, she's pregnant by whoring as well."

And Judah said, "Bring her out and let her be burned."

²⁵She was brought out. And she sent to her father-in-law, saying, "I'm pregnant by the man to whom these belong," and she said, "Recognize: to whom do these seal and cords and staff belong?"

²⁶And Judah recognized and said, "She's more right than I am, because of the fact that I didn't give her to my son Shelah." And he did not go on to know her again.

²⁷And it was at the time that she was giving birth, and here were twins in her womb. ²⁸And it was as she was giving birth, and one put out his hand, and the midwife took a scarlet thread and tied it on his hand, saying, "This one came out first." ²⁹And it was as he pulled his hand back, and here his brother came out. And she said, "What a breach you've made for yourself!" And he called his name Perez. ³⁰And his brother who had the scarlet thread on his hand came out after. And he called his name Zerah.

39

¹And Joseph had been brought down to Egypt. And an Egyptian man, Potiphar, an official of Pharaoh, chief of the guards, bought him from the hand of the Ishmaelites who had brought him down there. ²And YHWH was with Joseph, and he was a successful man, and he was in his Egyptian lord's house. ³And his lord saw that YHWH was with him, and YHWH made everything he was doing successful in his hand. ⁴And Joseph found favor in his eyes, and he attended him, and he appointed him over his house and put everything he had in his hand. ⁵And it was from the time that he appointed him in his house and over all that he had that YHWH blessed the Egyptian's house because of Joseph, and YHWH's blessing was in everything that he had, in the house and in the field. ⁶And he left everything that he had in Joseph's hand and did not know a thing about what he had except the bread that he was eating.

And Joseph had an attractive figure and was handsome. ⁷And it was after these things, and his lord's wife raised her eyes to Joseph and said, "Lie with me."

⁸And he refused, and he said to his lord's wife, "Here, my lord doesn't know what he has with me in the house, and he's put everything that he has in my hand. ⁹No one is bigger than I am in this house, and he hasn't held back a thing from me except you because you're his wife, and how could I do this great wrong? And I would sin against God." ¹⁰And it was, when she spoke to Joseph day after day, that he didn't listen to her, to lie by her, to be with her. ¹¹And it was on a day like this, and he came to the house to do his work, and not one of the people of the house was there in the house.

¹²And she grasped him by his garment, saying, "Lie with me!" And he left his garment in her hand and fled and went outside. ¹³And it was, when she saw that he had left his garment in her hand and run off outside, ¹⁴that she called to the people of her house and said to them, saying, "See, he brought us a Hebrew man to fool with us. He came to me, to lie with me, and I called in a loud voice. ¹⁵And it was when he heard that I raised my voice and called that he left his garment by me and fled and went outside." ¹⁶And she laid his garment down by her until his lord came to his house. ¹⁷And she spoke things like these to him, saying, "The Hebrew slave, whom you brought us, came to me, to fool with me. ¹⁸And it was when I raised my voice and called that he left his garment by me and fled outside." ¹⁹And it was, when his lord heard his wife's words that she spoke to him, saying, "Your servant did things like these to me," that his anger flared. ²⁰And Joseph's lord took him and put him in prison, a place where the king's prisoners were kept.

And he was there in the prison, ²¹and YHWH was with Joseph and extended kindness to him and gave him favor in the eyes of the warden. ²²And the warden put all the prisoners who were in the prison into Joseph's hand, and he was doing all the things that they do there. ²³The warden was not seeing anything in his hand because YHWH was with him, and YHWH would make whatever he did successful.

40

¹And it was, after these things, the drink-steward of the king of Egypt and the baker sinned against their lord, against the king of Egypt. ²And Pharaoh was angry at his two officers, at the chief of the drink-stewards and at the chief of the bakers, ³and he put them under watch at the house of the chief of the guards, into prison, the place where Joseph was held. ⁴And the chief of the guards assigned Joseph with them, and he attended them.

And they were under watch for days. ⁵And the two of them had a dream, each his own dream, in one night, each with his own dream's meaning, the drink-steward and the baker whom the king of Egypt had, who were held in the prison. ⁶And Joseph came to them in the morning and saw them, and here they were upset. ⁷And he asked Pharaoh's officers who were with him under watch at his lord's house, saying, "Why are your faces bad today?"

⁸And they said to him, "We had a dream, and there's no one who can tell the meaning of it."

And Joseph said to them, "Don't meanings belong to God? Tell me."

⁹And the chief of the drink-stewards told his dream to Joseph, and he said to him, "In my dream: And here was a vine in front of me, ¹⁰and in the vine were three branches, and it was like it was blooming: its blossom came up; its clusters produced grapes. ¹¹And Pharaoh's cup was in my hand. And I took the grapes and pressed them into Pharaoh's cup and set the cup on Pharaoh's hand."

¹²And Joseph said to him, "This is its meaning: The three branches, they're three days. ¹³In three more days Pharaoh will lift your head up, and he'll put you back at your station, and you'll set Pharaoh's cup in his hand—like the original manner when you were his drink-steward. ¹⁴So if you'll remember me with you when it will be good for you, and you'll practice kindness with me, then you'll bring up the memory of me to Pharaoh, and you'll bring me out of this house. ¹⁵Because I was stolen from the land of the Hebrews; and here, too, I haven't done anything that they should have put me in the pit."

¹⁶And the chief of the bakers saw that he told a good meaning, and he said to Joseph, "Me, too. In my dream: And here were three baskets of white bread on my head, ¹⁷and in the highest basket were some of all of Pharaoh's foods, baked goods. And the birds were eating them from the basket, from on my head."

¹⁸And Joseph answered, and he said, "This is its meaning: The three baskets, they're three days. ¹⁹In three more days Pharaoh will lift your head up from you, and he'll hang you on a tree, and the birds will eat your flesh from you."

²⁰And it was in the third day, Pharaoh's birthday, and Pharaoh made a feast for all his servants. And he held up the head of the chief of the drink-stewards and the head of the chief of the bakers among his servants. ²¹And he put the chief of the drink-stewards back over his stewardship, and he set the cup on Pharaoh's hand; ²²and he hanged the chief of the bakers—as Joseph had told the meaning for them. ²³And the chief of the drink-stewards did not remember Joseph. And he forgot him.

41

¹And it was at the end of two years' time, and Pharaoh was dreaming: and here he was standing by the Nile. ²And here, coming up from the Nile, were seven cows, beautiful-looking and fat-fleshed, and they fed in the reeds. ³And here were seven other cows coming up after them from the Nile, bad-looking and thin-fleshed, and they stood by the cows that were by the bank of the Nile. ⁴And the bad-looking and thin-fleshed cows ate the seven beautiful-looking and fat cows—and Pharaoh woke up.

⁵And he slept and dreamed a second time, and here were seven ears of grain coming up on one stalk, fat and good. ⁶And here were seven ears of grain, thin and scorched by the east wind, growing after them. ⁷And the thin ears of grain swallowed the seven fat and full ears of grain—and Pharaoh woke up, and here it was a dream.

⁸And it was in the morning, and his spirit was moved, and he sent and called all of Egypt's magicians and all its wise men. And Pharaoh told them his dream, and there was no one who could tell the meaning of them to Pharaoh.

⁹And the chief of the drink-stewards spoke to Pharaoh, saying, "I'm recalling my sins today: ¹⁰Pharaoh had been angry at his servants, and he put me under watch at the house of the chief of the guards, me and the chief of the bakers. ¹¹And we had a dream in one night, I and he; we each dreamed

with his own dream's meaning. ¹²And there, with us, was a Hebrew boy, a slave of the chief of the guards; and we told him, and he told us the meaning of our dreams. He told the meaning according to each one's dream. ¹³And it was—as he told the meaning for us, so it was: me he put back at my station, and him he hanged."

¹⁴And Pharaoh sent and called Joseph, and they rushed him from the pit, and he shaved and changed his clothing and came to Pharaoh. ¹⁵And Pharaoh said to Joseph, "I've had a dream, and there's no one who can tell the meaning of it, and I've heard about you, saying you hear a dream so as to tell the meaning of it."

¹⁶And Joseph answered Pharaoh, saying, "Not I. God will answer regarding Pharaoh's well-being."

¹⁷And Pharaoh spoke to Joseph, "In my dream, here I was standing by the bank of the Nile. ¹⁸And here, coming up from the Nile, were seven cows, fat-fleshed and beautiful-figured, and they fed in the reeds. ¹⁹And here were seven other cows coming up after them, weak and very bad-figured and scrawny-fleshed. I haven't seen any like these in all the land of Egypt for bad! ²⁰And the cows that were scrawny and bad ate the first seven cows that were fat, ²¹and they came inside, and it wasn't known that they had come inside! And their appearance was bad, as at first. And I woke up.

²²"And I saw in my dream, and here were seven ears of grain coming up on one stalk, full and good. ²³And here were seven ears of grain, dried up, thin, scorched by the east wind, growing after them. ²⁴And the thin ears of grain swallowed the seven good ears of grain.

"And I said it to the magicians, and there's no one who can tell me."

²⁵And Joseph said to Pharaoh, "Pharaoh's dream: it is one. It has told to Pharaoh what God is doing. ²⁶The seven good cows: they're seven years. And the seven good ears of grain: they're seven years. It's one dream. ²⁷And the seven cows that were scrawny and bad that were coming up after them: they're seven years. And the seven ears of grain that were scrawny, scorched by the east wind, will be seven years of famine. ²⁸That is the thing that I spoke to Pharaoh: it has shown Pharaoh what God is doing. ²⁹Here, seven years are coming: big bountifulness in all the land of Egypt. ³⁰And seven years of famine will rise after them, and all the bountifulness in the land of Egypt will be forgotten, and the famine will finish off the land. ³¹And the bountifulness won't be known in the land on account of that famine afterwards because it will be very heavy. ³²And about the recurrence of the dream to Pharaoh two times: because the thing is right from God, and God is hurrying to do it. ³³And now, let Pharaoh look out for an understanding and wise man and set him over the land of Egypt. ³⁴Let Pharaoh do it and appoint

overseers over the land and five-out the land of Egypt in the seven years of bountifulness. ³⁵And let them gather all the food of these coming good years and pile up grain under Pharaoh's hand, food in the cities, and watch over it. ³⁶And the food will become a deposit for the land for the seven years of famine that will be in the land of Egypt so the land won't be cut off in the famine."

³⁷And the thing was good in Pharaoh's eyes and in all his servants' eyes. ³⁸And Pharaoh said to his servants, "Will we find such a man as this, that God's spirit is in him?" ³⁹And Pharaoh said to Joseph, "Since God has made you know all this, there's no one as understanding and wise as you. ⁴⁰You shall be over my house, and at your mouth all my people shall conform. I shall be greater than you only in the throne." ⁴¹And Pharaoh said to Joseph, "See, I've put you over all the land of Egypt." ⁴²And Pharaoh took off his ring from his hand and put it on Joseph's hand, and he had him dressed in linen garments, and he set a gold chain on his neck, ⁴³and he had him driven in the chariot of the second-in-command whom he had, and they called in front of him, "Kneel," so putting him over all the land of Egypt. ⁴⁴And Pharaoh said to Joseph, "I am Pharaoh, and without you a man won't lift his hand and his foot in all the land of Egypt."

⁴⁵And Pharaoh called Joseph's name Zaphenath-paneah. And he gave him Asenath, daughter of Poti-phera, priest of On, as a wife. And Joseph went out over the land of Egypt. ⁴⁶And Joseph was thirty years old when he stood in front of Pharaoh, king of Egypt. And Joseph went out from in front of Pharaoh and passed through all the land of Egypt.

⁴⁷And the land produced in the seven years of bountifulness by fistfuls. ⁴⁸And he gathered all the food of the seven years, which were in the land of Egypt, and he put food in cities; he put the food of the city's fields that were around it inside of it. ⁴⁹And Joseph piled up grain like the sand of the sea, very much, until he stopped counting, because it was without number.

⁵⁰And two sons were born to Joseph before the year of famine came—to whom Asenath, daughter of Poti-phera, priest of On, gave birth for him. ⁵¹And Joseph called the firstborn's name Manasseh, "because God has made me forget all of my trouble and all of my father's house." ⁵²And he called the second one's name Ephraim, "because God has made me fruitful in the land of my degradation."

⁵³And the seven years of the bountifulness that was in the land of Egypt finished, ⁵⁴and the seven years of famine started to come, as Joseph had said. And there was famine in all the lands, and in all the land of Egypt there was bread. ⁵⁵And all the land of Egypt hungered, and the people cried to Pharaoh for the bread, and Pharaoh said to all Egypt, "Go to Joseph. Do what

he'll tell you." ⁵⁶And the famine was on all the face of the earth. And Joseph opened everything that was in them and sold to Egypt. And the famine was strong in the land of Egypt. ⁵⁷And all the earth came to Egypt to buy, to Joseph, because the famine was strong in all the earth.

42

¹And Jacob saw that there was grain in Egypt, and Jacob said to his sons, "Why do you look at each other?" ²And he said, "Here I've heard that there's grain in Egypt. Go down there and buy grain for us from there, and we'll live and not die." ³And ten of Joseph's brothers went down to buy grain from Egypt, ⁴and Jacob did not send Joseph's brother Benjamin with his brothers because, he said, "In case some harm will happen to him."

⁵**And the sons of Israel came to buy among those who were coming, because the famine was in the land of Canaan.** ⁶And Joseph was the one in charge over the land; he was the one who sold grain to all the people of the land. And Joseph's brothers came and bowed to him, noses to the ground. ⁷**And Joseph saw his brothers and recognized them, but he made himself unrecognizable to them, and he spoke with them in hard tones. And he said to them, "From where have you come?"**

And they said, "From the land of Canaan, to buy food."

⁸And Joseph recognized his brothers, but they did not recognize him, ⁹and Joseph remembered the dreams that he had had about them. And he said to them, "You're spies. You came to see the land exposed."

¹⁰And they said to him, "No, my lord, your servants came to buy food. ¹¹We're all sons of one man. We're honest men. Your servants weren't spying."

¹²And he said to them, "No, but you've come to see the land exposed."

¹³And they said, "Your servants are twelve brothers. We're sons of one man in the land of Canaan, and, here, the youngest is with our father today, and one is no more."

¹⁴And Joseph said to them, "It's as I spoke to you, saying: you're spies. ¹⁵By this you'll be tested: by Pharaoh's life, you won't go out of here except by your youngest brother's coming here. ¹⁶Send one from among you, and let him get your brother, and you remain in prison, and your words will be tested: is the truth with you? And if not, then by Pharaoh's life you're spies." ¹⁷And he gathered them under watch for three days. ¹⁸And Joseph said to them on the third day, "Do this and live, as I fear God: ¹⁹If you're honest, one brother from among you will be held at the place where you're under watch; and you, go, bring grain for the famine in your houses. ²⁰And you

will bring your youngest brother to me, and your words will be confirmed, and you won't die." And they did so.

²¹**And they said, each to his brother, "But we're guilty over our brother, because we saw his soul's distress when he implored us and we didn't listen. On account of that this distress has come to us!"**

²²**And Reuben answered them, saying, "Didn't I say to you, saying, 'Don't sin against the boy'? And you didn't listen. And his blood, too, is required here!"**

²³**And they did not know that Joseph was listening, because an interpreter was between them.** ²⁴**And he turned from them and wept. And he came back to them and spoke to them and took Simeon from them and shackled him before their eyes.** ²⁵**And Joseph commanded that they fill their containers with grain and to put their silver back in each man's sack and to give them provisions for the road. And he did that for them.**

²⁶And they loaded their grain on their asses and went from there.

²⁷And one opened his sack to give fodder to his ass at a lodging place, and he saw his silver, and here it was in the mouth of his bag. ²⁸And he said to his brothers, "My silver's been put back, and here it is in my bag, too."

And their heart went out, and the brothers trembled to one another, saying, "What is this that God has done to us?"

²⁹And they came to Jacob, their father, to the land of Canaan, and told him all the things that happened to them, saying, ³⁰"The man, the lord of the land, spoke with us hard and accused us of spying on the land. ³¹And we said to him, 'We're honest. We weren't spying. ³²We're twelve brothers, our father's sons, one is no more, and the youngest is with our father in the land of Canaan today.' ³³And the man, the lord of the land, said to us, 'By this I'll know that you're honest: leave one brother from among you with me, and take for the famine in your houses and go, ³⁴and bring your youngest brother to me, so I may know that you aren't spies, that you're honest. I'll give you your brother, and you'll go around in the land.'"

³⁵**And it was: they were emptying their sacks, and here was each man's bundle of silver in his sack, and they saw the bundles of their silver, they and their father, and they were afraid.** ³⁶**And their father, Jacob, said to them, "You've bereaved me! Joseph is gone, and Simeon's gone, and you'll take Benjamin. All these have happened to me!"**

³⁷**And Reuben said to his father, saying, "Kill my two sons if I don't bring him back to you. Put him in my hand, and I'll bring him back to you."**

³⁸And he said, "My son will not go down with you. Because his brother's dead, and he's left by himself, and if some harm would happen to him on the way in which you're going then you'll bring down my gray hair in anguish to Sheol."

43

¹And the famine was heavy in the land. ²And it was when they had finished eating the grain that they had brought from Egypt: and their father said to them, "Go back. Buy us a little food."

³And Judah said to him, saying, "The man certified to us, saying, 'You won't see my face unless your brother is with you.' ⁴If you're sending our brother with us, we'll go down and buy food for you, ⁵and if you're not sending, we won't go down, because the man said to us, 'You won't see my face unless your brother is with you.'"

⁶And Israel said, "Why have you done me wrong, to tell the man that you have another brother?"

⁷And they said, "The man asked about us and about our birthplace, saying, 'Is your father still alive? Do you have a brother?' And we told him about these things. Could we have known that he would say, 'Bring your brother down'?"

⁸And Judah said to Israel, his father, "Send the boy with me, so we may get up and go, and we'll live and not die, we and you and our infants as well. ⁹I'll be security for him. You'll seek him from my hand. If I don't bring him to you and set him before you, then I'll have sinned against you for all time. ¹⁰For, if we hadn't delayed, by now we would have come back twice."

¹¹And Israel, their father, said to them, "If that's how it is, then do this: Take some of the best fruit of the land in your containers and take a gift down to the man, a little balm and a little honey, gum and myrrh, pistachios and almonds. ¹²And take double the silver in your hand, and take back in your hand the silver that was put back in the mouth of your bags. Maybe it was a mistake. ¹³And take your brother. And get up, go back to the man. **¹⁴And may El Shadday give you mercy before the man, so he'll send your other brother and Benjamin to you. And I: if I'm bereaved I'm bereaved!"**

¹⁵And the men took this gift and took double the silver in their hand and Benjamin and got up and went down to Egypt and stood before Joseph. ¹⁶And Joseph saw Benjamin with them and said to the one who was over his house, "Bring the men to the house, and slaughter and prepare an animal, because the men will eat with me at noon." ¹⁷And the man did as Joseph said, and the man brought the men to Joseph's house.

¹⁸And the men were afraid because they were brought to Joseph's house, and they said, "We're being brought on account of the silver that came back in our bags the first time, in order to roll over us and to fall upon us and to take us as slaves—and our asses." ¹⁹And they went over to the man who was over Joseph's house and spoke to him at the entrance of the house

²⁰and said, "Please, my lord, we came down the first time to buy food, ²¹and it was when we came to the lodging place, and we opened our bags, and here was each man's silver in the mouth of his bag, our money in its full weight. And we've brought it in our hand, ²²and we've brought down additional silver in our hand to buy food. We don't know who put our silver in our bags."

²³And he said, "Peace to you. Don't be afraid. Your God and your father's God put treasure in your bags for you. Your silver came to me." **And he brought Simeon out to them.**

²⁴And the man brought the men to Joseph's house, and he gave water, and they washed their feet, and he gave fodder for their asses. ²⁵And they prepared the gift until Joseph's arrival at noon because they heard that they would eat bread there. ²⁶And Joseph came to the house, and they brought the gift for him that was in their hand to the house, and they bowed to him to the ground.

²⁷And he asked if they were well, and he said, "Is your old father whom you mentioned well? Is he still alive?"

²⁸And they said, "Your servant, our father, is well. He's still alive." And they knelt and bowed.

²⁹And he raised his eyes and saw Benjamin, his brother, his mother's son, and said, "Is this your youngest brother whom you mentioned to me?" And he said, "May God be gracious to you, my son." ³⁰And Joseph hurried because his feelings for his brother were boiling, and he looked for a place to weep and came to his room and wept there. ³¹And he washed his face and went out and restrained himself and said, "Put out bread." ³²And they put it out for him by himself and for them by themselves and for the Egyptians who were eating with him by themselves, because the Egyptians could not eat bread with the Hebrews because that is an offensive thing to Egypt. ³³And they sat before him, the firstborn according to his birthright and the youngest according to his youth. And the men looked amazed at one another. ³⁴And he conveyed portions from before him to them, and he made Benjamin's portion five times more than the portions of all of them, and they drank and were drunk with him.

44

¹And he commanded the one who was over his house, saying, "Fill the men's bags with as much food as they can carry and put each man's silver in the mouth of his bag, ²and put my cup, the silver cup, in the mouth of the youngest one's bag, and the silver for his grain." And he did according to Joseph's word that he spoke.

³The morning was light: and the men had been sent away, they and their asses. ⁴They had gone out of the city. They had not gone far, and Joseph had said to the one who was over his house, "Get up. Pursue the men, and you'll catch up with them and say to them, 'Why did you pay back bad for good? ⁵Isn't this the thing from which my lord drinks? And he divines by it! You've done bad, this thing that you've done.'" ⁶And he caught up with them and spoke these things to them.

⁷And they said to him, "Why would my lord speak things like these? Far be it from your servants to do a thing like this. ⁸Here, we brought the silver that we found in the mouth of our bags back to you from the land of Canaan, so how would we steal silver or gold from your lord's house?! ⁹The one among your servants with whom it's found, let him die, and also we'll become my lord's servants."

¹⁰And he said, "Now, also, it will be so according to your words: the one with whom it's found will become my servant. And you will be free."

¹¹And they hurried, and each man lowered his bag to the ground, and each man opened his bag. ¹²And he searched. With the oldest he began, and with the youngest he finished. And the cup was found in Benjamin's bag. ¹³And they ripped their clothes, and each man loaded his ass, and they went back to the city. ¹⁴And Judah and his brothers came to Joseph's house, and he was still there, and they fell to the ground before him.

¹⁵And Joseph said to them, "What is this thing that you've done? Didn't you know that a man like me would divine?"

¹⁶And Judah said, "What shall we say to my lord? What shall we speak? By what shall we justify ourselves? God has found your servants' crime. Here we're my lord's servants, both we and the one in whose hand the cup was found."

¹⁷And he said, "Far be it from me to do this. The man in whose hand the cup was found: he will be my servant; and you, go up in peace to your father."

¹⁸And Judah went over to him and said, "Please, my lord, let your servant speak something in my lord's ears, and let your anger not flare at your servant, because you're like Pharaoh himself. ¹⁹My lord asked his servants, saying, 'Do you have a father or brother?' ²⁰and we said to my lord, 'We have an old father and a young son of his old age, and his brother's dead, and he's left alone of his mother, and his father loves him.' ²¹And you said to your servants, 'Bring him down to me, so I may set my eye on him.' ²²And we said to my lord, 'The boy can't leave his father; if he left his father he'd die.' ²³And you said to your servants, 'If your youngest brother doesn't come down with you, you won't see my face again.' ²⁴And it was, when we

went up to your servant, my father, and told him my lord's words, ²⁵that our father said, 'Go back. Buy us a little food.' ²⁶And we said, 'We can't go down. If our youngest brother is with us then we'll go down, because we can't see the man's face if our youngest brother isn't with us.' ²⁷And your servant, my father, said to us, 'You know that my wife gave birth to two for me, ²⁸and one went away from me, and I said he's surely torn up, and I haven't seen him since. ²⁹And if you take this one from me as well and some harm happens to him, then you'll bring down my gray hair in wretchedness to Sheol.' ³⁰And now, when I come to your servant, my father, and the boy isn't with us, and he's bound to him soul to soul, ³¹it will be, when he sees that the boy isn't there, that he'll die. And your servants will have brought down your servant our father's gray hair in anguish to Sheol, ³²because your servant offered security for the boy to my father, saying, 'If I don't bring him to you then I'll have sinned against my father for all time.' ³³And now, let your servant stay as my lord's servant in place of the boy, and let the boy go up with his brothers— ³⁴for how could I go up to my father and the boy isn't with me—or else I'll see the wretchedness that will find my father."

45

¹And Joseph was not able to restrain himself in front of everyone who was standing by him, and he called, "Take everyone out from my presence." And not a man stood with him when Joseph made himself known to his brothers. ²And he wept out loud. And Egypt heard, and Pharaoh's house heard. **³And Joseph said to his brothers, "I'm Joseph. Is my father still alive?" And his brothers were not able to answer him, because they were terrified in front of him.** ⁴And Joseph said to his brothers, "Come over to me." And they went over. And he said, "I'm Joseph, your brother, whom you sold to Egypt. ⁵And now, don't be sad and let there be no anger in your eyes because you sold me here, because God sent me before you to preserve life. ⁶For it's two years that the famine is in the land, and for five more years there'll be no plowing and harvest. ⁷And God sent me ahead of you to provide a remnant for you in the earth and to keep you alive as a big, surviving community. ⁸And now, it wasn't you who sent me here, but God, and he made me into a father to Pharaoh and a lord to all his house and a ruler in all the land of Egypt. ⁹Hurry, and go up to my father and say to him: 'Your son Joseph said this: God has made me a lord to all Egypt. Come down to me. Don't stand back. ¹⁰And you'll live in the land of Goshen, and you'll be close to me, you and your children and your children's children and your flock and your

oxen and everything you have. [11]And I'll provide for you there, because there are five more years of famine, or else you and your house and everything you have will be impoverished.' [12]And here your eyes see, and the eyes of my brother Benjamin, that it's my mouth that speaks to you. [13]And you'll tell my father of all my glory in Egypt and of all that you've seen, and hurry and bring my father down here." [14]And he fell on his brother Benjamin's neck and wept, and Benjamin wept on his neck. [15]And he kissed all his brothers and wept over them. And after that his brothers spoke with him.

[16]And the report was heard at Pharaoh's house, saying, "Joseph's brothers have come." And it was good in Pharaoh's eyes and in his servants' eyes. [17]And Pharaoh said to Joseph, "Say to your brothers, 'Do this: load your beasts and go; come to the land of Canaan, [18]and take your father and your households and come to me, and I'll give you the best of the land of Egypt; and eat the fat of the land.' [19]And you are commanded, 'Do this: Take wagons from the land of Egypt for your infants and for your wives, and carry your father and come. [20]And let your eye not care about your possessions, for the best of all the land of Egypt is yours.'"

[21]And the children of Israel did so. And Joseph gave them wagons by order of Pharaoh and gave them provisions for the road. [22]For all of them he gave each man changes of clothes, and he gave Benjamin three hundred weights of silver and five changes of clothes. [23]And to his father he sent as follows: ten asses bearing Egypt's best, and ten she-asses bearing grain, bread, and food supply for his father for the road. [24]And he sent his brothers off, and they went, and he said to them, "Don't quarrel on the road."

[25]And they went up from Egypt and came to the land of Canaan, to Jacob, their father, [26]and told him, saying, "Joseph is still alive! And he rules all the land of Egypt!" And his heart grew numb because he did not believe them. [27]And they spoke to him all of Joseph's words that he had spoken to them, and he saw the wagons that Joseph had sent to carry him, and their father Jacob's spirit came alive.

[28]And Israel said, "So much! Joseph, my son, is still alive. Let me go and see him before I die."

46

[1]And Israel and everyone he had traveled and came to Beer-sheba, and he offered sacrifices to the God of his father, Isaac. [2]And God said to Israel in night visions, and He said, "Jacob, Jacob."

And he said, "I'm here."

³And He said, "I am God, your father's God. Don't be afraid of going down to Egypt, because I'll make you into a big nation there. ⁴I shall go down with you to Egypt, and I shall also bring you up. And Joseph will set his hand on your eyes."

⁵And Jacob got up from Beer-sheba. And the children of Israel carried Jacob, their father, and their infants and their wives in the wagons that Pharaoh had sent to carry him. ⁶And they took their cattle and their property that they had acquired in the land of Canaan, and they came to Egypt, Jacob and all his seed with him. ⁷He brought his sons and his grandsons with him, his daughters and his granddaughters and all his seed with him to Egypt.

⁸And these are the names of the children of Israel who came to Egypt, Jacob and his sons: Jacob's firstborn was Reuben. ⁹And Reuben's sons were Hanoch and Pallu and Hezron and Carmi. ¹⁰And Simeon's sons were Jemuel and Jamin and Ohad and Jachin and Zohar and Saul, the son of a Canaanite woman. ¹¹And Levi's sons were Gershon, Kohath, and Merari. ¹²And Judah's sons were Er and Onan and Shelah and Perez and Zerah. And Er and Onan died in the land of Canaan, and Perez's sons were Hezron and Hamul. ¹³And Issachar's sons were Tola and Puvah and Job and Shimron. ¹⁴And Zebulun's sons were Sered and Elon and Jahleel. ¹⁵These were the sons of Leah, to whom she gave birth for Jacob in Paddan Aram, and Dinah, his daughter, every person of his sons and his daughters, thirty-three. ¹⁶And Gad's sons were Ziphion and Haggai and Shuni and Ezbon, Eri and Arodi and Areli. ¹⁷And Asher's sons were Imnah and Ishvah and Ishvi and Beriah, and Serah was their sister. And Beriah's sons were Hever and Malchiel. ¹⁸These were the sons of Zilpah, whom Laban gave to Leah, his daughter, and she gave birth to these for Jacob, sixteen persons. ¹⁹The sons of Rachel, Jacob's wife, were Joseph and Benjamin. ²⁰And Manasseh and Ephraim were born to Joseph in the land of Egypt, to whom Asenath, daughter of Poti-phera, priest of On, gave birth for him. ²¹And Benjamin's sons were Bela and Becher and Ashbel, Gera and Naaman, Ehi and Rosh, Muppim and Huppim and Ard. ²²These were Rachel's sons, who were born to Jacob. All the persons were fourteen. ²³And Dan's sons: Hushim. ²⁴And Naphtali's sons were Jahzeel and Guni and Jezer and Shillem. ²⁵These were the sons of Bilhah, whom Laban gave to Rachel, his daughter, and she gave birth to these for Jacob. All the persons were seven. ²⁶All the persons of Jacob's who came to Egypt, who came out from his thigh, outside of Jacob's sons' wives, all the persons were sixty-six. ²⁷And Joseph's sons who were born to him in Egypt were two persons. All the persons of Jacob's house who came to Egypt were seventy.

²⁸And he sent Judah ahead of him to Joseph to direct him in advance to Goshen. And they came to the land of Goshen. ²⁹And Joseph hitched his

chariot and went up to Israel, his father, at Goshen. And he appeared to him and fell on his neck and wept on his neck a long time. ³⁰And Israel said to Joseph, "Let me die now after I've seen your face, that you're still alive."

³¹And Joseph said to his brothers and to his father's house, "Let me go up and tell Pharaoh and say to him, 'My brothers and my father's house that were in the land of Canaan have come to me. ³²And the people are shepherds, because they were livestock people, and they've brought their flock and their oxen and all they have.' ³³And it will be, when Pharaoh will call you and say, 'What is your occupation?' ³⁴that you'll say, 'Your servants were livestock people from our youth until now, both we and our fathers,' so that you'll live in the land of Goshen, because any shepherd is an offensive thing to Egypt."

47

¹And Joseph came and told Pharaoh and said, "My father and my brothers and their flock and their oxen and all that they own have come from the land of Canaan, and here they are in the land of Goshen." ²And he took several of his brothers, five men, and set them before Pharaoh.

³And Pharaoh said to his brothers, "What is your work?"

And they said to Pharaoh, "Your servants are shepherds, both we and our fathers," ⁴and they said to Pharaoh, "We came to reside in the land because there's no pasture for your servants' flock because the famine is heavy in the land of Canaan. And now may your servants live in the land of Goshen."

⁵And Pharaoh said to Joseph, saying, "Your father and your brothers have come to you. ⁶The land of Egypt is before you. Settle your father and your brothers in the best of the land. Let them live in the land of Goshen. And if you know—and if there are among them—worthy men, then you shall make them livestock officers over those that I have."

⁷And Joseph brought Jacob, his father, and stood him in front of Pharaoh. And Jacob blessed Pharaoh. ⁸And Pharaoh said to Jacob, "How many are the days of the years of your life?"

⁹And Jacob said to Pharaoh, "The days of the years of my residences are a hundred thirty years. The days of the years of my life have been few and bad, and they haven't attained the days of the years of my fathers' lives, in the days of their residences." ¹⁰And Jacob blessed Pharaoh and went out from in front of Pharaoh.

¹¹And Joseph settled his father and his brothers and gave them a possession in the land of Egypt, in the best of the land, in the land of Rameses,

as Pharaoh had commanded. ¹²And Joseph supported his father and his brothers and all of his father's household, bread by the number of infants.*

¹³And there was was no bread in all the land of Egypt, because the famine was very heavy, and the land of Egypt and the land of Canaan languished because of the famine.** ¹⁴And Joseph collected all the silver that was found in the land of Egypt and in the land of Canaan for the grain that they were buying, and Joseph brought the silver to Pharaoh's house. ¹⁵And the silver came to an end from the land of Egypt and from the land of Canaan. And all of Egypt came to Joseph, saying, "Give us bread! And why should we die in front of you? Because there's no more silver!"

¹⁶And Joseph said, "Give your livestock, and I'll give it to you for your livestock if there's no more silver."

¹⁷And they brought their livestock to Joseph, and Joseph gave them bread for the horses and for the livestock of the flocks and for the livestock of the oxen and for the asses, and he sustained them with bread for all their livestock in that year. ¹⁸And that year came to an end, and they came to him in the second year and said to him, "We won't conceal from my lord that the silver has come to an end and the cattle livestock have gone to my lord. Nothing is left in front of my lord except our body and our land. ¹⁹Why should we die before your eyes, both we and our land? Buy us and our land for bread, and we and our land will be servants to Pharaoh; and give seed so we'll live and not die, and the land won't be devastated." ²⁰And Joseph bought all the land of Egypt for Pharaoh, because Egypt, each man, sold his field, because the famine was strong on them. And the land became Pharaoh's. ²¹And the people: he moved them to cities, from one edge of

---

*This section, 47:5–12, comes in the middle of a J text. But Jacob says here that he is 130 years old and that Abraham and Isaac lived longer, while in J YHWH has decreed that no human will live more than 120 years. It is in P that ages are given and that Abraham and Isaac live longer. Moreover, this section has other characteristics of P: The phrases "the days of the years" and "the years of your life" occur only in P. The terms "residences" and "possession" occur only in P. The phrase "as he commanded" occurs fifty-three other times in Genesis–Numbers, and fifty-two are in P. And it is in P that the people live in Rameses.

Nonetheless, we should recognize that it is possible that the Redactor combined some material from J or E with P to form this section. The reference to Goshen (v. 6) may be in conflict with the reference to Rameses, and P never mentions Goshen elsewhere. The words "Let them live in Goshen" may have originally read "they lived in Goshen," which would look the same in the consonantal text. And Goshen is what the brothers requested in the J text (v. 4). Further, this matter is complicated by the fact that the Septuagint text is different, which may be related to the recurrence of the words "let them live in the land of Goshen" in vv. 4 and 6.

**It is difficult to determine whether this section, vv. 13–26, is J or E.

Egypt's border to its other edge. ²²Only the priests' land he did not buy, because it was a law for the priests from Pharaoh, and they ate their statutory share that Pharaoh had given them. On account of this they did not sell their land.

²³And Joseph said to the people, "Here, I've bought you and your land for Pharaoh today. Look: seed for you. And you'll sow the land; ²⁴and it will be, at the harvests, that you'll give a fifth to Pharaoh, and the four parts will be yours for field seed and for you to eat and for whoever is in your households and for your infants to eat."

²⁵And they said, "You've kept us alive! Let us find favor in my lord's eyes, and we'll be servants to Pharaoh."

²⁶And Joseph set it as a law to this day on Egypt's land: to Pharaoh the fifth. Only the land of the priests alone was not Pharaoh's.

²⁷And Israel lived in Egypt in the land of Goshen, and they held property in it.**And they were fruitful and multiplied very much.**

²⁸**And Jacob lived in the land of Egypt seventeen years. And Jacob's days, the years of his life, were seven years and a hundred forty years.**

²⁹And Israel's days to die drew close. And he called his son, Joseph, and said to him, "If I've found favor in your eyes, place your hand under my thigh and practice kindness and faithfulness with me: don't bury me in Egypt. ³⁰And I'll lie with my fathers, and you'll carry me out of Egypt and bury me in their burial place."

And he said, "I'll do according to your word."

³¹And he said, "Swear to me."

And he swore to him. And Israel bowed at the head of the bed.

48

¹And it was after these things, and one said to Joseph, "Here, your father is sick." And he took his two sons with him, Manasseh and Ephraim. ²And one told Jacob and said, "Here, your son Joseph is coming to you." And Israel fortified himself and sat up on the bed.

³And Jacob said to Joseph, "El Shadday appeared to me in Luz in the land of Canaan, and He blessed me ⁴and said to me, 'Here, I'm making you fruitful and multiplying you, and I'll make you into a community of peoples, and I'll give this land to your seed after you, an eternal possession.' ⁵And now, your two sons who were born to you in the land of Egypt by my arrival to you at Egypt: they're mine. Ephraim and Manasseh will be like Reuben and Simeon to me. ⁶And your offspring that you'll have after them will be yours. They shall be called by their brothers' names with regard to their inheritance. ⁷And

I: when I was coming from Paddan Aram, Rachel died by me in the land of Canaan on the way, when there was still a span of land to come to Ephrat, and I buried her there on the Ephrat road. That's Bethlehem."*

⁸And Israel saw Joseph's sons and said, "Who are these?"**

⁹And Joseph said to his father, "They're my sons, whom God has given me here."

And he said, "Bring them to me, and I'll bless them." ¹⁰And Israel's eyes were heavy from old age. He was not able to see. And he brought them close to him, and he kissed them and embraced them. ¹¹And Israel said to Joseph, "I didn't expect to see your face; and, here, God has shown me your seed as well." ¹²And Joseph brought them out from between his knees, and he bowed, his nose to the ground. ¹³And Joseph took the two of them, Ephraim in his right hand, at Israel's left; and Manasseh in his left hand, at Israel's right; and he brought them over to him. ¹⁴And Israel put out his right hand and placed it on Ephraim's head—and he was the younger—and his left hand on Manasseh's head. He crossed his hands—because Manasseh was the firstborn. ¹⁵And he blessed Joseph and said, "The God before whom my fathers, Abraham and Isaac, walked, who shepherded me from my start to this day, ¹⁶the angel who redeemed me from all bad, may He bless the boys. And may my name be called on them, and the name of my fathers, Abraham and Isaac. And may they spawn into a great number within the earth."

¹⁷And Joseph saw that his father had placed his right hand on Ephraim's head, and it was bad in his eyes, and he held up his father's hand to turn it from on Ephraim's head onto Manasseh's head, ¹⁸and Joseph said to his father, "Not like that, my father, because this is the firstborn. Set your right hand on his head."

---

*Verse 7 fits uncomfortably in its context, connecting neither to the preceding nor to the following verses. And it merges elements of two sources: It refers to Paddan Aram, which is characteristic of P, but it says "there was still a span of land to come to Ephrat," and it refers to Rachel's being buried on the Ephrat road, which comes from E (Gen 35:16–20). It therefore appears to be an addition that the Redactor made to the text. Perhaps its function was to separate the two conflicting passages about Ephraim and Manasseh that precede and follow it. See the next note.

Alternatively, this verse might after all be P, because it fits with the next P passage (49:29–33). As a unit these two passages could be saying: "As for me: Rachel died and was buried on the road, but when I die I want to be buried back in my ancestral tomb with the other patriarchs and matriarchs." It is therefore uncertain whether v. 7 is P or R.

**In v. 5 Jacob promotes Ephraim and Manasseh to full status, equal to his own sons. But now in v. 8 he looks at them and asks, "Who are these?"! The former verse is P, and the contradiction developed when this verse was placed in the middle of the E passage about Ephraim and Manasseh.

¹⁹And his father refused and said, "I know, my son, I know. He, too, will become a people; and he, too, will be great. But in fact his little brother will be greater than he, and his seed will be full-fledged of nations." ²⁰And he blessed them in that day, saying, "Israel will bless with you, saying: 'May God make you like Ephraim and like Manasseh.'" And he set Ephraim before Manasseh.

²¹And Israel said to Joseph, "Here, I'm dying. And God will be with you and will bring you back to your fathers' land. ²²And I've given you one shoulder* over your brothers, which I took from the Amorite's hand with my sword and my bow."

49

¹And Jacob called to his sons and said:**

    Gather, and I'll tell you what will happen to you in the future days.
2   Assemble and listen, sons of Jacob,
        and listen to Israel, your father.
3   Reuben, you're my firstborn,
        my power, and the beginning of my might,
        preeminent in bearing and preeminent in strength.
4   Unstable as water, you'll not be preeminent,
        for you ascended your father's bed;
        then you defiled, going up to my couch.

---

*The word for a "shoulder" here in the Hebrew is *šekem*. That is, it is a pun in which Jacob gives his Joseph an extra "Shechem." Shechem was Jeroboam's capital of the northern kingdom of Israel. It was located in one of the Joseph tribes' territory (1 Kgs 12:25). E, the northern source, thus conveys the favored status of the northern kingdom, just as J favors the status of the southern kingdom of Judah in Jacob's deathbed blessing of Judah in the following chapter. (See the next two notes.)

**This poem, known as the Blessing of Jacob, is an independent, old composition probably coming from the premonarchic period. See Frank Moore Cross and David Noel Freedman, *Studies in Ancient Yahwistic Poetry* (Grand Rapids, MI: Eerdmans, 1975), pp. 46–63. The author of J used the poem as a source of information on which to construct part of the history of the tribes of Reuben, Simeon, Levi, and Judah, then included the poem along with the history that he or she based on it. A similar use and inclusion of a poetic source in a prose text may be seen in the case of the Song of the Sea. The poem appears in Exodus 15; the prose account that used it as a source is the J portion of Exodus 14. (Another case of use and inclusion is the Song of Deborah in Judges 5 and the prose account that used it as a source in Judges 4. It is outside the limits of the present volume, but it is an additional demonstration of how ancient Israelite prose authors worked with poetic sources.)

5 Simeon and Levi are brothers:

6   Implements of violence are their tools of trade.
    Let my soul not come in their council;
    let my glory not be united in their society.
    For in their anger they killed a man,
    and by their will they crippled an ox.

7   Cursed is their anger, for it's strong,
    and their wrath, for it's hard.
    I'll divide them in Jacob,
    and I'll scatter them in Israel.

8 Judah: You, your brothers will praise you.
    Your hand on your enemies' neck,
    your father's sons will bow to you.

9   A lion's whelp is Judah;
    from prey, my son, you've risen.
    He bent, crouched, like a lion;
    and, like a feline, who will rouse him?

10   The scepter won't depart from Judah*
    or a ruler from between his legs
    until he comes to Shiloh,
    and peoples' obedience is his.

11   Tying his ass to the vine
    and his she-ass's foal to the choice vine,
    he washed in wine his clothing
    and in blood of grapes his garment,

12   eyes darker than wine
    and teeth whiter than milk.

13 Zebulun will dwell by seashores:
    and he'll be a shore for boats,
    and his border at Sidon.

14 Issachar is a strong ass
    crouching between the saddle-packs:

15   and he saw rest, that it was good,
    and the land, that it was pleasant,
    and he leaned his shoulder to bear
    and became a work-company servant.

---

*The poem, here in J, eliminates the first three brothers (Reuben, Simeon, Levi) from the succession and then gives the monarchy to Judah forever ("The scepter won't depart from Judah").

16   Dan will judge his people
          as one of the tribes of Israel:
17   Dan will be a snake on a road,
          a venomous snake on a path,
          that bites a horse's heels,
          and its rider falls backward.
18   I wait for your salvation, YHWH.
19   Gad: a troop will trap him,
          and he'll trap their heel.
20   Asher: his bread will be rich,
          and he'll provide a king's delights.
21   Naphtali: a hind let loose,
          who gives lovely words.
22   A fruitful bough is Joseph,
          a fruitful bough over a spring,
          branches running over a wall:
23   And archers bitterly attacked him,
          shot at him, and despised him.
24   And his bow stayed strong,
          and his forearms were nimble,
          from the hands of the Mighty One of Jacob,
          from there, the shepherd, the rock of Israel,
25   from your father's God, and He'll strengthen you,
          and Shadday, and He'll bless you,
          blessings of skies from above,
          blessings of deep, crouching below,
          blessings of breast and womb,
26   blessings of your father, the mighty and most high,
          blessings of the mountains of old
          desired object of the hills of antiquity.
          They'll be on Joseph's head,
          on the top of the head of the one separate from his brothers.
27   Benjamin is a tearing wolf:
          in the morning eating prey,
          and at evening dividing booty.

²⁸All these are the tribes of Israel, twelve, and this is what their father spoke to them, and he blessed them. He blessed them each according to his blessing. ²⁹And he commanded them and said to them, "I'm being gathered

to my people. Bury me: to my fathers, to the cave that's in the field of Ephron, the Hittite, ³⁰in the cave that's in the field of Machpelah, which faces Mamre in the land of Canaan, as Abraham bought the field from Ephron, the Hittite, as a possession for a tomb. ³¹There they buried Abraham and Sarah, his wife. There they buried Isaac and Rebekah, his wife. And there I buried Leah. ³²The field and the cave that's in it were a purchase from the children of Heth." ³³And Jacob finished commanding his sons, and he gathered his feet into the bed, and he expired, and he was gathered to his people.

50

¹And Joseph fell upon his father's face and wept over him and kissed him. ²And Joseph commanded his servants, the physicians, to embalm his father. And the physicians embalmed Israel, ³and they spent forty days on him, because that is the number of days they spent on the embalming, and Egypt mourned him seventy days. ⁴And his mourning days passed, and Joseph spoke to Pharaoh's house, saying, "If I've found favor in your eyes, speak in Pharaoh's ears, saying, ⁵'My father had me swear, saying, "Here I'm dying. In my tomb, which I dug for me in the land of Canaan: you shall bury me there." And now, let me go up so I may bury my father and come back.'"

⁶And Pharaoh said, "Go up and bury your father as he had you swear."

⁷And Joseph went up to bury his father, and all of Pharaoh's servants, the elders of his house, and all the elders of the land of Egypt, ⁸and all of Joseph's house and his brothers and his father's house. Only their infants and their flock and their oxen they left in the land of Goshen. ⁹And both chariots and horsemen went up with him. It was a very heavy camp. ¹⁰And they came to the threshing floor of Atad, which is across the Jordan, and they had a very big and heavy funeral, and he made a mourning for his father for seven days. ¹¹And the Canaanite residents of the land saw the mourning at the threshing floor of Atad and said, "This is a heavy mourning to Egypt." On account of this its name was called Abel of Egypt, which is beyond the Jordan. ¹²And his sons did so for him, as he had commanded them. ¹³And his sons carried him to the land of Canaan and buried him in the cave of the field of Machpelah, as Abraham had bought the field as a possession for a tomb from Ephron, the Hittite, facing Mamre.

¹⁴And, after his burial of his father, Joseph came back to Egypt, he and his brothers and all those who went up with him to bury his father.

¹⁵And Joseph's brothers saw that their father was dead, and they said, "If Joseph will despise us he'll pay us back all the bad that we dealt to him." ¹⁶And they commanded to Joseph, saying, "Your father had commanded before his death, saying, ¹⁷'You shall say this to Joseph: Please, bear your brothers' offense and their sin, because they dealt you bad.' And now bear the offense of the servants of your father's God."

And Joseph wept when they spoke to him.

¹⁸And his brothers also went and fell in front of him and said, "Here, we're yours as slaves."

¹⁹And Joseph said to them, "Don't be afraid, because am I in God's place? ²⁰And you thought bad against me. God thought for good: in order to do as it is today, to keep alive a numerous people. ²¹And now, don't be afraid. I'll provide for you and your infants." And he consoled them. And he spoke on their heart.

²²And Joseph lived in Egypt, he and his father's house. And Joseph lived a hundred ten years, ²³and Joseph saw children of Ephraim's of the third generation. Also children of Machir, son of Manasseh, were born on Joseph's knees.

²⁴And Joseph said to his brothers, "I'm dying. And God will take account of you and will bring you up from this land to the land that He swore to Abraham, to Isaac, and to Jacob." ²⁵And Joseph had the children of Israel swear, saying, "God will take account of you, and you'll bring up my bones from here."

²⁶And Joseph died, a hundred ten years old, and they embalmed him and set him in a coffin in Egypt.

EXODUS

1

¹And these are the names of the children of Israel who came to Egypt. With Jacob, each and his household had come: ²Reuben, Simeon, Levi, and Judah, ³Issachar, Zebulun, and Benjamin, ⁴Dan and Naphtali, Gad and Asher. ⁵And all the persons coming out from Jacob's thigh were seventy persons. And Joseph had been in Egypt.

⁶And Joseph and all of his brothers and all of that generation died. ⁷And the children of Israel were fruitful and teemed and multiplied and became very, very powerful, and the land was filled with them.

⁸And a new king rose over Egypt—who did not know Joseph. ⁹And he said to his people, "Here, the people of the children of Israel is more numerous and powerful than we. ¹⁰Come on, let's be wise toward it or else it will increase; and it will be, when war will happen, that it, too, will be added to our enemies and will war against us and go up from the land."

¹¹And they set commanders of work-companies* over it in order to degrade it with their burdens. And they built storage cities for Pharaoh: Pithom and Rameses. ¹²And the more they degraded it, the more it increased, and the more it expanded; and they felt a disgust at the children of Israel. ¹³And Egypt made the children of Israel serve with harshness; ¹⁴and they made their lives bitter with hard work, with mortar and with bricks and with all work in the field—all their work that they did for them—with harshness.

¹⁵And the king of Egypt said to the Hebrew midwives—of whom the name of one was Shiphrah and the name of the second was Puah— ¹⁶and he said, "When you deliver the Hebrew women, and you look at the two stones, if it's a boy then kill him, and if it's a girl then she'll live." ¹⁷And the midwives

---

*Here in E the taskmasters are termed "commanders of work-companies" (Hebrew *missîm*). King Solomon instituted work-companies in Israel. This phrase is part of a chain of elements that are critical of Solomon in E. See the Collection of Evidence, pp. 20–21.

feared God and did not do what the king of Egypt had spoken to them, and they kept the children alive. ¹⁸And the king of Egypt called the midwives and said to them, "Why have you done this thing and kept the children alive?"

¹⁹And the midwives said to Pharaoh, "Because the Hebrews aren't like the Egyptian women, because they're animals! Before the midwife comes to them, they've given birth!"

²⁰And God was good to the midwives. And the people increased, and they became very powerful, ²¹and it was because the midwives feared God, and He made them households.

²²And Pharaoh commanded all of his people, saying, "Every son who is born: you shall throw him into the Nile. And every daughter you shall keep alive."

2

¹And a man from the house of Levi went and took a daughter of Levi. ²And the woman became pregnant and gave birth to a son. And she saw him, that he was good, and she concealed him for three months. ³And she was not able to conceal him anymore, and she took an ark made of bulrushes for him and smeared it with bitumen and with pitch and put the boy in it and put it in the reeds by the bank of the Nile. ⁴And his sister stood still at a distance to know what would be done to him.* ⁵And the Pharaoh's daughter went down to bathe at the Nile, and her girls were going alongside the Nile, and she saw the ark among the reeds and sent her maid, and she took it. ⁶And she opened it and saw him, the child: and here was a boy crying, and she had compassion on him, and she said, "This is one of the Hebrews' children."

⁷And his sister said to Pharaoh's daughter, "Shall I go and call a nursing woman from the Hebrews for you, and she'll nurse the child for you?"

⁸And Pharaoh's daughter said to her, "Go." And the girl went and called the child's mother. ⁹And Pharaoh's daughter said to her, "Take this child and nurse him for me, and I'll give your pay." And the woman took the boy and nursed him. ¹⁰And the boy grew older, and she brought him to Pharaoh's daughter, and he became her son. And she called his name Moses, and she said, "Because I drew him from the water."

¹¹And it was in those days, and Moses grew older, and he went out to his brothers and saw their burdens, and he saw an Egyptian man striking a

---

*The sister is not identified as Miriam here. Her name is not given. In J, E, and D, Miriam is not identified as Moses' sister, and Aaron is not identified as Moses' brother. Only in P are they said to be Moses' siblings.

Hebrew man, one of his brothers. ¹²And he turned this way and that way and saw that there was no man, and he struck the Egyptian and hid him in the sand. ¹³And he went out on the second day, and here were two Hebrew men fighting. And he said to the one who was in the wrong, "Why do you strike your companion?"

¹⁴And he said, "Who made you a commander and judge over us? Are you saying you'd kill me—the way you killed the Egyptian?!"

And Moses was afraid and said, "The thing is known for sure." ¹⁵And Pharaoh heard this thing and sought to kill Moses, and Moses fled from Pharaoh's presence and lived in the land of Midian.

And he sat by a well. ¹⁶And a priest of Midian had seven daughters, and they came and drew water and filled the troughs to water their father's flock, ¹⁷and the shepherds came and drove them away. And Moses got up and saved them and watered their flock. ¹⁸And they came to Reuel, their father, and he said, "Why were you so quick to come today?"

¹⁹And they said, "An Egyptian man rescued us from the shepherds' hand, and he drew water for us and watered the flock, too."

²⁰And he said to his daughters, "And where is he? Why is this that you've left the man? Call him, and let him eat bread."

²¹And Moses was content to live with the man. And he gave Zipporah, his daughter, to Moses, ²²and she gave birth to a son, and he called his name Gershom, "because," he said, "I was an alien in a foreign land."

²³And it was after those many days, and the king of Egypt died.

And the children of Israel groaned from the work, and they cried out, and their wail went up to God from the work. ²⁴And God heard their moaning, and God remembered His covenant with Abraham, with Isaac, and with Jacob. ²⁵And God saw the children of Israel. And God knew!

3 **¹And Moses had been shepherding the flock of Jethro, his father-in-law, priest of Midian.*** And he drove the flock at the far side of the wilder-ness, and he came to the Mountain of God, to Horeb.** ²And an angel of YHWH appeared to him in a fire's flame from inside a bush. And he looked, and here: the bush was burning in the fire, and the bush was not consumed! ³And Moses said, "Let me turn and see this great sight. Why doesn't the bush burn?"

---

*Moses' father-in-law, priest of Midian, is named Jethro in Exod 3:1,18; 18:1–27 (E) but is named Reuel in Exod 2:16–18; Num 10:29 (J).

⁴And YHWH saw that he turned to see. **And God called to him from inside the bush, and He said, "Moses, Moses."**

And he said, "I'm here."

⁵And He said, "Don't come close here. Take off your shoes from your feet, because the place on which you're standing: it's holy ground." **⁶And He said, "I'm your father's God, Abraham's God, Isaac's God, and Jacob's God." And Moses hid his face, because he was afraid of looking at God.** ⁷And YHWH said, "I've seen the degradation of my people who are in Egypt, and I've heard their wail on account of their taskmasters, because I know their pains. ⁸And I've come down to rescue them from Egypt's hand and to bring them up from that land to a good and widespread land, to a land flowing with milk and honey, to the place of the Canaanite and the Hittite and the Amorite and the Perizzite and the Hivite and the Jebusite.

⁹"And now, here, the cry of the children of Israel has come to me, and also I've seen the oppression that Egypt is causing them.* **¹⁰And now go, and I'll send you to Pharaoh, and bring out my people, the children of Israel, from Egypt."**

¹¹And Moses said to God, "Who am I that I should go to Pharaoh and that I should bring out the children of Israel from Egypt?"

¹²And He said, "Because I'll be with you. And this is the sign for you that I have sent you. When you bring out the people from Egypt you shall serve God on this mountain."

---

*Both J and E are present in the scene at the burning bush, but there are a variety of views of exactly how they are divided. There is duplication; in both 3:7 and 3:9 God states that He has seen and heard the oppression. The statement in 3:7 is attributed to YHWH, indicating J; the statement in 3:9 continues into the instruction in v. 10 and Moses' response in v. 11, which refers to Elohim in narration, indicating E. Most of the dialogue between God and Moses that continues out of vv. 9–11 is also E because: (1) it has Elohim in narration six more times, and the staff through which the miracles will be performed is identified as "the staff of God (Elohim)," and the mountain is identified as "the mountain of God (Elohim)"; (2) the divine name is revealed in 3:15, which is the mark and turning point of E; (3) Moses returns to Jethro (not Reuel) in 4:19; (4) Moses is told to meet Aaron in 4:14, and Aaron then meets him at "the mountain of Elohim" in 4:27; (5) Moses and Aaron are to "gather the elders" (3:16; 4:29), and this expression, "to gather elders," occurs elsewhere only in E (Num 11:24), and elders in general are a concern of E (Exod 24:1,9,14; 17:5,6; 18:12; 19:3; Num 11:16,24,25,30), not J (only Num 16:25); (6) the term for dry ground here (4:9) is Hebrew *yabbāšāh*, but J uses a different term for this, Hebrew *ḥārābāh* (Gen 7:22; Exod 14:21); (7) in Exod 4:1–8 the two signs are: the stick becomes a snake, and his hand becomes "leprous like snow." These foreshadow Miriam's being "leprous, like snow" (Numbers 12) and Moses' bronze snake on a pole (Num 21:5–9). These two stories in Numbers are both E, and they are adjacent to each other when we leave out the intervening J and P texts. This is evidence of the correctness of the hypothesis, and it is further evidence that the Exodus burning bush material here is E, not J.

Many scholars claim that E is fragmented or even that it does not exist at all. But that is based on an error in method. See the note on Exod 5:3.

¹³And Moses said to God, "Here, I'm coming to the children of Israel, and I'll say to them, 'Your fathers' God sent me to you.' And they'll say to me, 'What is His name?' What shall I say to them?"

¹⁴And God said to Moses, "I am who I am." And He said, "You shall say this to the children of Israel: 'I Am' has sent me to you." ¹⁵And God said further to Moses, "You shall say this to the children of Israel: YHWH, your fathers' God, Abraham's God, Isaac's God, and Jacob's God has sent me to you. This is my name forever, and this is how I am to be remembered for generation after generation.*

¹⁶"Go and gather Israel's elders and say to them, 'YHWH, your fathers' God, has appeared to me—the God of Abraham, Isaac, and Jacob—saying: I have taken account of you and what has been done to you in Egypt, ¹⁷and I say I shall bring you up from the degradation of Egypt to the land of the Canaanite and the Hittite and the Amorite and the Perizzite and the Hivite and the Jebusite, to a land flowing with milk and honey.' ¹⁸And they'll listen to your voice, and you'll come, you and Israel's elders, to the king of Egypt, and you'll say to him, 'YHWH, God of the Hebrews, has communicated with us. And now, let us go on a trip of three days in the wilderness so we may sacrifice to YHWH, our God.' ¹⁹And I know that the king of Egypt won't allow you to go, and not by a strong hand, ²⁰and I'll put out my hand and strike Egypt with all my wonders that I'll do among them, and after that he'll let you go. ²¹And I'll put this people's favor in Egypt's eyes; and it will be, when you go, you won't go empty-handed. ²²And each woman will ask for silver articles and gold articles and clothes from her neighbor and from anyone staying in her house, and you'll put them on your sons and on your daughters, and you'll despoil Egypt."**

4

¹And Moses answered, and he said, "And here, they won't believe me and won't listen to my voice, because they'll say, 'YHWH hasn't appeared to you!'"

²And YHWH said to him, "What's this in your hand?"

And he said, "A staff."

---

*This is where YHWH first reveals the divine name in E. Hereafter, the presence of the divine name will not be an indicator that a passage need be from J.

**The account of the despoiling of Egypt appears in words very similar to these in Exod 11:1–3; 12:35–36, but those two passages are embedded in E contexts, whereas the present passage is joined to a J context. The identification of these three passages is therefore uncertain.

³And He said, "Throw it to the ground."

And he threw it to the ground. And it became a snake! And Moses fled from it.

⁴And YHWH said to Moses, "Put out your hand and take hold of its tail."

And he put out his hand and held on to it, and it became a staff in his hand.

⁵"So that they will believe that YHWH, their fathers' God, Abraham's God, Isaac's God, and Jacob's God, has appeared to you!"

⁶And YHWH said to him further, "Bring your hand into your bosom."

And he brought his hand into his bosom. And he brought it out; and, here, his hand was leprous like snow!

⁷And He said, "Put your hand back to your bosom."

And he put his hand back to his bosom. And he brought it out from his bosom; and, here, it had gone back like its flesh.

⁸"And it will be, if they won't believe you and won't listen to the voice of the first sign, then they'll believe the voice of the latter one. ⁹And it will be, if they also won't believe in these two signs and won't listen to your voice, then you'll take some of the water of the Nile and spill it on the dry ground. And it will be water that you'll take from the Nile, and it will become blood on the dry ground."

¹⁰And Moses said to YHWH, "Please, my Lord, I'm not a man of words. Neither yesterday nor the day before—nor since you spoke to your servant! Because I'm heavy of mouth and heavy of tongue."

¹¹And YHWH said to him, "Who set a mouth for humans? Or who will set a mute or deaf or seeing or blind? Is it not I, YHWH? ¹²And now go, and I'll be with your mouth, and I'll instruct you what you shall speak."

¹³And he said, "Please, my Lord, send by the hand you'll send."

¹⁴And YHWH's anger flared at Moses, and He said, "Isn't Aaron your Levite brother?* I knew that he will speak! And also here he is, coming out toward you! And he'll see you and be happy in his heart. ¹⁵And you'll speak to him and set the words in his mouth, and I, I shall be with your mouth and with his mouth, and I shall instruct you what you shall do. ¹⁶And he will speak for you to the people. And it will be: he will become a mouth for you, and you will become a god for him! ¹⁷And you shall take this staff in your hand, by which you'll do the signs."

---

*This does not mean that Moses and Aaron are brothers. On the contrary, if they were siblings it would naturally say "your brother." Why would it say "your *Levite* brother"? If they are actual brothers, they *must* both be Levites! "Your Levite brother" has to mean "fellow Levite," and in E Moses and Aaron are not siblings. See further Exod 15:20 and the note there.

¹⁸And Moses went.

And he went back to Jether, his father-in-law, and said to him, "Let me go so I may go back to my brothers who are in Egypt and see if they're still living."

And Jethro said to Moses, "Go in peace."

¹⁹And YHWH said to Moses in Midian, "Go. Go back to Egypt, because all the people who sought your life have died." ²⁰And Moses took his wife and his sons* and rode them on an ass, and he went back to the land of Egypt. **And Moses took the staff of God in his hand. ²¹And YHWH said to Moses, "When you're going to go back to Egypt, see all the wonders that I've set in your hand, and you shall do them in front of Pharaoh. And I: I'll strengthen his heart, and he won't let the people go.** ²²And you shall say to Pharaoh, 'YHWH said this: My child, my firstborn, is Israel. ²³And I've said to you: Let my child go and serve me. And should you refuse to let it go, here: I'm killing your child, your firstborn!' "**

---

*In J Moses has only one son, Gershom, and he takes this son and Zipporah with him to Egypt. This is consistent with the fact that only one son is circumcised in the episode at the lodging place. In E there is a second son, Eliezer, and Moses does not take his wife and sons with him to Egypt. See the note on Exod 18:4.

**Verse 21b is the first occurrence of a formula used by R to organize the E and P accounts of the plagues into a united narrative, thus: The E accounts of the plagues of the insect swarm and the livestock epidemic conclude, "And Pharaoh's heart was heavy, and he did not let the people go" (8:28; 9:7). The P accounts of the plagues of lice and boils and also the P account of the staffs becoming serpents conclude, "And Pharaoh's heart was strong, and he did not listen to them—as YHWH had spoken" (7:13; 8:15; 9:12). The plague of blood is both E and P, and it concludes with the P formulation: "And Pharaoh's heart was heavy, and he did not let the people go." The plague of frogs is also combined E and P, and it ends in 8:11 both with part of the E conclusion ("he made his heart heavy") and with part of the P conclusion ("he did not listen to them—as YHWH had spoken"). It is not surprising that P accounts have the P conclusion, E accounts have the E conclusion, and combined accounts have either a P or a combined conclusion. But then the E plague of hail has what has been the P conclusion, "And Pharaoh's heart was strong, and he did not let the children of Israel go—as YHWH had spoken" (9:35). Then the E plagues of locusts and darkness also conclude with a P formula (10:20,27), and the final meeting between Moses and Pharaoh that ensues is likewise an E text followed by a P conclusion. It appears that the Redactor has combined the P and the E accounts of the plagues and has united them by drawing on the P formula and distributing it through the combined version. This is confirmed by the fact that the formula also appears here in 4:21b. It is awkward in this context, and again it is a formula derived from P in the middle of an E text.

The Redactor used the "These are the records" formula from the Book of Records to organize the episodes of the patriarchal age, and he used the "And Israel traveled . . ." formula from the itinerary list in Numbers 33 to organize the episodes of the wilderness travels. The gap between those two editorial structures is filled by this "strengthening of Pharaoh's heart" formula, which the Redactor derived from the P plagues account. It is these three structures that give chronology and continuity to the Bible's first four books. (See the notes on Gen 2:4a and Num 9:23.)

²⁴And he was on the way, at a lodging place, and YHWH met him, and he asked to kill him. ²⁵And Zipporah took a flint and cut her son's foreskin and touched his feet, and she said, "Because you're a bridegroom of blood to me." ²⁶And he held back from Him. Then she said, "A bridegroom of blood for circumcisions."

²⁷And YHWH said to Aaron, "Go toward Moses, to the wilderness." And he went, and he met him in the Mountain of God, and he kissed him. ²⁸And Moses told Aaron all YHWH's words that He had sent him and all the signs that He had commanded him. ²⁹And Moses went, and Aaron, and they gathered all the elders of the children of Israel, ³⁰and Aaron spoke all the words that YHWH had spoken to Moses. And he did the signs before the people's eyes. ³¹And the people believed, and they heard that YHWH had taken account of the children of Israel and that He had seen their degradation. And they knelt and bowed.

5

¹And after that Moses and Aaron came and said to Pharaoh, "YHWH, God of Israel, said this: 'Let my people go, so they will celebrate a festival for me in the wilderness.'"

²And Pharaoh said, "Who is YHWH that I should listen to His voice, to let Israel go?! I don't know YHWH, and also I won't let Israel go."

³And they said, "The God of the Hebrews has communicated with us. Let us go on a trip of three days in the wilderness so we may sacrifice to YHWH, our God, or else He'll strike us with an epidemic or with the sword."*

---

*From this point on, the non-P account of the plagues is largely consistent in terminology and in the development of the story. There is no evidence requiring that it be more than one source. This text has few clues to establish whether it is E or J, but, since it connects to and flows from the E account of the burning bush, it is apparently E as well. It has frequently been thought to be J in the past, in large part because of the conscious or unconscious invocation of "Noth's law," which is: when in doubt, it's J. Since most scholars naturally start with Genesis, and since there is more J than E in Genesis (with no E at all until Genesis 20), scholars have tended to identify difficult passages as J. But there may be specific explanations for the predominance of J in Genesis. For example: the author of J was more interested in the patriarchal period while the author of E was more focused on the Exodus and wilderness age. This would in fact fit with the fact that the J patriarchal stories have visible connections to the stories of David in the Court History (which I have argued may even be by the same author); that is, the J author's literary interest lay in establishing the patriarchs as reflections or forerunners of the age of the monarchy. And it would also fit with the idea that E is especially focused on Moses because E comes from a Levite milieu, and perhaps even from a priest who traced his ancestry to Moses; and so the E author's interest lay in the Mosaic age. Indeed, if the non-P plagues account is E, then J and E are of approximately equal length.

⁴And the king of Egypt said to them, "Why, Moses and Aaron, do you turn the people loose from its work? Go to your burdens!" ⁵And Pharaoh said, "Here, the people of the land are now many, and you've made them cease from their burdens." ⁶And Pharaoh commanded the taskmasters among the people and its officers in that day, saying, ⁷"You shall not continue to give straw to the people to make bricks as yesterday and the day before. They shall go and collect straw for themselves. ⁸And you shall impose on them the quota of the bricks that they were making yesterday and the day before. You shall not subtract from it. Because they're lazy. On account of this they're crying, saying 'Let us go and sacrifice to our God.' ⁹Let the work be heavy on the people, and let them do it, and let them not pay attention to words that are a lie!"

¹⁰And the people's taskmasters and its officers went out and said to the people, saying, "Pharaoh said this: 'I am not giving you straw. ¹¹You, go, take straw for yourselves from wherever you'll find it, because not a thing is subtracted from your work.'"

¹²And the people scattered through all the land of Egypt to collect stubble for straw. ¹³And the taskmasters were prodding, saying, "Finish your work, the day's thing in that very day, as when there was the straw." ¹⁴And the officers of the children of Israel whom Pharaoh's taskmasters had set over them were beaten—saying, "Why haven't you finished your requirement to make brick like the day before yesterday, also yesterday, also today?"

¹⁵And the officers of the children of Israel came and cried to Pharaoh, saying, "Why do you do a thing like this to your servants? ¹⁶Straw isn't given to your servants, and they say to us: Make bricks. And here, your servants are beaten, and it's your people's sin."

¹⁷And he said, "You're lazy, lazy! On account of this you're saying, 'Let us go and sacrifice to YHWH.' ¹⁸And now go, work! And straw will not be given to you, and you shall give the quota of bricks!"

¹⁹And the officers of the children of Israel saw themselves in a bad state—saying, "You shall not subtract from your bricks, the day's thing in that very day." ²⁰And they met Moses and Aaron, standing opposite them when they came out from Pharaoh, ²¹and they said to them, "May YHWH look on you and judge, that you've made our smell odious in Pharaoh's eyes and in his servants' eyes, to give a sword in their hand to kill us!"

²²And Moses went back to YHWH and said, "My Lord, why have you done bad to this people? Why did you send me here? ²³And since I came to Pharaoh to speak in your name he has done bad to this people, and you haven't rescued your people!"

6 ¹And YHWH said to Moses, "Now you'll see what I shall do to Pharaoh, because with a strong hand he'll let them go, and with a strong hand he'll drive them from his land."

²And God spoke to Moses and said to him, "I am YHWH. ³And I appeared to Abraham, to Isaac, and to Jacob as El Shadday, and I was not known to them by my name, YHWH.* ⁴And I also established my covenant with them, to give them the land of Canaan, the land of their residences, in which they resided. ⁵And also: I've heard the cry of the children of Israel as Egypt is enslaving them, and I've remembered my covenant. ⁶Therefore, say to the children of Israel: 'I am YHWH, and I shall bring you out from under Egypt's burdens, and I shall rescue you from their toil, and I shall redeem you with an outstretched arm and with tremendous judgments, ⁷ and I shall take you to me as a people, and I shall become your God, and you'll know that I am YHWH, your God, who is bringing you out from under Egypt's burdens. ⁸And I shall bring you to the land that I raised my hand to give to Abraham, to Isaac, and to Jacob, and I shall give it to you as a possession. I am YHWH.'"

⁹And Moses spoke this to the children of Israel, and they did not listen to Moses because of shortage of spirit and because of hard work.

¹⁰And YHWH spoke to Moses, saying, ¹¹"Come, speak to Pharaoh, king of Egypt, that he should let the children of Israel go from his land."

¹²And Moses spoke in front of YHWH, saying, "Here, the children of Israel didn't listen to me, and how will Pharaoh listen to me?! And I'm uncircumcised of lips!"**

¹³And YHWH spoke to Moses and to Aaron‡ and commanded them regarding the children of Israel and regarding Pharaoh, king of Egypt, to

---

*God tells Moses here (P) that He was not known to the patriarchs by the name YHWH. However, the patriarchs did in fact know the name YHWH (Gen 18:14; 24:3; 26:22; 27:20,27; 28:16; and see Gen 4:26—all J). This P passage (Exod 6:2–3) is a doublet of the passage in E in which God first reveals the divine name (Exod 3:15).

The presence of the name YHWH in the text ceases to be an indicator of source identification from this point on. (However, the presence of the word "God" [Elohim] in narration continues to be an indicator that a source is not J.)

**This verse nearly duplicates 6:30 below. This is the Redactor's epanalepsis (a resumptive repetition) surrounding an insertion of a genealogy of Aaron and Moses in the middle of God's conversation with Moses. Since Moses says, "the children of Israel didn't listen to me" here in v. 12, but he has not yet spoken with the children of Israel in P, this first occurrence must be R, and the occurrence in v. 30 is P.

‡God does not speak to Aaron in P until much later (Lev 11:1). This is another sign that this section derives from R, in addition to the epanalepsis and the context-breaking genealogy mentioned in the preceding note.

bring out the children of Israel from the land of Egypt. *¹⁴These are the heads of their fathers' houses:**

The sons of Reuben, Israel's firstborn: Hanoch and Pallu, Hezron, and Carmi. These are the families of Reuben. ¹⁵And the sons of Simeon: Jemuel and Jamin and Ohad and Jachin and Zohar and Saul, son of a Canaanite woman. These are the families of Simeon. ¹⁶And these are the names of the sons of Levi by their records: Gershon and Kohath and Merari. And the years of Levi's life were a hundred thirty-seven years. ¹⁷The sons of Gershon: Libni and Shimei, by their families. ¹⁸And the sons of Kohath: Amram and Izhar and Hebron and Uzziel. And the years of Kohath's life were a hundred thirty-three years. ¹⁹And the sons of Merari: Mahli and Mushi.** These are the families of Levi by their records. ²⁰And Amram took Jochebed, his aunt, as a wife; and she gave birth to Aaron and Moses for him. And the years of Amram's life were a hundred thirty-seven years. ²¹And the sons of Izhar: Korah and Nepheg and Zichri. ²²And the sons of Uzziel: Mishael and Elzaphan and Sithri. ²³And Aaron took Elisheba, daughter of Amminadab, sister of Nahshon as a wife; and she gave birth to Nadab and Abihu, Eleazar, and Ithamar for him. ²⁴And the sons of Korah: Assir and Elkanah and Abiasaph. These are the families of the Korahites. ²⁵And Eleazar son of Aaron had taken one of the daughters of Putiel as a wife, and she gave birth for him to Phinehas. These are the heads of the fathers of the Levites according to their families.

²⁶That is Aaron and Moses,‡ to whom YHWH said, "Bring out the children of Israel from the land of Egypt by their masses." ²⁷They were the ones speaking to Pharaoh, king of Egypt, to bring out the children of Israel from Egypt. That is Moses and Aaron.

²⁸And it was in the day that YHWH spoke to Moses in the land of Egypt, ²⁹and YHWH spoke to Moses, saying, "I am YHWH. Speak to Pharaoh, king of Egypt, everything that I speak to you."

³⁰And Moses said in front of YHWH, "Here, I'm uncircumcised of lips, and how will Pharaoh listen to me?!"

---

*This list (6:14–25) comes from the Book of Records or from some other separate source document. The Redactor appears to have used only the first section of it, covering genealogies from Reuben to Levi, and then stopping at Aaron and his successors, thus leaving out the remaining nine tribes of Israel.

**Gershon (v. 17) and Mushi (v. 19). Only in the sources that are traced to Aaronid priests (here in this list and in P) do we find a Mushi and a Gershon. It appears that the Aaronid sources thus deny that the Mushite and Gershonite Levites were actually descendants, respectively, of Moses and his son Gershon.

‡This same structure is used in another passage that must be traced to the Redactor: "That is Dathan and Abiram . . . who . . ." (Num 26:9).

7

¹And YHWH said to Moses, "See, I've made you a god to Pharaoh, and Aaron, your brother, will be your prophet. ²You shall speak everything that I'll command you; and Aaron, your brother, shall speak to Pharaoh, that he let the children of Israel go from his land. ³And I, I'll harden Pharaoh's heart, and I'll multiply my signs and my wonders in the land of Egypt. ⁴And Pharaoh won't listen to you, and I'll set my hand in Egypt and bring out my masses, my people, the children of Israel, from the land of Egypt with great judgments. ⁵And Egypt will know that I am YHWH when I reach out my hand on Egypt, and I'll bring out the children of Israel from among them."

⁶And Moses and Aaron did as YHWH had commanded them. They did so. ⁷And Moses was eighty years old, and Aaron was eighty-three years old when they spoke to Pharaoh.

⁸And YHWH said to Moses and to Aaron, saying, ⁹"When Pharaoh will speak to you, saying, 'Produce a wonder!' then say to Aaron, 'Take your staff and throw it in front of Pharaoh. Let it become a serpent.'" ¹⁰And Moses and Aaron came to Pharaoh and did so, as YHWH had commanded, and Aaron threw his staff in front of Pharaoh and in front of his servants, and it became a serpent.* ¹¹And Pharaoh, too, called the wise men and the sorcerers; and they, too, Egypt's magicians, did so with their charms: ¹²and they each threw his staff, and they became serpents. And Aaron's staff swallowed their staffs!**

¹³And Pharaoh's heart was strong, and he did not listen to them—as YHWH had spoken.

¹⁴And YHWH said to Moses, "Pharaoh's heart is heavy.‡ He has refused to let the people go. ¹⁵Go to Pharaoh in the morning—here, he'll be going out to the water—and you'll stand opposite him on the bank of the Nile, and you shall take in your hand the staff that was changed into a snake. ¹⁶And you'll

---

*The staff becomes a serpent (*tannin*) here in P. In E it becomes a snake (*nāḥāš*). Also, it was Moses' staff that was supposed to be used to perform the miracles in E (Exod 4:17), but it is Aaron's staff in P.

**The P version develops the role of the Egyptian magicians: They are able to turn staffs into serpents and to perform the plagues of blood and frogs. But then they are unable to perform the plagues of lice, then they themselves are stricken with the plague of boils, and then they do not figure in the plague of death of the firstborn. So there is a directed development, showing God's defeat of Egypt's powers of magic. And the magicians appear only in sections that involve Aaron's staff, never Moses' staff. The E version has nothing about magicians.

‡In v.13 Pharaoh's heart is "strong" (P), but in v. 14 it is "heavy" (E). This distinction in expressing the hardening of Pharaoh's heart is maintained consistently, with the term *ḥzq*

say to him, 'YHWH, the God of the Hebrews, sent me to you, saying: "Let my people go so they may serve me in the wilderness." And here, you haven't listened so far. ¹⁷YHWH said this: "By this you'll know that I am YHWH." Here, I'm striking with the staff that's in my hand on the waters that are in the Nile, and they'll be changed into blood. ¹⁸And the fish that are in the Nile will die, and the Nile will stink, and Egypt will weary themselves to drink water from the Nile.'"

¹⁹And YHWH said to Moses, "Say to Aaron, 'Take your staff and reach your hand over Egypt's waters, over their rivers, over their canals, and over their pools, and over every concentration of their waters.' And they will be blood! And blood will be in all the land of Egypt—and in the trees and in the stones!" ²⁰And Moses and Aaron did so, as YHWH had commanded. And he raised the staff and struck the waters that were in the Nile before Pharaoh's eyes and before his servants' eyes, and all the waters that were in the Nile were changed into blood. ²¹And the fish in the Nile died, and the Nile had an odor, and Egypt was not able to drink water from the Nile. And the blood was in all the land of Egypt. ²²And Egypt's magicians did so with their charms. And Pharaoh's heart was strong, and he did not listen to them—as YHWH had spoken. ²³And Pharaoh turned and came into his house and did not pay heed to this as well. ²⁴And All Egypt dug around the Nile for water to drink, because they were not able to drink from the Nile's waters. ²⁵And seven days were filled after YHWH's striking the Nile.

²⁶And YHWH said to Moses, "Come to Pharaoh, and you'll say to him, 'YHWH said this: Let my people go, so they may serve me. ²⁷And if you refuse to let go, here, I'm plaguing all your border with frogs, ²⁸and the Nile will teem with frogs, and they'll go up and come in your house and in your bedroom and on your bed and in your servants' house and among your people and in your ovens and in your bowls, ²⁹and the frogs will go up on you and on your people and on all your servants.'"

(or *qšh*) used in P (7:13,22; 8:15; 9:12; 14:4,8,17) but the term *kbd* used in E (8:11,28; 9:7,34; 10:1). Moreover, the use of the term "heavy" in the E version is part of a chain of punning on this term throughout the E account of the exodus, from the burning bush to Mount Horeb. The description of Moses as "heavy of mouth and heavy of tongue" (4:10) initiates a chain of puns on the various shades of meaning of the word "heavy" (Hebrew: *kbd*, meaning weighty, difficult, or substantial). Pharaoh says, "Let the work be heavy" (5:9). Four of the plagues are described as "heavy": insects (8:20), pestilence (9:3), hail (9:18,24), and locusts (10:14). The Israelites leave with "a very heavy livestock" (12:38). When Moses holds up his arms as the Israelites fight the Amalekites, "Moses' hands were heavy" (17:12). Jethro tells Moses to get help in administering the people "because the thing is too heavy for you" (18:18). And E's chain of puns culminates at Horeb: there is "a heavy cloud on the mountain" during the revelation (19:16).

8

¹And YHWH said to Moses, "Say to Aaron, 'Reach out your hand with your staff over the rivers, over the canals, and over the pools, and bring up the frogs on the land of Egypt.'" ²And Aaron reached out his hand over Egypt's waters, and the frogs came up and covered the land of Egypt. ³And the magicians did so with their charms. And they brought up the frogs on the land of Egypt.

⁴And Pharaoh called Moses and Aaron and said, "Pray to YHWH that He will take away the frogs from me and from my people so I may let the people go, and they'll sacrifice to YHWH."

⁵And Moses said to Pharaoh, "Be honored over me as to when I'll pray for you and for your servants and for your people to cut off the frogs from you and from your houses—they'll be left only in the river."

⁶And he said, "As of tomorrow."

And he said, "According to your word: so that you'll know that there's none like YHWH, our God. ⁷And the frogs will turn away from you and from your houses and from your servants and from your people—they'll be left only in the river." ⁸And Moses and Aaron went out from Pharaoh. And Moses cried to YHWH over the matter of the frogs that he had set upon Pharaoh. ⁹And YHWH did according to Moses' word, and the frogs died from the houses, from the yards, and from the fields. ¹⁰And they piled them up, heaps and heaps, and the land smelled. ¹¹And Pharaoh saw that there was a break, and he made his heart heavy. And he did not listen to them—as YHWH had spoken.

¹²And YHWH said to Moses, "Say to Aaron, 'Reach out your staff and strike the dust of the earth, and it will become lice in all the land of Egypt.'" ¹³And they did so, and Aaron reached out his hand with his staff and struck the dust of the earth, and the lice were in the humans and in the animals. All the dust of the earth was lice in all the land of Egypt.

¹⁴And the magicians did so with their charms, to bring out the lice, and they were not able. And the lice were in the humans and in the animals. ¹⁵And the magicians said to Pharaoh, "It's the finger of God!" And Pharaoh's heart was strong, and he did not listen to them—as YHWH had spoken.

¹⁶And YHWH said to Moses, "Get up early in the morning and stand up in front of Pharaoh. Here, he's going out to the water. And you'll say to him, 'YHWH said this: Let my people go so they may serve me. ¹⁷Because if you're not letting my people go, here, I'm causing an insect swarm to be let go on you and on your servants and on your people and on your houses. And the houses of Egypt will be filled with the insect swarm, and also the ground

that they're on. ¹⁸And I shall distinguish in that day the land of Goshen, on which my people is standing, for no insect swarm to be there, so that you will know that I, YHWH, am within the land. ¹⁹And I shall set a distinction between my people and your people. This sign will be tomorrow.' "

²⁰And YHWH did so. And a heavy insect swarm came to Pharaoh's house and his servants' house, and in all the land of Egypt the land was corrupted because of the insect swarm. ²¹And Pharaoh called Moses and Aaron. And he said, "Go. Sacrifice to your God in the land." ²²And Moses said, "It's not right to do so, because we'll be sacrificing to YHWH, our God, an offensive thing to Egypt. Here, we'll be sacrificing an offensive thing to Egypt before their eyes; and will they not stone us?! ²³We'll go on a trip of three days in the wilderness, and we'll sacrifice to YHWH, our God, whatever He'll say to us."

²⁴And Pharaoh said, "I'll let you go, and you'll sacrifice to YHWH, your God, in the wilderness. Only you shall not go far. Pray for me."*

²⁵And Moses said, "Here, I'm going out from you, and I'll pray to YHWH, and the insect swarm will turn away from Pharaoh and from his servants and from his people tomorrow. Only let Pharaoh not continue to toy so as not to let the people go to sacrifice to YHWH."

²⁶And Moses went out from Pharaoh, and he prayed to YHWH. ²⁷And YHWH did according to Moses' word, and the insect swarm turned away from Pharaoh and from his servants and from his people. Not one was left. ²⁸And Pharaoh made his heart heavy this time as well, and he did not let the people go.

9

¹And YHWH said to Moses, "Come to Pharaoh and speak to him: 'YHWH, God of the Hebrews, said this: Let my people go, so they may serve me. ²Because if you refuse to let go and you are still holding on to them,

---

*In the E account of the plagues, there is a process of negotiations. At first Moses does not ask for the slaves' liberation, but only for a festival in the wilderness—neglecting to mention that they will not return! Pharaoh is not fooled, and he says to hold their festival in the land of Egypt. Moses counters that Israel's festival sacrifice would be offensive to Egypt. Pharaoh acquiesces but says, "Don't go far." Later Pharaoh says that only the males can go—thus guaranteeing that they will return; but Moses insists: "We'll go with our young and with our old, we'll go with our sons and with our daughters, with our sheep and with our oxen." Pharaoh's next position is that the women may go, too, but not the animals. Moses counters that the Israelites will need the animals for sacrifices. After the last plague, Pharaoh capitulates completely. In the P account there is none of this progression of negotiations.

³here, YHWH's hand is on your livestock that are in the field, on the horses, on the asses, on the camels, on the oxen, and on the flock—a very heavy epidemic. ⁴And YHWH will distinguish between Israel's livestock and Egypt's livestock, and not a thing out of all that Israel has will die. ⁵And YHWH has set an appointed time, saying: Tomorrow YHWH will do this thing in the land.'"

⁶And YHWH did this thing on the next day, and all Egypt's livestock died, and of all the livestock of the children of Israel not one died. ⁷And Pharaoh sent; and, here, not even one of Israel's livestock had died. And Pharaoh's heart was heavy, and he did not let the people go.

⁸And YHWH said to Moses and to Aaron, "Take handfuls of furnace ash, and let Moses fling it to the skies before Pharaoh's eyes. ⁹And it will become a powder on all the land of Egypt, and it will become a boil breaking out in sores on the humans and on the animals in all the land of Egypt." ¹⁰And they took the furnace ash and stood in front of Pharaoh, and Moses flung it to the skies, and it was a boil breaking out in sores in the humans and in the animals. ¹¹And the magicians were not able to stand in front of Moses on account of the boil, because the boil was in the magicians and in all Egypt.

¹²And YHWH strengthened Pharaoh's heart, and he did not listen to them—as YHWH had spoken to Moses.

¹³And YHWH said to Moses, "Get up early in the morning and stand in front of Pharaoh, and you'll say to him, 'YHWH, God of the Hebrews, said this: Let my people go so they may serve me. ¹⁴Because this time I am sending all my plagues at your heart and at your servants and at your people, so that you'll know that there is none like me in all the land. ¹⁵Because by now I could have put out my hand and struck you and your people with an epidemic, and you would have been obliterated from the land. ¹⁶And in fact I established you for this purpose, for the purpose of showing you my power—and in order to tell my name in all the earth. ¹⁷You are still elevating yourself against my people by not letting them go. ¹⁸Here, I'll be showering at this time tomorrow a very heavy hail, that there hasn't been one like it in Egypt from the day of its founding until now. ¹⁹And now send, protect your livestock and everything that you have in the field. Every human and animal that will be found in the field and will not be gathered to the house: the hail will come down on them, and they'll die.'"

²⁰Whoever feared YHWH's word among Pharaoh's servants had his servants and his livestock flee to the houses. ²¹And whoever did not pay heed to YHWH's word left his servants and his livestock in the field.

²²And YHWH said to Moses, "Reach out your hand at the skies, and let there be hail in all the land of Egypt: on human and on animal and on all vegetation of the field in the land of Egypt." ²³And Moses reached out his

staff at the skies, and YHWH gave out thunders and hail, and lightning went to the ground. And YHWH showered hail on the land of Egypt. ²⁴And it was hail with lightning flashing in the hail, very heavy, that there had not been anything like it in all the land of Egypt since the time it became a nation. ²⁵And the hail struck in all the land of Egypt everything that was in the field, from human to animal, and the hail struck all the vegetation of the field and shattered every tree of the field. ²⁶Only in the land of Goshen, where the children of Israel were, there was no hail.

²⁷And Pharaoh sent and called Moses and Aaron and said to them, "I sinned this time. YHWH is the virtuous one, and I and my people are the wicked ones. ²⁸Pray to YHWH, and enough of there being God's thunders and hail, so I may let you go, and you won't continue to stay."

²⁹And Moses said to him, "As I go out of the city I'll spread my hands to YHWH, the thunders will stop, and the hail won't be anymore, so that you'll know that the earth is YHWH's. ³⁰And you and your servants: I know that you don't yet fear in front of YHWH, God."* ³¹And the flax and the barley were struck, because the barley was fresh and the flax was in bud. ³²And the wheat and the spelt were not struck, because they were late crops." ³³And Moses went out from Pharaoh, from the city, and spread his hands to YHWH, and the thunders and the hail stopped, and a shower did not pour to the earth. ³⁴And Pharaoh saw that the shower and the hail and the thunder stopped, and he continued to sin, and he made his heart heavy, he and his servants. ³⁵And Pharaoh's heart was strong, and he did not let the children of Israel go—as YHWH had spoken by Moses' hand.

10

¹And YHWH said to Moses, "Come to Pharaoh, because I have made his heart and his servants' heart heavy for the purpose of my setting these signs of mine among them ²and for the purpose that you will tell in the ears of your son and your son's son about how I abused Egypt and about my signs that I set among them, and you will know that I am YHWH."

³And Moses and Aaron came to Pharaoh and said to him, "YHWH, God of the Hebrews, said this: 'How long do you refuse to be humbled in front of me? Let my people go, so they may serve me. ⁴Because if you refuse to let

---

*This is the first occurrence of the phrase "YHWH God" since Genesis 2. There it appears to be the work of the Redactor, in order to soften the change from the consistent use of "God" in Genesis 1 (P) to the consistent use of "YHWH" in Genesis 2–3 (J). It occurs nowhere else in the Torah except here in Exod 9:30, and it is suspect here because the word "God" does not occur in this verse in the Septuagint.

my people go, here, I'm bringing a locust swarm in your border tomorrow, ⁵and it will cover the eye of the land, and one won't be able to see the land! And it will eat the remains of what has survived that is left to you from the hail, and it will eat every tree that is growing for you from the field. ⁶And they'll fill your houses and the houses of all your servants and the houses of all Egypt, which your fathers and your fathers' fathers did not see, from the day they were on the land until this day.'" And he turned and went out from Pharaoh.

⁷And Pharaoh's servants said to him, "How long will this be a trap for us? Let the people go, so they may serve YHWH, their God. Don't you know yet that Egypt has perished?!"

⁸And Moses and Aaron were brought back to Pharaoh. And he said to them, "Go. Serve YHWH, your God. Who are the ones who are going?"

⁹And Moses said, "We'll go with our young and with our old, we'll go with our sons and with our daughters, with our sheep and with our oxen, because we have a festival of YHWH."

¹⁰And he said to them, "YHWH would be with you like that, when I would let you and your infants go, see, because bad is in front of your faces. ¹¹It is not like that. Go—the men!—and serve YHWH, because that is what you're asking." And he drove them out from Pharaoh's face.

¹²And YHWH said to Moses, "Reach out your hand at the land of Egypt for the locust, and it will come up on the land of Egypt and eat all the land's vegetation, everything that the hail has left." ¹³And Moses reached out his staff at the land of Egypt, and YHWH drove an east wind through the land all that day and all the night. It was the morning: and the east wind had carried the locust swarm. ¹⁴And the locust swarm came up over all the land of Egypt and lingered in all of Egypt's border, very heavy: before it there was no such locust swarm like it, and after it there will not be such. ¹⁵And it covered the eye of all the land, and the land was dark; and it ate all the land's vegetation and the fruit of every tree that the hail had left, and not any plant was left, in the tree and in the field's vegetation, in all the land of Egypt.

¹⁶And Pharaoh hurried to call Moses and Aaron, and he said, "I've sinned against YHWH, your God, and against you. ¹⁷And now, bear my sin just this one time and pray to YHWH, your God, that He'll turn just this death away from me." ¹⁸And he went out from Pharaoh and prayed to YHWH, ¹⁹and YHWH turned back a very strong west wind, and it picked up the locust swarm and blew it to the Red Sea. Not one locust was left in all of Egypt's border. ²⁰And YHWH strengthened Pharaoh's heart, and he did not let the children of Israel go.

²¹And YHWH said to Moses, "Reach out your hand at the skies, and let there be darkness on the land of Egypt, and one will feel darkness. ²²And Moses reached out his hand at the skies, and there was dismal darkness in all the land of Egypt—three days. ²³Each man did not see his brother, and each man did not get up from under it—three days. And for all the children of Israel there was light in their homes.

²⁴And Pharaoh called Moses, and he said, "Go. Serve YHWH. Only your sheep and your oxen will stay put. Your infants will go with you as well."

²⁵And Moses said, "You shall put sacrifices and offerings in our hand as well, so we'll do them for YHWH, our God. ²⁶And our livestock will go with us as well. Not a hoof will be left. Because we'll take from it to serve YHWH, our God, and we won't know how we'll serve YHWH until we come there."

²⁷And YHWH strengthened Pharaoh's heart, and he was not willing to let them go.

²⁸And Pharaoh said to him, "Go away from me! Watch yourself! Don't continue to see my face. Because in the day you see my face you'll die!"

²⁹And Moses said, "So you've spoken: I won't continue to see your face anymore."

11

¹And YHWH said to Moses, "I'll bring one more plague on Pharaoh and on Egypt. After that he'll let you go from here. When he lets go completely he'll drive you out from here! ²Speak in the people's ears that each man will ask of his neighbor and each woman of her neighbor items of silver and items of gold." ³And YHWH put the people's favor in the Egyptians' eyes. Also, the man Moses was very big in the land of Egypt in the eyes of Pharaoh's servants and in the people's eyes.

⁴And Moses said, "YHWH said this: In the middle of the night I am going out through Egypt, ⁵and every firstborn in the land of Egypt will die, from the firstborn of Pharaoh who is sitting on his throne to the firstborn of the maid who is behind the mill and every firstborn of an animal. ⁶And there will be a big cry in all the land of Egypt, that there has been none like it and there won't continue to be like it. ⁷But not a dog will move its tongue at any of the children of Israel, from man to animal, so that you'll know that YHWH will distinguish between Egypt and Israel. ⁸And all these servants of yours will come down to me, and they'll bow to me, saying: 'Go out, you and all the people who are at your feet.' And after that I'll go out!" And he went out from Pharaoh in a flaring of anger.

⁹And YHWH said to Moses, "Pharaoh won't listen to you—in order to multiply my wonders in the land of Egypt." ¹⁰And Moses and Aaron had done all these wonders in front of Pharaoh, and YHWH strengthened Pharaoh's heart, and he did not let the children of Israel go from his land.

12

¹And YHWH said to Moses and to Aaron in the land of Egypt, saying, ²"This month is the beginning of months for you. It is first of the months of the year for you. ³Speak to all of the congregation of Israel, saying: On the tenth of this month, let them each take a lamb for the fathers' houses, a lamb per house. ⁴And if the household will be too few for a lamb, then he and his neighbor who is close to his house will take it according to the count of persons; you shall count each person according to what he eats for the lamb. ⁵You shall have an unblemished, male, year-old lamb; you shall take it from the sheep or from the goats. ⁶And it will be for you to watch over until the fourteenth day of this month. And all the community of the congregation of Israel will slaughter it 'between the two evenings.' ⁷And they will take some of the blood and place it on the two doorposts and on the lintel on the houses in which they will eat it. ⁸And they will eat the meat in this night; they will eat it fire-roasted and with unleavened bread on bitter herbs. ⁹Do not eat any of it raw or cooked in water, but fire-roasted: its head with its legs and with its innards. ¹⁰And do not leave any of it until morning; and you shall burn what is left of it until morning in fire. ¹¹And you shall eat it like this: your hips clothed, your shoes on your feet, and your staff in your hand; and you shall eat it in haste. It is YHWH's Passover.

¹²"And I shall pass through the land of Egypt in this night, and I shall strike every firstborn in the land of Egypt, from human to animal, and I shall make judgments on all the gods of Egypt. I am YHWH. ¹³And the blood will be as a sign for you on the houses in which you are, and I shall see the blood, and I shall halt at you, and there won't be a plague among you as a destroyer when I strike in the land of Egypt.

¹⁴"And this day will become a commemoration for you, and you shall celebrate it, a festival to YHWH; you shall celebrate it through your generations, an eternal law: ¹⁵Seven days you shall eat unleavened bread. Indeed, on the first day you shall make leaven cease from your houses. Because anyone who eats leavened bread: that person will be cut off from Israel—from the first day to the seventh day. ¹⁶And you will have a holy assembly on the first day and a holy assembly on the seventh day. Not any work will be done on them. Just what will be eaten by each person: that alone will be done for you.

¹⁷And you shall observe the unleavened bread, because in this very day I brought out your masses from the land of Egypt, and you shall observe this day through your generations, an eternal law. ¹⁸In the first month, on the fourteenth day of the month, in the evening, you shall eat unleavened bread, until the twenty-first day of the month, in the evening. ¹⁹Seven days leaven shall not be found in your houses, because anyone who eats something leavened: that person will be cut off from the congregation of Israel, whether the alien or the citizen of the land. ²⁰You shall not eat anything leavened; in all your homes you shall eat unleavened bread."

²¹And Moses called all Israel's elders, and he said to them, "Pull out and take a sheep for your families and slaughter the Passover. ²²And you'll take a bunch of hyssop and dip in the blood that is in a basin and touch some of the blood that is in the basin to the lintel and to the two doorposts. And you shall not go out, each one, from his house's entrance until morning. ²³And YHWH will pass to strike Egypt, and He'll see the blood on the lintel and on the two doorposts, and YHWH will halt at the entrance and will not allow the destroyer to come to your houses to strike. ²⁴And you shall observe this thing as a law for you and your children forever.* ²⁵And it will be, when you will come to the land that YHWH will give to you as He has spoken, that you shall observe this service. ²⁶And it will be, when your children will say to you, 'What is this service to you?' ²⁷that you shall say, 'It is the Passover sacrifice to YHWH, because He halted at the houses of the children of Israel in Egypt when He struck Egypt, and He saved our houses.'"

And the people knelt and bowed. ²⁸And the children of Israel went and did as YHWH had commanded Moses and Aaron. They did so.

²⁹And it was in the middle of the night, and YHWH struck every firstborn in the land of Egypt, from the firstborn of Pharaoh who was sitting on his throne to the firstborn of the prisoner who was in the prison house and every firstborn of an animal. ³⁰And Pharaoh got up at night, he and all his servants and all Egypt, and there was a big cry in Egypt, because there was not a house in which there was not one dead. ³¹And he called Moses and Aaron at

---

*Exod 12:24–27 and 13:1–16 are sometimes thought to be insertions by a Deuteronomistic editor. The reason for this is that there are some similarities to Deuteronomistic passages. This is possible but still unlikely. The similarities are few and slight, and they may well owe to the fact that E and D both have apparent connections back to the same circle: the priesthood that is identified as Shilonite or Mushite. Also, there is a question of why, out of all the laws and stories of Genesis through Numbers, this unknown Deuteronomistic editor should have chosen to make only these particular insertions in these two places. (See *Who Wrote the Bible?* p. 258.) See also the note on Exod 15:26.

night, and he said, "Get up. Go out from among my people, both you and the children of Israel, and go, serve YHWH as you spoke. ³²Take your sheep also, your oxen also, as you spoke, and go. And you'll bless me as well!"

³³And Egypt was forceful on the people to hurry to let them go from the land, because they said, "We're all dead!" ³⁴And the people carried off its dough before it leavened, their bowls being wrapped in their garments on their shoulder. ³⁵And the children of Israel had done according to Moses' word, and they asked items of silver and items of gold and garments from Egypt. ³⁶And YHWH had put the people's favor in the Egyptians' eyes, and they lent to them, and they despoiled Egypt.

³⁷And the children of Israel traveled from Rameses to Succoth.* The men, apart from infants, were about six hundred thousand on foot. ³⁸And also a great mixture had gone up with them, and sheep and oxen, a very heavy livestock. ³⁹And they baked the dough that they brought out of Egypt: cakes of unleavened bread, because it had not leavened, because they were driven from Egypt and were not able to delay, and they also had not made provisions for themselves.

⁴⁰And the duration of the children of Israel that they lived in Egypt was thirty years and four hundred years. ⁴¹And it was at the end of thirty years and four hundred years, and it was in that very day: all of YHWH's masses went out from the land of Egypt. ⁴²It is a night to be observed for YHWH for bringing them out from the land of Egypt. It is this night, to be observed for YHWH for all the children of Israel through their generations.

⁴³And YHWH said to Moses and Aaron, "This is the law of the Passover: any foreigner shall not eat from it. ⁴⁴And every slave of a man, purchased with money: you shall circumcise him; then he shall eat from it. ⁴⁵A visitor and an employee shall not eat from it. ⁴⁶It shall be eaten in one house; you shall not take any of the meat from the house outside. And you shall not break a bone from it. ⁴⁷All of the congregation of Israel shall do it. ⁴⁸And if an alien will reside with you and will make a Passover to YHWH, let him be circumcised, every male, and then he may come forward to do it, and he will be like a citizen of the land, but everyone who is uncircumcised shall not eat from it. ⁴⁹There shall be one instruction for the citizen and for the alien who resides among you."

---

*The Redactor used the "And Israel traveled . . ." formula from the itinerary list in Numbers 33 to organize the episodes of the wilderness travels, just as he had used the "These are the records" formula from the Book of Records to organize the episodes of the patriarchal age. The notice here that "the children of Israel traveled from Rameses to Succoth" is the first use of this formula as an organizing heading. See Num 33:5.

⁵⁰And all the children of Israel did as YHWH had commanded Moses and Aaron. They did so. ⁵¹And it was in this very day: YHWH brought out the children of Israel from the land of Egypt by their masses.

13

¹And YHWH spoke to Moses, saying,* ²"Consecrate every first-born for me. The first birth of every womb of the children of Israel, of a human and of an animal: it is mine."

³And Moses said to the people, "Remember this day in which you went out from Egypt, from a house of slaves, because YHWH brought you out of here by strength of hand: And no leavened bread shall be eaten. ⁴Today you are going out, in the month of Abib. ⁵And it will be, when YHWH will bring you to the land of the Canaanite and the Hittite and the Amorite and the Hivite and the Jebusite, which He swore to your fathers to give you, a land flowing with milk and honey, that you will perform this service in this month. ⁶You shall eat unleavened bread seven days, and on the seventh day is a festival to YHWH. ⁷Unleavened bread will be eaten for the seven days, and leavened bread shall not be seen for you, and leaven shall not be seen for you within all your borders. ⁸And you shall tell your child in that day, saying, 'Because of that which YHWH did for me when I went out from Egypt.' ⁹And it will become a sign on your hand and a reminder between your eyes for you so that YHWH's instruction will be in your mouth, because YHWH brought you out from Egypt with a strong hand. ¹⁰And you shall observe this law at its appointed time, regularly. ¹¹And it will be, when YHWH will bring you to the land of the Canaanite as He swore to you and to your fathers and will give it to you, ¹²that you will pass every first birth of a womb to YHWH; and every first birth, offspring of an animal, that you will have—the males—is YHWH's. ¹³And you shall redeem every first birth of an ass with a lamb, and if you will not redeem, then you shall break its neck. And you shall redeem every human firstborn among your sons. ¹⁴And it will be, when your child will ask you tomorrow, saying, 'What is this?' that you'll say to him, 'With strength of hand YHWH brought us out from Egypt, from a house of slaves. ¹⁵And it was when Pharaoh hardened against letting us go, and YHWH killed every firstborn in the land of Egypt, from firstborn of a human to firstborn of an animal. On account of this I am sacrificing to YHWH every first birth of a womb—the

---

*See the note on Exod 12:24–27.

males—and I shall redeem every firstborn of my sons.' ¹⁶And it will become a sign on your hand and bands between your eyes, because with strength of hand YHWH brought us out from Egypt."

¹⁷And it was, when Pharaoh let the people go, that God did not lead them by way of the Philistines' land—because it was close—because God said, "In case the people will be dissuaded when they see war, and they'll go back to Egypt." ¹⁸And God turned the people by way of the wilderness of the Red Sea. And the children of Israel went up armed from the land of Egypt. ¹⁹And Moses took Joseph's bones with him, because he had had the children of Israel swear, saying, "God will take account of you, and you'll bring up my bones from here with you."

²⁰And they traveled from Succoth and camped in Etham at the edge of the wilderness. ²¹And YHWH was going in front of them by day in a column of cloud to show them the way, and by night in a column of fire to shed light for them, so as to go by day and by night. ²²The column of cloud by day and the column of fire by night did not depart in front of the people.*

14

¹And YHWH spoke to Moses, saying, ²"Speak to the children of Israel that they should go back and camp in front of Pi-Hahiroth, between Migdol and the sea, in front of Baal-Zephon. You shall camp facing it, by the sea. ³And Pharaoh will say about the children of Israel: 'They're muddled in the land! The wilderness has closed them in.' ⁴And I'll strengthen Pharaoh's heart, and he'll pursue them, and I'll be glorified against Pharaoh and against all of his army, and Egypt will know that I am YHWH." And they did so.

⁵And it was told to the king of Egypt that the people had fled. **And the heart of Pharaoh and his servants was changed toward the people. And they said, "What is this that we've done, that we let Israel go from serving us?!"** ⁶And he hitched his chariot and took his people with him. ⁷**And he took six**

---

*The J and P accounts picture two different scenarios of the event at the sea. In J, while the Egyptians pursue the Israelites, God pushes back the sea with a wind. Then God throws the Egyptian camp into tumult, and when the Egyptians try to flee they run right into the dried seabed as God releases the seawaters, which return to swallow the fleeing Egyptians. In P, meanwhile, the sea splits, with a path of dry ground between walls of water, and the Israelites cross through this path. The Egyptians try to cross through this path as well, but the water closes up over them. Both the J and P accounts read as complete stories when the two are separated. The P story repeats details of locations and of the Egyptian forces. P also includes the repeated notation of God's "strengthening Pharaoh's heart."

hundred chosen chariots—and all the chariotry of Egypt—and officers over all of it. ⁸**And YHWH strengthened the heart of Pharaoh, king of Egypt, and he pursued the children of Israel. And the children of Israel were going out with a high hand.** ⁹And Egypt pursued them. **And they caught up to them, camping by the sea—every chariot horse of Pharaoh and his horsemen and his army—at Pi-Hahiroth, in front of Baal-Zephon.** ¹⁰**And Pharaoh came close!** And the children of Israel raised their eyes, and here was Egypt coming after them, and they were very afraid. **And the children of Israel cried out to YHWH.**

¹¹**And they said to Moses, "Was it because of an absence—none!—of graves in Egypt that you took us to die in the wilderness?! What is this that you've done to us to bring us out of Egypt?** ¹²**Isn't this the thing that we spoke to you in Egypt, saying: Stop from us! And let's serve Egypt. Because serving Egypt is better for us than our dying in the wilderness!"**

¹³And Moses said to the people, "Don't be afraid. Stand still and see YHWH's salvation that He'll do for you today. For, as you've seen Egypt today, you'll never see them again, ever. ¹⁴YHWH will fight for you, and you'll keep quiet!"

¹⁵**And YHWH said to Moses, "Why do you cry out to me? Speak to the children of Israel that they should move!** ¹⁶**And you, lift your staff and reach your hand out over the sea—and split it! And the children of Israel will come through the sea on the dry ground.** ¹⁷**And I, here, I'm strengthening Egypt's heart, and they'll come after them, and I'll be glorified against Pharaoh and against all of his army, against his chariots and against his horsemen.** ¹⁸**And Egypt will know that I am YHWH when I'm glorified against Pharaoh, against his chariots and against his horsemen."**

¹⁹**And the angel of God who was going in front of the camp of Israel moved and went behind them.** And the column of cloud went from in front of them and stood behind them. ²⁰**And it came between the camp of Egypt and the camp of Israel.** And there was the cloud and darkness [for the Egyptians], while it [the column of fire] lit the night [for the Israelites], and one did not come near the other all night. ²¹**And Moses reached his hand out over the sea.** And YHWH drove back the sea with a strong east wind all night and turned the sea into dry ground.* **And the water was split.** ²²**And the children of Israel came through the sea on the dry ground. And the water was a wall to them at their right and at their left.** ²³And Egypt pursued

---

*In the J Red Sea story, the Hebrew uses the same term for dry ground (*ḥārābāh*) that is used in the J flood story (Gen 7:22). Meanwhile, in the P Red Sea story, the Hebrew uses the same term for dry ground (*yabbāšāh*) that is used in the P flood (and creation) story (Gen 1:9,10; 8:14).

and came after them, every horse of Pharaoh, his chariots and his horse-men, through the sea. ²⁴And it was in the morning watch, and YHWH gazed at Egypt's camp through a column of fire and cloud and threw Egypt's camp into tumult ²⁵and turned its chariots' wheel so that it drove it with heaviness.

And Egypt said, "Let me flee from Israel, because YHWH is fighting for them against Egypt!"

²⁶And YHWH said to Moses, "Reach your hand out over the sea, and the water will go back over Egypt, over his chariots and over his horsemen."

²⁷And Moses reached his hand out over the sea. And the sea went back to its strong flow toward morning, and Egypt was fleeing toward it. And YHWH tossed the Egyptians into the sea. ²⁸and the waters went back and covered the chariots and the horsemen—all of Pharaoh's army who were coming after them in the sea. Not even one of them was left. ²⁹And the children of Israel had gone on the dry ground through the sea, and the water had been a wall to them at their right and at their left.

³⁰And YHWH saved Israel from Egypt's hand that day. And Israel saw Egypt dead on the seashore, ³¹and Israel saw the big hand that YHWH had used against Egypt, and the people feared YHWH, and they trusted in YHWH and in Moses His servant.

15

¹Then Moses and the children of Israel sang this song to YHWH. And they said, saying:*

> Let me sing to YHWH, for He triumphed!
> Horse and its rider He cast in the sea.
> ² My strength and song are Yah,
> and He became a salvation for me.
> This is my God, and I'll praise Him,
> my father's God, and I'll hail Him.

---

*This poem, known as the Song of the Sea (or Song of Miriam), is an independent, old composition, possibly the oldest composition in the Hebrew Bible. As in the case of the Blessing of Jacob, the author of J both used it as a source of information and included it in his work. See the note on Gen 49:1 and Frank Moore Cross and David Noel Freedman, *Studies in Ancient Yahwistic Poetry* (Grand Rapids, MI: Eerdmans, 1975), pp. 31–45; Cross, *Canaanite Myth and Hebrew Epic* (Cambridge: Harvard Univ. Press, 1973), pp. 112–144; Baruch Halpern, "Doctrine by Misadventure: Between the Israelite Source and the Biblical Historian," in R. E. Friedman, ed., *The Poet and the Historian* (Atlanta: Scholars Press, 1983), pp. 49–53.

3 YHWH is a warrior.
YHWH is His name.

4 Pharaoh's chariots and his army He plunged in the sea
and the choice of his troops drowned in the Red Sea.

5 The deeps covered them.
They sank in the depths like a stone.

6 Your right hand, YHWH, awesome in power,
your right hand, YHWH, crushed the foe.

7 And in your triumph's greatness you threw down your adversaries.
You let go your fury: it consumed them like straw.

8 And by wind from your nostrils water was massed,
surf piled up like a heap,
the deeps congealed in the heart of the sea.

9 The enemy said, "I'll pursue!
I'll catch up!
I'll divide spoil!
My soul will be sated!
I'll unsheathe my sword!
My hand will deprive them!"

10 You blew with your wind. Sea covered them.
They sank like lead in the awesome water.

11 Who is like you among the gods, YHWH!
Who is like you:
awesome in holiness!
fearsome with splendors!
making miracles!

12 You reached your right hand: earth swallowed them.

13 You led, in your kindness, the people you redeemed;
you ushered, in your strength, to your holy abode.

14 Peoples heard—they shuddered.
Shaking seized Philistia's residents.

15 Then Edom's chiefs were terrified.
Moab's chieftains: trembling seized them.
All Canaan's residents melted.

16 Terror and fear came over them.
At the power of your arm they're silent like stone.
'Til your people passed, YHWH,
'til the people you created passed.

17 You'll bring them and plant them in your legacy's mountain,
your throne's platform, that you made, YHWH;

a holy place, Lord, that your hands reared.
¹⁸ YHWH will reign forever and ever!

¹⁹Because Pharaoh's horses with his chariots and with his horsemen came in the sea, and YHWH brought back the water of the sea over them, and the children of Israel had gone on the dry ground through the sea.

²⁰And Miriam, the prophetess, Aaron's sister,* took a drum in her hand, and all the women went out behind her with drums and with dances. ²¹And Miriam sang to them:

Sing to YHWH for He triumphed!
Horse and its rider He cast in the sea.

²²And Moses had Israel travel from the Red Sea, and they went out to the wilderness of Shur. And they went three days in the wilderness. And they did not find water. ²³And they came to Marah, and they were not able to drink water from Marah because it was bitter. On account of this he called its name Marah. ²⁴And the people complained at Moses, saying, "What shall we drink?" ²⁵And he cried to YHWH, and YHWH showed him a tree, and he threw it into the water, and the water sweetened.

He set law and judgment for them there, and He tested them there. ²⁶And He said, "If you'll listen to the voice of YHWH, your God, and you'll do what is right in His eyes and turn your ear to His commandments and observe all His laws, I won't set on you any of the sickness that I set on Egypt, because I, YHWH, am your healer."**

²⁷And they came to Elim. And twelve springs of water and seventy palm trees were there. And they camped there by the water.

16

¹And they traveled from Elim, and all of the congregation of the children of Israel came to the wilderness of Sîn, which is between Elim and Sinai, on the fifteenth day of the second month after their exodus from the land of Egypt. **²And all of the congregation of the children of Israel com-**

---

*Miriam is identified as Aaron's sister, but not as the sister of Moses. In E, Miriam and Aaron are not Moses' siblings. Only in P are Aaron and Moses identified as brothers.

**Exod 15:26 has more phrases that sound Deuteronomistic than any other passage in Genesis through Numbers. Still, it is uncertain and may be E, which has other similarities to Deuteronomistic language. (See the note on Exod 12:24.)

plained at Moses and at Aaron in the wilderness. ³And the children of Israel said to them, "Who would make it so that we had died by YHWH's hand in the land of Egypt, when we sat by a pot of meat, when we ate bread to the full! Because you brought us out to this wilderness to kill this whole community with starvation!"

⁴And YHWH said to Moses, "Here, I'm raining bread from the skies for you, and let the people go out and gather the daily ration in its day in order that I can test them: will they go by my instruction or not. ⁵And it will be that on the sixth day they'll prepare what they bring in, and it will be twice as much as they'll gather on regular days."

⁶And Moses and Aaron said to all the children of Israel, "At evening you'll know that YHWH brought you out from the land of Egypt, ⁷and in the morning you'll see YHWH's glory, because He has heard your complaints about YHWH. And what are we, that you complain at us?!" ⁸And Moses said, "When YHWH gives you meat to eat in the evening and bread to the full in the morning, because YHWH has heard your complaints that you're making at Him! And what are we? Your complaints are not at us but at YHWH!" ⁹And Moses said to Aaron, "Say to all of the congregation of the children of Israel, 'Come close in front of YHWH, because He has heard your complaints.'"

¹⁰And it was as Aaron was speaking to all of the congregation of the children of Israel: and they turned to the wilderness, and here was YHWH's glory appearing in a cloud.

¹¹And YHWH spoke to Moses, saying, ¹²"I've heard the complaints of the children of Israel. Speak to them, saying, 'between the two evenings you shall eat meat, and in the morning you shall be filled with bread, and you will know that I am YHWH, your God.'"

¹³And it was in the evening, and quail went up and covered the camp. And in the morning there was a layer of dew around the camp. ¹⁴And the layer of dew went up, and here, on the face of the wilderness: scaly thin, thin as frost on the ground. ¹⁵And the children of Israel saw, and each said to his brother, "What is it?"—because they did not know what it was.

And Moses said to them, "That is the bread that YHWH has given you for food. ¹⁶This is the thing that YHWH has commanded: Collect some of it, each according to what he eats; you shall take an omer per head, the number of your persons, each for whoever is in his tent." ¹⁷And the children of Israel did so. And they collected—the one who took the most and the one who took the least. ¹⁸And they measured by the omer, and the one who took the most had not exceeded, and the one who took the least had not fallen short. Each had collected according to what he eats. ¹⁹And Moses said to them, "Let no one leave any of it over until morning." ²⁰And they did not listen to Moses, and people left some of it over until morning, and it yielded worms and stank. And Moses was angry at them. ²¹And they collected it morning by morning, each by what he eats, and when the sun was hot it melted. ²²And it was: on the sixth day they collected double bread, two times the omer for each one, and all the chiefs of the congregation came and told Moses. ²³And he said to them, "That is what YHWH spoke. Tomorrow is a ceasing, a holy Sabbath to YHWH. Bake what you'll bake, and cook what you'll cook, and leave what is left over for keeping until the morning." ²⁴And they left it until the morning, as Moses had commanded, and it did not stink, and there was not a worm in it. ²⁵And Moses said, "Eat it today, because today is a Sabbath to YHWH. Today you won't find it in the field. ²⁶Six days you shall collect it. And on the seventh day is a Sabbath; there will not be any in it." ²⁷And it was: on the seventh day some of the people went out to collect, and they did not find any.

²⁸And YHWH said to Moses, "How long do you refuse to observe my commandments and my instructions? ²⁹See that YHWH has given you the Sabbath. On account of this He is giving you two days' bread on the sixth day. Stay, each in his place. Let no man go out from his place in the seventh day." ³⁰And the people ceased in the seventh day.

³¹And the house of Israel called its name "manna." And it was like a coriander seed, white, and its taste was like a wafer in honey.

³²And Moses said, "This is the thing that YHWH has commanded: 'an omer-ful of it is for watching over through your generations so that they will see the bread that I fed you in the wilderness when I brought you out from the land of Egypt.'" ³³And Moses said to Aaron, "Take one jar and place an omer-ful of manna there and lay it in front of YHWH for watching over through your generations," ³⁴as YHWH had commanded Moses. And Aaron laid it in front of the Testimony for watching over. ³⁵And the children of Israel ate the manna forty years until they came to settled land. They ate the manna until they came to the edge of the land of Canaan.

³⁶(And an omer is a tenth of an ephah.)

17

¹And all of the congregation of the children of Israel traveled from the wilderness of Sîn on their travels by YHWH's word, and they camped in Rephidim. And there was no water for the people to drink. ²And the people quarreled with Moses. And they said, "Give us water, and let us drink."

And Moses said to them, "Why do you quarrel with me? Why do you test YHWH?!"

³And the people thirsted for water there, and the people complained at Moses and said, "Why is this that you brought us up from Egypt: to kill me and my children and my cattle with thirst?!"

⁴And Moses cried to YHWH, saying, "What shall I do to this people? A little more and they'll stone me!"

⁵And YHWH said to Moses, "Pass in front of the people and take some of Israel's elders with you, and take your staff with which you struck the Nile in your hand, and you'll go. ⁶Here, I'll be standing in front of you there on a rock at Horeb. And you'll strike the rock, and water will come out of it, and the people will drink." And Moses did so before the eyes of Israel's elders. ⁷And he called the place's name Massah and Meribah because of the quarrel of the children of Israel and because of their testing YHWH, saying, "Is YHWH among us or not?"

⁸And Amalek came and fought with Israel in Rephidim. ⁹And Moses said to Joshua,* "Choose men for us and go, fight against Amalek. Tomorrow I'll be standing up on the hilltop, and the staff of God in my hand." ¹⁰And Joshua did as Moses said to him, to fight against Amalek; and Moses, Aaron, and Hur went up to the hilltop. ¹¹And it was: when Moses would lift his hand, then Israel would predominate; and when he would rest his hand, then Amalek would predominate. ¹²And Moses' hands were heavy. And they took a stone and set it under him, and he sat on it, and Aaron and Hur held up his hands, one from this side and one from this side, and his hands were supported until the sunset. ¹³And Joshua defeated Amalek and his people by the sword.

¹⁴And YHWH said to Moses, "Write this—a memorial—in a scroll and set it in Joshua's ears, because I shall wipe out the memory of Amalek from under the skies!" ¹⁵And Moses built an altar and called its name "YHWH is my standard." ¹⁶And he said, "Because—hand on YH's throne—YHWH has war against Amalek from generation to generation."

18

¹And Jethro, priest of Midian, Moses' father-in-law, heard everything that God had done for Moses and for Israel, His people, that YHWH

---

*Joshua is mentioned eleven times in E but never in J. This is consistent with the idea that E is associated with the northern kingdom of Israel and J is associated with the southern kingdom of Judah. Joshua is a northern hero, from the tribe of Ephraim.

had brought Israel out from Egypt. ²And Jethro, Moses' father-in-law, took Zipporah, Moses' wife, after her being sent off, ³and her two sons, of whom one's name was Gershom, because he said, "I was an alien in a foreign land," ⁴and one's name was Eliezer, "because my father's God was my help and rescued me from Pharaoh's sword."* ⁵And Jethro, Moses' father-in-law, and his sons and his wife came to Moses, to the wilderness in which he was camping, at the Mountain of God. ⁶And he said to Moses, "I, your father-in-law, Jethro, have come to you, and your wife and her two sons with her." ⁷And Moses went out to his father-in-law, and he bowed, and he kissed him, and they asked each other how they were, and they came to the tent. ⁸And Moses told his father-in-law everything that YHWH had done to Pharaoh and to Egypt with regard to Israel, all the hardship that had found them on the way, and YHWH rescued them. ⁹And Jethro rejoiced over all the good that YHWH had done for Israel, that He had rescued it from Egypt's hand. ¹⁰And Jethro said, "Blessed is YHWH, who rescued you from Egypt's hand and from Pharaoh's hand, who rescued the people from under Egypt's hand: ¹¹now I know that YHWH is bigger than all the gods, because of the thing that they plotted against them." ¹²And Jethro, Moses' father-in-law, took a burnt offering and sacrifices to God. And Aaron and all of Israel's elders came to eat bread with Moses' father-in-law before God.

¹³And it was the next day, and Moses sat to judge the people. And the people stood by Moses from the morning to the evening. ¹⁴And Moses' father-in-law saw all that he was doing for the people, and he said, "What's this thing that you're doing for the people? Why are you sitting by yourself, and the entire people is standing up by you from morning until evening?"

¹⁵And Moses said to his father-in-law, "Because the people come to me to inquire of God. ¹⁶When they have a matter, it comes to me, and I judge between each one and his companion, and I make known God's laws and His instructions."

¹⁷And Moses' father-in-law said to him, "The thing that you're doing isn't good. ¹⁸You'll be worn out, both you and this people who are with you, because the thing is too heavy for you. You won't be able to do it by yourself.

---

*The explanation of the name Gershom here in E is a doublet of Exod 2:22, which is J. The existence of a second son, Eliezer, is reported only here in E, not in J. In J there was only one son. Also, in J Moses took his son and Zipporah with him to Egypt. But now, in E, Jethro shows up bringing Zipporah and their sons, who have been in Midian all along. The words "after her being sent off" appear to have been added by RJE to solve this contradiction.

¹⁹Now listen to my voice, and I'll advise you, and may God be with you. You be for the people toward God, and you will bring the matters to God. ²⁰And you'll enlighten them with the laws and the instructions, and you'll make known to them the way in which they'll go and the thing that they'll do. ²¹And you will envision, out of all the people, worthy men, who fear God, men of truth, who hate bribery, and you'll set chiefs of thousands, chiefs of hundreds, chiefs of fifties, and chiefs of tens over them. ²²And they'll judge the people at all times. And it will be: they'll bring every matter that is big to you, and they will judge every matter that is small. And make it lighter on you, and they'll bear it with you. ²³If you'll do this thing, and YHWH will command you, then you'll be able to stand, and also this entire people will come to its place in peace."

²⁴And Moses listened to his father-in-law's voice and did everything that he had said. ²⁵And Moses chose worthy men out of all of Israel and made them heads over the people: chiefs of thousands, chiefs of hundreds, chiefs of fifties, and chiefs of tens. ²⁶And they judged the people at all times. They would bring the matter that was hard to Moses, and they would judge every matter that was small.

²⁷And Moses let his father-in-law go, and he went to his land.

19

¹In the third month after the exodus of the children of Israel from the land of Egypt, on this day, they came to the wilderness of Sinai. ²And they traveled from Rephidim and came to the wilderness of Sinai and camped in the wilderness. And Israel camped there opposite the mountain.

³And Moses had gone up to God. And YHWH called to him from the mountain, saying, "This is what you shall say to the house of Jacob and tell to the children of Israel: ⁴'You've seen what I did to Egypt, and I carried you on eagles' wings and brought you to me. ⁵And now, if you'll listen to my voice and observe my covenant, then you'll be a treasure to me out of all the peoples, because all the earth is mine. ⁶And you'll be a kingdom of priests and a holy nation to me.' These are the words that you shall speak to the children of Israel."

⁷And Moses came and called the people's elders and set before them all these words that YHWH had commanded him. ⁸And all the people responded together, and they said, "We'll do everything that YHWH has spoken." And Moses brought back the people's words to YHWH.

⁹And YHWH said to Moses, "Here, I am coming to you in a mass of cloud for the purpose that the people will hear when I am speaking with you, and they will believe in you as well forever." And Moses told the people's words to YHWH. ¹⁰And YHWH said to Moses, "Go to the people and consecrate them today and tomorrow; and they shall wash their clothes ¹¹and be ready for the third day, because on the third day YHWH will come down on Mount Sinai before the eyes of all the people. ¹²And you shall limit the people all around, saying, 'Watch yourselves about going up in the mountain and touching its edge. Anyone who touches the mountain shall be put to death. ¹³A hand shall not touch him, but he shall be stoned or shot. Whether animal or man, he will not live.' At the blowing of the horn they shall go up the mountain."

¹⁴And Moses went down from the mountain to the people. And he consecrated the people, and they washed their clothes. ¹⁵And he said to the people, "Be ready for three days. Don't come close to a woman."

¹⁶And it was on the third day, when it was morning, **and it was: thunders and lightning and a heavy cloud on the mountain, and a sound of a horn, very strong. And the entire people that was in the camp trembled. ¹⁷And Moses brought out the people toward God from the camp, and they stood up at the bottom of the mountain.** ¹⁸And Mount Sinai was all smoke because YHWH came down on it in fire, and its smoke went up like the smoke of a furnace, and the whole mountain trembled greatly. **¹⁹And the sound of the horn was getting much stronger. Moses would speak, and God would answer him in a voice.** ²⁰And YHWH came down on Mount Sinai, at the top of the mountain, and YHWH called to Moses at the top of the mountain, and Moses went up. ²¹And YHWH said to Moses, "Go down. Warn the people in case they break through to YHWH, to see, and many of them fall. ²²And also let the priests who approach YHWH consecrate themselves, or else YHWH will break out against them."

²³And Moses said to YHWH, "The people is not able to go up to Mount Sinai, because you warned us, saying, 'Limit the mountain and consecrate it.'"

²⁴And YHWH said to him, "Go. Go down. Then you'll come up, you and Aaron with you.* And let the priests and the people not break through to come up to YHWH, or else He'll break out against them." ²⁵And Moses went down to the people, and he said it to them.

---

*The command that Aaron is to go up together with Moses is unexpected here in J. Aaron has never been mentioned up to this point in J. In fact, Aaron is never mentioned at all in J outside of this verse. Moreover, Aaron does not in fact go up with Moses in J. The

20

¹And God spoke all these words, saying:*

²*I am YHWH, your God, who brought you out from the land of Egypt, from a house of slaves.*

³*You shall not have other gods before my face.*

⁴*You shall not make a statue or any form that is in the skies above or that is in the earth below or that is in the water below the earth.* ⁵*You shall not bow to them, and you shall not serve them. Because I, YHWH, your God, am a jealous God, counting parents' crime on children, on the third generation, and on the fourth generation for those who hate me,* ⁶*but practicing kindness to thousands for those who love me and for those who observe my commandments.*

⁷*You shall not bring up the name of YHWH, your God, for a falsehood, because YHWH will not make one innocent who will bring up His name for a falsehood.*

⁸*Remember the Sabbath day, to make it holy.* ⁹*Six days you shall labor and do all your work,* ¹⁰*and the seventh day is a Sabbath to YHWH, your God. You shall not do any work: you and your son and your daughter, your servant and your maid and your animal and your alien who is in your gates.* ¹¹Because for six days YHWH made the skies and the earth, the sea, and everything that is in them, and He rested on the seventh day. On account of this, YHWH blessed the Sabbath day and made it holy.**

---

next time that Moses goes up the mountain in J, God tells him, "No man shall go up with you" (Exod 34:3). It is rather in E that Aaron (and others) will go up with Moses (24:1). Therefore, it appears that a redactor has added here in order to deal with the fact that Moses' ascent in E along with Aaron and other persons is now inserted before the J account of an ascent that Moses makes alone in Exodus 34. The redactor who made this addition could be either R or RJE.

*The text of the Ten Commandments here does not appear to belong to any of the major sources. It is likely to be an independent document, which was inserted here by the Redactor. A slightly different version was used by the Deuteronomistic historian in Deuteronomy 5.

**The most striking difference between the text of the Decalog as it appears here and as it appears in Deuteronomy 5 is the reason that is given as the basis of the Sabbath command. Here it is "because for six days YHWH made the skies and the earth, the sea, and everything that is in them, and He rested on the seventh day. On account of this, YHWH blessed the Sabbath day and made it holy," referring to the P creation story. In Deuteronomy it is so "you shall remember that you were a slave in the land of Egypt and YHWH, your God, brought you out from there with a strong hand and an outstretched arm. On account of this, YHWH, your God, has commanded you to do the Sabbath day."

¹² *Honor your father and your mother, so that your days will be extended on the land that YHWH, your God, is giving you.*

¹³ *You shall not murder.*

¹⁴ *You shall not commit adultery.*

¹⁵ *You shall not steal.*

¹⁶ *You shall not testify against your neighbor as a lying witness.*

¹⁷ *You shall not covet your neighbor's house. You shall not covet your neighbor's wife or his servant or his maid or his ox or his ass or anything that your neighbor has.*

¹⁸And all the people were seeing the thunders and the flashes and the sound of the horn and the mountain smoking. And the people saw, and they moved and stood at a distance, ¹⁹and they said to Moses, "You speak with us so we may listen, but let God not speak with us or else we'll die."

²⁰And Moses said to the people, "Don't be afraid, because God is coming for the purpose of testing you and for the purpose that his fear will be on your faces so that you won't sin."

²¹And the people stood at a distance, and Moses went over to the nimbus where God was. ²²And YHWH said to Moses, "You shall say this to the children of Israel: You have seen that I have spoken with you from the skies. ²³You shall not make gods of silver with me, and and you shall not make gods of gold for yourselves. ²⁴You shall make an altar of earth for me, and you shall sacrifice on it your burnt offerings and your peace offerings, your sheep and your oxen. In every place where I'll have my name commemorated I'll come to you, and I'll bless you. ²⁵And if you'll make an altar of stones for me, you shall not make them cut. When you have elevated your sword over it, then you have desecrated it. ²⁶And you shall not go up by stairs on my altar, so that your nudity will not be exposed over it."

21

¹"And these are the judgments that you shall set before them:*

²"When you will buy a Hebrew slave, he shall work six years, and in the seventh he shall go out liberated for free. ³If he will come by himself,

---

*Exod 21:1–23:19 is a law code known as the Covenant Code. It was originally a separate, independent document, but it was used by the author of E as part of the E work.

he shall go out by himself. If he is a woman's husband, then his wife shall go out with him. ⁴If his master will give him a wife, and she will give birth to sons or daughters for him, the wife and her children will be her master's, and he shall go out by himself. ⁵And if the slave will say: 'I love my master, my wife, and my children; I won't go out liberated!' ⁶then his master shall bring him over to God and bring him over to the door or to the doorpost, and his master shall pierce his ear with an awl, and he shall serve him forever.

⁷"And if a man will sell his daughter as a maid, she shall not go out as the slaves go out. ⁸If she is bad in the eyes of her master who has designated her for himself, then he shall let her be redeemed. He shall not dominate so as to sell her to a foreign people in his betrayal of her. ⁹And if he will designate her for his son, he shall treat her according to the manner of daughters. ¹⁰If he will take another for himself, he shall not subtract from her food, her apparel, and her hygiene. ¹¹And if he will not do these three for her, then she shall go out free. There is no money.

¹²"One who strikes a man, and he dies, he shall be put to death. ¹³And one who did not scheme, but God conveyed it to his hand, I shall set a place for you, that he shall flee there. ¹⁴But if a man will plot against his neighbor, to kill him with treachery, you shall take him from my altar to die.

¹⁵"And one who strikes his father and his mother shall be put to death.

¹⁶"And one who steals a man and has sold him, or he was found in his hand, will be put to death.

¹⁷"And one who curses his father and his mother shall be put to death.

¹⁸"And if people will quarrel, and a man strikes his neighbor with a stone or with a fist, and he does not die, and he falls to bed, ¹⁹if he will get up and walk himself outside on his staff, then the one who struck will be innocent. Only he shall compensate for his staying home and shall have him healed.

²⁰"And if a man will strike his slave or his maid with a rod, and he dies by his hand, he shall be avenged. ²¹Just: if he will stand for a day or two days, he shall not be avenged, because he is his money.

²²"And if people will fight, and they strike a pregnant woman, and her children go out, and there will not be an injury, he shall be penalized according to what the woman's husband will impose on him, and he will give it by the judges. ²³And if there will be an injury, then you shall give a life for a life, ²⁴an eye for an eye, a tooth for a tooth, a hand for a hand, a foot for a foot, ²⁵a burn for a burn, a wound for a wound, a hurt for a hurt.

²⁶"And if a man will strike his slave's eye or his maid's eye and destroy it, he shall let him go, liberated, for his eye. ²⁷And if he will knock out his slave's tooth or his maid's tooth, he shall let him go liberated for his tooth.

²⁸"And if an ox will gore a man or a woman and they die, the ox shall be stoned, and its meat shall not be eaten—and the ox's owner is innocent. ²⁹And if it was a goring ox from the day before yesterday, and it had been so testified to its owner, and he did not watch it, and it killed a man or a woman, the ox will be stoned, and its owner will be put to death as well. ³⁰If a ransom will be set on him, then he shall give everything that will be set on him for the redemption of his life. ³¹Whether it will gore a son or it will gore a daughter, according to this judgment shall be done to it. ³²If the ox will gore a slave or a maid, he shall pay thirty silver shekels to his owner, and the ox shall be stoned.

³³"And if a man will open a pit, or if a man will dig a pit, and he will not cover it, and an ox or an ass will fall there, ³⁴the owner of the pit shall pay; he shall pay back money to its owner, and the dead one will be his. ³⁵And if a man's ox will strike his neighbor's ox, and it dies, then they shall sell the live ox and split the money for it, and they shall split the dead one as well. ³⁶Or: if it was known that it was a goring ox from the day before yesterday, and its owner did not watch it, he shall pay an ox for the ox, and the dead one shall be his.

³⁷"If a man will steal an ox or a sheep and slaughter it or sell it, he shall pay five oxen for the ox and four sheep for the sheep.

22

¹"If the thief will be found while breaking in and will be struck, and he dies, there is no blood for him. ²If the sun has risen on him there is blood for him. He shall pay. If he does not have it, then he shall be sold for his theft. ³It the theft will be found in his hand—from ox to ass to sheep—alive, he shall pay two.

⁴"If a man will have a field or a vineyard grazed, and he will let his beast go and graze in another person's field, he shall pay the best of his field and the best of his vineyard.

⁵"If fire will break out and find thorns and stacked grain or standing grain or a field is consumed, the one who set the blaze shall pay.

⁶"If a man will give his neighbor money or items to watch, and it will be stolen from the man's house, if the thief will be found he shall pay two. ⁷If

the thief will not be found, then the owner of the house shall be brought near to God: that he has not put out his hand into his neighbor's property.

⁸"Over every case of an offense, over an ox, over an ass, over a sheep, over clothing, over every loss about which one will say that 'This is it,' the word of the two of them shall come to God. The one whom God will implicate shall pay two to his neighbor.

⁹"If a man will give an ass or an ox or a sheep or any animal to his neighbor to watch, and it dies or is injured or is seized—no one seeing— ¹⁰an oath of YHWH shall be between the two of them: that he has not put out his hand into his neighbor's property; and its owner shall take it, and he shall not pay. ¹¹And if it will be stolen from him, he shall pay its owner. ¹²If it will be torn, he shall bring it in witness; he shall not pay for the torn one. ¹³And if a man will ask it of his neighbor, and it is injured or dies, its owner not being with it, he shall pay. ¹⁴If its owner is with it, he shall not pay. If it was hired, he has its hire coming to him.

¹⁵"And if a man will deceive a virgin who is not betrothed, and he lies with her, he shall espouse her by a bride-price to him as a wife. ¹⁶If her father will refuse to give her to him, he shall weigh out money corresponding to the bride-price of virgins.

¹⁷"You shall not let a witch live.

¹⁸"Anyone who lies with an animal shall be put to death.

¹⁹"One who sacrifices to gods shall be completely destroyed—except to YHWH alone.

²⁰"And you shall not persecute an alien, and you shall not oppress him, because you were aliens in the land of Egypt.

²¹"You shall not degrade any widow or orphan. ²²If you will degrade them, when they will cry out to me I'll hear their cry, ²³and my anger will flare, and I'll kill you with a sword, and your wives will be widows and your children orphans!

²⁴"If you will lend money to my people, to the poor who is with you, you shall not be like a creditor to him; you shall not impose interest on him. ²⁵If you take your neighbor's clothing as security, you shall give it back to him by the sunset, ²⁶ because it is his only apparel; it is his clothing for his skin. In what will he sleep? And it will be, when he will cry out to me, that I shall listen, because I am gracious.

²⁷"You shall not blaspheme God, and you shall not curse a chieftain among your people.

²⁸"You shall not delay your fulfillment and your flowing.

"You shall give me the firstborn of your sons.

²⁹"You shall do this to your ox and to your sheep: Seven days it will be with its mother. On the eighth day you shall give it to me.

³⁰"And you shall be holy people to me.

"And you shall not eat meat in the field that is torn. You shall throw it to the dog.

23

¹"You shall not bring up a false report. Do not join your hand with a wicked person to be a malevolent witness. ²You shall not be following many to do bad. And you shall not testify about a dispute to bend following many, to bend it. ³And you shall not favor a weak person in his dispute.

⁴"If you will happen upon your enemy's ox or his ass straying, you shall bring it back to him. ⁵If you will see the ass of someone who hates you sagging under its burden, and you would hold back from helping him: you shall help with him.

⁶"You shall not bend the judgment of your poor in his dispute.

⁷"You shall keep far from a word of a lie, and do not kill an innocent and a virtuous person, because I shall not vindicate a wicked person.

⁸"And you shall not take a bribe, because bribery will blind those who can see and will undermine the words of the virtuous.

⁹"And you shall not oppress an alien—since you know the alien's soul, because you were aliens in the land of Egypt.

¹⁰"And six years you shall sow your land and gather its produce; ¹¹and the seventh: you shall let it lie fallow and leave it, and your people's indigent will eat, and what they leave the animal of the field will eat. You shall do this to your vineyard, to your olives.

¹²"Six days you shall do the things you do, and on the seventh day you shall cease, so that your ox and your ass will rest, and your maid's son and the alien will be refreshed.

¹³"And you shall be watchful in everything that I have said to you. And you shall not commemorate the name of other gods. Let it not be heard on your mouth.

¹⁴"You shall celebrate three pilgrimages for me in the year:

¹⁵"You shall observe the Festival of Unleavened Bread. Seven days you shall eat unleavened bread, as I commanded you, at the appointed time of the month of Abib, because you went out of Egypt in it. And none shall appear before me empty.

¹⁶"And the Festival of Harvest, the firstfruits of what you do, of what you will sow in the field.

"And the Festival of Gathering, at the end of the year, when you gather what you have done from the field.

¹⁷"Three times in the year every male of yours shall appear in front of the Lord YHWH.

¹⁸"You shall not offer the blood of my sacrifice on leavened bread. And the fat of my festival shall not remain until morning.

¹⁹"You shall bring the first of the firstfruits of your land to the house of YHWH, your God.

"You shall not cook a kid in its mother's milk.

²⁰"Here, I'm sending an angel ahead of you to watch over you on the way and to bring you to the place that I've prepared. ²¹Be watchful in front of him and listen to his voice. Don't rebel against him, because he will not bear your offense, because my name is within him. ²²But if you will listen to his voice and do everything that I speak, then I'll be an enemy to your enemies and an opponent to your opponents. ²³When my angel will go ahead of you and will bring you to the Amorite and the Hittite and the Perizzite and the Canaanite, the Hivite, and the Jebusite, and I obliterate them, ²⁴you shall not bow to their gods, and you shall not serve them, and you shall not do like the things they do; but you shall tear them down and shatter their pillars. ²⁵And you will serve YHWH, your God, and He will bless your bread and your water, and I shall turn sickness away from within you. ²⁶There won't be a bereaved woman and an infertile woman in your land. I shall fulfill the number of your days. ²⁷I shall have my terror go ahead of you, and I shall throw all the people against whom you come into tumult, and I shall give all your enemies to you by the back. ²⁸And I shall send the hornet ahead of you, and it will drive out the Hivite, the Canaanite, and the Hittite from in front of you. ²⁹I won't drive them out from in front of you in one year, or else the land will be a devastation, and the animal of the field will be many at you. ³⁰Little by little I shall drive them out from in front of you, until you will be fruitful, and you will have a legacy of the land. ³¹And I shall set your border from the Red Sea to the sea of the Philistines and from the wilderness to the river, because I shall put the residents of the land in your hand, and you'll drive them out from in front of you. ³²You shall not make a covenant with them and with their gods. ³³They shall not live in your land, in case they will make you sin against me when you'll serve their gods, because it will be a trap for you."

24

¹And He said to Moses, "Come up to YHWH: you and Aaron, Nadab and Abihu,* and seventy of Israel's elders, and bow from a distance.** ²And Moses will come over alone to YHWH, and they shall not come over, and the people shall not come up with him."

³And Moses came and told the people all of YHWH's words and all the judgments. And all the people answered, one voice, and they said, "We'll do all the things that YHWH has spoken." ⁴And Moses wrote all of YHWH's words. And he got up early in the morning and built an altar below the mountain and twelve pillars for twelve tribes of Israel. ⁵And he sent young men of the children of Israel, and they made burnt offerings, and they made peace-offering sacrifices to YHWH: bulls. ⁶And Moses took half of the blood and set it in basins and threw half of the blood on the altar. ⁷And he took the scroll of the covenant and read in the people's ears. And they said, "We'll do everything that YHWH has spoken, and we'll listen."

⁸And Moses took the blood and threw it on the people, and he said, "Here is the blood of the covenant that YHWH has made with you regarding all these things."

---

*Note the curious fact that King Jeroboam's sons are Nadab and Abiyah (1 Kgs 14:1,20) and Aaron's sons are Nadab and Abihu. The names of the sons of the two makers of golden calves in the Bible are nearly the same. This is just part of a string of connections between the golden calves of Aaron and of Jeroboam. See the note on Exod 32:4.

Note also: In E only these two sons of Aaron are known: Nadab and Abihu. In P, Nadab and Abihu are killed, and there is a third son, Eleazar, who becomes Aaron's heir as high priest. See Lev 10:1–2.

**There is an extensive string of connections between this E account of a revelation on Mount Horeb in Exodus 24 and the E account of the sacrifice of Isaac in Genesis 22. The two stories have a chain of ten verbs in common: "and he said," "and he took . . . and he set," "and he got up early," "and he built an altar," "and he put out his hand," "and he/it was," "and he/they got up," "and he/they came," "and he/they saw." Here in Exodus Moses says to the elders, "Sit here . . . we'll come back to you." There Abraham says the same words to the servant boys. And here servant boys (*nĕ'ārîm*) appear as well. Both accounts use the term "from a distance" (*mērāhōq*). Both use the term "to bow" (*hištaḥăwōt*). Both Moses and Abraham come up a mountain. Both have a burnt offering (*ha'ălōt 'ōlāh*). In Genesis Abraham is rewarded because "you did this thing"; and the people in Exodus here promise that "We'll do all the things." Abraham is rewarded because "you listened to my voice"; and here in Exodus the people "said with one voice," and they say, "we'll listen."

Such a large number of connections is further confirmation of E as an independent source. E is a long work, fashioned with literary connections. Here the author used reminiscences of terms, phrases, and narrative elements to link two great scenes of divine communication.

⁹And Moses and Aaron, Nadab and Abihu, and seventy of Israel's elders went up. ¹⁰And they saw the God of Israel. And below His feet it was like a structure of sapphire brick and like the essence of the skies for clarity. ¹¹And He did not put out His hand to the chiefs of the children of Israel. And they envisioned God. And they ate and drank.

¹²And YHWH said to Moses, "Come up to me, to the mountain, and be there, and I'll give you stone tablets and the instruction and the commandment that I've written to instruct them."

¹³And Moses and Joshua, his attendant, got up, and Moses went up to the Mountain of God. ¹⁴And he said to the elders, "Sit for us here until we'll come back to you. And here, Aaron and Hur are with you. Let whoever has any matters go over to them." ¹⁵And Moses went up to the mountain. And the cloud covered the mountain. ¹⁶And YHWH's glory settled on Mount Sinai, and the cloud covered it six days. And He called to Moses on the seventh day from inside the cloud. ¹⁷And the appearance of YHWH's glory was like a consuming fire in the mountaintop before the eyes of the children of Israel. ¹⁸And Moses came inside the cloud and went up into the mountain.* And Moses was in the mountain forty days and forty nights.

25

¹And YHWH spoke to Moses, saying, ²"Speak to the children of Israel that they shall take a donation for me. You shall take my donation from every man whose heart will move him. ³And this is the donation that you shall take from them: gold and silver and bronze ⁴and blue and purple and scarlet and linen and goats' hair ⁵and rams' skins dyed red and leather skins and acacia wood, ⁶oil for lighting, spices for the anointing oil and for the incense fragrances, ⁷onyx stones and stones to be set for the ephod and for the breastplate. ⁸And they shall make me a holy place, and I shall tent among them. ⁹According to everything that I show you: the design of the Tabernacle and the design of all of its equipment. And you shall do so.

¹⁰"And they shall make an ark of acacia wood, its length two and a half cubits and its width a cubit and a half and its height a cubit and a half. ¹¹And you shall plate it with pure gold. You shall plate it inside and outside. And you shall make a border of gold all around on it. ¹²And you shall cast four rings of gold for it and place them on its four bases: and two rings on its one

---

*Note the resumptive repetition of the words "and he went up into the mountain" in vv. 15 and 18, and the text inside these bookends changes from E's "Mountain of God" to P's Mount Sinai, and it refers to the "glory of YHWH," which is known from P.

side and two rings on its second side. ¹³And you shall make poles of acacia wood and plate them with gold, ¹⁴and bring the poles through the rings on the ark's sides, in order to carry the ark with them. ¹⁵The poles shall be in the ark's rings; they shall not depart from it. ¹⁶And you shall place in the ark the Testimony that I shall give you. ¹⁷And you shall make an atonement dais of pure gold, its length two and a half cubits and its width a cubit and a half. ¹⁸And you shall make two cherubs of gold—you shall make them of hammered work—at the two ends of the atonement dais. ¹⁹And make one cherub at this end and one cherub at that end. You shall make the cherubs from the atonement dais on its two sides. ²⁰And the two cherubs will be spreading wings above, covering over the atonement dais with their wings, and their faces each toward its brother: the cherubs' faces shall be toward the atonement dais. ²¹And you shall place the atonement dais on the ark, from above, and you shall place in the ark the Testimony that I shall give you. ²²And I shall meet with you there and speak with you from above the atonement dais, from between the two cherubs that are on the Ark of the Testimony, everything that I shall command you to the children of Israel.

²³"And you shall make a table of acacia wood, its length two cubits and its width a cubit and its height a cubit and a half. ²⁴And you shall plate it with pure gold and make a border of gold all around for it ²⁵and make a rim of a handbreadth for it all around and make a border of gold for its rim all around. ²⁶And you shall make four rings of gold for it and put the rings on the four corners that its four legs have. ²⁷The rings shall be in juxtaposition to the rim as housings for the poles in order to carry the table. ²⁸And you shall make the poles of acacia wood and plate them with gold, and the table will be carried with them. ²⁹And you shall make its dishes and its pans and its jars and its bowls with which libations will be poured. You shall make them of pure gold. ³⁰And you shall place show bread on the table in front of me always.

³¹"And you shall make a menorah of pure gold. The menorah shall be made of hammered work—its shaft and its branch, its cups, its ornaments, and its flowers shall be part of it— ³²and six branches coming out from its sides, three of the menorah's branches from its one side and three of the menorah's branches from its second side, ³³three almond-shaped cups in the one branch, with ornament and flower, and three almond-shaped cups in the other branch, with ornament and flower. So it is for the six branches that come out from the menorah, ³⁴and four almond-shaped cups within the menorah, with its ornaments and its flowers, ³⁵and an ornament under the two branches from it, and an ornament under the two branches from it, and an ornament under the two branches from it, for the six branches that come out from the menorah. ³⁶Their ornaments and their branches shall be part of

it, all of it one hammered work of pure gold. [37]And you shall make its lamps seven, and it will hold up its lamps and light the area in front of it. [38]And its tongs and its fire-holders of pure gold. [39]He shall make it—all of these items—of a talent of pure gold. [40]And see and make them by their design that you are shown in the mountain.

26.

[1]"And you shall make the Tabernacle* with ten curtains of woven linen and blue and purple and scarlet, with cherubs—you shall make them designer's work. [2]The length of one curtain shall be twenty-eight in cubits, and the width of one curtain four in cubits: one size to all the curtains. [3]Five curtains will be connected, each to its sister-piece, and five curtains connected, each to its sister-piece. [4]And you shall make loops of blue on the side of the one curtain at the end of the connected group, and you shall do so in the side of the end curtain in the second connected group. [5]You shall make fifty loops in the one curtain, and you shall make fifty loops in the end of the curtain that is in the second connected group, with the loops parallel: each to its sister-piece. [6]And you shall make fifty clasps of gold and connect the curtains, each to its sister-piece, with the clasps. And the Tabernacle will be one.

[7]"And you shall make curtains of goats' hair for a tent over the Tabernacle. You shall make them eleven curtains. [8]The length of one curtain shall be thirty in cubits, and the width of one curtain four in cubits: one size for eleven curtains. [9]And you shall connect five of the curtains by themselves and six of the curtains by themselves. And you shall double-fold the sixth curtain opposite the front of the tent. [10]And you shall make fifty loops on the side of the one end curtain in the connected group and fifty loops on the side of the curtain of the second connected group. [11]And you shall make fifty clasps of bronze and bring the clasps into the loops and connect the tent. And it will be one. [12]And the hanging one that is left over among the tent's curtains: you shall hang half of the leftover curtain on the back parts of the Tabernacle.

---

*I have presented evidence that the Tabernacle, as described in this chapter, corresponded in size to the space under the wings of the cherubs inside the Holy of Holies inside the Temple of Solomon. This, together with other textual, historical, and archaeological evidence, contributed to the conclusion that the Tabernacle was historical and was located in that Temple—but not in the second, postexilic Jerusalem Temple. This in turn argued that the P texts that require the presence of the Tabernacle for the performance of sacrifices and ceremonies had to have been written while the first Jerusalem Temple was still standing: before the Babylonian exile and destruction of the Temple. For discussion and bibliography, see the Collection of Evidence, pp. 22–24.

¹³And the cubit on this side and the cubit on that side in the leftover in the length of the tent's curtains shall be hung on the sides of the Tabernacle, on this side and on that side, to cover it. ¹⁴And you shall make a covering for the tent of rams' skins dyed red and a covering of leather skins above.

¹⁵"And you shall make the frames for the Tabernacle of acacia wood, standing. ¹⁶The frame's length shall be ten cubits, and the width of one frame a cubit and a half cubit. ¹⁷One frame has two projections, each aligned with its sister-piece: so you shall make for all the Tabernacle's frames. ¹⁸And you shall make the frames for the Tabernacle: twenty frames for the south side—to the south. ¹⁹And you shall make forty bases of silver under the twenty frames: two bases under one frame for its two projections and two bases under each other frame for its two projections. ²⁰And for the Tabernacle's second side, for the north side: twenty frames ²¹and their forty bases of silver, two bases under one frame and two bases under each other frame. ²²And for the rear of the Tabernacle, to the west, you shall make six frames. ²³And you shall make two frames for the Tabernacle's corners in the rear, ²⁴and they shall be doubles from below, and together they shall be integrated on its top to one ring. It shall be so for the two of them; they will be for the two corners. ²⁵And they shall be eight frames and their bases of silver, sixteen bases, two bases under one frame and two bases under each other frame. ²⁶And you shall make bars of acacia wood: five for the frames of one side of the Tabernacle ²⁷and five bars for the frames of the second side of the Tabernacle and five bars for the frames of the side of the Tabernacle at the rear, to the west, ²⁸and the middle bar through the frames extending from end to end. ²⁹And you shall plate the frames with gold, and you shall make their rings gold, housings for the bars, and you shall plate the bars with gold. ³⁰And you shall set up the Tabernacle according to the model of it that you were shown in the mountain.

³¹"And you shall make a pavilion of blue and purple and scarlet and woven linen; he shall make them designer's work with cherubs. ³²And you shall place it on four acacia columns plated with gold, their hooks of gold, on four bases of silver. ³³And you shall place the pavilion under the clasps. And you shall bring the Ark of the Testimony there, inside the pavilion, and the pavilion will distinguish for you between the Holy and the Holy of Holies. ³⁴And you shall place the atonement dais on the Ark of the Testimony in the Holy of Holies. ³⁵And you shall place the table outside the pavilion, and the menorah opposite the table on the south side of the Tabernacle, and you shall place the table on the north side.

³⁶"And you shall make a cover for the entrance of the tent: blue and purple and scarlet and woven linen—embroiderer's work. ³⁷And you shall

make five acacia columns for the cover and plate them with gold, their hooks of gold, and cast five bases of bronze for them.

27

[1]"And you shall make the altar of acacia wood. Five cubits long and five cubits wide, the altar shall be square—and its height three cubits. [2]And you shall make its horns on its four corners. Its horns shall be part of it. And you shall plate it with bronze. [3]And you shall make its pots to remove ashes from it, and its shovels and its basins and its forks and its fire-holders. You shall make all of its equipment bronze. [4]And you shall make a grate for it, a network of bronze, and on the net you shall make four rings of bronze on its four ends. [5]And you shall place it under the altar's ledge below so that the net will be up to the middle of the altar. [6]And you shall make poles for the altar, poles of acacia wood, and plate them with bronze. [7]And its poles shall be brought through rings so that the poles shall be on the altar's two sides when carrying it. [8]You shall make it hollow of boards, as it was shown to you in the mountain. They shall do it so.

[9]"And you shall make the Tabernacle's courtyard: for the south side—to the south, hangings for the courtyard of woven linen, one side having a hundred in cubits, [10]and its columns twenty, and their bases twenty of bronze, and the columns' hooks and their rods of silver. [11]And so for the north side: in length, hangings of a hundred long, and its columns twenty, and their bases twenty of bronze, and the columns' hooks and their bands of silver. [12]And the courtyard's width for the west side: hangings of fifty cubits, their columns ten and their bases ten. [13]And the courtyard's width for the east side—to the east—fifty cubits. [14]And the panel shall have fifteen cubits of hangings, their columns three and their bases three; [15]and the second panel shall have fifteen of hangings, their columns three and their bases three. [16]And the courtyard's gate shall have a cover of twenty cubits: blue and purple and scarlet and woven linen, embroiderer's work, their columns four and their bases four. [17]All of the courtyard's columns all around shall be banded with silver, their hooks of silver and their bases bronze. [18]The courtyard's length a hundred in cubits, and width consistently fifty, and height five cubits of woven linen, and their bases of bronze. [19]For all of the Tabernacle's equipment in all of the service of it, and all of its pegs and all of the courtyard's pegs: bronze.

[20]"And you: you shall command the children of Israel that they shall bring clear pressed olive oil to you for the light, to keep up a lamp always.

²¹In the Tent of Meeting, outside the pavilion that is over the Testimony, Aaron and his sons shall arrange it from evening until morning in front of YHWH, an eternal law through their generations from the children of Israel.

28

¹"And you, bring Aaron, your brother, forward to you, and his sons with him, from among the children of Israel, for him to function as a priest for me: Aaron, Nadab and Abihu, Eleazar and Ithamar, Aaron's sons. ²And you shall make holy clothes for Aaron, your brother, for glory and for beauty. ³And you shall speak to all the wise of heart whom I have filled with a spirit of wisdom, that they shall make Aaron's clothes, to sanctify him for him to function as a priest for me. ⁴And these are the clothes that they shall make: breastplate and ephod and robe and patterned coat, a headdress and a sash. And they shall make holy clothes for Aaron, your brother, and for his sons, for him to function as a priest for me. ⁵And they shall take the gold and the blue and the purple and the scarlet and the linen.

⁶"And they shall make the ephod: gold, blue, and purple, scarlet, and woven linen, designer's work. ⁷It shall have two connected shoulder-pieces at its two ends, and it will be connected. ⁸And the ephod's designed belt that is on it shall be like its work and be a part of it: gold, blue, and purple, and scarlet and woven linen. ⁹And you shall take two onyx stones and inscribe the names of the children of Israel on them: ¹⁰six of their names on one stone and the names of the remaining six on the second stone, according to their birth orders. ¹¹By a stone engraver's work you shall inscribe the two stones with signet inscriptions according to the names of the children of Israel. You shall make them surrounded by settings of gold. ¹²And you shall set the two stones on the ephod's shoulder-pieces, commemorative stones for the children of Israel, and Aaron shall carry their names in front of YHWH on his two shoulders as a commemoration.

¹³"And you shall make settings of gold ¹⁴and two chains of pure gold. You shall make them twisted, rope work, and put the rope chains on the settings.

¹⁵"And you shall make a breastplate of judgment, designer's work. You shall make it like the work of the ephod. You shall make it gold, blue, and purple and scarlet and woven linen. ¹⁶It shall be square when doubled, its length a span and its width a span. ¹⁷And you shall put a mounting of stones in it: four rows of stone. A row of a carnelian, a topaz, and an emerald: the one row. ¹⁸And the second row: a ruby, a sapphire, and a diamond. ¹⁹And the third row: a jacinth, an agate, and an amethyst. ²⁰And the fourth row: a beryl and an onyx and a jasper. They shall be set in gold in their mountings. ²¹And

the stones shall be with the names of the children of Israel, twelve with their names; they shall be signet engravings, each with its name, for twelve tribes. ²²And you shall make twisted chains, rope work, of pure gold, on the breastplate. ²³And you shall make two rings of gold on the breastplate and put the two rings on the two ends of the breastplate ²⁴and put the two ropes of gold on the two rings at the ends of the breastplate. ²⁵And you shall put the two ends of the two ropes on the two settings, and you shall put them on the ephod's shoulder-pieces opposite the front of it. ²⁶And you shall make two rings of gold and set them on the breastplate's two ends on its side that is adjacent to the ephod, inward. ²⁷And you shall make two rings of gold and put them on the ephod's two shoulder-pieces below, opposite the front of it, by its connection, above the ephod's designed belt. ²⁸And they shall attach the breastplate from its rings to the ephod's rings with a blue string so it will be on the ephod's designed belt and the breastplate will not be detached from the ephod. ²⁹And Aaron shall carry the names of the children of Israel in the breastplate of judgment on his heart when he comes into the Holy, as a commemorative in front of YHWH always. ³⁰And you shall put the Urim and Tummim in the breastplate of judgment, and they shall be on Aaron's heart when he comes in front of YHWH, and Aaron shall carry the judgment of the children of Israel on his heart in front of YHWH always.

³¹"And you shall make the robe of the ephod all of blue. ³²And its head-opening shall be within it. It shall have a binding for its opening all around, weaver's work. It shall be like the opening of a coat of mail for him; it will not be torn. ³³And you shall make on its skirts pomegranates of blue and purple and scarlet, on its skirts all around, and bells of gold within them all around: ³⁴a golden bell and a pomegranate, a golden bell and a pomegranate, on the robe's skirts all around. ³⁵And it shall be on Aaron for ministering: and the sound of it will be heard when he comes to the Holy in front of YHWH and when he goes out, so he will not die.

³⁶"And you shall make a plate of pure gold and make signet inscriptions on it: 'Holiness to YHWH.' ³⁷And you shall set it on a blue string, and it shall be on the headdress. It shall be opposite the front of the headdress. ³⁸And it shall be on Aaron's forehead, and Aaron shall bear the crime of the holy things that the children of Israel will sanctify, for all their holy gifts. And it shall be on his forehead always for acceptance for them in front of YHWH. ³⁹And you shall weave the coat in a pattern of linen and make a headdress of linen. And you shall make a sash, embroiderer's work, ⁴⁰and you shall make coats for Aaron's sons, and you shall make sashes for them, and you shall make hats for them—for glory and for beauty. ⁴¹And you shall dress them— Aaron, your brother, and his sons with him—and you shall anoint them and

fill their hand and sanctify them, and they shall function as priests for me. ⁴²And make shorts of linen for them, to cover naked flesh; they shall be from hips to thighs. ⁴³And they shall be on Aaron and on his sons when they come to the Tent of Meeting or when they come close to the altar to minister in the Holy, so they will not bear a crime and die. It is an eternal law for him and for his seed after him.

29

¹"And this is the thing that you shall do to them to sanctify them to function as priests for me: Take one bull of the cattle and two unblemished rams ²and unleavened bread and unleavened cakes mixed with oil and unleavened wafers with oil poured on them—you shall make them of fine flour of wheat. ³And you shall put them on one basket and bring them forward in the basket—and the bull and the two rams. ⁴And you shall bring Aaron and his sons forward to the Tent of Meeting and wash them with water. ⁵And you shall take the clothes and dress Aaron with the coat and with the ephod's robe and with the ephod and with the breastplate, and you shall put on the ephod for him with the ephod's designed belt. ⁶And you shall set the headdress on his head and put the crown of Holiness on the headdress. ⁷And you shall take the anointing oil and pour it on his head and anoint him. ⁸And you shall bring his sons forward, and you shall dress them in coats ⁹and you shall belt them with a sash, Aaron and his sons, and put hats on for them. And they shall have priesthood as an eternal law. And you shall fill Aaron's hand and his sons' hand. ¹⁰And you shall bring the bull forward in front of the Tent of Meeting, and Aaron and his sons shall lay their hands on the bull's head. ¹¹And you shall slaughter the bull in front of YHWH at the entrance of the Tent of Meeting. ¹²And you shall take some of the bull's blood and put it on the horns of the altar with your finger, and you shall spill all of the blood at the base of the altar. ¹³And you shall take all of the fat that covers the inside and the appendage on the liver and the two kidneys and the fat that is on them, and you shall burn them into smoke at the altar. ¹⁴And you shall burn the meat of the bull and its skin and its dung in fire outside the camp. It is a sin offering. ¹⁵And you shall take the one ram, and Aaron and his sons shall lay their hands on the ram's head. ¹⁶And you shall slaughter the ram and take its blood and fling it on the altar all around. ¹⁷And you shall cut up the ram into its parts, and you shall wash its inside and its legs and put them on its parts and on its head. ¹⁸And you shall burn all of the ram to smoke at the altar. It is a burnt offering to YHWH. It is a pleasant smell, an offering by

fire to YHWH. ¹⁹And you shall take the second ram, and Aaron and his sons shall lay their hands on the ram's head. ²⁰And you shall slaughter the ram and take some of its blood and put it on Aaron's earlobe and on his sons' earlobe, the right one, and on the thumb of their right hand and on the big toe of their right foot. And you shall fling the blood on the altar all around. ²¹And you shall take some of the blood that is on the altar and some of the anointing oil and sprinkle it on Aaron and on his clothes and on his sons and on his sons' clothes with him. And he and his clothes and his sons and his sons' clothes with him will be holy. ²²And you shall take the fat from the ram and the fat tail and the fat that covers the inside and the appendage of the liver and the two kidneys and the fat that is on them and the right thigh—because it is a ram of ordination— ²³and one loaf of bread and one cake of bread with oil and one wafer from the basket of unleavened bread that is in front of YHWH. ²⁴And you shall put it all on Aaron's hands and on his sons' hands and elevate them as an elevation offering in front of YHWH. ²⁵And you shall take them from their hand and burn them to smoke at the altar in addition to the burnt offering as a pleasant smell in front of YHWH. It is an offering by fire to YHWH. ²⁶And you shall take the breast from the ram of ordination that is Aaron's and elevate it as an elevation offering in front of YHWH, and it shall be a portion for you. ²⁷And you shall sanctify the breast that is an elevation offering and the thigh that is a donation, that is elevated and that is donated, from the ram of ordination, from Aaron's and from his sons'. ²⁸And it shall be Aaron's and his sons' as an eternal law from the children of Israel, because it is a donation, and it will be a donation from the children of Israel from the sacrifices of their peace offerings, their donation to YHWH. ²⁹And the holy clothes that are Aaron's shall be his sons' after him, to be anointed in them and to fill their hand in them. ³⁰The priest in his place from among his sons, who will come to the Tent of Meeting to minister in the Holy, shall wear them for seven days. ³¹And you shall take the ram of ordination and cook its meat in a holy place, ³²and Aaron and his sons shall eat the meat of the ram and the bread that is in the basket at the entrance of the Tent of Meeting. ³³And those who have acquired atonement by them shall eat them, to fill their hand, to make them holy; and an outsider shall not eat, because they are holy. ³⁴And if some of the meat of the ordination or some of the bread will be left until the morning, then you shall burn what is left in fire. It shall not be eaten, because it is holy.

³⁵"And you shall do thus to Aaron and to his sons, according to all that I have commanded you. You shall fill their hand for seven days. ³⁶And you shall do a bull sin offering per day for atonement, and you shall make a sin

offering on the altar when you make atonement for it, and you shall anoint it to make it holy. [37]Seven days you shall make atonement on the altar and make it holy, and the altar shall be holy of holies. Anyone who touches the altar will be holy.

[38]"And this is what you shall do on the altar: year-old lambs, two per day, always. [39]You shall do the one sheep in the morning and do the second sheep between the two evenings. [40]And a tenth of a measure of fine flour mixed with a fourth of a hin of pressed oil and a libation of a fourth of a hin of wine for the first lamb. [41]And you shall do the second lamb between the two evenings. You shall do it like the morning grain offering and like its libation for a pleasant smell, an offering by fire to YHWH, [42]a continual burnt offering through your generations at the entrance of the Tent of Meeting in front of YHWH, where I shall meet with you to speak to you there. [43]And I shall meet there with the children of Israel, and it will be made holy through my glory. [44]And I shall make the Tent of Meeting and the altar holy, and I shall make Aaron and his sons holy to function as priests for me. [45]And I shall tent among the children of Israel, and I shall be God to them. [46]And they will know that I am YHWH, their God, who brought them out from the land of Egypt for me to tent among them. I am YHWH, their God.

30

[1]"And you shall make an altar for burning incense. You shall make it of acacia wood. [2]Its length a cubit and its width a cubit, it shall be square, and its height two cubits, its horns a part of it. [3]And you shall plate it with pure gold, its roof and its walls all around and its horns. And you shall make a border of gold for it all around. [4]And you shall make two rings of gold for it below its rim on its two sides; you shall make it on its two sidewalls, and it will be for housings for poles with which to carry it. [5]And you shall make the poles of acacia wood and plate them with gold. [6]And you shall put it in front of the pavilion that is over the Ark of the Testimony, in front of the atonement dais that is over the Testimony, where I shall meet with you. [7]And Aaron shall burn incense of fragrances on it. Morning by morning, when he attends to the lamps, he shall burn it, [8]and when Aaron puts up the lamps between the two evenings he shall burn it: a continual incense in front of YHWH through your generations. [9]You shall not offer unfitting incense or a burnt offering or a grain offering on it, and you shall not pour a libation on it. [10]And Aaron shall make atonement on its horns once per year; he shall make atonement on it with the blood of the sin offer-

ing of atonement once per year through your generations. It is holy of holies to YHWH."

¹¹And YHWH spoke to Moses, saying, ¹²"When you add up the heads of the children of Israel by their counts, each of them shall give a ransom for his life to YHWH when counting them, so there will not be a plague among them when counting them. ¹³Everyone who passes through the counts shall give this: half of a shekel, by the shekel of the Holy (the shekel is twenty gerah); half of a shekel as a donation to YHWH. ¹⁴Everyone who passes through the counts, from twenty years old and up, shall give YHWH's donation. ¹⁵The rich one shall not multiply, and the poor one shall not diminish from the half of a shekel, to give YHWH's donation, to make atonement for your lives. ¹⁶And you shall take the atonement money from the children of Israel and give it for the service of the Tent of Meeting, and it shall become a commemorative for the children of Israel in front of YHWH, to make atonement for your lives."

¹⁷And YHWH spoke to Moses, saying, ¹⁸"And you shall make a basin of bronze and its stand of bronze for washing, and you shall put it between the Tent of Meeting and the altar and put water there. ¹⁹And Aaron and his sons will wash their hands and their feet from it. ²⁰When they come to the Tent of Meeting they shall wash with water, and they will not die—or when they come near to the altar to minister, to burn an offering by fire to YHWH to smoke. ²¹And they shall wash their hands and their feet, and they will not die. And it will be an eternal law for them—for him and for his seed through their generations."

²²And YHWH spoke to Moses, saying, ²³"And you, take spices, choice: flowing myrrh, five hundred; and aromatic cinnamon, half as much, two hundred fifty; and aromatic reed, two hundred fifty; ²⁴and cassia, five hundred—by the shekel of the Holy—and olive oil, a hin. ²⁵And you shall make it oil of holy anointing, an ointment mixture, the work of an ointment-maker. It shall be oil of holy anointing. ²⁶And you shall anoint the Tent of Meeting and the Ark of the Testimony with it, ²⁷and the table and all its equipment and the menorah and its equipment and the incense altar ²⁸and the altar of burnt offering and all its equipment and the basin and its stand. ²⁹And you shall make them holy, and they shall be holy of holies. Anyone who touches them will be holy. ³⁰And you shall anoint Aaron and his sons and make them holy to function as priests for me. ³¹And you shall speak to the children of Israel, saying, 'This shall be oil of holy anointing for me through your generations. ³²It shall not be poured on human flesh, and you shall not make anything else like it in its quantities. It is a holy thing. It shall be a holy thing to you. ³³Anyone who will make a compound like it and who will give some of it to an outsider: he will be cut off from his people.'"

³⁴And YHWH said to Moses, "Take fragrances—stacte and onycha and galbanum—fragrances and clear frankincense; it shall be part for part. ³⁵And you shall make it ointment incense, the work of an ointment-maker: salted, pure, holy. ³⁶And you shall pound some of it, making it thin, and put some of it in front of the Testimony in the Tent of Meeting where I shall meet with you. It shall be holy of holies to you. ³⁷And the incense that you will make: you shall not make for yourselves in its quantities. It shall be a holy thing to you for YHWH. ³⁸Anyone who will make anything like it to make a fragrance with it will be cut off from his people."

31

¹And YHWH spoke to Moses, saying, ²"See, I've called by name Bezalel, son of Uri, son of Hur, of the tribe of Judah. ³And I've filled him with the spirit of God in wisdom and in understanding and in knowledge and in every kind of work, ⁴to form conceptions to make in gold and in silver and in bronze ⁵and in cutting stone for setting and in cutting wood—for making things in every kind of work. ⁶And I: here, I've put Oholiab, son of Ahisamach, of the tribe of Dan, with him. And in the heart of every wise-hearted person I've put wisdom. And they'll make everything that I've commanded you: ⁷the Tent of Meeting and the Ark of the Testimony and the atonement dais that is on it and all the equipment of the tent ⁸and the table and its equipment and the pure menorah and all its equipment and the incense altar ⁹and the burnt offering altar and all its equipment and the basin and its stand ¹⁰and the fabric clothes and the holy clothes for Aaron, the priest, and his sons' clothes for functioning as priests ¹¹and the anointing oil and the incense of fragrances for the Holy. According to everything that I've commanded you, they shall do."

¹²And YHWH said to Moses, saying, ¹³"And you, speak to the children of Israel, saying, 'Just: you shall observe my Sabbaths, because it is a sign between me and you through your generations: to know that I, YHWH, make you holy. ¹⁴And you shall observe the Sabbath, because it is a holy thing to you. One who desecrates it shall be put to death. Because anyone who does work in it: that person will be cut off from among his people. ¹⁵Six days work shall be done, and in the seventh day is a Sabbath, a ceasing, a holy thing to YHWH. Anyone who does work in the Sabbath day shall be put to death. ¹⁶And the children of Israel shall observe the Sabbath, to make the Sabbath through their generations, an eternal covenant. ¹⁷Between me and the children of Israel it is a sign forever, because for six days YHWH made the skies and the earth, and in the seventh day He ceased and was refreshed.'"

¹⁸And when He finished speaking with him in Mount Sinai, He gave the two tablets of the Testimony to Moses, tablets of stone, written by the finger of God.*

32

¹And the people saw that Moses was delaying to come down from the mountain, and the people assembled at Aaron and said to him, "Get up. Make gods for us who will go in front of us, because this Moses, the man who brought us up from the land of Egypt: we don't know what has become of him!"

²And Aaron said to them, "Take off the gold rings that are in your wives', your sons', and your daughters' ears, and bring them to me." ³And all the people took off the gold rings that were in their ears and brought them to Aaron. ⁴And he took them from their hand and fashioned it with a stylus and made it a molten calf.**

And they said, "These are your gods, Israel, who brought you up from the land of Egypt!"‡

⁵And Aaron saw, and he built an altar in front of it, and Aaron called, and he said, "A festival to YHWH tomorrow!" ⁶And they got up early the next day, and they made burnt offerings and brought over peace offerings, and the people sat down to eat and drink, and they got up to fool around.

⁷And YHWH spoke to Moses: "Go. Go down. Because your people, whom you brought up from the land of Egypt, has corrupted. ⁸They've turned quickly from the way that I commanded them. They've made themselves a molten calf, and they've bowed to it and sacrificed to it and said, 'These are your gods, Israel, who brought you up from the land of Egypt!'" ⁹And YHWH said to Moses, "I've seen this people; and, here, it's a hard-necked people. ¹⁰And now, leave off from me, and my anger will flare at them, and I'll finish them, and I'll make you into a big nation!"

¹¹And Moses conciliated in front of YHWH, his God, and said, "Why, YHWH, should your anger flare at your people whom you brought out from the land of Egypt with big power and with a strong hand? ¹²Why should

---

*The phrase "finger of God" occurs in another P passage (Exod 8:15) but never in J or E. The reference to the "testimony" also is characteristic of P. Further, the mountain is referred to as Sinai, which occurs only in P and J, never in E or D. This passage connects to the next P passage, Exod 34:29.

**On the string of connections between Aaron's golden calf and King Jeroboam's golden calf, see the Collection of Evidence, p. 21 and p. 25, as well as the note on Exod 24:1 above and the note following this one.

‡These are the words that Jeroboam says at his golden calf at Beth-El (1 Kgs 12:28).

Egypt say, saying, 'He brought them out for bad, to kill them in the mountains, and to finish them from on the face of the earth'? Turn back from your flaring anger, and relent about the bad to your people. ¹³Remember Abraham, Isaac, and Israel, your servants, that you swore to them by yourself, and you spoke to them: 'I'll multiply your seed like the stars of the skies, and I'll give to your seed all this land that I've said, and they'll possess it forever.'" ¹⁴And YHWH relented about the bad that He had spoken, to do to His people.

¹⁵And Moses turned and went down from the mountain. And the two tablets of witness were in his hand, tablets written from their two sides: from this side and from this side they were written. ¹⁶And the tablets: they were God's doing. And the writing: it was God's writing, inscribed on the tablets.

¹⁷And Joshua heard the sound of the people in its shouting, and he said to Moses, "A sound of war is in the camp."

¹⁸And he said, "It's not a sound of singing of victory, and it's not a sound of singing of defeat. It's just the sound of singing I hear!"

¹⁹And it was when he came close to the camp, and he saw the calf and dancing: and Moses' anger flared, and he threw the tablets from his hands and shattered them below the mountain. ²⁰And he took the calf that they had made, and he burned it in fire and ground it until it was thin, and he scattered it on the face of the water, and he made the children of Israel drink!

²¹And Moses said to Aaron, "What did this people do to you, that you've brought a big sin on it?!"

²²And Aaron said, "Let my lord's anger not flare. You know the people, that it's in a bad state. ²³And they said to me, 'Make gods for us who will go in front of us, because this Moses, the man who brought us up from the land of Egypt: we don't know what has become of him!' ²⁴And I said to them, 'Whoever has gold: take it off.' And they gave it to me, and I threw it into the fire, and this calf came out!"

²⁵And Moses saw the people, that it was turned loose, because Aaron had turned it loose*—to denigration among their adversaries! ²⁶And Moses stood in the gate of the camp and said, "Whoever is for YHWH: to me!" And all the children of Levi were gathered to him. ²⁷And he said to them, "YHWH, God of Israel, said this: 'Set, each man, his sword on his thigh; cross over and come back from gate to gate in the camp; and kill, each man, his brother and, each man, his neighbor and, each man, his relative.'" ²⁸And the chil-

---

*The word for "turned it loose" is *pr'h,* which is spelled the same as the Hebrew for "pharaoh"! This is an example of punning in E. It is also common in J, but not in P or D.

dren of Levi did according to Moses' word, and about three thousand men fell from the people in that day. ²⁹And Moses said, "Fill your hand to YHWH today—because each man was at his son and at his brother—and to put a blessing on you today."

³⁰And it was on the next day, and Moses said to the people, "You've committed a big sin. And now I'll go up to YHWH. Perhaps I may make atonement for your sin." ³¹And Moses went back to YHWH and said, "Please, this people has committed a big sin and made gods of gold for themselves. ³²And now, if you will bear their sin—and if not, wipe me out from your scroll that you've written."

³³And YHWH said to Moses, "The one who has sinned against me, I'll wipe him out from my scroll. ³⁴And now, go. Lead the people to where I spoke to you. Here, my angel will go ahead of you. And, in the day that I take account, I'll account their sin on them." ³⁵And YHWH struck the people because they had made the calf, which Aaron had made.

33

¹And YHWH spoke to Moses: "Go. Go up from here, you and the people whom you brought up from the land of Egypt, to the land that I swore to Abraham, to Isaac, and to Jacob, saying, 'I'll give it to your seed.' ²And I'll send an angel ahead of you—and I'll drive out the Canaanite, the Amorite, and the Hittite and the Perizzite and the Hivite and the Jebusite— ³to a land flowing with milk and honey, because I won't go up among you, because you're a hard-necked people, or else I'll finish you on the way." ⁴And the people heard this bad thing, and they mourned, and not a man put his jewelry on him. ⁵And YHWH said to Moses, "Say to the children of Israel: 'You're a hard-necked people. If I would go up among you for one moment, I would finish you! And now, put your jewelry down from on you, so I may know what I'll do with you.'" ⁶And the children of Israel divested their jewelry from Mount Horeb.

⁷And Moses would take the tent and pitch it outside of the camp, going far from the camp, and he called it the Tent of Meeting.* And it would be: everyone seeking YHWH would go out to the Tent of Meeting, which was outside of the camp. ⁸And it would be, when Moses would go out to the Tent, all the people would get up, and they would stand up, each one at the entrance

---

*Moses moves the Tent outside the camp here in Exod 33:7–11 (E), but the Tent is not built until Exodus 36 (P)!

of his tent, and they would look after Moses until he came to the Tent. ⁹And it would be, when Moses came to the Tent, the column of cloud would come down, and it would stand at the entrance of the Tent, and He would speak with Moses. ¹⁰And all the people would see the column of cloud standing at the entrance of the Tent, and all the people would get up and bow, each at the entrance of his tent. ¹¹And YHWH would speak to Moses face-to-face, the way a man speaks to his fellow man. And he would come back to the camp. And his attendant, Joshua, son of Nun, a young man, would not depart from inside the Tent.*

¹²And Moses said to YHWH, "See, you say to me, 'Bring this people up,' and you haven't made known to me whom you will send with me. And you've said, 'I've known you by name,' and also 'you've found favor in my eyes.' ¹³And now, if I've found favor in your eyes, make your way known to me, so I may know you, so that I'll find favor in your eyes. And see that this nation is your people."

¹⁴And He said, "My face will go, and I'll let you rest."

¹⁵And he said to Him, "If your face isn't going, don't take us up from here. ¹⁶And by what then will it be known that I've found favor in your eyes, I and your people? Is it not by your going with us? And we'll be distinguished, I and your people, from every people that is on the face of the earth."

¹⁷And YHWH said to Moses, "I'll do this thing that you've spoken as well, because you've found favor in my eyes, and I've known you by name."

¹⁸And he said, "Show me your glory!"

¹⁹And He said, "I shall have all my good pass in front of you, and I shall invoke the name YHWH in front of you. And I shall show grace to whomever I shall show grace, and I shall show mercy to whomever I shall show mercy." ²⁰And He said, "You won't be able to see my face, because a human will not see me and live." ²¹And YHWH said, "Here is a place with me, and you'll stand up on a rock; ²²and it will be, when my glory passes, that I'll set you in a cleft of the rock, and I'll cover my hand over you until I've passed, ²³and I'll turn my hand away, and you'll see my back, but my face won't be seen."**

---

*Here in E Joshua is pictured as being inside the Tent of Meeting. But this is a contradiction of P, where it is forbidden for anyone who is not a priest ever to be in the Tent, the penalty for which is to be put to death (Num 1:51; 3:10,38; 18:5,7).

**The divine revelation to Moses is foretold here in E, but it takes place in J (in the next chapter). RJE may have merged the J and E accounts in 33:12–23 in such a way that it is now difficult, perhaps impossible, to distinguish them.

34

¹And YHWH said to Moses, "Carve two tablets of stones like the first ones, and I'll write on the tablets the words that were on the first tablets, which you shattered.* ²And be ready for the morning, and you shall go up in the morning to Mount Sinai and present yourself to me there on the top of the mountain. ³And no man shall go up with you, and also let no man be seen in all of the mountain. Also let the flock and the oxen not feed opposite that mountain." ⁴And he carved two tablets of stones like the first ones, and Moses got up early in the morning and went up to Mount Sinai as YHWH had commanded him, and he took in his hand two tablets of stones. ⁵And YHWH came down in a cloud and stood with him there, and he invoked the name YHWH. ⁶And YHWH passed in front of him and called,

> YHWH, YHWH, merciful and gracious God, slow to anger and abounding in kindness and faithfulness, ⁷keeping kindness for thousands, bearing crime and offense and sin; though not making one innocent: reckoning fathers' crime on children and on children's children, on third generations and on fourth generations.**

⁸And Moses hurried and knelt to the ground and bowed, ⁹and he said, "If I've found favor in your eyes, my Lord, may my Lord go among us, because it is a stiff-necked people, and forgive our crime and our sin, and make us your legacy."

---

*The tablets in E are shattered. Now comes the J account of the tablets. In the combined JE text, it would be awkward to picture God just commanding Moses to make some tablets, as if there were no history to this matter, so RJE adds the explanation that these are a replacement for the earlier tablets that were shattered.

In E the tablets that are shattered are never said to be replaced. This suggests that, according to E, the ark that is housed in the Temple in Judah to the south either contains broken tablets or no tablets at all. As in other places, the northern Israel source E has clashing religious symbols from those of the southern kingdom of Judah. See the Collection of Evidence, pp. 19, 21.

**This famous formula in J emphasizes the merciful over the just side of God: mercy, grace, kindness. As noted in the Collection of Evidence (p. 12), P never uses these words or several other words relating to mercy. P rather emphasizes the just side of God. This is an important example of the pervasive way in which the Bible became more than the sum of its parts when the Redactor combined the sources. J (and E and D) emphasized the merciful side of God; P emphasized the just side. The final version of the united Torah now brings the two sides together in a new balance, conveying a picture of God who is torn between His justice and His mercy—which has been a central element of the conception of God in Judaism and Christianity ever since.

¹⁰And He said, "Here, I'm making a covenant. Before all your people I'll do wonders that haven't been created in all the earth and among all the nations; and all the people whom you're among will see YHWH's deeds, because that which I'm doing with you is awesome. ¹¹Watch yourself regarding what I command you today. Here, I'm driving out from before you the Amorite and the Canaanite and the Hittite and the Perizzite and the Hivite and the Jebusite. ¹²Be watchful of yourself that you don't make a covenant with the resident of the land onto which you're coming, that he doesn't become a trap among you. ¹³But you shall demolish their altars and shatter their pillars and cut down their Asherahs.

¹⁴For you shall not bow to another god—because YHWH: His name is Jealous, He is a jealous God— ¹⁵that you not make a covenant with the resident of the land, and they will prostitute themselves after their gods and sacrifice to their gods, and he will call to you, and you will eat from his sacrifice. ¹⁶And you will take some of his daughters for your sons, and his daughters will prostitute themselves after their gods and cause your sons to prostitute themselves after their gods.

¹⁷You shall not make molten gods for yourself.

¹⁸You shall observe the Festival of Unleavened Bread. Seven days you shall eat unleavened bread, which I commanded you, at the appointed time, the month of Abib; because in the month of Abib you went out of Egypt.

¹⁹Every first birth of a womb is mine, and all your animals that have a male first birth, ox or sheep. ²⁰And you shall redeem an ass's first birth with a sheep, and if you do not redeem it then you shall break its neck. You shall redeem every firstborn of your sons. And none shall appear before me empty-handed.

²¹Six days you shall work, and in the seventh day you shall cease. In plowing time and in harvest, you shall cease.

²²And you shall make a Festival of Weeks, of the firstfruits of the wheat harvest, and the Festival of Gathering at the end of the year. ²³Three times in the year every one of your males shall appear before the Lord YHWH, God of Israel. ²⁴For I shall dispossess nations before you and widen your border, and no man will covet your land while you are going up to appear before YHWH, your God, three times in the year.

²⁵You shall not offer the blood of my sacrifice on leavened bread. And the sacrifice of the Festival of Passover shall not remain until the morning.

²⁶You shall bring the first of the firstfruits of your land to the house of YHWH, your God.

You shall not cook a kid in its mother's milk."

²⁷And YHWH said to Moses, "Write these words for yourself, because I've made a covenant with you and with Israel based on these words." ²⁸And he was there with YHWH forty days and forty nights. He did not eat bread, and he did not drink water. And he wrote on the tablets the words of the covenant, the Ten Commandments.*

²⁹And it was when Moses was coming down from Mount Sinai, and the two tablets of the Testimony were in Moses' hand when he was coming down from the mountain.** And Moses had not known that the skin of his face was transformed when He was speaking with him. ³⁰And Aaron and all the children of Israel saw Moses; and, here, the skin of his face was transformed, and they were afraid of going over to him. ³¹And Moses called to them. And Aaron and all the chiefs in the congregation came back to him, and he spoke to them. ³²And after that all the children of Israel went over. And he commanded them everything that YHWH had spoken with him in Mount Sinai. ³³And Moses finished speaking with them, and he put a veil on his face. ³⁴And when Moses would come in front of YHWH to speak with Him, he would turn away the veil until he would go out; and he would go out and speak to the children of Israel what he had been commanded. ³⁵And the children of Israel would see Moses' face, that the skin of Moses' face was transformed, and Moses would put back the veil on his face until he would come to speak with Him.

---

*Exod 34:14–26 is the J text of the Ten Commandments. This is made absolutely explicit in vv. 27–28: "'Write these words for yourself, because I've made a covenant with you and with Israel based on these words' . . . And he wrote on the tablets the words of the covenant, the Ten Commandments." The first two commandments and the Sabbath commandment have parallels in the other versions of the Ten Commandments (Exodus 20 and Deuteronomy 5), though the wording is different. The other seven commandments here are completely different.

**Several marks of P are present in this passage: the reference to the "tablets of Testimony," the prominence of Aaron, the identification of the mountain as Sinai, the reference to the "congregation" and to its "chiefs." This P passage picks up where the last P passage left off. It flows as a continuous text when the intervening J and E narrative is removed.

Note that here and in Exod 31:18 P does not speak of the Ten Commandments. The tablets are called the "tablets of the Testimony," and we are not informed what the "Testimony" is.

35

¹And Moses assembled all of the congregation of the children of Israel and said to them, "These are the things that YHWH commanded, to do them: ²Six days work shall be done, and in the seventh day you shall have a holy thing, a Sabbath, a ceasing to YHWH. Anyone who does work in it shall be put to death. ³You shall not burn a fire in all of your homes on the Sabbath day."

⁴And Moses said to all of the congregation of the children of Israel, saying, "This is the thing that YHWH commanded, saying, ⁵'Take a donation for YHWH from among you. Everyone whose heart is moved shall bring it, YHWH's donation: gold and silver and bronze ⁶and blue and purple and crimson and linen and goats' hair ⁷and rams' skins dyed red and leather skins and acacia wood ⁸and oil for lighting and spices for the anointing oil and for the incense fragrances ⁹and onyx stones and stones to be set for the ephod and for the breastplate. ¹⁰And let everyone wise of heart among you come and make everything that YHWH has commanded: ¹¹the Tabernacle, its tent and its cover and its clasps and its frames, its bars, its columns and its bases, ¹²the ark and its poles, the atonement dais and the covering pavilion, ¹³the table and its poles and all of its equipment and the show bread ¹⁴and the menorah for lighting and its equipment and its lamps and the oil for lighting ¹⁵and the incense altar and its poles and the anointing oil and the incense fragrances and the entrance cover for the Tabernacle's entrance, ¹⁶the altar of burnt offering and the bronze grate that it has, its poles and all of its equipment, the basin and its stand, ¹⁷the courtyard's hangings, its columns and its bases and the cover of the courtyard's gate, ¹⁸the Tabernacle's pegs and the courtyard's pegs and their cords, ¹⁹the fabric clothes for ministering in the Holy, the holy clothes for Aaron the priest, and his sons' clothes for functioning as priests.'"

²⁰And all of the congregation of the children of Israel went out from in front of Moses. ²¹And everyone whose heart inspired him came, and everyone whose spirit moved him brought a contribution for YHWH for the work of the Tent of Meeting and for all of its construction and for the holy clothes. ²²And the men came together with the women. All whose hearts moved them had brought brooches and earrings and rings and ornaments, every kind of gold item. And every man who brought an elevation offering of gold to YHWH ²³and every man with whom was found blue and purple and scarlet and linen and goats' hair and rams' skins dyed red and leather skins had brought them. ²⁴Everyone making a donation of silver and bronze had brought YHWH's donation. And everyone with whom was found acacia wood for all the work of the construction had brought it. ²⁵And every woman who was wise of heart with her hands had spun, and they brought yarn, the blue and

the purple, the scarlet and the linen. ²⁶And all the women whose hearts inspired them with wisdom had spun the goats' hair. ²⁷And the chieftains had brought onyx stones and stones to be set for the ephod and for the breastplate ²⁸and the spice and the oil for lighting and for the anointing oil and for the incense fragrances. ²⁹Every man and woman whose heart moved them to bring for all the work that YHWH had commanded to do by the hand of Moses: the children of Israel brought a contribution for YHWH.

³⁰And Moses said to the children of Israel, "See, YHWH has called Bezalel, son of Uri, son of Hur, of the tribe of Judah by name, ³¹and He has filled him with the spirit of God in wisdom, in understanding and in knowledge and in every kind of work ³²and to form conceptions to make in gold and in silver and in bronze ³³and in cutting stone for setting and in cutting wood, for making every kind of conceived work. ³⁴And He has put it in his heart to instruct: he and Oholiab, son of Ahisamach, of the tribe of Dan. ³⁵He has filled them with wisdom of heart to do all the work of the cutter and the designer and the embroiderer in the blue and in the purple, in the scarlet and in the linen and the weaver: those who do every kind of work and form conceptions.

36

¹And Bezalel and Oholiab and every man who is wise of heart, in whom YHWH has put wisdom and understanding to know how to do all the work of the service of the Holy shall do it, for everything that YHWH has commanded."

²And Moses called Bezalel and Oholiab and every man who was wise of heart, in whose heart YHWH had put wisdom, everyone whose heart inspired him to come forward for the work, to do it. ³And they took from in front of Moses all of the donation that the children of Israel had brought for the work of the construction of the Holy, to do it. And they had brought him more contribution, morning by morning. ⁴And all the wise persons who were doing all the work of the Holy came, each from his kind of work that they were doing, ⁵and they said to Moses, saying, "The people are bringing more than enough for the construction, for the work that YHWH has commanded, to do it!"

⁶And Moses commanded, and they passed an announcement through the camp saying, "Man and woman: let them not do any more work for the donation for the Holy." And the people were held back from bringing. ⁷And the work had been enough for them, for all the work, to do it and more. ⁸And all those who were wise of heart among those who were doing the work made the Tabernacle with ten curtains of woven linen and blue and purple and scarlet, with cherubs. They made them designer's work. ⁹The length of one curtain was twenty-eight in cubits, and the width of one curtain four in

cubits: one size to all the curtains. ¹⁰And he connected five of the curtains, one to one; and he connected five curtains, one to one. ¹¹And he made loops of blue on the side of one curtain at the end of the connected group. He did so in the side of the end curtain in the second connected group. ¹²He made fifty loops in the one curtain and made fifty loops in the end of the curtain that was in the second connected group with the loops parallel: one to one. ¹³And he made fifty clasps of gold and connected the curtains, one to one, with the clasps. And the Tabernacle was one.

¹⁴And he made curtains of goats' hair for the tent over the Tabernacle. He made them eleven curtains. ¹⁵The length of one curtain was thirty in cubits, and the width of one curtain was four cubits: one size for eleven curtains. ¹⁶And he connected five of the curtains by themselves and six of the curtains by themselves. ¹⁷And he made fifty loops on the side of the end curtain in the connected group and made fifty loops on the side of the curtain of the second connected group. ¹⁸And he made fifty bronze clasps to connect the tent, to be one. ¹⁹And he made a covering for the tent of rams' skins dyed red and a covering of leather skins above.

²⁰And he made the frames for the Tabernacle of acacia wood, standing. ²¹The frame's length was ten cubits, and the width of one frame was a cubit and a half cubit. ²²One frame had two projections, aligned one to one: so he made for all of the Tabernacle's frames. ²³And he made the frames for the Tabernacle: twenty frames for the south side—to the south. ²⁴And he made forty bases of silver under the twenty frames: two bases under one frame for its two projections and two bases under each other frame for its two projections. ²⁵And for the Tabernacle's second side, for the north side, he made twenty frames ²⁶and their forty bases of silver, two bases under one frame and two bases under each other frame. ²⁷And for the rear of the Tabernacle, to the west, he made six frames. ²⁸And he made two frames for the Tabernacle's corners in the rear, ²⁹and they were doubles from below, and together they were integrated on its top to one ring. He made it so for the two of them, for the two corners. ³⁰And they were eight frames and their bases of silver, sixteen bases, two bases and two bases under each one frame. ³¹And he made bars of acacia wood: five for the frames of one side of the Tabernacle ³²and five bars for the frames of the second side of the Tabernacle and five bars for the frames of the side of the Tabernacle at the rear, to the west. ³³And he made the middle bar to extend through the frames from end to end. ³⁴And he plated the frames with gold, and he made their rings gold, housings for the bars, and he plated the bars with gold.

³⁵And he made the pavilion of blue and purple and scarlet and woven linen; he made it designer's work with cherubs. ³⁶And he made four acacia columns for it and plated them with gold, their hooks of gold, and he cast

four bases of silver for them. ³⁷And he made a cover for the entrance of the tent: blue and purple and scarlet and woven linen—embroiderer's work—³⁸and its five columns and their hooks, and he plated their tops and their bands with gold, and their five bases were bronze.

37

¹And Bezalel made the ark of acacia wood, its length two and a half cubits and its width a cubit and a half and its height a cubit and a half. ²And he plated it with pure gold inside and outside. And he made a border of gold all around for it. ³And he cast four rings of gold for it on its four bottoms: and two rings on its one side and two rings on its second side. ⁴And he made poles of acacia wood and plated them with gold ⁵and brought the poles through the rings on the ark's sides, in order to carry the ark. ⁶And he made an atonement dais of pure gold, its length two and a half cubits and its width a cubit and a half. ⁷And he made two cherubs of gold—he made them of hammered work—at the two ends of the atonement dais, ⁸one cherub at this end and one cherub at that end. He made the cherubs from the atonement dais at its two sides. ⁹And the two cherubs were spreading wings above, covering over the atonement dais with their wings, and their faces each toward its brother: the cherubs' faces were toward the atonement dais.

¹⁰And he made the table of acacia wood, its length two cubits and its width a cubit and its height a cubit and a half. ¹¹And he plated it with pure gold and made a border of gold all around for it ¹²and made a rim of a handbreadth for it all around and made a border of gold for its rim all around. ¹³And he cast four rings of gold for it and put the rings on the four corners that its four legs had. ¹⁴The rings were in juxtaposition to the rim, housings for the poles in order to carry the table. ¹⁵And he made the poles of acacia wood and plated them with gold in order to carry the table. ¹⁶And he made the items that were on the table—its dishes and its pans and its bowls and its jars with which libations would be poured—of pure gold.

¹⁷And he made the menorah of pure gold. He made the menorah of hammered work—its shaft and its branch, its cups, its ornaments, and its flowers were part of it— ¹⁸and six branches coming out from its sides, three of the menorah's branches from its one side and three of the menorah's branches from its second side, ¹⁹three almond-shaped cups in the one branch, with ornament and flower, and three almond-shaped cups in the other branch, with ornament and flower. So it was for the six branches that came out from the menorah, ²⁰and four almond-shaped cups within the menorah, with its ornaments and its flowers, ²¹and an ornament under the two branches from it, and an ornament under the two branches from it, and an ornament under

the two branches from it, for the six branches that came out from it. ²²Their ornaments and their branches were part of it, all of it one hammered work of pure gold. ²³And he made its lamps, seven, and its tongs and its fire-holders of pure gold. ²⁴He made it and all of its equipment out of a talent of pure gold.

²⁵And he made the incense altar of acacia wood: its length a cubit and its width a cubit, square, and its height two cubits, its horns were a part of it. ²⁶And he plated it with pure gold, its roof and its walls all around and its horns. And he made a border of gold for it all around. ²⁷And he made two rings of gold for it below its rim on its two sides, on its two sidewalls, for housings for poles with which to carry it. ²⁸And he made the poles of acacia wood and plated them with gold. ²⁹And he made the holy anointing oil and the pure incense fragrances, the work of an ointment-maker.

38

¹And he made the altar of burnt offering of acacia wood, its length five cubits and its width five cubits, square, and its height three cubits. ²And he made its horns on its four corners. Its horns were part of it. And he plated it with bronze. ³And he made all of the altar's equipment: the pots, the shovels and the basins, the forks and the fire-holders. He made all of its equipment bronze. ⁴And he made a grate for the altar, a network of bronze, under its ledge up to the middle of it. ⁵And he cast four rings in the bronze grate's four ends: housings for the poles. ⁶And he made the poles of acacia wood and plated them with bronze ⁷and brought the poles through the rings on the altar's sides in order to carry it with them. He made it hollow of boards.

⁸And he made the basin of bronze and its stand of bronze with the mirrors of the women who served at the entrance of the Tent of Meeting.

⁹And he made the courtyard: for the south side—to the south, the courtyard's hangings of woven linen, a hundred in cubits, ¹⁰their columns twenty, and their bases twenty of bronze, and the columns' hooks and their rods of silver. ¹¹And for the north side: a hundred in cubits, their columns twenty, and their bases twenty of bronze, and the columns' hooks and their bands of silver. ¹²And for the west side: hangings of fifty in cubits, their columns ten, and their bases ten, the columns' hooks and their bands of silver. ¹³And the courtyard's width for the east side—to the east—fifty cubits. ¹⁴Fifteen cubits of hangings to the panel, their columns three and their bases three; ¹⁵and the second panel—on this side and that side of the courtyard's gate—hangings of fifteen cubits, their columns three and their bases three. ¹⁶All of the courtyard's hangings, all around, were woven linen. ¹⁷And the column's bases were bronze, the columns' hooks and their bands were silver, and the plating of

their tops was silver, and they were banded with silver: all of the courtyard's columns. ¹⁸And the cover of the courtyard's gate was embroiderer's work, blue and purple and scarlet and woven linen, and twenty cubits in length, and five cubits in height in the width, in juxtaposition to the courtyard's hangings. ¹⁹And their columns were four and their bases four of bronze, their hooks silver, and the plating of their tops and their bands silver. ²⁰And all of the pegs of the Tabernacle and the courtyard all around were bronze.

²¹These are the accounts of the Tabernacle, the Tabernacle of the Testimony, that were made by Moses' word, the work of the Levites by the hand of Ithamar, son of Aaron, the priest. ²²And Bezalel, son of Uri, son of Hur, of the tribe of Judah, made everything that YHWH had commanded Moses. ²³And with him was Oholiab, son of Ahisamach, of the tribe of Dan, an engraver and designer and embroiderer in blue and in purple and in scarlet and in linen. ²⁴All the gold that was used for the work, in all the work of the Holy: and the gold of the elevation offering was twenty-nine talents and seven hundred thirty shekels by the shekel of the Holy.

²⁵And the silver of the congregation's accounts was a hundred talents and a thousand seven hundred seventy-five shekels by the shekel of the Holy: ²⁶a beqa per head, half of a shekel by the shekel of the Holy, for everyone who passed through the counts, from twenty years old and up, for six hundred thousand and three thousand five hundred fifty. ²⁷And the hundred talents of silver were for casting the bases of the Holy and the bases of the pavilion, a hundred bases to the hundred talents, a talent per base. ²⁸And he made the thousand seven hundred seventy-five into hooks for the columns, and he plated their tops and banded them.

²⁹And the bronze of the elevation offering was seventy talents and two thousand four hundred shekels. ³⁰And with it he made the bases of the entrance of the Tent of Meeting and the bronze altar and the bronze network that it had and all of the altar's equipment ³¹and the bases of the courtyard all around and the bases of the courtyard's gate and all of the Tabernacle's pegs and all of the courtyard's pegs all around.

39

¹And from the blue and the purple and the scarlet they made fabric clothes for ministering in the Holy, and they made the holy clothes that were Aaron's, as YHWH had commanded Moses.

²And he made the ephod: gold, blue, and purple and scarlet and woven linen. ³And they hammered out foil sheets of the gold, and he cut threads to use among the blue and among the purple and among the scarlet and among

the linen—designer's work. ⁴They made shoulder-pieces for it, connected: on its two ends it was connected. ⁵And its ephod designed belt that was on it was a part of it, like its work, gold, blue, and purple and scarlet and woven linen, as YHWH had commanded Moses. ⁶And they made the onyx stones surrounded by settings of gold, inscribed with signet inscriptions with the names of the children of Israel. ⁷And he set them on the ephod's shoulder-pieces, commemorative stones for the children of Israel, as YHWH had commanded Moses.

⁸And he made the breastplate, designer's work, like the work of the ephod: gold, blue, and purple and scarlet and woven linen. ⁹It was square. They made the breastplate doubled, its length a span and its width a span, doubled. ¹⁰And they mounted four rows of stones in it: a row of a carnelian, a topaz, and an emerald: the one row; ¹¹and the second row: a ruby, a sapphire, and a diamond; ¹²and the third row: a jacinth, an agate, and an amethyst; ¹³and the fourth row: a beryl, an onyx, and a jasper—set in gold in their mountings. ¹⁴And the stones: they were with the names of the children of Israel, twelve with their names, signet engravings, each with its name, for twelve tribes. ¹⁵And they made twisted chains, rope work, of pure gold, on the breastplate. ¹⁶And they made two settings of gold and two rings of gold and put the two rings on the two ends of the breastplate ¹⁷and put the two ropes of gold on the two rings at the ends of the breastplate. ¹⁸And they put the two ends of the two ropes on the two settings and put them on the ephod's shoulder-pieces opposite the front of it. ¹⁹And they made two rings of gold and put them on the breastplate's two ends on its side that is adjacent to the ephod, inward. ²⁰And they made two rings of gold and put them on the ephod's two shoulder-pieces below, opposite the front of it, by its connection, above the ephod's designed belt. ²¹And they attached the breastplate from its rings to the ephod's rings with a blue string so it would be on the ephod's designed belt and the breastplate would not be detached from the ephod, as YHWH had commanded Moses.

²²And he made the robe of the ephod, weaver's work, all of blue, ²³and the robe's opening within it like the opening of a coat of mail, a binding for its opening all around so it would not be torn. ²⁴And they made on the robe's skirts pomegranates of blue and purple and scarlet, woven. ²⁵And they made bells of pure gold and put the bells among the pomegranates on the robe's skirts all around among the pomegranates: ²⁶bell and pomegranate, bell and pomegranate, on the robe's skirts all around, for ministering, as YHWH had commanded Moses.

²⁷And they made the coats of linen, weaver's work, for Aaron and for his sons, ²⁸and the headdress of linen and the beautiful hats of linen and the

shorts of linen, woven linen, ²⁹and the sash of woven linen and blue and purple and scarlet, embroiderer's work, as YHWH had commanded Moses.

³⁰And they made the plate of the crown of Holiness of pure gold, and they wrote on it a text of signet inscriptions: "Holiness to YHWH." ³¹And they put a blue string on it for putting it on the headdress above, as YHWH had commanded Moses.

³²And all of the construction of the Tabernacle of the Tent of Meeting was finished. And the children of Israel did according to everything that YHWH had commanded Moses. They did so. ³³And they brought the Tabernacle to Moses: the tent and all of its equipment, its clasps, its frames, its bars, and its columns and its bases, ³⁴and the covering of rams' skins dyed red and the covering of leather skins, and the covering pavilion, ³⁵the Ark of the Testimony and its poles and the atonement dais, ³⁶the table and all of its equipment and the show bread, ³⁷the pure menorah, its lamps, lamps for the row, and all of its equipment, and the oil for lighting, ³⁸and the golden altar and the anointing oil and the incense of fragrances and the cover of the entrance of the Tent, ³⁹the bronze altar and the bronze grate that it had, its poles and all of its equipment, the basin and its stand, ⁴⁰the courtyard's hangings, its columns and its bases and the cover for the courtyard's gate, its cords and its pegs, and all the equipment for the service of the Tabernacle of the Tent of Meeting, ⁴¹the fabric clothes for ministering in the Holy, the holy clothes for Aaron, the priest, and his sons' clothes for functioning as priests. ⁴²According to everything that YHWH had commanded Moses: so the children of Israel did all of the construction. ⁴³And Moses saw all of the work; and, here, they had done it as YHWH had commanded. They did so. And Moses blessed them.

40

¹And YHWH spoke to Moses, saying, ²"On the day of the first month, on the first of the month, you shall set up the Tabernacle of the Tent of Meeting. ³And you shall set the Ark of the Testimony there and have the pavilion cover over the ark. ⁴And you shall bring the table and make its arrangement, and bring the menorah and put up its lamps. ⁵And you shall put the golden altar for incense in front of the Ark of the Testimony, and you shall set the cover of the entrance of the Tabernacle. ⁶And you shall put the altar of burnt offering in front of the entrance of the Tabernacle of the Tent of Meeting. ⁷And you shall put the basin between the Tent of Meeting and the altar and put water there. ⁸And you shall set the courtyard all around and put on the cover of the courtyard's gate. ⁹And you shall take the anointing oil and anoint the Tabernacle and everything that is in it, and you shall make it and

all of its equipment holy, and it will be holiness. ¹⁰And you shall anoint the altar of burnt offering and all of its equipment, and you shall make the altar holy: and the altar will be holy of holies. ¹¹And you shall anoint the basin and its stand and make it holy.

¹²"And you shall bring Aaron and his sons forward to the entrance of the Tent of Meeting and wash them with water. ¹³And you shall dress Aaron with the holy clothes and anoint him and make him holy, and he shall function as a priest for me. ¹⁴And you shall bring his sons forward and dress them with coats ¹⁵and anoint them as you anointed their father, and they shall function as priests for me. And it will be for their anointing to be theirs as an eternal priesthood through their generations." ¹⁶And Moses did it. According to everything that YHWH commanded him, he did so.

¹⁷And it was: in the first month, in the second year, on the first of the month, the Tabernacle was set up. ¹⁸And Moses set up the Tabernacle and put on its bases and set its frames and put on its bars and set up its columns. ¹⁹And he spread the Tent over the Tabernacle and set the Tent's covering on it above, as YHWH had commanded Moses. ²⁰And he took the Testimony and put it into the ark, and he set the poles on the ark, and he put the atonement dais on the ark above. ²¹And he brought the ark into the Tabernacle and set the covering pavilion and covered over the Ark of the Testimony, as YHWH had commanded Moses.

²²And he put the table in the Tent of Meeting on the northward side of the Tabernacle, outside of the pavilion. ²³And he made the arrangement of bread on it in front of YHWH, as YHWH had commanded Moses.

²⁴And he set the menorah in the Tent of Meeting opposite the table, on the southward side of the Tabernacle, ²⁵and he put up the lamps in front of YHWH, as YHWH had commanded Moses.

²⁶And he set the golden altar in the Tent of Meeting in front of the pavilion, ²⁷and he burned the incense of fragrances on it, as YHWH had commanded Moses.

²⁸And he set the cover of the entrance of the Tabernacle. ²⁹And he set the altar of burnt offering at the entrance of the Tabernacle of the Tent of Meeting, and he offered up the burnt offering and the grain offering on it, as YHWH had commanded Moses.

³⁰And he set the basin between the Tent of Meeting and the altar, and he put water for washing there. ³¹And Moses and Aaron and his sons washed their hands and their feet from it. ³²When they came to the Tent of Meeting and when they came forward to the altar they would wash, as YHWH had commanded Moses.

³³And he set up the courtyard all around the Tabernacle and the altar, and he put on the cover of the courtyard's gate.

And Moses finished the work.

³⁴And the cloud covered the Tent of Meeting, and YHWH's glory filled the Tabernacle. ³⁵And Moses was not able to come into the Tent of Meeting, because the cloud had settled on it and YHWH's glory filled the Tabernacle. ³⁶And when the cloud was lifted from on the Tabernacle, the children of Israel would travel—in all their travels— ³⁷and if the cloud would not be lifted, then they would not travel until the day that it would be lifted. ³⁸Because YHWH's cloud was on the Tabernacle by day, and fire would be in it at night, before the eyes of all the house of Israel in all their travels.

LEVITICUS

1

¹And He called to Moses, and YHWH spoke to him from the Tent of Meeting, saying, ²"Speak to the children of Israel. And you shall say to them: A human from you who will make an offering to YHWH—you shall make your offering from the domestic animals: from the herd and from the flock.

³"If his offering is a burnt offering from the herd, he shall make it an unblemished male. He shall bring it forward to the entrance of the Tent of Meeting for his acceptance in front of YHWH. ⁴And he shall lay his hand on the head of the burnt offering, and it will be accepted for him, to atone for him. ⁵And he shall slaughter the herd animal in front of YHWH, and the sons of Aaron, the priests, shall bring the blood forward and fling the blood on the altar, all around, which is at the entrance of the Tent of Meeting. ⁶And he shall flay the burnt offering and cut it into its parts. ⁷And the sons of Aaron, the priest, shall put fire on the altar and arrange wood on the fire. ⁸And the sons of Aaron, the priests, shall arrange the parts, the head, and the suet on the wood that is on the fire that is on the altar. ⁹And he shall wash its innards and its legs with water. And the priest shall burn it all to smoke at the altar, a burnt offering, an offering by fire of a pleasant smell to YHWH.

¹⁰"And if his offering is from the flock—from the sheep or from the goats—for a burnt offering, he shall make it an unblemished male. ¹¹And he shall slaughter it on the northward side of the altar in front of YHWH. And the sons of Aaron, the priests, shall fling its blood on the altar, all around. ¹²And he shall cut it into its parts and its head and its suet. And the priest shall arrange them on the wood that is on the fire that is on the altar. ¹³And he shall wash the innards and the legs with water. And the priest shall bring it all forward and burn it to smoke at the altar. It is a burnt offering, an offering by fire of a pleasant smell to YHWH.

¹⁴"And if his offering to YHWH is a burnt offering from birds, then he shall make his offering from turtledoves or from pigeons. ¹⁵And the priest shall bring it forward to the altar and wring its head and burn it to smoke at the altar, and its blood shall be drained on the wall of the altar. ¹⁶And he shall take away its crop with its feathers and throw it beside the altar eastward to the place of the ashes. ¹⁷And he shall tear it open by its wings—he shall not divide it—and the priest shall burn it to smoke at the altar on the wood that is on the fire. It is a burnt offering, an offering by fire of a pleasant smell to YHWH.

2

¹"And a person who will make an offering of a grain offering to YHWH, his offering shall be of fine flour, and he shall pour oil on it and put frankincense on it. ²And he shall bring it to the sons of Aaron, the priests. And he shall take the fill of his fist from there: from its fine flour and from its oil in addition to all of its frankincense. And the priest shall burn a representative portion of it to smoke at the altar, an offering by fire of a pleasant smell to YHWH. ³And the remainder from the grain offering is Aaron's and his sons', the holy of holies from YHWH's offerings by fire.

⁴"And if he will make an offering of an oven-baked grain offering: fine flour, unleavened cakes mixed with oil and unleavened wafers with oil poured on them.

⁵"And if your offering is a grain offering on a griddle, it shall be fine flour, mixed with oil, unleavened. ⁶Break it into pieces and pour oil on it. It is a grain offering.

⁷"And if your offering is a grain offering from a pan, it shall be made of fine flour in oil.

⁸"And you shall bring the grain offering that one will make from these things to YHWH, and one shall bring it forward to the priest, and he shall bring it over to the altar. ⁹And the priest shall lift from the grain offering a representative portion of it and burn it to smoke at the altar, an offering by fire of a pleasant smell to YHWH. ¹⁰And the remainder from the grain offering is Aaron's and his sons', the holy of holies from YHWH's offerings by fire. ¹¹Every grain offering that you will bring forward to YHWH shall not be made with leavening, because all leaven and all honey: you shall not burn any of it to smoke as an offering by fire to YHWH. ¹²You shall bring them forward to YHWH as an offering of a first thing, but they shall not go up to the altar as a pleasant smell. ¹³And you shall sprinkle every offering of a grain offering with salt. And you shall not let the salt of your God's covenant cease from on your grain offering; you shall bring salt on all your offerings.

¹⁴"And if you will bring a grain offering of firstfruits to YHWH, you shall bring the grain offering of your firstfruits ripe, parched with fire, groats of fresh grain. ¹⁵And you shall put oil on it and set frankincense on it. It is a grain offering. ¹⁶And the priest shall burn a representative portion of it to smoke, from its groats and from its oil, in addition to all of its frankincense, an offering by fire to YHWH.

3

¹"And if his offering is a peace-offering sacrifice, if he is offering from the herd, whether male or female, he shall make it unblemished in front of YHWH. ²And he shall lay his hand on the head of his offering and slaughter it at the entrance of the Tent of Meeting. And the sons of Aaron, the priests, shall fling the blood on the altar all around. ³And he shall bring forward from the peace-offering sacrifice an offering by fire to YHWH: the fat that covers the innards and all the fat that is on the innards ⁴and the two kidneys and the fat that is on them, that is on the loins; and the lobe on the liver: he shall take it away with the kidneys. ⁵And the sons of Aaron shall burn it to smoke at the altar upon the burnt offering that is on the wood that is on the fire, an offering by fire of a pleasant smell to YHWH.

⁶"And if his offering as a peace-offering sacrifice to YHWH is from the flock, male or female, he shall make it unblemished. ⁷If he is making his offering a sheep, then he shall bring it forward in front of YHWH ⁸and lay his hand on the head of his offering and slaughter it in front of the Tent of Meeting. And the sons of Aaron shall fling its blood on the altar all around. ⁹And he shall bring forward from the peace-offering sacrifice an offering by fire to YHWH: its fat, the entire fat tail—he shall take it away from the backbone—and the fat that covers the innards and all the fat that is on the innards ¹⁰and the two kidneys and the fat that is on them, that is on the loins; and the lobe on the liver: he shall take it away with the kidneys. ¹¹And the priest shall burn it to smoke at the altar: food, an offering by fire to YHWH.

¹²"And if his offering is a goat, then he shall bring it forward in front of YHWH ¹³and lay his hand on its head and slaughter it in front of the Tent of Meeting. And the sons of Aaron shall fling its blood on the altar all around. ¹⁴And he shall make his offering from it, an offering by fire to YHWH: the fat that covers the innards and all the fat that is on the innards ¹⁵and the two kidneys and the fat that is on them, that is on the loins; and the lobe on the liver: he shall take it away with the kidneys. ¹⁶And the priest shall burn them to smoke at the altar: food, an offering by fire as a pleasant smell. All fat is YHWH's. ¹⁷It is an eternal law, through your generations, in all your homes: you shall not eat any fat and any blood."

4

¹And YHWH spoke to Moses, saying, ²"Speak to the children of Israel, saying: A person who sins by mistake—of any of YHWH's commandments that are not to be done—and does any one of them:

³"If the anointed priest will sin, causing the people's guilt, then he shall bring forward for his sin that he committed: a bull of the cattle, unblemished, for YHWH as a sin offering. ⁴And he shall bring the bull to the entrance of the Tent of Meeting in front of YHWH. And he shall lay his hand on the bull's head and slaughter the bull in front of YHWH. ⁵And the anointed priest shall take some of the bull's blood and bring it to the Tent of Meeting. ⁶And the priest shall dip his finger in the blood and sprinkle some of the blood seven times in front of YHWH before the pavilion of the Holy. ⁷And the priest shall put some of the blood on the horns of the altar of the incense of fragrances, in front of YHWH, which is in the Tent of Meeting. And he shall spill all of the bull's blood at the base of the altar of burnt offering, which is at the entrance of the Tent of Meeting. ⁸And he shall take off all the fat of the bull of the sin offering from it: the fat that covers the innards and all the fat that is on the innards ⁹and the two kidneys and the fat that is on them, that is on the loins; and the lobe on the liver: he shall take it away with the kidneys ¹⁰when it will be taken off from the ox of the peace-offering sacrifice. And the priest shall burn them to smoke on the altar of burnt offering. ¹¹And the bull's skin and all of its meat with its head and with its legs and its innards and its dung: ¹²and he shall bring all of the bull outside the camp, to a pure place, to the place where ash is spilled, and burn it on wood in fire. It shall be burned at the place where ash is spilled.

¹³"And if all the congregation of Israel will make a mistake, and something will be hidden from the community's eyes, and they do one of any of YHWH's commandments that are not to be done, and they are guilty, ¹⁴and the sin over which they have sinned will become known, then the community shall bring forward a bull of the cattle as a sin offering, and they shall bring it in front of the Tent of Meeting. ¹⁵And the community's elders shall lay their hands on the bull's head in front of YHWH, and he shall slaughter the bull in front of YHWH. ¹⁶And the anointed priest shall bring some of the bull's blood to the Tent of Meeting. ¹⁷And the priest shall dip his finger from the blood and sprinkle seven times in front of YHWH before the pavilion. ¹⁸And he shall put some of the blood on the horns of the altar that is in front of YHWH, that is in the Tent of Meeting, and he shall spill all of the blood at the base of the altar of burnt offering, which is at the entrance of the Tent of Meeting. ¹⁹And

he shall take off all of its fat from it and burn it to smoke at the altar. ²⁰And he shall do to the bull as he did to the bull of the sin offering. So he shall do to it. And the priest shall make atonement over them, and it will be forgiven for them. ²¹And he shall bring the bull outside the camp and burn it as he burned the first bull. It is the community's sin offering.

²²"When a chieftain will sin and do one of any of the commandments of YHWH, his God, that are not to be done, by mistake, and he is guilty, ²³or his sin by which he has sinned has been made known to him, then he shall bring his offering, a goat, male, unblemished. ²⁴And he shall lay his hand on the goat's head and slaughter it at the place where he would slaughter a burnt offering in front of YHWH. It is a sin offering. ²⁵And the priest shall take some of the blood of the sin offering with his finger and put it on the horns of the altar of burnt offering, and he shall spill its blood at the base of the altar of burnt offering. ²⁶And he shall burn all of its fat to smoke at the altar like the fat of the peace-offering sacrifice. And the priest shall make atonement over him from his sin, and it will be forgiven for him.

²⁷"And if one person from the people of the land will sin by mistake by doing one of YHWH's commandments that are not to be done and is guilty, ²⁸or his sin that he has committed has been made known to him, then he shall bring his offering, a goat, unblemished, female, for his sin that he committed. ²⁹And he shall lay his hand on the head of the sin offering and slaughter the sin offering at the place of burnt offering. ³⁰And the priest shall take some of its blood with his finger and put it on the horns of the altar of burnt offering, and he shall spill all of its blood at the base of the altar. ³¹And he shall take away all of its fat as the fat was taken away from on the peace-offering sacrifice, and the priest shall burn it to smoke at the altar as a pleasant smell to YHWH, and the priest shall make atonement over him, and it will be forgiven for him.

³²"And if he will bring a lamb as his offering for a sin offering, he shall bring a female, unblemished. ³³And he shall lay his hand on the head of the sin offering and slaughter it as a sin offering at the place where he would slaughter a burnt offering. ³⁴And the priest shall take some of the blood of the sin offering with his finger and put it on the horns of the altar of burnt offering, and he shall spill all of its blood at the base of the altar. ³⁵And he shall take away all of its fat as the sheep's fat was taken away from the peace-offering sacrifice, and the priest shall burn them to smoke at the altar with YHWH's offerings by fire, and the priest shall make atonement over him, over his sin that he committed, and it will be forgiven for him.

5

[1]"And a person who will sin in that he has heard a pronouncement of an oath, and he was a witness—whether he saw or he knew: if he will not tell, then he shall bear his crime.

[2]"Or a person who will touch any impure thing or the carcass of an impure wild animal or the carcass of an impure domestic animal or the carcass of an impure swarming creature, and it was hidden from him, so he had become impure and had become guilty; [3]or when he will touch a human's impurity—for any impurity of his through which he will become impure—and it was hidden from him, and then he had come to know and had become guilty; [4]or a person who will swear so as to let out of his lips to do bad or to do good—for anything that a human would let out in an oath—and it was hidden from him, and then he had come to know and had become guilty by one of these: [5]And it will be that when he becomes guilty by one of these he shall confess that he has sinned over it [6]and he shall bring his guilt offering to YHWH over his sin that he has committed: a female from the flock, a sheep or a goat, as a sin offering, and the priest shall make atonement over him from his sin.

[7]"And if his hand will not attain enough for a sheep, then he shall bring as his guilt offering for having sinned two turtledoves or two pigeons to YHWH: one for a sin offering and one for a burnt offering. [8]And he shall bring them to the priest, and he shall bring forward the one that is for the sin offering first and will wring but not separate its head at the point opposite its neck. [9]And he shall sprinkle some of the blood of the sin offering on the wall of the altar, and what remains of the blood shall be drained at the base of the altar. It is a sin offering. [10]And he shall make the second one a burnt offering according to the required manner. And the priest shall make atonement over him from his sin that he committed, and it shall be forgiven for him.

[11]"And if his hand cannot attain enough for two turtledoves or two pigeons, then he shall bring as his offering for having sinned a tenth of an ephah of fine flour for a sin offering. He shall not set oil on it, and he shall not put frankincense on it, because it is a sin offering. [12]And he shall bring it to the priest, and the priest shall take the fill of his fist from it, a representative portion of it, and he shall burn it to smoke at the altar with YHWH's offerings by fire. It is a sin offering. [13]And the priest shall make atonement over him, over his sin that he committed, from one of these, and it shall be forgiven for him. And it shall be the priest's, like the grain offering."

[14]And YHWH spoke to Moses, saying, [15]"A person who will make a breach and sin by mistake among YHWH's holy things: he shall bring his guilt offering to YHWH, an unblemished ram from the flock by your evalua-

tion of silver by shekels, by the shekel of the Holy, as a guilt offering. ¹⁶And for what he sinned from the Holy he shall pay and add to it a fifth of it and give it to the priest, and the priest shall make atonement over him with the ram of the guilt offering, and it shall be forgiven for him.

¹⁷"And if a person who will sin and commit one of any of YHWH's commandments that are not to be done and did not know and became guilty, then he shall bear his crime. ¹⁸And he shall bring an unblemished ram from the flock by your evaluation as a guilt offering to the priest, and the priest shall make atonement over him, over his mistake that he made and had not known, and it shall be forgiven for him. ¹⁹It is a guilt offering. He is guilty to YHWH."

²⁰And YHWH spoke to Moses, saying, ²¹"A person who will sin and make a breach against YHWH and tell a lie against his fellow in a matter of a deposit or something set in hand or by robbery, or has exploited his fellow ²²or has found something that was lost and has lied about it or sworn to a falsehood—for one of any of these that a human will do to sin: ²³it will be, when he sins and is guilty, that he shall bring back the thing that he robbed or the thing that he coerced or the thing that was deposited with him or the lost thing that he found ²⁴or anything about which he swore as a falsehood, and he shall pay it in its worth and add to it a fifth of it. He shall give it to the one whose it is on the day of his being guilty, ²⁵and he shall bring his guilt offering to YHWH: an unblemished ram from the flock by your evaluation as a guilt offering, to the priest. ²⁶And the priest shall atone over him in front of YHWH, and it will be forgiven for him, for any one out of all that he will do to become guilty through it."

6 ¹And YHWH spoke to Moses, saying, ²"Command Aaron and his sons, saying: This is the instruction for the burnt offering. It is the one that goes up on its place of burning on the altar all night until morning, and the altar's fire shall be kept burning through it. ³And the priest shall wear his linen garment and shall wear linen drawers on his flesh. And he shall lift the ashes to which the fire will consume the burnt offering on the altar, and he shall set them beside the altar. ⁴And he shall take off his clothes and wear other clothes, and he shall take the ashes outside the camp, to a pure place. ⁵And the fire on the altar shall be kept burning through it. It shall not go out. And the priest shall burn wood on it morning by morning, and he shall arrange the burnt offering on it, and he shall burn the fat of the peace offerings to smoke on it. ⁶Fire always shall be kept burning on the altar. It shall not go out.

[7]"And this is the instruction for the grain offering. The sons of Aaron shall bring it forward in front of YHWH to the front of the altar. [8]And he shall lift some of it in his fist, some of the fine flour of the grain offering and some of its oil and all of the frankincense that is on the grain offering, and he shall burn a representative portion of it to smoke at the altar as a pleasant smell to YHWH. [9]And Aaron and his sons shall eat the remainder of it. It shall be eaten as unleavened bread, in a holy place. They shall eat it in the courtyard of the Tent of Meeting. [10]It shall not be baked with leaven. I have given it as their portion from my offerings by fire. It is the holy of holies, like the sin offering and like the guilt offering. [11]Every male among the sons of Aaron shall eat it—an eternal law through your generations—from YHWH's offerings by fire. Anything that will touch them will become holy."

[12]And YHWH spoke to Moses, saying, [13]"This is the offering of Aaron and his sons that they shall bring to YHWH in the day of his being anointed: a tenth of an ephah of fine flour as a continual grain offering, half of it in the morning and half of it in the evening. [14]It shall be made on a griddle in oil. You shall bring it well mixed. You shall offer it as cakes of a grain offering of pieces, a pleasant smell to YHWH. [15]And the anointed priest in his place from among his sons shall do it, an eternal law, for YHWH: it shall be burnt to smoke entirely. [16]And every grain offering of a priest shall be done entirely. It shall not be eaten."

[17]And YHWH spoke to Moses, saying, [18]"Speak to Aaron and to his sons, saying: This is the instruction for the sin offering. In the place where the burnt offering will be slaughtered, the sin offering shall be slaughtered, in front of YHWH. It is the holy of holies. [19]The priest who makes it a sin offering shall eat it. It shall be eaten in a holy place, in the courtyard of the Tent of Meeting. [20]Anything that will touch the meat of it will become holy. And if some of its blood will spatter on clothing, you shall wash the thing on which it will spatter in a holy place. [21]And a clay container in which it will be boiled shall be broken. And if it was boiled in a brass container then it shall be scoured and rinsed with water. [22]Every male among the priests shall eat it. It is the holy of holies. [23]And every sin offering some of whose blood will be brought to the Tent of Meeting for atoning in the Holy shall not be eaten. It shall be burned in fire.

7

[1]"And this is the instruction for the guilt offering. It is the holy of holies. [2]They shall slaughter the guilt offering in the place where they slaughter the

burnt offering. And he shall fling its blood on the altar all around. ³And he shall bring forward from it all of its fat, the fat tail and the fat that covers the innards, ⁴and the two kidneys and the fat that is on them, that is on the loins; and the lobe on the liver: he shall take it away with the kidneys. ⁵And the priest shall burn them to smoke at the altar, an offering by fire to YHWH. It is a guilt offering. ⁶Every male among the priests shall eat it. It shall be eaten in a holy place. It is the holy of holies. ⁷As with the sin offering, so with the guilt offering: they have one instruction. The priest who will make atonement with it: it shall be his. ⁸And the priest who brings forward a man's burnt offering: the skin of the burnt offering that he brought forward is for the priest; it shall be his. ⁹And every grain offering that will be baked in an oven and every one made in a pan and on a griddle shall be for the priest who brings it; it shall be his. ¹⁰And every grain offering mixed with oil or dry shall be for all the sons of Aaron, each like his brother.

¹¹"And this is the instruction of the peace-offering sacrifice that one shall bring forward to YHWH. ¹²If he will bring it forward out of thanks, then he shall bring forward with the sacrifice of thanks unleavened cakes mixed with oil and unleavened wafers with oil poured on them and fine flour well mixed, cakes, mixed with oil. ¹³He shall make his offering with cakes of leavened bread, with his peace-offering sacrifice of thanks. ¹⁴And he shall bring forward from it one of each offering as a donation for YHWH. For the priest who flings the blood of the peace offerings: it shall be his. ¹⁵And the meat of his peace-offering sacrifice shall be eaten on the day of his offering. He shall not leave any of it until morning. ¹⁶And if his sacrificial offering is a vow or a contribution, it shall be eaten on the day that he brings forward his sacrifice, and on the next day what is left of it may be eaten. ¹⁷And what is left of the meat of the sacrifice on the third day shall be burned in fire. ¹⁸And if any of the meat of his peace-offering sacrifice will be eaten on the third day, it shall not be acceptable. The one who brings it forward: it shall not be counted for him. It shall be a repugnant thing. And the person who eats any of it shall bear his crime. ¹⁹And meat that will touch any impure thing shall not be eaten. It shall be burned in fire. And meat: everyone who is pure may eat meat, ²⁰but the person who will eat meat from the peace-offering sacrifice that is YHWH's while his impurity is on him, that person will be cut off from his people. ²¹And a person who will touch any impure thing, human impurity or an impure animal or any impure detestable thing, and will eat some of the meat of the peace-offering sacrifice that is YHWH's: that person will be cut off from his people."

²²And YHWH spoke to Moses, saying, ²³"Speak to the children of Israel, saying: You shall not eat any fat of an ox or sheep or goat. ²⁴And fat of a

carcass and fat of a torn animal may be used for any work, but you shall not eat it. ²⁵Because anyone who eats fat from an animal from which one would bring forward an offering by fire to YHWH, the person who eats it will be cut off from his people. ²⁶And you shall not eat any blood in all of your homes, a bird's or an animal's. ²⁷Any person who will eat any blood, that person will be cut off from his people."

²⁸And YHWH spoke to Moses, saying, ²⁹"Speak to the children of Israel, saying: The one who brings forward his peace-offering sacrifice to YHWH shall bring his offering to YHWH from his peace-offering sacrifice: ³⁰his hands shall bring YHWH's offerings by fire. He shall bring it, the fat with the breast: the breast so as to elevate it, an elevation offering in front of YHWH. ³¹And the priest shall burn the fat to smoke at the altar, and the breast shall be Aaron's and his sons'. ³²And you shall give the right thigh as a donation to the priest from your peace-offering sacrifices. ³³The one from the sons of Aaron who brings forward the blood of the peace offerings and the fat: the right thigh shall be his as a portion. ³⁴Because I have taken the breast of the elevation offering and the thigh of the donation from the children of Israel, from their peace-offering sacrifices, and I have given them to Aaron the priest and to his sons as an eternal law from the children of Israel."

³⁵This is the anointing of Aaron and the anointing of his sons from YHWH's offerings by fire in the day He brought them forward to function as priests for YHWH, ³⁶which YHWH commanded to give to them in the day of His anointing them from among the children of Israel, an eternal law through their generations.

³⁷This is the instruction* of the burnt offering, of the grain offering, and of the sin offering and of the guilt offering and of the ordination and of the peace-offering sacrifice, ³⁸which YHWH commanded Moses in Mount Sinai in the day that He commanded the children of Israel to make their offerings to YHWH in the wilderness of Sinai.**

---

*P claims to have the divine instruction (Hebrew *tôrāh*) sixteen times in Leviticus. But in the book of Jeremiah (which is connected with the Deuteronomistic literature), Jeremiah says, "How do you say, 'We're wise, and YHWH's *torah* is with us'? In fact, here, it was made for a lie, the lying pen of scribes!" See the next note and *Who Wrote the Bible?* p. 209.

**This conclusion (vv. 37–38) summarizes seven full chapters about offerings and sacrifices that are given "in the day" that Moses was commanded. Like other P passages, this P passage is rejected and reversed in the book of Jeremiah. Jeremiah says, "I did not speak with your fathers and I did not command them in the day that I brought them out of the land of Egypt about matters of offerings and sacrifices" (Jer 7:22). See the note on Gen 1:2 and *Who Wrote the Bible?* p. 168.

8

¹And YHWH spoke to Moses, saying, ²"Take Aaron and his sons with him and the clothes and the anointing oil and the bull for the sin offering and the two rams and the basket of unleavened bread, ³and assemble all of the congregation to the entrance of the Tent of Meeting."

⁴And Moses did as YHWH commanded him. And the congregation was gathered to the entrance of the Tent of Meeting. ⁵And Moses said to the congregation, "This is the thing that YHWH has commanded to do."

⁶And Moses brought Aaron and his sons forward, and he washed them with water. ⁷And he put the coat on him and belted him with the sash and dressed him with the robe and put the ephod on him and belted him with the ephod's designed belt and put on the ephod for him with it. ⁸And he set the breastplate on him and put the Urim and Tummim into the breastplate. ⁹And he set the headdress on his head and set the gold plate, the crown of Holiness, on the headdress opposite the front of it, as YHWH had commanded Moses.

¹⁰And Moses took the anointing oil, and he anointed the Tabernacle and everything that was in it, so he consecrated them. ¹¹And he sprinkled some of it on the altar seven times and anointed the altar and all of its equipment and the basin and its stand to consecrate them. ¹²And he poured some of the anointing oil on Aaron's head and anointed him to consecrate him. ¹³And Moses brought forward Aaron's sons and dressed them in coats and belted them with a sash and put on hats for them, as YHWH had commanded Moses.

¹⁴And he brought up the bull for the sin offering. And Aaron and his sons laid their hands on the head of the bull for the sin offering. ¹⁵And Moses slaughtered it and took the blood and put it on the altar's horns all around with his finger and purified the altar from sin, and he poured the blood at the base of the altar, and he consecrated it to make atonement on it. ¹⁶And he took all the fat that was on the innards and the lobe of the liver and the two kidneys and their fat, and Moses burnt them to smoke at the altar. ¹⁷And he burnt the bull and its skin and its meat and its dung in fire outside the camp, as YHWH had commanded Moses.

¹⁸And he brought forward the ram for the burnt offering. And Aaron and his sons laid their hands on the ram's head. ¹⁹And he slaughtered it, and Moses flung the blood on the altar all around. ²⁰And he cut the ram into its parts, and Moses burned the head and the parts and the suet to smoke. ²¹And he washed the innards and the legs with water. And Moses burned all of the ram to smoke at the altar. It was a burnt offering as a pleasant smell. It was an offering by fire to YHWH, as YHWH had commanded Moses.

²²And he brought forward the second ram, the ram of ordination. And Aaron and his sons laid their hands on the ram's head. ²³And he slaughtered it, and Moses took some of its blood and put it on Aaron's right earlobe and on the thumb of his right hand and on the big toe of his right foot. ²⁴And he brought Aaron's sons forward, and Moses put some of the blood on their right earlobe and on the thumb of their right hand and on the big toe of their right foot. And Moses flung the blood on the altar all around. ²⁵And he took the fat and the fat tail and all the fat that was on the innards and the lobe of the liver and the two kidneys and their fat and the right thigh. ²⁶And from the basket of unleavened bread that was in front of YHWH he took one cake of unleavened bread and one cake of bread with oil and one wafer, and he set them on the fats and on the right thigh. ²⁷And he put it all on Aaron's hands and on his sons' hands and elevated them, an elevation offering in front of YHWH. ²⁸And Moses took them from on their hands and burned them to smoke at the altar with the burnt offering. They were an ordination offering as a pleasant smell. It was an offering by fire to YHWH. ²⁹And Moses took the breast and elevated it, an elevation offering in front of YHWH from the ram of ordination. It was Moses' for a portion, as YHWH had commanded Moses.

³⁰And Moses took some of the anointing oil and some of the blood that was on the altar and sprinkled them on Aaron, on his clothes, and on his sons and on his sons' clothes with him, and he consecrated Aaron, his clothes, and his sons and his sons' clothes with him.

³¹And Moses said to Aaron and to his sons, "Cook the meat at the entrance of the Tent of Meeting and eat it and the bread that's in the basket of ordination there, as I commanded, saying, 'Aaron and his sons shall eat it.' ³²And you shall burn what is left of the meat and of the bread in fire. ³³And you shall not go out from the Tent of Meeting for seven days, until the day of completion of the days of your ordination, because He will fill your hand for seven days. ³⁴What has been done on this day YHWH commanded to do, to make atonement over you. ³⁵And you shall sit at the entrance of the Tent of Meeting day and night, seven days, and you shall keep YHWH's charge, and you will not die, because that is what I was commanded."

³⁶And Aaron and his sons did all the things that YHWH commanded by Moses' hand.

9

¹And it was, on the eighth day, Moses called to Aaron and to his sons and to Israel's elders. ²And he said to Aaron, "Take a calf of the cattle for a

sin offering and a ram for a burnt offering—unblemished—and bring them forward in front of YHWH. ³And you shall speak to the children of Israel, saying, 'Take a goat for a sin offering and a calf and a lamb, unblemished one-year-olds, for a burnt offering ⁴and an ox and a ram for peace offerings to sacrifice in front of YHWH, and a grain offering mixed with oil, because today YHWH is appearing to you.'"

⁵And they took what Moses had commanded to the front of the Tent of Meeting, and they brought forward all of the congregation, and they stood in front of YHWH.

⁶And Moses said, "This is the thing that YHWH has commanded that you shall do, and YHWH's glory will appear to you." ⁷And Moses said to Aaron, "Come forward to the altar and make your sin offering and your burnt offering and make atonement for yourself and for the people, and make the people's offering and make atonement for them as YHWH commanded."

⁸And Aaron came forward to the altar and slaughtered the calf for the sin offering that he had. ⁹And Aaron's sons brought forward the blood to him, and he dipped his finger in the blood and put it on the altar's horns, and he poured the blood to the base of the altar. ¹⁰And he burned the fat and the kidneys and the lobe from the liver from the sin offering to smoke at the altar, as YHWH had commanded Moses. ¹¹And he burned the meat and the skin in fire outside the camp. ¹²And he slaughtered the burnt offering. And Aaron's sons presented the blood to him, and he flung it on the altar all around. ¹³And they presented the burnt offering to him in its parts and the head, and he burnt it to smoke on the altar. ¹⁴And he washed the innards and the legs and burnt them to smoke with the burnt offering at the altar.

¹⁵And he made the people's offering: and he took the goat for the sin offering that was the people's, and he slaughtered it and made a sin offering with it like the first one. ¹⁶And he brought forward the burnt offering and made it according to the required manner. ¹⁷And he brought forward the grain offering and filled his hand from it and burned it to smoke on the altar—apart from the morning's burnt offering. ¹⁸And he slaughtered the ox and the ram, the peace-offering sacrifice that was the people's. And Aaron's sons presented the blood to him, and he flung it on the altar all around, ¹⁹and the fats from the ox and from the ram, the fat tail and the covering and the kidneys and the lobe of the liver. ²⁰And they set the fats on the breasts, and he burned the fats to smoke at the altar. ²¹And Aaron elevated the breasts and the right thigh, an elevation offering in front of YHWH, as Moses had commanded. ²²And Aaron raised his hands to the people and blessed them. And he went down from making the sin offering and the burnt offering and the peace offering.

²³And Moses and Aaron came to the Tent of Meeting, and they went out and blessed the people. And YHWH's glory appeared to all the people. ²⁴And fire came out from in front of YHWH and consumed the burnt offering and the fats on the altar! ²⁵And all the people saw, and they shouted, and they fell on their faces!

10

¹And Aaron's sons, Nadab and Abihu, each took his fire-holder, and they put fire in them and set incense on it. And they brought forward unfitting fire, which He had not commanded them, in front of YHWH. ²And fire came out from in front of YHWH and consumed them! And they died in front of YHWH.*

³And Moses said to Aaron, "That is what YHWH spoke, saying, 'I shall be made holy through those who are close to me, and I shall be honored in front of all the people.'"

And Aaron was silent.

⁴And Moses called to Mishael and to Elzaphan, sons of Uzziel, Aaron's uncle, and said to them, "Come forward. Carry your brothers from in front of the Holy to the outside of the camp."

⁵And they came forward and carried them by their coats to the outside of the camp as Moses had spoken.

⁶And Moses said to Aaron and to Eleazar and to Ithamar, his sons, "Don't let loose the hair of your heads and don't tear your clothes, so you won't die and He'll be angry at all the congregation. And your brothers, all the house of Israel, will weep for the burning that YHWH has made. ⁷And you shall not go out from the entrance of the Tent of Meeting, or else you'll die, because YHWH's anointing oil is on you."

And they did according to Moses' word.

⁸And YHWH spoke to Aaron, saying, ⁹"You shall not drink wine and beer, you and your sons with you, when you come to the Tent of Meeting, so you won't die. It is an eternal law through your generations, ¹⁰and to distinguish between the holy and the secular, and between the impure and the pure, ¹¹and to instruct the children of Israel all the laws that YHWH has spoken to them by the hand of Moses."

---

*The author of P traced the Aaronid priesthood through Aaron's son Eleazar, but the received tradition (still retained in E) was that Aaron's sons were Nadab and Abihu. P therefore included this story of how Nadab and Abihu came to be replaced by the next two sons, Eleazar and Ithamar. Verse 12 below identifies them as "his sons who were left." See the note on Exod 24:1.

¹²And Moses said to Aaron and to Eleazar and to Ithamar, his sons who were left, "Take the grain offering that is left from YHWH's offerings by fire and eat it as unleavened bread beside the altar, because it is the holy of holies. ¹³And you shall eat it in a holy place, because it is your statutory share, and it is your sons' statutory share from YHWH's offerings by fire, because that is what I was commanded. ¹⁴And you shall eat the breast of the elevation offering and the thigh of the donation in a pure place—you and your sons and your daughters with you—because they have been given as your statutory share and your sons' statutory share from the peace-offering sacrifices of the children of Israel. ¹⁵They shall bring the thigh of the donation and the breast of the elevation offering with the offerings by fire of the fats to elevate, an elevation offering in front of YHWH; and it will be yours and your sons' with you as an eternal law, as YHWH commanded."

¹⁶And Moses inquired about the goat of the sin offering, and here it was burnt! And he was angry at Eleazar and at Ithamar, Aaron's sons who were left, saying, ¹⁷"Why didn't you eat the sin offering in the place of the Holy—because it's the holy of holies, and He gave it to you for bearing the congregation's crime, for making atonement over them in front of YHWH! ¹⁸Here, its blood hasn't been brought to the Holy, inside. You should have eaten it in the Holy as I commanded!"

¹⁹And Aaron spoke to Moses: "Here, today they brought forward their sin offering and their burnt offering in front of YHWH. When things like these have happened to me, if I had eaten a sin offering today would it be good in YHWH's eyes?"

²⁰And Moses listened, and it was good in his eyes.

11

¹And YHWH spoke to Moses and to Aaron, saying to them, ²"Speak to the children of Israel, saying: This is the animal that you shall eat out of all the domestic animals that are on the earth: ³every one that has a hoof and that has a split of hooves, that regurgitates cud among animals, you shall eat it. ⁴Except you shall not eat this out of those that regurgitate the cud and out of those that have a hoof: The camel, because it regurgitates cud and does not have a hoof; it is impure to you. ⁵And the rock-badger, because it regurgitates cud and does not have a hoof; it is impure to you. ⁶And the hare, because it regurgitates cud and does not have a hoof; it is impure to you. ⁷And the pig, because it has a hoof and has a split of hooves, and it does not chew cud; it is impure to you. ⁸You shall not eat from their meat, and you shall not touch their carcass. They are impure to you.

⁹"You shall eat this out of all that are in the water: every one that has fins and scales in the water—in the seas and in the streams—you shall eat them. ¹⁰And any one that does not have fins and scales in the seas and in the streams—out of every swarming thing of the water and out of every living being that is in the water—they are a detestable thing to you, ¹¹and they shall be a detestable thing to you. You shall not eat from their meat, and you shall detest their carcass. ¹²Every one that does not have scales and fins in the water, it is a detestable thing to you.

¹³"And you shall detest these out of the flying creatures. They shall not be eaten. They are a detestable thing: the eagle and the vulture and the black vulture ¹⁴and the kite and the falcon by its kind, ¹⁵every raven by its kind ¹⁶and the eagle owl and the nighthawk and the seagull and the hawk by its kind ¹⁷and the little owl and the cormorant and the great owl ¹⁸and the white owl and the pelican and the fish hawk ¹⁹and the stork and the heron by its kind and the hoopoe and the bat. ²⁰Every swarming thing of flying creatures that goes on four—it is a detestable thing to you. ²¹Except you shall eat this out of every swarming thing of flying creatures that goes on four: that which has jointed legs above its feet, to leap by them on the earth. ²²You shall eat these out of them: the locust by its kind and the bald locust by its kind and the cricket by its kind and the grasshopper by its kind. ²³And every swarming thing of flying creatures that has four legs—it is a detestable thing to you.

²⁴"And you will become impure by these—everyone who touches their carcass will be impure until evening, ²⁵and everyone who carries their carcass shall wash his clothes and be impure until evening— ²⁶by every animal that has a hoof and does not have a split of hooves and does not regurgitate its cud. They are impure to you. Everyone who touches them will be impure. ²⁷And every one that goes on its paws among all the animals that go on four, they are impure to you. Every one who touches their carcass will be impure until evening, ²⁸and one who carries their carcass shall wash his clothes and be impure until evening. They are impure to you.

²⁹"And this is the impure to you among the things that swarm on the earth: the rat, the mouse, and the great lizard by its kind ³⁰and the gecko and the spotted lizard and the lizard and the sand lizard and the chameleon. ³¹These are the impure to you among all the swarming things. Everyone who touches them when they are dead will be impure until evening. ³²And everything on which one of them will fall when they are dead will be impure, out of every wooden item or clothing or leather or sack, every item with which work may be done shall be put in water and will be impure until evening and then will be pure. ³³And every clay container into which any of them will fall: everything that is inside it will be impure, and you shall break it. ³⁴Every

food that may be eaten on which water will come will be impure, and every liquid that may be drunk in any container will be impure. ³⁵And everything on which some of their carcass will fall will be impure. An oven or stove shall be demolished. They are impure, and they shall be impure to you. ³⁶Except a spring or a cistern with a concentration of waters will be pure. And one who touches their carcass will be impure. ³⁷And if some of their carcass will fall on any sowing seed that will be sown, it is pure. ³⁸And if water will be put on a seed, and some of their carcass will fall on it, it is impure to you.

³⁹"And if any of the animals that are yours for food will die, the one who touches its carcass will be impure until evening, ⁴⁰and the one who eats some of its carcass shall wash his clothes and is impure until evening, and the one who carries its carcass shall wash his clothes and is impure until evening.

⁴¹"And every swarming creature that swarms on the earth, it is a detestable thing. It shall not be eaten. ⁴²Everything going on a belly and everything going on four as well as everything having a great number of legs of every swarming creature that swarms on the earth: you shall not eat them because they are a detestable thing. ⁴³Do not make yourselves detestable with any swarming creature that swarms, and you shall not become impure with them, so that you will be impure through them. ⁴⁴Because I am YHWH, your God, and you shall make yourselves holy, and you shall be holy because I am holy. And you shall not make yourselves impure with any swarming creature that creeps on the earth. ⁴⁵Because I am YHWH, who brought you up from the land of Egypt to be God to you, and you shall be holy because I am holy.

⁴⁶"This is the instruction for animal and bird and every living being that moves in the water and for every being that swarms on the earth, ⁴⁷to distinguish between the impure and the pure, and between the living thing that is eaten and the living thing that shall not be eaten."

12

¹And YHWH spoke to Moses, saying, ²"Speak to the children of Israel, saying: A woman, when she will bear seed and give birth to a male, will be impure seven days. She will be impure like the days of the impurity of her menstruation. ³And on the eighth day the flesh of his foreskin shall be circumcised. ⁴And thirty days and three days she shall remain in blood of purity. She shall not touch any holy thing, and she shall not come to the holy place until the completion of the days of her purification. ⁵And if she will give birth to a female, then she will be impure two weeks, like her impurity. And sixty days and six days she shall remain with blood of purity. ⁶And at the

completion of the days of her purification, for a son or for a daughter, she shall bring a lamb in its first year for a burnt offering and a pigeon or a turtledove for a sin offering to the entrance of the Tent of Meeting, to the priest. ⁷And he shall bring it forward in front of YHWH and make atonement over her, and she will be purified from the source of her blood. This is the instruction for the one giving birth to a male or to a female. ⁸And if her hand will not find enough for a sheep, then she shall take two turtledoves or two pigeons, one for a burnt offering and one for a sin offering, and the priest shall make atonement over her, and she will be purified."

13

¹And YHWH spoke to Moses and to Aaron, saying, ²"When a person will have a swelling or a rash or a bright spot in his flesh's skin, and it becomes an affliction of leprosy in his flesh's skin, and he will be brought to Aaron, the priest, or to one of his sons, the priests, ³and the priest will see the affliction in the flesh's skin, and hair in the affliction will have turned white, and the affliction's appearance is deeper than his flesh's skin, it is an affliction of leprosy. And when the priest will see it he shall identify him as impure. ⁴And if it is a white bright spot in his flesh's skin, and its appearance is not deeper than the skin, and its hair has not turned white, then the priest shall shut in the one with the affliction seven days. ⁵And the priest shall see him on the seventh day; and, here, in his eyes the affliction will have stayed the same—the affliction has not spread in the skin—then the priest shall shut him in seven days a second time. ⁶And the priest shall see him on the seventh day a second time; and, here, the affliction has become dim, and the affliction has not spread in the skin, then the priest shall identify him as pure. It is a rash. And he shall wash his clothes and be pure. ⁷But if the rash has spread in the skin after his being seen by the priest for pronouncing him pure, and he is seen a second time by the priest, ⁸and the priest sees, and, here, the rash has spread in the skin, then the priest shall identify him as impure. It is leprosy.

⁹"When an affliction of leprosy will be in a human, and he will be brought to the priest, ¹⁰and the priest will see; and, here, a white swelling will be in the skin, and it will have turned hair white, and some vital flesh will be in the swelling, ¹¹it is chronic leprosy in his flesh's skin, and the priest shall identify him as impure. He shall not shut him in, because he is impure. ¹²And if the leprosy will develop in the skin, and the leprosy will cover all the skin of the one with the affliction from his head to his feet, to wherever it is within sight of the priest's eyes, ¹³and the priest will see, and, here, the leprosy has cov-

ered all his flesh, then he shall identify the one with the affliction as pure. All of him has turned white. He is pure. ¹⁴And on the day that vital flesh will appear in him he will be impure. ¹⁵And the priest will see the vital flesh and shall identify him as impure. The vital flesh: it is impure. It is leprosy. ¹⁶Or when the vital flesh will go back and turn to white, and he will come to the priest, ¹⁷and the priest will see him, and, here, the affliction has turned to white, then the priest shall identify the affliction as pure. He is pure.

¹⁸"And when flesh will have a boil in it, in its skin, and will be healed, ¹⁹and in place of the boil there will be a white swelling or a reddish white bright spot, and he will be seen by the priest, ²⁰and the priest will see, and, here, its appearance is lower than the skin, and its hair has turned white, then the priest shall identify him as impure. It is an affliction of leprosy. It has developed in the boil. ²¹And if the priest will see it, and, here, there is not white hair in it, and it is not lower than the skin, and it has become dim, then the priest shall shut him in seven days. ²²And if it will spread in the skin, then the priest shall identify him as impure. It is an affliction. ²³And if the bright spot will have stayed the same in its place—it has not spread—it is the scar of the boil, and the priest shall identify him as pure.

²⁴"Or when flesh will have a burn from a fire in its skin, and the vital part of the burn is a bright spot of reddish white or white, ²⁵and the priest will see it, and, here, hair has turned white in the bright spot, and its appearance is lower than the skin, it is leprosy. It has developed in the burn. And the priest shall identify him as impure. It is an affliction of leprosy. ²⁶And if the priest will see it, and, here, there is not white hair in the bright spot, and it is not lower than the skin, and it has become dim, then the priest shall shut him in seven days. ²⁷And the priest shall see him on the seventh day. If it will spread in the skin, then the priest shall identify him as impure. It is an affliction of leprosy. ²⁸And if the bright spot will have stayed the same in its place—it has not spread in the skin—and it has become dim, it is the swelling of the burn, and the priest shall identify him as pure, because it is the scar of the burn.

²⁹"And when a man or woman will have an affliction in the head or beard, ³⁰and the priest will see the affliction, and, here, its appearance is deeper than the skin, and there is thin yellow hair in it, then the priest shall identify him as impure. It is a scab. It is leprosy of the head or the beard. ³¹And when the priest will see the affliction of the scab, and, here, its appearance is not deeper than the skin, and there is not black hair in it, then the priest shall shut in the affliction of the scab seven days. ³²And the priest shall see the affliction on the seventh day. And, here, the scab has not spread, and there is not yellow hair in it, and the scab's appearance is not deeper than the skin. ³³Then he shall shave himself, and he shall not shave

the scab. And the priest shall shut in the one with the scab seven days a second time. [34]And the priest shall see the scab on the seventh day. And, here, the scab has not spread in the skin, and its appearance is not deeper than the skin. Then the priest shall identify him as pure. And he shall wash his clothes, and he shall be pure. [35]But if the scab has spread in the skin, after his purification, [36]and the priest will see him, and, here, the scab has spread in the skin, the priest shall not inspect for the yellow hair. He is impure. [37]And if, in his eyes, the scab has stayed the same, and black hair has developed in it, the scab has been healed. He is pure. And the priest shall identify him as pure.

[38]"And when a man or woman will have bright spots in the skin of their flesh, white bright spots, [39]and the priest will see, and, here, bright spots in the skin of their flesh are dim white, it is a tetter. It has developed in the skin. He is pure.

[40]"And when a man's head will become hairless, he is bald. He is pure. [41]And if his head will become hairless from the corner of his face, he has a bald forehead. He is pure. [42]And when there will be in the bald head or in the bald forehead a reddish white affliction, it is leprosy developing in his bald head or in his bald forehead. [43]And the priest will see it, and, here, the affliction's swelling is reddish white in his bald head or in his bald forehead, like the appearance of leprosy of skin of flesh, [44]he is a leprous man. He is impure. The priest shall identify him as impure. His affliction is in his head. [45]And the leper in whom is the affliction: his clothes shall be torn, and the hair of his head shall be loosed, and he shall cover over his mustache. And he shall call, 'Impure! Impure!' [46]All the days that the affliction is in him he will be impure. He is impure. He shall live separate. His home is outside of the camp.

[47]"And when clothing will have an affliction of leprosy in it—in clothing of wool or in clothing of linen, [48]either in the warp or in the woof of the linen or of the wool, or in leather or in anything made of leather: [49]if the affliction will be greenish or reddish in the clothing or in the leather or in the warp or in the woof or in any item of leather, it is an affliction of leprosy—and it will be shown to the priest, [50]and the priest will see the affliction, and he shall shut in the thing with the affliction seven days. [51]And he shall see the affliction on the seventh day: if the affliction has spread in the clothing or in the warp or in the woof or in the leather, or any work into which the leather will be made, the affliction is malignant leprosy. It is impure. [52]And he shall burn the clothing or the warp or the woof in the wool or in the linen or any item of leather in which the affliction will be, because it is malignant leprosy. It shall be burned in fire. [53]And if the priest will look, and, here, the affliction has not spread in the clothing or in the warp or in the woof or any item of leather,

⁵⁴then the priest shall command, and they shall wash the thing in which the affliction is, and he shall shut it in seven days a second time. ⁵⁵And the priest shall see the affliction after it will be washed, and, here, the affliction has not changed its appearance, and the affliction will not have spread, it is impure. You shall burn it in fire. It is a deterioration, in its 'bald head' or in its 'forehead.' ⁵⁶If the priest will see, and, here, the affliction has become dim after it was washed, then he shall rip it from the clothing or from the leather or from the warp or from the woof. ⁵⁷And if it will appear again in the clothing or in the warp or in the woof or in any item of leather, it is developing. You shall burn it, the thing in which the affliction is, in fire. ⁵⁸And the clothing or the warp or the woof or any item of leather that you will wash: if the affliction will turn away from them, then it shall be washed a second time, and it will be pure.

⁵⁹"This is the instruction for the affliction of leprosy of clothing of wool or linen or warp or woof or any item of leather, to identify it as pure or to identify it as impure."

14

¹And YHWH spoke to Moses, saying, ²"This shall be the instruction for the leper in the day of his purification: And he shall be brought to the priest, ³and the priest shall go outside the camp, and the priest shall see, and if, here, the affliction of leprosy has been healed from the leper, ⁴then the priest shall command, and one shall take two live, pure birds and cedarwood and scarlet and hyssop for the one being purified. ⁵And the priest shall command, and he shall slaughter one of the birds in a clay container over living water. ⁶The live bird: he shall take it and the cedarwood and the scarlet and the hyssop, and he shall dip them and the live bird in the slaughtered bird's blood over the living water. ⁷And he shall sprinkle it on the one being purified from the leprosy seven times. And he shall identify him as pure. And he shall let the live bird go at the open field. ⁸And the one being purified shall wash his clothes and shave all his hair and wash in water, and he will be pure, and after that he shall come to the camp. And he shall live outside his tent seven days. ⁹And it will be, on the seventh day: he shall shave all his hair—he shall shave his head and his beard and his eyebrows and all his hair—and he shall wash his clothes and wash his flesh in water, and he will be pure. ¹⁰And on the eighth day he shall take two unblemished he-lambs and one unblemished ewe-lamb in its first year and three-tenths of a measure of fine flour as a grain offering mixed with oil and one log of oil. ¹¹And the priest who is purifying shall have the man being purified and them stand

in front of YHWH at the entrance of the Tent of Meeting. ¹²And the priest shall take one of the lambs and bring it forward as a guilt offering and the log of oil, and he shall elevate them, an elevation offering in front of YHWH. ¹³And he shall slaughter the lamb in the place where he slaughters the sin offering and the burnt offering, in the place of the Holy, because, like the sin offering, the guilt offering is the priest's. It is the holy of holies. ¹⁴And the priest shall take some of the blood of the guilt offering, and the priest shall put it on the right earlobe of the one being purified and on the thumb of his right hand and on the big toe of his right foot. ¹⁵And the priest shall take some of the log of oil and pour it on the priest's left hand. ¹⁶And the priest shall dip his right finger in some of the oil that is on his left hand and sprinkle some of the oil with his finger seven times in front of YHWH. ¹⁷And the priest shall put some of the remaining oil that is on his hand on the right earlobe of the one being purified and on the thumb of his right hand and on the big toe of his right foot, over the blood of the guilt offering. ¹⁸And he shall put what is left of the oil that is on the priest's hand on the head of the one being purified. And the priest shall make atonement over him in front of YHWH. ¹⁹And the priest shall make the sin offering and make atonement over the one being purified from his impurity, and after that he shall slaughter the burnt offering. ²⁰And the priest shall make the burnt offering and the grain offering at the altar. And the priest shall make atonement over him, and he will be pure.

²¹"And if he is poor, and his hand cannot attain enough, then he shall take one lamb, a guilt offering, for elevation, for making atonement over him, and one-tenth of a measure of fine flour mixed with oil for a grain offering and a log of oil ²²and two turtledoves or two pigeons, whichever his hand can attain, and one shall be a sin offering and one a burnt offering. ²³And he shall bring them on the eighth day of his purification to the priest, to the entrance of the Tent of Meeting, in front of YHWH. ²⁴And the priest shall take the lamb of the guilt offering and the log of oil, and the priest shall elevate them, an elevation offering in front of YHWH. ²⁵And he shall slaughter the lamb of the guilt offering, and the priest shall take some of the blood of the guilt offering and put it on the right earlobe of the one being purified and on the thumb of his right hand and on the big toe of his right foot. ²⁶And the priest shall pour some of the oil on the priest's left hand, ²⁷and the priest shall sprinkle some of the oil that is on his left hand with his right finger seven times in front of YHWH. ²⁸And the priest shall put some of the oil that is on his hand on the right earlobe of the one being purified and on the thumb of his right hand and on the big toe of his right foot, over the place of the blood of the guilt offering. ²⁹And what is left of the oil that is on the priest's hand he shall put on the head of the one being purified to make atonement over him

in front of YHWH. ³⁰And he shall make one of the turtledoves or the pigeons, from those which his hand can attain— ³¹whichever his hand will attain— one a sin offering and one a burnt offering, with the grain offering, and the priest shall make atonement over the one being purified in front of YHWH.

³²"This is the instruction for one who has an affliction of leprosy in him, whose hand cannot attain enough for his purification."

³³And YHWH spoke to Moses and to Aaron, saying, ³⁴"When you will come to the land of Canaan, which I am giving to you as a possession, and I shall put an affliction of leprosy in a house at the land of your possession, ³⁵and the one whose house it is will come and tell the priest, saying, 'It appears like an affliction to me in the house,' ³⁶then the priest shall command, and they shall clear the house before the priest will come to see the affliction, so everything that is in the house will not become impure. And, after that, the priest shall come to see the house. ³⁷And he shall see the affliction, and, here, the affliction in the walls of the house is greenish or reddish streaks, and their appearance is deeper than the wall; ³⁸then the priest shall come out from the house, to the entrance of the house, and he shall shut the house up seven days. ³⁹And the priest shall go back on the seventh day and see, and, here, the affliction has spread in the walls of the house; ⁴⁰then the priest shall command, and they shall extract the stones in which is the affliction, and they shall throw them outside the city, to an impure place. ⁴¹And he shall have the house scraped inside, all around, and they shall spill the dust that they have scraped outside the city, to an impure place. ⁴²And they shall take other stones and bring them in place of the stones, and he shall take other dust and coat the house. ⁴³And if the affliction will come back and develop in the house after he has extracted the stones and after scraping the house and after being coated, ⁴⁴then the priest shall come and see, and, here, the affliction has spread in the house, it is malignant leprosy in the house. It is impure. ⁴⁵And he shall demolish the house: its stones and its wood and all the dust of the house; and he shall take it outside the city, to an impure place. ⁴⁶And one who comes into the house all the days that it is shut up will be impure until evening, ⁴⁷and one who lies in the house shall wash his clothes, and one who eats in the house shall wash his clothes. ⁴⁸And if the priest will come and see, and, here, the affliction has not spread in the house after coating the house, then the priest shall identify the house as pure, because the affliction has been healed. ⁴⁹And, to decontaminate the house, he shall take two birds and cedarwood and scarlet and hyssop, ⁵⁰and he shall slaughter one of the birds in a clay container over living water. ⁵¹And he shall take the cedarwood and the hyssop and the scarlet and the live bird and dip them in the blood of the

slaughtered bird and in the living water, and he shall sprinkle it at the house seven times. ⁵²And he shall decontaminate the house with the bird's blood and with the living water and with the live bird and with the cedarwood and with the hyssop and with the scarlet. ⁵³And he shall let the live bird go outside the city at the open field. And he shall make atonement over the house, and it will be pure.

⁵⁴"This is the instruction for every affliction of leprosy and for a scab ⁵⁵and for leprosy of clothing and for a house ⁵⁶and for a swelling and for a rash and for a bright spot, ⁵⁷to instruct on the day of the impure and on the day of the pure. This is the instruction for leprosy."

15

¹And YHWH spoke to Moses and to Aaron, saying, ²"Speak to the children of Israel, and you shall say to them: When any man will have an emission from his flesh, his emission: it is impure. ³And this shall be his impurity when he has an emission: his flesh leaks with his emission, or his flesh is obstructed from his emission. It is his impurity. ⁴Any bed on which the one with the emission will lie will be impure, and any item on which he will sit will be impure. ⁵And a man who will touch his bed shall wash his clothes and shall wash in water and will be impure until evening. ⁶And one who sits on an item on which the one with the emission has sat shall wash his clothes and shall wash in water and will be impure until evening. ⁷And one who touches the flesh of the one with the emission shall wash his clothes and shall wash in water and will be impure until evening. ⁸And if the one with the emission will spit on one who is pure, then he shall wash his clothes and shall wash in water and will be impure until evening. ⁹And any conveyance on which the one with the emission will ride will be impure. ¹⁰And anyone who touches anything that has been under him will be impure until evening. And one who carries them shall wash his clothes and shall wash in water and will be impure until evening. ¹¹And anyone whom the one with the emission will touch when he has not rinsed his hands in water shall wash his clothes and shall wash in water and will be impure until evening. ¹²And a clay container that the one with the emission will touch shall be broken, and any wood container shall be rinsed in water. ¹³And when the one with the emission will be purified from his emission, he shall count seven days for his purification and shall wash his clothes and shall wash his flesh in living water and will be pure. ¹⁴And on the eighth day he shall take two turtledoves or two pigeons and shall come in front of YHWH, to the entrance of the Tent of Meeting, and shall give them to the priest. ¹⁵And the priest shall

do them: one a sin offering and one a burnt offering, and the priest shall make atonement over him in front of YHWH from his emission. ¹⁶"And when a man's intercourse seed will come out from him: he shall wash all his flesh in water and will be impure until evening. ¹⁷And any clothing and any leather on which there will be intercourse seed: it shall be washed with water and will be impure until evening. ¹⁸And a woman with whom a man will lie—an intercourse of seed—they shall wash with water and will be impure until evening.

¹⁹"And when a woman will have an emission—her emission will be blood in her flesh—she shall be in her impurity seven days. And anyone who touches her will be impure until evening. ²⁰And anything on which she will lie during her impurity will be impure, and anything on which she will sit will be impure. ²¹And anyone who touches her bed shall wash his clothes and shall wash in water and will be impure until evening. ²²And anyone who touches any item on which she will sit shall wash his clothes and shall wash in water and will be impure until evening. ²³And if he is on the bed or on the item on which she sits while he is touching it, he will be impure until evening. ²⁴And if a man will lie with her, and her impurity will be on him, then he will be impure seven days. And any bed on which he will lie will be impure.

²⁵"And when a woman will have an emission of her blood many days when it is not the time of her impurity, or when she will have an emission beyond her impurity, for all the days of her impure emission she shall be like the days of her impurity. She is impure. ²⁶Any bed on which she will lie all the days of her emission will be like a bed of her impurity for her, and any item on which she will sit will be impure like the impurity of her menstruation. ²⁷And anyone who touches them will be impure. And he shall wash his clothes and shall wash with water and will be impure until evening.

²⁸"And if she has become purified from her emission, then she shall count seven days, and after that she will be pure. ²⁹And on the eighth day she shall take two turtledoves or two pigeons, and she shall bring them to the priest at the entrance of the Tent of Meeting. ³⁰And the priest shall make one a sin offering and one a burnt offering, and the priest shall make atonement over her in front of YHWH from her impure emission.

³¹"And you shall alert the children of Israel regarding their impurity so they will not die through their impurity when they defile my Tabernacle that is among them. ³²This is the instruction for one who has an emission and for one from whom seed of intercourse will come out, so as to become impure by it, ³³and one who is in her menstrual impurity and one who has an emission—for a male and for a female—and for a man who will lie with a woman who is impure."

16

¹And YHWH spoke to Moses after the death of Aaron's two sons— when they came forward in front of YHWH and died. ²And YHWH said to Moses, "Speak to Aaron, your brother, and let him not come at all times to the Holy, inside the pavilion, in front of the atonement dais that is over the ark, so he will not die, because I shall appear in a cloud over the atonement dais. ³Aaron shall come to the Holy with this: with a bull of the cattle for a sin offering and a ram for a burnt offering. ⁴He shall wear a holy linen coat, and linen drawers shall be on his flesh, and he shall be belted with a linen sash, and he shall wear a linen headdress. They are holy clothes: and he shall wash his flesh with water and put them on. ⁵And he shall take from the congregation of the children of Israel two goats for a sin offering and one ram for a burnt offering. ⁶And Aaron shall bring forward the bull of the sin offering that is his and shall make atonement for himself and for his house. ⁷And he shall take the two goats and stand them in front of YHWH, at the entrance of the Tent of Meeting. ⁸And Aaron shall cast lots on the two goats, one lot for YHWH and one lot for Azazel. ⁹And Aaron shall bring forward the goat on which the lot for YHWH arose, and he shall make it a sin offering. ¹⁰And the goat on which the lot for Azazel arose shall be stood alive in front of YHWH to make atonement over it, to let it go to Azazel, into the wilderness. ¹¹And Aaron shall bring forward the bull of the sin offering that is his and shall make atonement for him and for his house, and he shall slaughter the bull of the sin offering that he has. ¹²And he shall take a fire-holder-full of coals of fire from on the altar, from in front of YHWH, and handfuls of fine incense of fragrances, and he shall bring it inside the pavilion ¹³and put the incense on the fire in front of YHWH so that the cloud of the incense will cover the atonement dais that is over the Testimony, and he will not die. ¹⁴And he shall take some of the bull's blood and sprinkle with his finger on the front of the atonement dais eastward, and he shall sprinkle some of the blood with his finger in front of the atonement dais seven times. ¹⁵And he shall slaughter the goat of the sin offering that is the people's and shall bring its blood inside the pavilion and shall do its blood as he did to the bull's blood: and he shall sprinkle it on the atonement dais and in front of the atonement dais. ¹⁶And he shall make atonement over the Holy from the impurities of the children of Israel and from their offenses, for all their sins, and he shall do so for the Tent of Meeting that tents with them among their impurities. ¹⁷And no human shall be in the Tent of Meeting when he comes to make atonement in the Holy until he comes out. And he shall make atonement for him and for his house and for all the community of Israel.

¹⁸"And he shall go out to the altar that is in front of YHWH and make atonement over it, and he shall take some of the bull's blood and some of the goat's blood and put it on the altar's horns all around. ¹⁹And he shall sprinkle some of the blood on it with his finger seven times and purify it and make it holy from the impurities of the children of Israel.

²⁰"And when he will finish making atonement for the Holy and the Tent of Meeting and the altar, then he shall bring forward the live goat. ²¹And Aaron shall lay his two hands on the live goat's head and confess over it all the crimes of the children of Israel and all their offenses, for all their sins, and he shall put them on the goat's head and let it go by the hand of an appointed man to the wilderness. ²²And the goat will carry all their crimes on it to an inaccessible land. And he shall let the goat go in the wilderness.

²³"And Aaron shall come to the Tent of Meeting and take off the linen clothes that he wore when he came to the Holy, and he shall leave them there. ²⁴And he shall wash his flesh with water in a holy place and put on his clothes, and he shall go out and make his burnt offering and the people's burnt offering and make atonement for him and for the people. ²⁵And he shall burn the fat of the sin offering into smoke at the altar. ²⁶And the one who let the goat go to Azazel shall wash his clothes and wash his flesh with water, and after that he shall come to the camp. ²⁷And he shall take the bull of the sin offering and the goat of the sin offering, whose blood was brought to make atonement in the Holy, outside the camp; and they shall burn their skin and their meat and their dung in fire. ²⁸And the one who burns them shall wash his clothes and wash his flesh with water, and after that he shall come to the camp.

²⁹"And it shall be an eternal law for you: in the seventh month, on the tenth of the month, you shall degrade yourselves, and you shall not do any work: the citizen and the alien who resides among you. ³⁰Because on this day he shall make atonement over you, to purify you. You will be pure from all your sins in front of YHWH. ³¹It is a Sabbath, a ceasing, to you. And you shall degrade yourselves—an eternal law. ³²And the priest whom one will anoint and who will fill his hand to function as a priest in his father's place shall make atonement. And he shall wear the linen clothes, the holy clothes. ³³And he shall make atonement for the holy place of the Holy, and he shall make atonement for the Tent of Meeting and for the altar, and he shall make atonement over the priests and over all the people of the community. ³⁴And this shall become an eternal law for you, to make atonement over the children of Israel from all their sins, once in the year."

And he did as YHWH had commanded Moses.

17

¹And YHWH spoke to Moses, saying,* ²"Speak to Aaron and to his sons and to all the children of Israel and say to them: This is the thing that YHWH has commanded, saying: ³Any man from the house of Israel who slaughters an ox or a sheep or a goat in the camp or who slaughters outside the camp ⁴and has not brought it to the entrance of the Tent of Meeting to bring forward an offering to YHWH in front of YHWH's Tabernacle: blood will be counted to that man. He has spilled blood. And that man will be cut off from among his people. ⁵So that the children of Israel will bring their sacrifices—which they are making at the open field—and will bring them to YHWH, to the entrance of the Tent of Meeting, to the priest, and make them sacrifices of peace offerings to YHWH. ⁶And the priest shall fling the blood on YHWH's altar at the entrance of the Tent of Meeting and burn the fat to smoke as a pleasant smell to YHWH. ⁷And they shall not make their sacrifices anymore to the satyrs, after whom they are whoring. This shall be an eternal law to them through their generations.

⁸"And you shall say to them: Any man from the house of Israel and from the aliens who will reside among them who will make a burnt offering or a sacrifice ⁹and will not bring it to the entrance of the Tent of Meeting to make it to YHWH: that man will be cut off from his people.

¹⁰"And any man from the house of Israel and from the aliens who will reside among them who will eat any blood: then I shall set my face against the person who eats the blood, and I shall cut him off from among his people. ¹¹Because the flesh's life is in the blood, and I have given it to you on the altar to make atonement over your lives, because it is the blood that makes atonement for life. ¹²On account of this I have said to the children of Israel: every person among you shall not eat blood, and the alien who resides among you shall not eat blood.

¹³"And any man from the children of Israel and from the aliens who reside among them who will hunt game, animal or bird, that may be eaten: he shall spill out its blood and cover it with dust. ¹⁴Because all flesh's life: its

---

*The section from Leviticus 17 to 26 is called the Holiness Code, or H. In much of its language it is related to P. There is considerable agreement that it has some sort of distinctiveness in its language but considerable disagreement over what that distinctiveness is, what this means, and what the relationship between H and P is. Also, scholars draw different lines of what is contained in H; some see additional portions of H elsewhere in Leviticus and even in Exodus and Numbers. For many, someone who was associated with P was the redactor of H. For Knohl and Milgrom in recent works, someone who was associated with H was the redactor of P. At minimum, as they stand in the text, P and H are integrally related. Material that is identified as H is thus marked in the typeface that is used for P texts in this book. On the view of Knohl, see the note on Num 30:1.

blood is one with its life. So I say to the children of Israel: you shall not eat the blood of all flesh—because all flesh's life: it is its blood. Everyone of those who eat it will be cut off. ¹⁵And any living being, whether a citizen or an alien, who will eat carcass or a torn animal shall wash his clothes and shall wash with water and will be impure until evening and then will be pure. ¹⁶And if he will not wash them and will not wash his flesh, then he shall bear his crime."

18

¹And YHWH spoke to Moses, saying, ²"Speak to the children of Israel, and you shall say to them: I am YHWH, your God. ³You shall not do like what is done in the land of Egypt, in which you lived; and you shall not do like what is done in the land of Canaan, to which I'm bringing you; and you shall not go by their laws. ⁴You shall do my judgments, and you shall observe my laws, to go by them. I am YHWH, your God. ⁵And you shall observe my laws and my judgments which, when a human will do them, he'll live through them! I am YHWH.

⁶"Any man, to any close relative of his: you shall not come close to expose nudity. I am YHWH. ⁷You shall not expose your father's nudity and your mother's nudity. She is your mother. You shall not expose her nudity. ⁸You shall not expose your father's wife's nudity. It is your father's nudity. ⁹Your sister's nudity—your father's daughter or your mother's daughter, born home or born outside—you shall not expose their nudity. ¹⁰The nudity of your son's daughter or your daughter's daughter—you shall not expose their nudity, because they are your nudity. ¹¹The nudity of your father's wife's daughter, born of your father: she is your sister; you shall not expose her nudity. ¹²You shall not expose your father's sister's nudity. She is your father's close relative. ¹³You shall not expose your mother's sister's nudity. She is your mother's close relative. ¹⁴You shall not expose your father's brother's nudity: you shall not come close to his wife. She is your aunt. ¹⁵You shall not expose your daughter-in-law's nudity. She is your son's wife. You shall not expose her nudity. ¹⁶You shall not expose your brother's wife's nudity. It is your brother's nudity. ¹⁷You shall not expose the nudity of a woman and her daughter. You shall not take her son's daughter or her daughter's daughter to expose her nudity. They are close relatives. It is perversion. ¹⁸And you shall not take a woman to her sister to rival, to expose her nudity along with her in her lifetime. ¹⁹And you shall not come close to a woman during her menstrual impurity to expose her nudity. ²⁰And you shall not give your intercourse of seed to your fellow's wife, to become impure by it. ²¹And you shall not give any of your seed for passing to the Molech, and you shall

not desecrate your God's name. I am YHWH. ²²And you shall not lie with a male like lying with a woman. It is an offensive thing. ²³And you shall not give your intercourse with any animal, to become impure by it. And a woman shall not stand in front of an animal to mate with it. It is an aberration.

²⁴"You shall not become impure by all of these, because the nations that I am putting out from in front of you became impure by all of these, ²⁵and the land became impure, and I reckoned its sin on it, and the land vomited out its residents. ²⁶But you: you shall observe my laws and my judgments and not do any of all of these offensive things, the citizen and the alien who resides among you— ²⁷because the people of the land who were before you did all of these offensive things, and the land became impure— ²⁸so the land will not vomit you out for your making it impure as it vomited out the nation that was before you. ²⁹Because anyone who will do any of these offensive things: the persons who do will be cut off from among their people. ³⁰And you shall keep my charge: not to do any of the abominable customs that were done before you; and you will not become impure by them. I am YHWH, your God."

19

¹And YHWH spoke to Moses, saying, ²"Speak to all the congregation of the children of Israel, and you shall say to them: You shall be holy, because I, YHWH, your God, am holy.

³"You shall each fear his mother and his father, and you shall observe my Sabbaths. I am YHWH, your God.

⁴"Do not turn to idols, and you shall not make molten gods for yourselves. I am YHWH, your God.

⁵"And when you will make a peace-offering sacrifice to YHWH, you shall sacrifice it so that it will be accepted for you. ⁶It shall be eaten on the day of your sacrifice and on the next day; and what is left until the third day shall be burned in fire. ⁷And if it will be eaten on the third day it is a repugnant thing. It shall not be acceptable. ⁸And anyone who eats it shall bear his crime, because he desecrated YHWH's holy thing, and that person will be cut off from his people. ⁹And when you reap your land's harvest, you shall not finish harvesting your field's corner, and you shall not gather your harvest's gleaning. ¹⁰And you shall not strip your vineyard, and you shall not collect the vineyard's fallen fruit. You shall leave them for the poor and for the alien. I am YHWH, your God.

¹¹"You shall not steal, and you shall not lie, and you shall not act false, each against his fellow. ¹²And you shall not swear by my name falsely, so that you would desecrate your God's name. I am YHWH.

¹³"You shall not exploit your neighbor, and you shall not rob. An employee's wages shall not stay through the night with you until morning. ¹⁴You shall not curse a deaf person, and you shall not place a stumbling block in front of a blind person. And you shall fear your God. I am YHWH.

¹⁵"You shall not do an injustice in judgment. You shall not be partial to a weak person, and you shall not favor a big person. You shall judge your fellow with justice. ¹⁶You shall not go with slander among your people. You shall not stand by at your neighbor's blood. I am YHWH.

¹⁷"You shall not hate your brother in your heart. You shall criticize your fellow, so you shall not bear sin over him. ¹⁸You shall not take revenge, and you shall not keep on at the children of your people. And you shall love your neighbor as yourself. I am YHWH.

¹⁹"You shall observe my laws. Your animal: you shall not mate two kinds. Your field: you shall not seed two kinds. And a garment of two kinds, sha'atnez: it shall not go on you.

²⁰"And when a man will lie with a woman—an intercourse of seed—and she is a maid designated to a man, and she has not been redeemed, or freedom has not been given to her, there will be a reparation. They shall not be put to death, because she was not freed. ²¹And he shall bring his guilt offering to YHWH, to the entrance of the Tent of Meeting, a ram for a guilt offering. ²²And the priest shall atone over him with the ram for the guilt offering in front of YHWH over his sin that he committed, and it will be forgiven for him from his sin that he committed.

²³"And when you will come to the land, and you will plant any tree for eating, you shall leave its top with its fruit uncircumcised. It shall be uncircumcised for three years for you. It shall not be eaten. ²⁴And in the fourth year all of its fruit shall be holy, tributes for YHWH. ²⁵And in the fifth year you shall eat its fruit, to increase its produce for you. I am YHWH, your God.

²⁶"You shall not eat with the blood. You shall not practice divination, and you shall not practice soothsaying. ²⁷You shall not trim your head's edge, and you shall not destroy your beard's edge. ²⁸You shall not put a cut in your flesh for a person, and you shall not put an inscription of a tattoo in you. I am YHWH.

²⁹"Do not desecrate your daughter to make her a prostitute, so the land will not go to prostitution, and the land will fill with perversion. ³⁰You shall observe my Sabbaths and fear my holy place. I am YHWH.

³¹"Do not turn to ghosts, and do not seek spirits of acquaintances, to become impure by them. I am YHWH, your God.

³²"You shall get up in front of an aged person, and you shall show respect in front of an elderly person. And you shall fear your God. I am YHWH.

³³"And if an alien will reside with you in your land, you shall not perse-cute him. ³⁴The alien who resides with you shall be to you like a citizen of yours, and you shall love him as yourself, because you were aliens in the land of Egypt. I am YHWH, your God.

³⁵"You shall not do an injustice in judgment, in measurement, in weight, and in quantity. ³⁶You shall have just scales, just weights, a just ephah, and a just hin. I am YHWH, your God, who brought you out from the land of Egypt.

³⁷"And you shall observe all my laws and all my judgments and do them. I am YHWH."

20

¹And YHWH spoke to Moses, saying, ²"And to the children of Israel you shall say: Any man from the children of Israel and from the alien who resides in Israel who will give any of his seed to the Molech shall be put to death. The people of the land shall batter him with stone. ³And I shall set my face against that man, and I shall cut him off from among his people because he gave any of his seed for the Molech so as to make my holy place impure and to desecrate my holy name. ⁴And if the people of the land will hide their eyes from that man when he gives any of his seed for the Molech, not to put him to death, ⁵then I shall set my face at that man and at his fam-ily, and I shall cut off him and all who whore after him, to whore after the Molech, from among their people. ⁶And the person who will turn to ghosts and to spirits of acquaintances to whore after them: I shall set my face against that person and cut him off from among his people.

⁷"And you shall make yourselves holy, and you shall be holy, because I am YHWH, your God. ⁸And you shall observe my laws and do them. I am YHWH, who makes you holy.

⁹"Because any man who will curse his father and his mother shall be put to death. He has cursed his father and his mother: his blood is on him!

¹⁰"And a man who will commit adultery with a man's wife—who will commit adultery with his neighbor's wife!—shall be put to death: the adul-terer and the adulteress. ¹¹And a man who will lie with his father's wife, he has exposed his father's nudity: the two of them shall be put to death. Their blood is on them. ¹²And a man who will lie with his daughter-in-law: the two of them shall be put to death. They have done an aberration. Their blood is on them. ¹³And a man who will lie with a male like lying with a woman: the two of them have done an offensive thing. They shall be put to death. Their blood is on them. ¹⁴And a man who will take a woman and her mother: it is a perversion. You shall burn him and them in fire, so there will not be perver-

sion among you. ¹⁵And a man who will have his intercourse with an animal shall be put to death. And you shall kill the animal. ¹⁶And a woman who will go up to any animal to mate with it: you shall kill the woman and the animal. They shall be put to death. Their blood is on them. ¹⁷And a man who will take his sister, his father's daughter or his mother's daughter, and see her nudity, and she will see his nudity, it is shame; and they will be cut off in the eyes of the children of their people. He has exposed his sister's nudity. He shall bear his crime. ¹⁸And a man who will lie with a menstruating woman and will expose her nudity: he has uncovered her source, and she has exposed the source of her blood. And the two of them will be cut off from among their people. ¹⁹And you shall not expose the nudity of your mother's sister or your father's sister, because one has thus uncovered his close relative. They shall bear their crime. ²⁰And a man who will lie with his aunt: he has exposed his uncle's nudity. They shall bear their sin. They shall die childless. ²¹And a man who will take his brother's wife: it is an impurity. He has exposed his brother's nudity. They will be childless.

²²"And you shall observe all my laws and all my judgments and do them, and the land to which I am bringing you to live in it will not vomit you out. ²³And you shall not go by the laws of the nation that I am ejecting from in front of you, because they have done all of these, and I am disgusted with them. ²⁴And I have said to you: You shall possess their land, and I shall give it to you to possess it, a land flowing with milk and honey. I am YHWH, your God, who has distinguished* you from the peoples, ²⁵and you shall distinguish between the pure animal and the impure, and between the impure bird and the pure, and you shall not make yourselves detestable by an animal or by a bird or by anything that creeps on the ground that I have distinguished as impure for you. ²⁶And you shall be holy to me because I, YHWH, am holy, and I have distinguished you from the peoples to be mine.

²⁷"And a man or woman: if there will be among them a ghost or a spirit of an acquaintance, they shall be put to death. They shall batter them with stone. Their blood is on them."

21

¹And YHWH said to Moses, "Say to the priests, the sons of Aaron, and say to them: One shall not become impure for a person among his people ²except for his relative who is close to him: for his mother and for his

---

*Three more times in this passage (20:24–26) the P term for "distinguishing" occurs, describing what God does and what the people must do so as to be holy, because their God is holy.

father and for his son and for his daughter and for his brother ³and for his virgin sister who is close to him, who has not been a husband's; he may become impure for her. ⁴He shall not become impure as a husband among his people, for him to be desecrated. ⁵They shall not make a bald place on their head and shall not shave the corner of their beard and not make a cut in their flesh. ⁶They shall be holy to their God and shall not desecrate their God's name, because they are bringing forward YHWH's offerings by fire, their God's bread, so they shall be a holy thing. ⁷They shall not take a woman who is a prostitute and desecrated, and they shall not take a woman who is divorced from her husband, because he is holy to his God. ⁸And you shall regard him as holy because he is bringing forward your God's bread. He shall be holy to you because I, YHWH, who makes you holy, am holy. ⁹And the daughter of a man who is a priest who will become desecrated, to whore: she is desecrating her father. She shall be burned in fire.

¹⁰"And the priest who is the most senior of his brothers, on whose head the anointing oil will be poured and who has filled his hand to wear the clothes, he shall not let loose the hair of his head and not tear his clothes ¹¹and he shall not come to any dead persons; he shall not become impure for his father and for his mother. ¹²And he shall not go out from the holy place, so he will not desecrate his God's holy place, because the crown with his God's anointing oil is on him. I am YHWH.

¹³"And he shall take a woman in her virginity. ¹⁴A widow and a divorcee and a desecrated woman, a prostitute: he shall not take these; he shall take none except a virgin from his people. ¹⁵And he shall not desecrate his seed among his people, because I, YHWH, make him holy."

¹⁶And YHWH spoke to Moses, saying, ¹⁷"Speak to Aaron, saying: A man from your seed, through their generations, in whom will be an injury shall not come forward to bring forward his God's bread. ¹⁸Because any man in whom is an injury shall not come forward: a blind man or a cripple or mutilated or has an elongated limb ¹⁹or a man who has a break of the leg or a break of the arm in him ²⁰or a hunchback or a dwarf or who has a spotting in his eye or is scabbed or scurvied or has crushed testicles. ²¹Any man from the seed of Aaron the priest in whom is an injury shall not come near to bring forward YHWH's offerings by fire. He has an injury in him. He shall not come near to bring forward his God's bread. ²²He shall eat his God's bread, from the holies of holies and from the holies. ²³Just: he shall not come to the pavilion, and he shall not come near to the altar, because he has an injury in him. And he shall not desecrate my holy places, because I, YHWH, make them holy."

²⁴So Moses spoke to Aaron and to his sons and to all the children of Israel.

22

¹And YHWH spoke to Moses, saying, ²"Speak to Aaron and to his sons that they be alerted regarding the holy things of the children of Israel that they consecrate to me, so they will not desecrate my holy name. I am YHWH. ³Say to them: Through your generations, any man who will come close, from all of your seed, to the holy things that the children of Israel will consecrate to YHWH, while his impurity is on him: that person will be cut off from in front of me. I am YHWH.

⁴"Any man from Aaron's seed and who is a leper or has an emission shall not eat any of the holy things until he becomes pure. And one who touches anything that is impure by a person, or a man from whom intercourse seed will come out, ⁵or a man who will touch any swarming creature by which he will become impure or a human by whom he will become impure, whatever his impurity: ⁶a person who will touch him will be impure until evening; and he shall not eat from the holy things unless he has washed his flesh in water. ⁷And when the sun has set, he shall be pure, and after that he shall eat from the holy things, because it is his food. ⁸He shall not eat a carcass or a torn animal, to become impure by it. I am YHWH.

⁹"And they shall keep my charge so they will not bear sin over it and die through it when they desecrate it. I, YHWH, make them holy.

¹⁰"And any outsider shall not eat what is holy: a priest's visitor and an employee shall not eat what is holy. ¹¹But when a priest buys a person as a possession by his money, he may eat it; and one who is born in his household: they may eat his bread. ¹²And a priest's daughter who will become an outsider's: she shall not eat the donated holy things; ¹³but a priest's daughter who will be a widow or a divorcée and has no seed and returns to her father's house as in her youth, she may eat from her father's bread. But any outsider shall not eat it. ¹⁴And a man who eats what is holy by mistake shall add to it a fifth of it and shall give the holy thing to the priest. ¹⁵And they shall not desecrate the holy things of the children of Israel that they will donate to YHWH ¹⁶so that they would make them bear a crime requiring a guilt offering by their eating their holy things, because I, YHWH, make them holy."

¹⁷And YHWH spoke to Moses, saying, ¹⁸"Speak to Aaron and to his sons and to all the children of Israel, and you shall say to them: Any man from the house of Israel or from the aliens in Israel who will make his offering—for all their vows and all their contributions that they bring forward to YHWH as a burnt offering— ¹⁹for acceptance for you it is to be unblemished, male of the cattle, of the sheep, or of the goats. ²⁰You shall not bring forward any that

has an injury in it, because it will not be acceptable for you. ²¹And a man who will bring forward a peace-offering sacrifice to YHWH to express a vow or as a contribution of the cattle or of the flock: it shall be unblemished for acceptance; there shall not be any injury in it. ²²Blind or broken or slashed or sore or scabbed or scurvied: you shall not bring these forward to YHWH, and you shall not give an offering by fire of them on the altar to YHWH. ²³An ox or a sheep that has an elongated limb or a short limb: you may make it a contribution, but it shall not be accepted for a vow. ²⁴And you shall not bring forward to YHWH one that is bruised, crushed, torn, or cut. And you shall not do it in your land, ²⁵and you shall not bring forward your God's bread from any of these from a foreigner's hand, because their flaw is in them, an injury is in them; they shall not be accepted for you."

²⁶And YHWH spoke to Moses, saying, ²⁷"When an ox or a sheep or a goat will be born, it will be under its mother seven days, and from the eighth day on it will be accepted as an offering, an offering by fire to YHWH. ²⁸And an ox or a sheep: you shall not slaughter it and its child on one day. ²⁹And if you will make a sacrifice of thanks to YHWH, you shall sacrifice it so it will be acceptable for you. ³⁰It shall be eaten on that day. Do not leave any of it until morning. I am YHWH.

³¹"And you shall observe my commandments and do them. I am YHWH.

³²"And you shall not desecrate my holy name, so I shall be sanctified among the children of Israel. I am YHWH, who makes you holy, ³³who brought you out from the land of Egypt to be God to you. I am YHWH."

23

¹And YHWH spoke to Moses, saying, ²"Speak to the children of Israel, and you shall say to them: YHWH's appointed times, which you shall call holy assemblies—these are my appointed times: ³Six days work shall be done, and in the seventh day is a Sabbath, a ceasing, a holy assembly. You shall not do any work. It is a Sabbath to YHWH in all your homes.

⁴"These are YHWH's appointed times, holy assemblies that you shall proclaim at their appointed time: ⁵In the first month, on the fourteenth of the month, 'between the two evenings,' is YHWH's Passover. ⁶And on the fifteenth day of this month is YHWH's Festival of Unleavened Bread. You shall eat unleavened bread seven days. ⁷On the first day you shall have a holy assembly. You shall not do any act of work. ⁸And you shall bring forward an offering by fire to YHWH for seven days. On the seventh day you shall have a holy assembly. You shall not do any act of work."

⁹And YHWH spoke to Moses, saying, ¹⁰"Speak to the children of Israel, and you shall say to them: When you will come to the land that I am giving to you and you reap its harvest, you shall bring the first sheaf of your harvest to the priest, ¹¹and he shall elevate the sheaf in front of YHWH for acceptance for you. The priest shall elevate it on the day after the Sabbath. ¹²And on the day of your elevating the sheaf, you shall do an unblemished lamb in its first year as a burnt offering to YHWH, ¹³and its grain offering shall be two-tenths of a measure of fine flour mixed with oil, an offering by fire to YHWH, a pleasant smell, and its libation shall be wine, a fourth of a hin. ¹⁴And you shall not eat bread or parched or fresh grain until that very day, until you have brought your God's offering. It is an eternal law through your generations in all your homes. ¹⁵And you shall count from the day after the Sabbath, from the day of your bringing the sheaf for an elevation offering, seven Sabbaths. They shall be complete. ¹⁶You shall count until the day after the seventh Sabbath: fifty days. And you shall bring forward a new grain offering to YHWH. ¹⁷From your homes you shall bring bread for an elevation offering: two of them. They shall be two-tenths of a measure of fine flour, baked with leaven, firstfruits to YHWH. ¹⁸And you shall bring forward with the bread seven lambs, unblemished one-year-olds, and one bull of the cattle and two rams. They shall be a burnt offering to YHWH, with their grain offering and their libations, an offering by fire, a pleasant smell to YHWH. ¹⁹And you shall do one goat as a sin offering and two one-year-old lambs as a peace-offering sacrifice. ²⁰And the priest shall elevate them with the bread of firstfruits, an elevation offering in front of YHWH with the two sheep. They shall be a holy thing to YHWH: for the priest. ²¹And you shall proclaim on that very day: you shall have a holy assembly. You shall not do any act of work: an eternal law in all your homes through your generations. ²²And when you reap your land's harvest, you shall not finish your field's corner when you harvest, and you shall not gather your harvest's gleaning. You shall leave them for the poor and for the alien. I am YHWH, your God."

²³And YHWH spoke to Moses, saying, ²⁴"Speak to the children of Israel, saying: In the seventh month, on the first of the month you shall have a ceasing, a commemoration with horn-blasting, a holy assembly. ²⁵You shall not do any act of work. And you shall bring forward an offering by fire to YHWH."

²⁶And YHWH spoke to Moses, saying, ²⁷"Just: On the tenth of this seventh month, it is the Day of Atonement. You shall have a holy assembly, and you shall degrade yourselves. And you shall bring forward an offering by fire to YHWH. ²⁸And you shall not do any work on this very day, because it is a day of atonement, to atone for you in front of YHWH, your God. ²⁹Because any person who will not be degraded on this very day will be cut off from his

people. ³⁰And any person who will do any work in this very day: I shall destroy that person from among his people. ³¹You shall not do any work: an eternal law through your generations in all your homes. ³²It is a Sabbath, a ceasing, for you, and you shall degrade yourselves: on the ninth of the month in the evening, from evening to evening, you shall keep your Sabbath."

³³And YHWH spoke to Moses, saying, ³⁴"Speak to the children of Israel, saying: On the fifteenth day of this seventh month is the Festival of Booths, seven days, for YHWH. ³⁵On the first day is a holy assembly. You shall not do any act of work. ³⁶For seven days you shall bring forward an offering by fire to YHWH. On the eighth day you shall have a holy assembly, and you shall bring forward an offering by fire to YHWH. It is a convocation. You shall not do any act of work.

³⁷"These are YHWH's appointed times, which you shall call holy assemblies, to bring forward an offering by fire to YHWH: burnt offering and grain offering, sacrifice and libations, each day's thing on its day, ³⁸aside from YHWH's Sabbaths and aside from your gifts and aside from all of your vows and aside from all of your contributions that you will give to YHWH.

³⁹"Just: On the fifteenth day of the seventh month when you gather the land's produce, you shall celebrate YHWH's holiday seven days. On the first day is a ceasing, and on the eighth day is a ceasing. ⁴⁰And on the first day you shall take fruit of appealing trees, branches of palms, boughs of thick trees, and willows of a wadi, and you shall be happy in front of YHWH, your God, seven days. ⁴¹And you shall celebrate it, a holiday to YHWH, seven days in the year, an eternal law through your generations; you shall celebrate it in the seventh month. ⁴²You shall live in booths seven days. Every citizen in Israel shall live in booths, ⁴³so your generations will know that I had the children of Israel live in booths when I brought them out from the land of Egypt. I am YHWH, your God."*

⁴⁴And Moses spoke YHWH's appointed times to the children of Israel.

---

*The list of holidays appears in this chapter in vv. 4–36 and concludes that "These are YHWH's appointed times" (v. 37). But then this passage (vv. 39–43) comes as a strange addition, going back to discussing the Festival of Booths (Sukkot), which had already been covered in the list (vv. 33–36). This added text informs the Israelites for the first time that they are actually commanded to live in booths during this holiday and that they are supposed to take certain species of plants. This curious addition is explained by a passage in the book of Nehemiah (8:13–18). There, when Ezra and the people's leaders study the Torah "they found it written in the Torah that YHWH had commanded by Moses' hand that the children of Israel should live in booths on the holiday." And it has a notation of bringing species of plants similar to those in the passage here in Leviticus. (There is a scribal change of the word *hădas* in Nehemiah for the word *hādār* here in Leviticus.) And the passage in Nehemiah states that this commandment had never been followed in

24

¹And YHWH spoke to Moses, saying, ²"Command the children of Israel that they shall take clear pressed olive oil to you for the light, to keep up a lamp always. ³Outside of the pavilion of the Testimony, in the Tent of Meeting, Aaron shall arrange it from evening until morning in front of YHWH always, an eternal law through your generations. ⁴He shall arrange the lamps on the pure menorah in front of YHWH always.

⁵"And you shall take fine flour and bake it into twelve loaves: each loaf shall be two-tenths of a measure. ⁶And you shall set them in two rows, six to a row, on the pure table in front of YHWH. ⁷And you shall put clear frankincense on each row, and it will be a representative portion for the bread, an offering by fire to YHWH. ⁸On the Sabbath day, on the Sabbath day, he shall arrange it in front of YHWH always from the children of Israel, an eternal covenant. ⁹And it shall be Aaron's and his sons', and they shall eat it in a holy place, because it is the holy of holies to him from YHWH's offerings by fire, an eternal law."

¹⁰And a son of an Israelite woman—and he was a son of an Egyptian man—went out among the children of Israel, and the son of the Israelite woman fought with an Israelite man in the camp. ¹¹And the son of the Israelite woman profaned the name and cursed. And they brought him to Moses. And his mother's name was Shelomith, daughter of Dibri, of the tribe of Dan. ¹²And they left him under watch, to determine it for them by YHWH's word.

¹³And YHWH spoke to Moses, saying, ¹⁴"Take out the one who cursed to the outside of the camp, and let all who heard lay their hands on his head, and all the congregation shall batter him.

¹⁵"And you shall speak to the children of Israel, saying: Any man who curses his God: he shall bear his sin. ¹⁶And one who profanes YHWH's name shall be put to death. All the congregation shall batter him. The same for the alien and the citizen: when he profanes the name he shall be put to death.

¹⁷"And a man who will strike any human's life shall be put to death, ¹⁸and one who strikes an animal's life shall pay for it: a life for a life. ¹⁹And a man who will make an injury in his fellow: as he has done, so it shall be done to him. ²⁰A break for a break, an eye for an eye, a tooth for a tooth: as he will

---

Israel's history in the land ("since the days of Joshua"). This indicates that the commandment about booths was not established together with the other laws of the holidays and that this passage was composed separately and then added to the list. This fits with the conclusion that the redaction of the Torah took place by the time of Ezra and that the P text, to which this addition was made, was composed at an earlier stage of Israel's history.

make an injury in a human, so it shall be made in him. ²¹And one who strikes an animal shall pay for it, and one who strikes a human shall be put to death. ²²You shall have one judgment: it will be the same for the alien and the citizen; because I am YHWH, your God."

²³And Moses spoke to the children of Israel. And they brought out the one who cursed to the outside of the camp, and they battered him with stone.

And the children of Israel had done as YHWH commanded Moses.

25

¹And YHWH spoke to Moses in Mount Sinai, saying, ²"Speak to the children of Israel. And you shall say to them: When you will come to the land that I am giving to you, then the land shall have a Sabbath for YHWH. ³Six years you shall seed your field, and six years you shall prune your vineyard, and you shall gather its produce. ⁴And in the seventh year the land shall have a Sabbath, a ceasing, a Sabbath for YHWH: you shall not seed your field, and you shall not prune your vineyard, ⁵you shall not reap your harvest's free growth, and you shall not cut off your untrimmed grapes. The land shall have a year of ceasing. ⁶And the land's Sabbath shall be yours for food: for you and for your servant and for your maid and for your employee and for your visitor who are residing with you ⁷and for your domestic animal and for the wild animal that are in your land shall be all of its produce to eat.

⁸"And you shall count seven Sabbaths of years: seven years, seven times. And the days of the seven Sabbaths of years shall be for you forty-nine years. ⁹And you shall pass a blasting horn in the seventh month on the tenth of the month: on the Day of Atonement you shall have the horn pass through all your land. ¹⁰And you shall consecrate the year that makes fifty years and proclaim liberty in the land, to all its inhabitants. It shall be a jubilee for you. And you shall go back, each to his possession; and you shall go back, each to his family. ¹¹It, the year that makes fifty years, shall be a jubilee for you. You shall not seed, and you shall not harvest its free growths, and you shall not cut off its untrimmed fruits, ¹²because it is a jubilee; it shall be a holy thing to you. You shall eat its produce from the field. ¹³In this jubilee year you shall go back, each to his possession. ¹⁴And when you will make a sale to your fellow or buy from your fellow's hand: each of you, do not persecute his brother. ¹⁵You shall buy from your fellow by the number of

years after the jubilee. He shall sell to you by the number of years of yields— [16]corresponding to a greater amount of the years, you shall make its price greater; and corresponding to a smaller amount of the years, you shall make its price smaller—because it is a number of yields that he is selling to you. [17]And you shall not persecute—each of you—his brother, but you shall fear your God, because I am YHWH, your God.

[18]"And you shall do my laws and observe my judgments and do them, so you will live on the land in security. [19]And the land will give its fruit, and you will eat to the full, and you will live in security on it. [20]And if you will say, 'What shall we eat in the seventh year? Here, we won't seed and won't gather our produce,' [21]I shall command my blessing for you in the sixth year, and it will make the produce for the three years. [22]And you will seed the eighth year and eat from the old produce until the ninth year; you will eat the old until its produce comes. [23]But the land shall not be sold permanently, because the land is mine, because you are aliens and visitors with me! [24]So in all the land in your possession you shall give a redemption for the land. [25]When your brother will be low so that he will sell any of his possession, then his redeemer who is the closest relative to him shall come and redeem his brother's sale. [26]And when a man will not have a redeemer, but his hand has come to attain it and he has found enough for his redemption, [27]then he shall figure the years of his sale and pay back what is left over to the man to whom he sold it, and he shall go back to his possession. [28]And if his hand has not found enough to pay it back to him, then his sale shall be in the hand of the one who bought it until the jubilee year, and it shall come out in the jubilee, and he shall go back to his possession.

[29]"And when a man will sell a home in a walled city, then its redemption shall be until the end of the year of its sale. Its redemption shall be for days. [30]And if it will not be redeemed by the completion of a full year for it, then the house that is in a city that has a wall shall be established permanently for the one who bought it, through his generations. It shall not come out in the jubilee.

[31]"As for houses of the villages that do not have a wall around them: it shall be figured along with the land's field. It shall have redemption, and it shall come out in the jubilee.

[32]"As for the Levites' cities, the houses in the cities of their possession: the Levites shall have eternal redemption. [33]And that which one from the Levites will redeem: it shall come out, a sale of a house and of a city of his possession, in the jubilee, because that—the houses of the Levites' cities—is

their possession among the children of Israel. [34]But a field of their cities' surrounding land shall not be sold, because it is an eternal possession for them.

[35]"And when your brother will be low so that his hand is slipping with you, then you shall take hold of him—an alien and a visitor—and he shall live with you. [36]Do not take interest or a charge from him; but you shall fear your God, and your brother will live with you. [37]You shall not give him your money for interest, and you shall not give him your food for a charge. [38]I am YHWH, your God, who brought you out from the land of Egypt to give you the land of Canaan, to be God to you.

[39]"And when your brother will be low with you so that he is sold to you, you shall not have him work a slave's work. [40]He shall be like an employee, like a visitor, with you. He shall work with you until the jubilee year. [41]And he shall go out from you, he and his children with him, and go back to his family, and he shall go back to his fathers' possession. [42]Because they are my servants, whom I brought out from the land of Egypt; they shall not be sold like the sale of a slave. [43]You shall not dominate him with harshness, but you shall fear your God.

[44]"And your slave and your maid that you will have: from the nations that are around you, you shall buy a slave or a maid from them. [45]And also from the children of the visitors who reside with you—you shall buy from them and from their families that are with you—to whom they gave birth in your land. And they shall become a possession for you. [46]And you shall make them a legacy for your children after you to inherit as a possession. You may have them work forever, but as for your brothers, the children of Israel—a man toward his brother—you shall not dominate him with harshness.

[47]"And if the hand of an alien and visitor with you will attain it, and your brother is low with him and is sold to the alien and visitor with you or to an offshoot of an alien's family, [48]after he is sold he shall have redemption. One of his brothers shall redeem him, [49]or his uncle or his uncle's son shall redeem him, or some close relative of his from his family shall redeem him; or if his hand can attain it then he can redeem himself. [50]And he shall figure with the one who buys him: from the year he was sold to him to the jubilee year; and the price of his sale shall be by the number of years. It shall be with him like the days of an employee: [51]If there are still a great number of years, he shall pay back his redemption according to them from his purchase price. [52]And if a small amount of years remain until the jubilee year, then he shall figure it for him. He shall pay back his redemption according to his years. [53]He shall be with him like a year-by-year employee. He shall not dominate him with harshness before your eyes. [54]And if he will not be

redeemed by these, then he shall go out in the jubilee year, he and his children with him. ⁵⁵Because the children of Israel are servants to me. They are my servants, whom I brought out from the land of Egypt. I am YHWH, your God.

26

¹"You shall not make idols, and and you shall not set up an image or a pillar, and you shall not put a carved stone in your land to bow at it, because I am YHWH, your God.

²"You shall observe my Sabbaths and fear my sanctuary. I am YHWH.

³"If you will go by my laws, and if you will observe my commandments, and you will do them:

⁴then I shall give your rains in their time,
and the earth will give its crop,
and the tree of the field will give its fruit,
⁵and threshing will extend to vintage for you,
and vintage will extend to seeding,
and you will eat your bread to the full,
and you will live in security in your land,
⁶and I shall give peace in the land,
and you will lie down with no one making you afraid,
and I shall make wild animals cease from the land,
and a sword will not pass through your land,
⁷and you will chase your enemies,
and they will fall in front of you by the sword,
⁸and five of you will chase a hundred,
and a hundred of you will chase ten thousand,
and your enemies will fall in front of you by the sword,
⁹and I shall turn to you,
and I shall make you fruitful and make you multiply,
and I shall establish my covenant with you,
¹⁰and you will eat the oldest of the old,
and you will take out the old because of the new,
¹¹and I shall put my Tabernacle among you,
and my soul will not scorn you,
¹²and I shall walk among you,
and I shall be God to you,
and you will be a people to me.

¹³I am YHWH, your God, who brought you out from the land of Egypt, from being slaves to them, and I broke the beams of your yoke and had you go standing tall.

¹⁴"But if you will not listen to me and not do all these commandments, ¹⁵and if you will reject my laws, and if your souls will scorn my judgments so as not to do all my commandments, so that you break my covenant, ¹⁶I, too, I shall do this to you:

> then I shall appoint terror over you with consumption and with fever,
> > exhausting eyes and grieving the soul,
> and you will sow your seed in vain, for your enemies will eat it,
> ¹⁷and I shall set my face against you,
> and you will be struck before your enemies,
> and ones who hate you will dominate you,
> and you will flee though no one is pursuing you.

¹⁸And if, even after these, you will not listen to me, then I shall add seven times more to discipline you for your sins:

> ¹⁹and I shall break your strong pride,
> and I shall make your skies like iron and your land like bronze,
> ²⁰and your power will be used up in vain,
> and your land will not give its crop,
> and the tree of the land will not give its fruit.

²¹And if you will go on with me in defiance and will not be willing to listen to me, then I shall add seven times more striking on you, corresponding to your sins:

> ²²and I shall let loose the wild animal among you,
> and it will bereave you,
> and it will cut off your cattle,
> and it will diminish you,
> and your roads will be desolated.

²³And if you will not be disciplined for me by these, and you will go on with me in defiance, ²⁴then I shall go on with you, I also, in defiance. And I shall strike you, I too, seven times more for your sins:

> ²⁵and I shall bring a sword over you, requiting covenant retribution,
> and you will be gathered to your cities,
> and I shall let an epidemic go among you,
> and you will be put in your enemy's hand.
> ²⁶When I break the staff of bread for you,
> then ten women will bake your bread in one oven,
> and they will give back your bread by weight,
> and you will eat and not be full.

²⁷And if, through this, you will not listen to me, and you will go on with me in defiance, ²⁸then I shall go on with you in a fury of defiance, and I shall discipline you, I also, seven times more for your sins:

²⁹and you will eat your sons' flesh,

and your daughters' flesh you will eat,

³⁰and I shall destroy your high places,

and I shall cut off your incense altars,

and I shall put your carcasses on your idols' carcasses,

and my soul will scorn you,

³¹and I shall make your cities a ruin,

and I shall devastate your holy places,

and I shall not smell your pleasant smell,

³²and I, I, shall devastate the land,

so your enemies who live in it will be astonished,

³³and you: I shall scatter among the nations,

and I shall unsheath my sword after you,

and your land will be a devastation,

and your cities will be a ruin.

³⁴Then the land will accept its Sabbaths: all the days of devastation, while you are in your enemies' land. Then the land will cease and accept its Sabbaths. ³⁵All the days of the desolation it will cease, the amount that it did not cease on your Sabbaths when you lived on it. ³⁶And those of you who remain:

I shall bring faintness in their hearts in their enemies' lands,

and the sound of a driven leaf will chase them,

and they will flee like the flight from a sword,

and they will fall when there is no one pursuing,

³⁷and they will stumble, each over his brother, as in front of a sword, when there is no one pursuing,

and you will not have a footing in front of your enemies,

³⁸and you will perish among the nations,

and your enemies' land will eat you up.

³⁹And those of you who remain* will rot for their crime in your enemies' lands,

and also for their fathers' crimes with them they will rot.

---

*The last entry of the curse list (v. 39) threatens exile. That does not in itself establish that this passage was written after the Babylonian exile. Exile was a reality in the ancient Near East, and one could imagine it as a curse in any period. The full passage, however, also promises a return from exile, which seems to address an actual community in exile. It is therefore more probably an addition to the list, composed after the Babylonian exile, though we might also consider the possibility that it is original to P and was written with the Assyrian exiles from the northern kingdom of Israel in mind.

⁴⁰"When they will confess their crime and their fathers' crime for their breach that they made against me, and also that they went on with me in defiance, ⁴¹so I, I also, would go on with them in defiance, and I brought them into their enemies' land; or if then their uncircumcised heart will be humbled and then they will accept their crime, ⁴²then I shall remember my covenant of Jacob, and I shall remember also my covenant of Isaac and also my covenant of Abraham, and I shall remember the land. ⁴³And the land will be left from them, and it will accept its Sabbaths while it is devastated from them, and they will accept their crime, because and only because they rejected my judgments and their soul scorned my laws.

⁴⁴"And even despite this, when they were in their enemies' land I did not reject them and did not scorn them, to finish them, to break my covenant with them, because I am YHWH, their God! ⁴⁵So I shall remember for them the covenant of the first ones, whom I brought out from the land of Egypt before the eyes of the nations to be God to them. I am YHWH."

⁴⁶These are the laws and the judgments and the instructions that YHWH gave between Him and the children of Israel in Mount Sinai by Moses' hand.

27

¹And YHWH spoke to Moses, saying, ²"Speak to the children of Israel. And you shall say to them: When a man will express a vow by your appraisal of persons for YHWH, ³then your appraisal shall be:

"A male from twenty years old up to sixty years old: then your appraisal shall be fifty shekels of silver by the shekel of the Holy. ⁴And if it is a female, then your appraisal shall be thirty shekels. ⁵And if one is from five years old up to twenty years old, then your appraisal for a male shall be twenty shekels and for a female ten shekels. ⁶And if one is from a month old up to five years old, then your appraisal for a male shall be five shekels of silver and your appraisal for a female three shekels. ⁷And if one is from sixty years old and up, if a male then your appraisal shall be fifteen shekels, and for a female ten shekels. ⁸And if he is lower than your estimate, then one shall stand him in front of the priest, and the priest shall appraise him. The priest shall appraise him on the basis of what the hand of the one making the vow can attain.

⁹"And if it is an animal from which people would bring an offering to YHWH, everything that he will give of it to YHWH will be a holy thing. ¹⁰And he shall not exchange it and shall not trade it, good for bad or bad for good;

and if he does trade an animal for an animal, then both it and the one traded for it shall be a holy thing. ¹¹And if it is any impure animal, from which people would not bring an offering to YHWH, then he shall stand the animal in front of the priest, ¹²and the priest shall appraise it. Whether good or bad: according to your appraisal by the priest, so it shall be. ¹³And if he will redeem it, then he shall add a fifth of it to your appraisal.

¹⁴"And when a man will consecrate his house to be a holy thing to YHWH, then the priest shall appraise it. Whether good or bad: as the priest will appraise it, so it shall stand. ¹⁵And if the one who consecrates it will redeem his house, then he shall add a fifth of the money of your appraisal to it, and it shall be his.

¹⁶"And if a man will consecrate any of a field of his possession to YHWH, then your appraisal shall be on the basis of its seed: the seed of a homer of barley at fifty shekels of silver. ¹⁷If he will consecrate his field from the jubilee year, it shall stand according to your appraisal; ¹⁸and if he will consecrate his field after the jubilee, then the priest shall figure the money for him on the basis of the years that are left until the jubilee year, and it shall be subtracted from your appraisal. ¹⁹And if the one who consecrates it will redeem the field, then he shall add a fifth of the money of your appraisal to it, and it will stand as his. ²⁰And if he will not redeem the field, or if he has sold the field to another man, it shall not be redeemed anymore. ²¹And when it goes out in the jubilee, the field shall be a holy thing to YHWH, like a devoted field; his possession shall be the priest's.

²²"And if he will consecrate any of a field that he has bought, that is not from a field of his possession, to YHWH, ²³then the priest shall figure for him the count of your appraisal up to the jubilee year, and he shall give your appraisal on that day, a holy thing to YHWH. ²⁴In the jubilee year the field shall go back to the one from whom it was bought, to the one to whom the possession of the land belongs. ²⁵And all of your appraisal shall be by the shekel of the Holy. (The shekel shall be twenty gerah.)

²⁶"Except: a firstling of the animals—which as a firstling is committed to YHWH—no man shall consecrate it. Whether an ox or a sheep, it is YHWH's. ²⁷And if it is of the impure animals, then he shall redeem it at your appraisal, and he shall add to it a fifth of it. And if it will not be redeemed then it shall be sold at your appraisal.

²⁸"Except: any devoted thing that a man will devote to YHWH from anything that he has—from human or animal or from a field of his possession—shall not be sold and shall not be redeemed. Any devoted thing: it is a holy of holies to YHWH. ²⁹Anyone who will be devoted from humans shall not be redeemed. He shall be put to death.

³⁰"And all the tithe of the land, from the land's seed, from the tree's fruit: it is YHWH's, a holy thing to YHWH. ³¹And if a man will redeem some of his tithe, he shall add to it a fifth of it. ³²And all the tithe of a herd or a flock, everything that passes under the rod: the tenth shall be a holy thing to YHWH. ³³He shall not inspect it either for good or for bad. And he shall not trade it. And if he will trade it, then both it and the one traded for it shall be a holy thing. It shall not be redeemed."

³⁴These are the commandments that YHWH commanded Moses for the children of Israel in Mount Sinai.

NUMBERS

1

¹And YHWH spoke to Moses in the wilderness of Sinai in the Tent of Meeting on the first day of the second month in the second year of their exodus from the land of Egypt, saying, ²"Add up the heads of all of the congregation of Israel by their families, by their fathers' houses, with the number of names of every male by their heads. ³From twenty years old and up, everyone going out to the army in Israel: you shall count them by their army units, you and Aaron.

⁴"And a man for each tribe shall be with you; each is the head of his fathers' house. ⁵And these are the names of the men who will stand with you: For Reuben, Elizur son of Shedeur. ⁶For Simeon, Shelumiel son of Zurishadday. ⁷For Judah, Nahshon son of Amminadab. ⁸For Issachar, Nethanel son of Zuar. ⁹For Zebulun, Eliab son of Helon. ¹⁰For the children of Joseph: for Ephraim, Elishama son of Ammihud; for Manasseh, Gamaliel son of Pedahzur. ¹¹For Benjamin, Abidan son of Gideoni. ¹²For Dan, Ahiezer son of Ammishadday. ¹³For Asher, Pagiel son of Ochran. ¹⁴For Gad, Eliasaph son of Deuel. ¹⁵For Naphtali, Ahira son of Enan." ¹⁶These were the prominent ones of the congregation, chieftains of their fathers' tribes. They were heads of Israel's thousands. ¹⁷And Moses and Aaron took these men who were designated by name, ¹⁸and they assembled all of the congregation on the first day of the second month, and they were recorded by their families, by their fathers' houses, with the number of names, from twenty years old and up, by their heads, ¹⁹as YHWH commanded Moses. And he counted them in the wilderness of Sinai.

²⁰And the children of Reuben, Israel's firstborn, were: by their records, by their families, by their fathers' house, with the number of names, by their heads, every male from twenty years old and up, everyone going out to the army, ²¹the tribe of Reuben's counts were forty-six thousand five hundred.

²²For the children of Simeon: by their records, by their families, by their fathers' house, their counts with the number of names, by their heads, every male from twenty years old and up, everyone going out to the army, ²³the tribe of Simeon's counts were fifty-nine thousand three hundred.

²⁴For the children of Gad: by their records, by their families, by their fathers' house, with the number of names, from twenty years old and up, everyone going out to the army, ²⁵the tribe of Gad's counts were forty-five thousand six hundred fifty.

²⁶For the children of Judah: by their records, by their families, by their fathers' house, with the number of names, from twenty years old and up, everyone going out to the army, ²⁷the tribe of Judah's counts were seventy-four thousand six hundred.

²⁸For the children of Issachar: by their records, by their families, by their fathers' house, with the number of names, from twenty years old and up, everyone going out to the army, ²⁹the tribe of Issachar's counts were fifty-four thousand four hundred.

³⁰For the children of Zebulun: by their records, by their families, by their fathers' house, with the number of names, from twenty years old and up, everyone going out to the army, ³¹the tribe of Zebulun's counts were fifty-seven thousand four hundred.

³²For the children of Joseph:

For the children of Ephraim: by their records, by their families, by their fathers' house, with the number of names, from twenty years old and up, everyone going out to the army, ³³the tribe of Ephraim's counts were forty thousand five hundred.

³⁴For the children of Manasseh: by their records, by their families, by their fathers' house, with the number of names, from twenty years old and up, everyone going out to the army, ³⁵the tribe of Manasseh's counts were thirty-two thousand two hundred.

³⁶For the children of Benjamin: by their records, by their families, by their fathers' house, with the number of names, from twenty years old and up, everyone going out to the army, ³⁷the tribe of Benjamin's counts were thirty-five thousand four hundred.

³⁸For the children of Dan: by their records, by their families, by their fathers' house, with the number of names, from twenty years old and up, everyone going out to the army, ³⁹the tribe of Dan's counts were sixty-two thousand seven hundred.

⁴⁰For the children of Asher: by their records, by their families, by their fathers' house, with the number of names, from twenty years old and up, everyone going out to the army, ⁴¹the tribe of Asher's counts were forty-one thousand five hundred.

⁴²The children of Naphtali: by their records, by their families, by their fathers' house, with the number of names, from twenty years old and up, everyone going out to the army, ⁴³the tribe of Naphtali's counts were fifty-three thousand four hundred.

⁴⁴These are the counts that Moses and Aaron and Israel's chieftains made. (They were twelve men, one each for his fathers' house.) ⁴⁵And they were all of the counts of the children of Israel, by their fathers' house, from twenty years old and up, everyone going out to the army in Israel. ⁴⁶And all of the counts were six hundred three thousand five hundred fifty.

⁴⁷And the Levites, by their fathers' tribe, were not counted among them, ⁴⁸for YHWH spoke to Moses, saying, ⁴⁹"Except: you shall not count the tribe of Levi, and you shall not add up their heads among the children of Israel. ⁵⁰And you: appoint the Levites over the Tabernacle of the Testimony and over all its equipment and over everything it has. They shall carry the Tabernacle and all its equipment, and they shall attend to it, and they shall camp around the Tabernacle. ⁵¹And when the Tabernacle travels, the Levites shall take it down; and when the Tabernacle camps, the Levites shall set it up. And an outsider who comes close shall be put to death. ⁵²And the children of Israel shall camp, each at his camp, each at his flag, by their army units, ⁵³and the Levites shall camp all around the Tabernacle of the Testimony, so there will not be a rage on the congregation of the children of Israel, and the Levites shall keep the charge of the Tabernacle of the Testimony."

⁵⁴And the children of Israel did according to everything that YHWH had commanded Moses. They did so.

2 ¹And YHWH spoke to Moses and to Aaron, saying, ²"The children of Israel shall camp, each by his flag with the signs of their fathers' house; they shall camp opposite, all around the Tent of Meeting.* ³And the ones camping on the east: to the east is the flag of Judah's camp by their armies. And the chieftain of the children of Judah is Nahshon son of Amminadab, ⁴and his army and its counts are seventy-four thousand six hundred. ⁵And the ones camping next to it are: the tribe of Issachar. And the chieftain of the children of Issachar is Nethanel son of Zuar, ⁶and his army and its counts are fifty-four thousand four hundred. ⁷The tribe of Zebulun. And the chieftain of the children of Zebulun is Eliab son of Helon, ⁸and his army and its counts are

---

*The Tabernacle is erected inside the camp in Numbers 2 (P), but it is still outside the camp in Num 12:4–15 (E). In E the Tabernacle had been moved outside the camp following the golden-calf incident. See Exod 33:7–11 and the note there.

fifty-seven thousand four hundred. ⁹All the counts of Judah's camp are one hundred eighty-six thousand four hundred by their army units. They shall travel first.

¹⁰"The flag of Reuben's camp on the south by their armies. And the chieftain of the children of Reuben is Elizur son of Shedeur, ¹¹and his army and its counts are forty-six thousand five hundred. ¹²And the ones camping next to it are: the tribe of Simeon. And the chieftain of the children of Simeon is Shelumiel son of Zurishadday, ¹³and his army and their counts are fifty-nine thousand three hundred. ¹⁴And the tribe of Gad. And the chieftain of the children of Gad is Eliasaph son of Reuel, ¹⁵and his army and their counts are forty-five thousand six hundred fifty. ¹⁶All the counts of Reuben's camp are one hundred fifty-one thousand four hundred fifty by their army units. And they shall travel second.

¹⁷"And the Tent of Meeting, the Levites' camp, shall travel inside the camps. As they camp, so they shall travel: each at his position by their flags.

¹⁸"The flag of Ephraim's camp by their armies on the west. And the chieftain of the children of Ephraim is Elishama son of Ammihud, ¹⁹and his army and their counts are forty thousand five hundred. ²⁰And next to it: the camp of Manasseh. And the chieftain of the children of Manasseh is Gamaliel son of Pedahzur, ²¹and his army and their counts are thirty-two thousand two hundred. ²²And the tribe of Benjamin. And the chieftain of the children of Benjamin is Abidan son of Gideoni, ²³and his army and their counts are thirty-five thousand four hundred. ²⁴All the counts of Ephraim's camp are one hundred eight thousand one hundred by their army units. And they shall travel third.

²⁵"The flag of Dan's camp on the north by their armies. And the chieftain of the children of Dan is Ahiezer son of Ammishadday, ²⁶and his army and their counts are sixty-two thousand seven hundred. ²⁷And the ones camping next to it are: the tribe of Asher. And the chieftain of the children of Asher is Pagiel son of Ochran, ²⁸and his army and their counts are forty-one thousand five hundred. ²⁹And the tribe of Naphtali. And the chieftain of the children of Naphtali is Ahira son of Enan, ³⁰and his army and their counts are fifty-three thousand four hundred. ³¹All the counts of Dan's camp are one hundred fifty-seven thousand six hundred. They shall travel last, by their flags."

³²These are the counts of the children of Israel by their fathers' house, all the counts of the camps by their armies: six hundred three thousand five hundred fifty. ³³And the Levites were not counted among the children of Israel, as YHWH had commanded Moses. ³⁴And the children of Israel did according to all that YHWH commanded Moses. So they camped by their flags, and so they traveled, each by his families, by his fathers' house.

3

¹These are the records of Aaron and Moses in the day YHWH spoke to Moses in Mount Sinai. ²And these are the names of Aaron's sons: the firstborn Nadab, and Abihu and Eleazar and Ithamar. ³These are the names of Aaron's sons, the anointed priests, who filled their hand to function as priests. ⁴And Nadab and Abihu died in front of YHWH when they brought forward unfitting fire in front of YHWH in the wilderness of Sinai, and they had no sons; and Eleazar and Ithamar functioned as priests in front of Aaron, their father.

⁵And YHWH spoke to Moses, saying, ⁶"Bring forward the tribe of Levi and stand it in front of Aaron, the priest, so they will attend to him. ⁷And they shall keep his charge and the charge of all the congregation in front of the Tent of Meeting, to do the work of the Tabernacle. ⁸And they shall keep all the equipment of the Tent of Meeting and the charge of the children of Israel, to do the work of the Tabernacle. ⁹And you shall give the Levites to Aaron and to his sons. They are given—given—to him from the children of Israel. ¹⁰And you shall appoint Aaron and his sons, that they shall keep their priesthood, and an outsider who comes close shall be put to death."

¹¹And YHWH spoke to Moses, saying, ¹²"And I, here, I have taken the Levites from among the children of Israel in place of every firstborn, the first birth of the womb, from the children of Israel. And the Levites shall be mine. ¹³Because every firstborn is mine. In the day that I struck every firstborn in the land of Egypt, I consecrated every firstborn in Israel to me, from human to animal. They shall be mine. I am YHWH."

¹⁴And YHWH spoke to Moses in the wilderness of Sinai, saying, ¹⁵"Count the children of Levi by their fathers' house, by their families. You shall count them: every male from a month old and up." ¹⁶And Moses counted them by YHWH's word as he was commanded. ¹⁷And these were Levi's sons by their names: Gershon and Kohath and Merari. ¹⁸And these are the names of Gershon's sons by their families: Libni and Shimei. ¹⁹And Kohath's sons by their families: Amram and Izhar, Hebron and Uzziel. ²⁰And Merari's sons by their families: Mahli and Mushi. These are the Levite families by their fathers' house.

²¹Gershon had the Libnite family and the Shimeite family. These are the Gershonite families. ²²Their counts by the number of every male from a month old and up: their counts were seven thousand five hundred. ²³The Gershonite families were to camp behind the Tabernacle, to the west. ²⁴And the chieftain of the Gershonite father's house was Eliasaph son of Lael. ²⁵And the charge of the sons of Gershon in the Tent of Meeting was the Tabernacle

and the tent, its covering and the cover of the entrance of the Tent of Meeting
²⁶and the courtyard's hangings and the cover for the entrance of the court-
yard that is all around the Tabernacle and the altar, and its cords, for all of its
service.

²⁷And Kohath had the Amramite family and the Izharite family and the
Hebronite family and the Uzzielite family. These are the Kohathite families.
²⁸By the number of every male from a month old and up: eight thousand six
hundred keeping the charge of the Holy. ²⁹The families of the children of
Kohath were to camp to the south. ³⁰And the chieftain of the father's house
for the Kohathite families was Elizaphan son of Uzziel. ³¹And their charge
was the ark and the table and the menorah and the altars and the equipment
of the Holy with which they minister and the cover and all of its service.

³²And the chieftain of chieftains of the Levites was Eleazar son of Aaron,
the priest, with responsibility for those who keep the charge of the Holy.

³³And Merari had the Mahlite family and the Mushite family. These are
the Merarite families. ³⁴And their counts by the number of every male from a
month old and up: six thousand two hundred. ³⁵And the chieftain of the
father's house for the Merarite families was Zuriel son of Abihail. They were
to camp on the side of the Tabernacle to the north. ³⁶And the responsibility of
the charge of the children of Merari was the Tabernacle's frames and its bars
and its columns and its bases and all of its equipment and all of its service
³⁷and the courtyard's columns all around and their bases and their pegs and
their cords.

³⁸And those who camped in front of the Tabernacle, on the east, in front
of the Tent of Meeting, to the east, were Moses and Aaron and his sons,
keeping the charge of the holy place, for the charge of the children of Israel.
And the outsider who will come close shall be put to death.

³⁹All the counts of the Levites that Moses and Aaron made by YHWH's
word, by their families, every male from a month old and up were twenty-two
thousand.

⁴⁰And YHWH said to Moses, "Count every male firstborn of the children
of Israel from a month old and up, and add up the number of their names.
⁴¹And you shall take the Levites for me—I am YHWH—in place of every first-
born in the children of Israel, and the Levites' animals in place of every firstborn in the animals of the children of Israel." ⁴²And Moses counted, as YHWH
commanded him, every firstborn in the children of Israel. ⁴³And every male
firstborn, by the number of names, from a month old and up, by their counts
were twenty-two thousand two hundred seventy-three. ⁴⁴And YHWH spoke
to Moses, saying, ⁴⁵"Take the Levites in place of every firstborn in the children of Israel, and the Levites' animals in place of their animals, and the

Levites shall be mine. I am YHWH. ⁴⁶And for the redemption of the two hundred seventy-three who are left over above the Levites from the firstborn of
the children of Israel, ⁴⁷you shall take five shekels each per head; you shall
take it by the shekel of the Holy. (The shekel is twenty gerah.) ⁴⁸And you
shall give the money to Aaron and to his sons for the redemption of those left
over among them." ⁴⁹And Moses took the money of the redemption from
those left over above those who were redeemed by the Levites. ⁵⁰He took the
money from the firstborn of the children of Israel: one thousand three hundred sixty-five by the shekel of the Holy. ⁵¹And Moses gave the money for
those who were redeemed to Aaron and to his sons by YHWH's word, as
YHWH commanded Moses.

4

¹And YHWH spoke to Moses and to Aaron, saying, ²"Add up the heads
of the children of Kohath from among the children of Levi by their families, by
their fathers' house, ³from thirty years old and up to fifty years old, everyone
who would come to the army to do work in the Tent of Meeting. ⁴This is the
work of the sons of Kohath in the Tent of Meeting: the Holy of Holies.

⁵"And Aaron and his sons shall come when the camp is to travel, and
they shall take down the covering pavilion and cover the ark of the testimony
with it. ⁶And they shall put a cover of leather and shall spread a fabric all of
blue above it and put in its poles. ⁷And on the table of show bread they shall
spread a blue fabric, and they shall put on it the dishes and the pans and the
bowls and the libation jars; and the continual bread shall be on it. ⁸And they
shall spread a scarlet fabric over them and cover it with a leather covering
and set its poles. ⁹And they shall take a blue fabric and cover the menorah
for lighting and its lamps and its tongs and its fire-holders and all of its
equipment for oil with which they will minister for it. ¹⁰And they shall put it
and all its equipment into a leather covering and put it on a beam. ¹¹And on
the gold altar they shall spread a blue fabric, and they shall cover it with a
leather covering and set its poles. ¹²And they shall take all the equipment for
ministering with which they minister in the Holy and put them into a blue
fabric and cover them with a leather covering and put them on a beam. ¹³And
they shall clear the ashes from the altar and spread a purple fabric over it.
¹⁴And they shall put on it all its equipment with which they minister at it—
the fire-holders, the forks and the shovels and the basins—all the altar's
equipment, and they shall spread a leather covering on it and set its poles.
¹⁵And Aaron and his sons will finish covering the Holy and all the equipment
of the Holy when the camp is to travel, and after that the children of Kohath

shall come to carry, so they shall not touch the holy and die. These are what the children of Kohath are to carry in the Tent of Meeting.

¹⁶"And the responsibility of Eleazar son of Aaron, the priest, is the oil for lighting and the incense of fragrances and the continual grain offering and the anointing oil—the responsibility for all of the Tabernacle and everything that is in it, in the Holy and in its equipment."

¹⁷And YHWH spoke to Moses and to Aaron, saying, ¹⁸"You shall not cut off the tribe of the Kohathite families from among the Levites, ¹⁹but do this to them so they will live and not die when they come close to the Holy of Holies: Aaron and his sons shall come, and they shall set them each at his work and to what he is to carry, ²⁰and they shall not come to see as the Holy is covered up and die."

²¹And YHWH spoke to Moses, saying, ²²"Add up the heads of the children of Gershon, them as well, by their fathers' house, by their families. ²³You shall count them from thirty years old and up to fifty years old, everyone who would come to do army service, to do work in the Tent of Meeting. ²⁴This is the work of the Gershonite families, for work and for carrying: ²⁵And they shall carry the curtains of the Tabernacle, and the Tent of Meeting, its covering, and the leather covering that is on it above, and the cover of the entrance of the Tent of Meeting ²⁶and the courtyard's hangings and the cover for the entrance of the gate of the courtyard that is all around the Tabernacle and the altar, and their cords and all the equipment for their service. And everything that will be done for them: they shall do the work. ²⁷All the work of the children of the Gershonites shall be by the word of Aaron and his sons, for all their carrying and all their work. And you shall supervise them in the task: all their carrying. ²⁸This is the work of the families of the children of the Gershonites in the Tent of Meeting. And their charge is in the hand of Ithamar son of Aaron, the priest.

²⁹"The children of Merari by their families, by their fathers' house: you shall count them. ³⁰You shall count them from thirty years old and up to fifty years old, everyone who would come to the army, to do the work of the Tent of Meeting. ³¹And this is their carrying task, for all their work in the Tent of Meeting: the Tabernacle's frames and its bars and its columns and its bases ³²and the courtyard's columns all around and their bases and their pegs and their cords, for all their equipment and all their service. And you shall take account of the equipment for their carrying task by name. ³³This is the work of the families of the children of Merari, for all their work in the Tent of Meeting in the hand of Ithamar son of Aaron, the priest."

³⁴And Moses and Aaron and the congregation's chieftains counted the Kohathite children by their families and by their fathers' house ³⁵from thirty years old and up to fifty years old, everyone who would come to the army for the work of the Tent of Meeting. ³⁶And their counts by their families were two

thousand seven hundred fifty. [37]These are the counts of the Kohathite families, everyone who worked in the Tent of Meeting, whom Moses and Aaron counted by YHWH's word through Moses' hand.

[38]And the counts of the children of Gershon by their families and by their fathers' house [39]from thirty years old and up to fifty years old, everyone who would come to the army for work in the Tent of Meeting: [40]And their counts by their families, by their fathers' house, were two thousand six hundred thirty. [41]These are the counts of the families of the children of Gershon, everyone who worked in the Tent of Meeting, whom Moses and Aaron counted by YHWH's word.

[42]And the counts of the families of the children of Merari by their families, by their fathers' house [43]from thirty years old and up to fifty years old, everyone who would come to the army for work in the Tent of Meeting: [44]And their counts by their families were three thousand two hundred. [45]These are the counts of the families of the children of Merari whom Moses and Aaron counted by YHWH's word through Moses' hand.

[46]All the counts that Moses and Aaron and Israel's chieftains made of the Levites by their families and by their fathers' house [47]from thirty years old and up to fifty years old, everyone who was coming to do the service of work and the service of carrying in the Tent of Meeting: [48]And their counts were eight thousand five hundred eighty. [49]By YHWH's word he counted them by Moses' hand, each man by his work or by his carrying, and his counts were as YHWH commanded Moses.

5

[1]And YHWH spoke to Moses, saying, [2]"Command the children of Israel that they shall have every leper and everyone who has an emission and everyone who is impure by a person go from the camp. [3]Male or female, you shall have them go; you shall have them go outside the camp so they will not make their camps, among which I tent, impure." [4]And the children of Israel did so, and they had them go outside the camp. As YHWH spoke to Moses, so the children of Israel did.

[5]And YHWH spoke to Moses, saying, [6]"Speak to the children of Israel: A man or a woman—when they will do any of the sins of humans, to make a breach against YHWH—so that person has guilt, [7]then they shall confess their sin that they have done. And he shall pay back for his guilt with its principal, and he shall add to it a fifth of it, and he shall give it to the one whom he wronged. [8]And if the man does not have a redeemer, to pay him back for the guilt, the guilt that is paid back is YHWH's, for the priest, apart from the ram of atonement by which he will make atonement for him. [9]And every

donation of all the holy things of the children of Israel that they will bring forward to the priest shall be his. [10]And each man's holy things shall be his; what each man gives to the priest shall be his."

[11]And YHWH spoke to Moses, saying, [12]"Speak to the children of Israel, and you shall say to them: Any man whose wife will go astray and will make a breach of faith with him, [13]and a man has lain with her—an intercourse of seed—and it has been hidden from her husband's eyes, and she has kept concealed, and she has been made impure, and there is no witness against her, and she has not been caught, [14]and a spirit of jealousy has come over him, and he is jealous about his wife, and she has been made impure, or a spirit of jealousy has come over him, and he is jealous about his wife, and she has not been made impure: [15]then the man shall bring his wife to the priest and shall bring her offering along with her: a tenth of an ephah of barley flour. He shall not pour oil on it and shall not put frankincense on it, because it is an offering about jealousies, an offering about being recalled: causing a crime to be recalled.

[16]"And the priest shall bring her forward and stand her in front of YHWH. [17]And the priest shall take holy water in a clay container, and the priest shall take some of the dust that will be on the Tabernacle's floor and put it into the water. [18]And the priest shall stand the woman in front of YHWH and loosen the hair of the woman's head and put the offering of bringing to mind on her hands; it is an offering of jealousies. And in the priest's hand shall be the bitter cursing water. [19]And the priest shall have her swear, and he shall say to the woman: 'If a man has not lain with you, and if you have not gone astray in impurity with someone in place of your husband, be cleared by this bitter cursing water. [20]But you, if you have gone astray with someone in place of your husband and if you have been made impure, and if a man other than your husband has had his intercourse with you,' [21]then the priest shall have the woman swear a curse oath, and the priest shall say to the woman, 'Let YHWH make you a curse and an oath among your people when YHWH sets your thigh sagging and your womb swelling, [22]and this cursing water will come in your insides, to swell the womb and make the thigh sag.'

"And the woman shall say, 'Amen, amen.'

[23]"And the priest shall write these curses in a scroll and rub them into the bitter water. [24]And he shall have the woman drink the bitter cursing water, and the bitter cursing water will come into her. [25]And the priest shall take the offering of jealousies from the woman's hand and elevate the offering in front of YHWH, and he shall bring her forward to the altar. [26]And the priest shall take a fistful from the grain offering, a representative portion of it, and burn it to smoke at the altar, and after that he shall have the woman

drink the water. ²⁷When he has had her drink the water, then it will be, if she has been made impure and has made a breach of faith with her husband, when the bitter cursing water will come into her, and her womb will swell and her thigh will sag, then the woman will become a curse among her people. ²⁸And if the woman has not been made impure, and she is pure, then she shall be cleared and shall conceive seed.

²⁹"This is the instruction for jealousies, when a woman will go astray with someone in place of her husband and be made impure, ³⁰or when a spirit of jealousy will come over a man and he will be jealous about his wife. And the priest shall stand the woman in front of YHWH and do all of this instruction to her. ³¹And the man shall be clear of a crime, and that woman shall bear her crime."

6 ¹And YHWH spoke to Moses, saying, ²"Speak to the children of Israel, and you shall say to them: When a man or a woman will expressly make a Nazirite vow to make a separation for YHWH, ³he shall separate from wine and beer; he shall not drink any vinegar of wine or vinegar of beer, and he shall not drink any juice of grapes, and he shall not eat fresh or dried grapes. ⁴All the days of his being a Nazirite, he shall not eat anything that is made from the grapevine, from seeds to skin. ⁵All the days of his Nazirite vow, a razor shall not pass on his head; until the fulfillment of the days that he will make a separation for YHWH, he shall be holy, growing the hair of his head loose. ⁶All the days of his making a separation for YHWH he shall not come to a dead person. ⁷For his father and for his mother, for his brother and for his sister: he shall not become impure for them when they die, because the crown of his God is on his head. ⁸All the days of his being a Nazirite he is holy to YHWH. ⁹And if someone will die by chance suddenly by him and will make his head's crown impure, then he shall shave his head on the day of his purification: he shall shave it on the seventh day. ¹⁰And on the eighth day he shall bring two turtledoves or two pigeons to the priest, to the entrance of the Tent of Meeting. ¹¹And the priest shall do one as a sin offering and one as a burnt offering and shall make atonement over him in that he has sinned over a person. And he shall make his head holy on that day. ¹²And he shall make a separation for YHWH for the days of his being a Nazirite, and he shall bring a lamb in its first year for a guilt offering, and the first days shall fall because his Nazirite state became impure.

¹³"And this is the instruction for the Nazirite: On the day of the fulfillment of the days of his being a Nazirite, one shall bring him to the entrance

of the Tent of Meeting. ¹⁴And he shall make his offering to YHWH: one unblemished lamb in its first year for a burnt offering and one unblemished ewe-lamb in its first year for a sin offering and one unblemished ram for a peace offering ¹⁵and a basket of unleavened bread of fine flour, cakes mixed with oil and unleavened wafers with oil poured on them with their grain offering and their libations. ¹⁶And the priest shall bring it forward in front of YHWH and shall do his sin offering and his burnt offering. ¹⁷And he shall make the ram a peace-offering sacrifice to YHWH with the basket of unleavened bread, and the priest shall do his grain offering and his libation. ¹⁸And the Nazirite shall shave his head's crown at the entrance of the Tent of Meeting and shall take the hair of his head's crown and put it on the fire that is under the peace-offering sacrifice. ¹⁹And the priest shall take the cooked shoulder from the ram and one unleavened cake from the basket and one unleavened wafer and put them on the Nazirite's hands after his crown is shaved. ²⁰And the priest shall elevate them, an elevation offering in front of YHWH. It is holy for the priest along with the breast of the elevation offering and the thigh of the donation. And after that the Nazirite may drink wine. ²¹This is the instruction for the Nazirite who will vow his offering to YHWH for his being a Nazirite outside of what his hand may attain. According to his vow that he will make, so he shall do along with the instruction of his being a Nazirite."

²²And YHWH spoke to Moses, saying, ²³"Speak to Aaron and to his sons, saying, This is how you shall bless the children of Israel; say to them:

²⁴ May YHWH bless you and watch over you.
²⁵ May YHWH make His face shine to you and be gracious to you.
²⁶ May YHWH raise His face to you and give you peace.

²⁷And they shall set my name on the children of Israel, and I shall bless them."

7

¹And it was on the day that Moses finished setting up the Tabernacle, and he anointed it and made it and all its equipment and the altar and all its equipment holy. He anointed them and made them holy. ²And Israel's chieftains, the heads of their fathers' house brought forward—they were the tribes' chieftains; they were the ones standing over those who were counted— ³and they brought their offering in front of YHWH: six covered wagons and twelve oxen, a wagon for two chieftains and an ox for each one. And they brought them in front of the Tabernacle.

⁴And YHWH said to Moses, saying, ⁵"Take them from them, and they will be for doing the work of the Tent of Meeting. And you shall give them to the Levites, to each man according to his work."

⁶And Moses took the wagons and the oxen and gave them to the Levites. ⁷He gave two wagons and four oxen to the sons of Gershon according to their work. ⁸And he gave four wagons and eight oxen to the sons of Merari according to their work in the hand of Ithamar son of Aaron, the priest. ⁹And he did not give to the sons of Kohath, because the service of the Holy is their responsibility. They would carry on the shoulder. ¹⁰And the chieftains brought forward the altar's dedication offering on the day it was anointed, and the chieftains made their offering in front of the altar.

¹¹And YHWH said to Moses, "One chieftain on a day, one chieftain on the next day, they shall make their offering for the altar's dedication offering."

¹²And the one who made his offering on the first day was Nahshon son of Amminadab for the tribe of Judah. ¹³And his offering was one silver dish, its weight in shekels a hundred thirty; one silver basin, seventy shekels by the shekel of the Holy; both of them were full of fine flour mixed with oil for a grain offering; ¹⁴one gold pan, ten shekels, full of incense; ¹⁵one bull of the cattle, one ram, one lamb in its first year for a burnt offering; ¹⁶one goat for a sin offering; ¹⁷and for a peace-offering sacrifice two oxen, five rams, five he-goats, five lambs a year old. This was the offering of Nahshon son of Amminadab.

¹⁸On the second day, Nethanel son of Zuar, chieftain of Issachar, brought forward. ¹⁹He made his offering: one silver dish, its weight in shekels a hundred thirty; one silver basin, seventy shekels by the shekel of the Holy; both of them were full of fine flour mixed with oil for a grain offering; ²⁰one gold pan, ten shekels, full of incense; ²¹one bull of the cattle, one ram, one lamb in its first year for a burnt offering; ²²one goat for a sin offering; ²³and for a peace-offering sacrifice two oxen, five rams, five he-goats, five lambs a year old. This was the offering of Nethanel son of Zuar.

²⁴On the third day, the chieftain of the children of Zebulun, Eliab son of Helon. ²⁵His offering was one silver dish, its weight in shekels a hundred thirty; one silver basin, seventy shekels by the shekel of the Holy; both of them were full of fine flour mixed with oil for a grain offering; ²⁶one gold pan, ten shekels, full of incense; ²⁷one bull of the cattle, one ram, one lamb in its first year for a burnt offering; ²⁸one goat for a sin offering; ²⁹and for a peace-offering sacrifice two oxen, five rams, five he-goats, five lambs a year old. This was the offering of Eliab son of Helon.

³⁰On the fourth day, the chieftain of the children of Reuben, Elizur son of Shedeur. ³¹His offering was one silver dish, its weight in shekels a hundred thirty; one silver basin, seventy shekels by the shekel of the Holy; both of

them were full of fine flour mixed with oil for a grain offering; [32]one gold pan, ten shekels, full of incense; [33]one bull of the cattle, one ram, one lamb in its first year for a burnt offering; [34]one goat for a sin offering; [35]and for a peace-offering sacrifice two oxen, five rams, five he-goats, five lambs a year old. This was the offering of Elizur son of Shedeur.

[36]On the fifth day, the chieftain of the children of Simeon, Shelumiel son of Zurishadday. [37]His offering was one silver dish, its weight in shekels a hundred thirty; one silver basin, seventy shekels by the shekel of the Holy; both of them were full of fine flour mixed with oil for a grain offering; [38]one gold pan, ten shekels, full of incense; [39]one bull of the cattle, one ram, one lamb in its first year for a burnt offering; [40]one goat for a sin offering; [41]and for a peace-offering sacrifice two oxen, five rams, five he-goats, five lambs a year old. This was the offering of Shelumiel son of Zurishadday.

[42]On the sixth day, the chieftain of the children of Gad, Eliasaph son of Deuel. [43]His offering was one silver dish, its weight in shekels a hundred thirty; one silver basin, seventy shekels by the shekel of the Holy; both of them were full of fine flour mixed with oil for a grain offering; [44]one gold pan, ten shekels, full of incense; [45]one bull of the cattle, one ram, one lamb in its first year for a burnt offering; [46]one goat for a sin offering; [47]and for a peace-offering sacrifice two oxen, five rams, five he-goats, five lambs a year old. This was the offering of Eliasaph son of Deuel.

[48]On the seventh day, the chieftain of the children of Ephraim, Elishama son of Ammihud. [49]His offering was one silver dish, its weight in shekels a hundred thirty; one silver basin, seventy shekels by the shekel of the Holy; both of them were full of fine flour mixed with oil for a grain offering; [50]one gold pan, ten shekels, full of incense; [51]one bull of the cattle, one ram, one lamb in its first year for a burnt offering; [52]one goat for a sin offering; [53]and for a peace-offering sacrifice two oxen, five rams, five he-goats, five lambs a year old. This was the offering of Elishama son of Ammihud.

[54]On the eighth day, the chieftain of the children of Manasseh, Gamaliel son of Pedahzur. [55]His offering was one silver dish, its weight in shekels a hundred thirty; one silver basin, seventy shekels by the shekel of the Holy; both of them were full of fine flour mixed with oil for a grain offering; [56]one gold pan, ten shekels, full of incense; [57]one bull of the cattle, one ram, one lamb in its first year for a burnt offering; [58]one goat for a sin offering; [59]and for a peace-offering sacrifice two oxen, five rams, five he-goats, five lambs a year old. This was the offering of Gamaliel son of Pedahzur.

[60]On the ninth day, the chieftain of the children of Benjamin, Abidan son of Gideoni. [61]His offering was one silver dish, its weight in shekels a hundred thirty; one silver basin, seventy shekels by the shekel of the Holy; both of

them were full of fine flour mixed with oil for a grain offering; ⁶²one gold pan, ten shekels, full of incense; ⁶³one bull of the cattle, one ram, one lamb in its first year for a burnt offering; ⁶⁴one goat for a sin offering; ⁶⁵and for a peace-offering sacrifice two oxen, five rams, five he-goats, five lambs a year old. This was the offering of Abidan son of Gideoni.

⁶⁶On the tenth day, the chieftain of the children of Dan, Ahiezer son of Ammishadday. ⁶⁷His offering was one silver dish, its weight in shekels a hundred thirty; one silver basin, seventy shekels by the shekel of the Holy; both of them were full of fine flour mixed with oil for a grain offering; ⁶⁸one gold pan, ten shekels, full of incense; ⁶⁹one bull of the cattle, one ram, one lamb in its first year for a burnt offering; ⁷⁰one goat for a sin offering; ⁷¹and for a peace-offering sacrifice two oxen, five rams, five he-goats, five lambs a year old. This was the offering of Ahiezer son of Ammishadday.

⁷²On the eleventh day, the chieftain of the children of Asher, Pagiel son of Ochran. ⁷³His offering was one silver dish, its weight in shekels a hundred thirty; one silver basin, seventy shekels by the shekel of the Holy; both of them were full of fine flour mixed with oil for a grain offering; ⁷⁴one gold pan, ten shekels, full of incense; ⁷⁵one bull of the cattle, one ram, one lamb in its first year for a burnt offering; ⁷⁶one goat for a sin offering; ⁷⁷and for a peace-offering sacrifice two oxen, five rams, five he-goats, five lambs a year old. This was the offering of Pagiel son of Ochran.

⁷⁸On the twelfth day, the chieftain of the children of Naphtali, Ahira son of Enan. ⁷⁹His offering was one silver dish, its weight in shekels a hundred thirty; one silver basin, seventy shekels by the shekel of the Holy; both of them were full of fine flour mixed with oil for a grain offering; ⁸⁰one gold pan, ten shekels, full of incense; ⁸¹one bull of the cattle, one ram, one lamb in its first year for a burnt offering; ⁸²one goat for a sin offering; ⁸³and for a peace-offering sacrifice two oxen, five rams, five he-goats, five lambs a year old. This was the offering of Ahira son of Enan.

⁸⁴This was the dedication offering of the altar from Israel's chieftains on the day of its being anointed: Twelve silver dishes, twelve silver basins, twelve gold pans, ⁸⁵each dish being a hundred thirty of silver, and each basin seventy; all the silver of the items was two thousand four hundred by the shekel of the Holy. ⁸⁶Twelve gold pans full of incense, the pans being ten each by the shekel of the Holy; all the gold of the pans was a hundred twenty. ⁸⁷All the oxen for the burnt offering were twelve bulls, twelve rams, twelve lambs a year old and their grain offering and twelve goats for a sin offering. ⁸⁸And all the oxen of the peace-offering sacrifice were twenty-four bulls, sixty rams, sixty he-goats, sixty lambs a year old. This was the dedication offering of the altar after its being anointed.

⁸⁹And when Moses came into the Tent of Meeting to speak with Him, then he heard the voice speaking to him from above the atonement dais that was on the Ark of the Testimony, from between the two cherubs, and He spoke to him.

8 ¹And YHWH spoke to Moses, saying, ²"Speak to Aaron, and you shall say to him: 'When you put up the lamps, the seven lamps shall shed light opposite the front of the menorah.'" ³And Aaron did so. He put up its lamps opposite the front of the menorah as YHWH had commanded Moses. ⁴And this was the menorah's construction: hammered work of gold; including its shaft, including its flower, it was hammered work. According to the appearance that YHWH had shown Moses, so he made the menorah.

⁵And YHWH spoke to Moses, saying, ⁶"Take the Levites from among the children of Israel, and make them pure. ⁷And this is what you shall do to them to make them pure: you shall sprinkle water of sin expiation on them, and they shall pass a razor over all of their flesh, and they shall wash their clothes, and so they will be made pure. ⁸And they shall take a bull of the cattle and its grain offering, fine flour mixed with oil; and you shall take a second bull of the cattle for a sin offering. ⁹And you shall bring the Levites forward in front of the Tent of Meeting, and you shall assemble all of the congregation of the children of Israel. ¹⁰And you shall bring the Levites forward in front of YHWH, and the children of Israel shall lay their hands on the Levites. ¹¹And Aaron shall make the Levites an elevation offering in front of YHWH from the children of Israel, and they shall be to do YHWH's service. ¹²And the Levites shall lay their hands on the bulls' heads. And make one a sin offering and one a burnt offering for YHWH to make atonement for the Levites. ¹³And you shall stand the Levites in front of Aaron and in front of his sons and make them an elevation offering for YHWH. ¹⁴And you shall distinguish the Levites from among the children of Israel, and the Levites shall be mine. ¹⁵And after that the Levites shall come to work at the Tent of Meeting, when you have made them pure and made them an elevation offering. ¹⁶Because they are given, given, to me from among the children of Israel. I have taken them to me in place of the first birth of every womb, the firstborn of everyone from the children of Israel. ¹⁷Because every firstborn of the children Israel is mine, of human and of animal; on the day that I struck every firstborn in the land of Egypt I consecrated them to me. ¹⁸And I took the Levites in place of every firstborn of the children of Israel ¹⁹and gave the

Levites—they are given—to Aaron and to his sons from among the children of Israel to do the work of the children of Israel in the Tent of Meeting and to make atonement for the children of Israel, so there will not be a plague in the children of Israel when the children of Israel would come near to the Holy."

²⁰And Moses and Aaron and all the congregation of the children of Israel did to the Levites according to all that YHWH commanded Moses about the Levites; the children of Israel did so to them. ²¹And the Levites did sin expiation and washed their clothes, and Aaron made them an elevation offering in front of YHWH, and Aaron made atonement for them to make them pure. ²²And after that the Levites came to do their work in the Tent of Meeting in front of Aaron and in front of his sons. As YHWH commanded Moses about the Levites, so they did to them.

²³And YHWH spoke to Moses, saying, ²⁴"This is what the Levites have: from twenty-five years old and up each shall come to do army service by the work of the Tent of Meeting; ²⁵and from fifty years old he shall go back from the army service and shall not work anymore; ²⁶and he shall minister with his brothers in the Tent of Meeting to keep the charge, but he shall not do work. You shall do thus to the Levites regarding their charge."

9

¹And YHWH had spoken to Moses in the wilderness of Sinai in the second year of their exodus from the land of Egypt, in the first month, saying, ²"And the children of Israel shall do the Passover at its appointed time. ³On the fourteenth day in this month 'between the two evenings' you shall do it at its appointed time. You shall do it according to all of its law and according to all of its judgments."

⁴And Moses had spoken to the children of Israel to do the Passover, ⁵and they had done the Passover in the first month on the fourteenth day of the month "between the two evenings" in the wilderness of Sinai. According to all that YHWH had commanded Moses, so the children of Israel had done.

⁶And there had been people who were impure by a human being and so had not been able to do the Passover on that day, and they had come forward in front of Moses and in front of Aaron on that day, ⁷and those people had said to him, "We're impure by a human being. Why should we be excluded so as not to make YHWH's offering at its appointed time among the children of Israel?"

⁸And Moses had said, "Stay, and let me hear what YHWH will command about you."

⁹And YHWH had spoken to Moses, saying, ¹⁰"Speak to the children of Israel, saying: Any man who will be impure by a person or on a faraway journey—among you or through your generations—and will do the Passover for YHWH, ¹¹they shall do it in the second month on the fourteenth day 'between the two evenings.' They shall eat it with unleavened bread and bitter herbs. ¹²They shall not leave any of it until morning, and they shall not break a bone of it. They shall do it according to all of the law of the Passover. ¹³But a man who is pure and has not been on a journey and has failed to do the Passover: that person will be cut off from his people, because he did not make YHWH's offering at its appointed time. That man shall bear his sin. ¹⁴And if an alien will reside with you and will do the Passover for YHWH: according to the law of the Passover and according to its required manner, so he shall do it. You shall have one law, for the alien and for the citizen of the land."

¹⁵And on the day that the Tabernacle was set up, the cloud covered the Tabernacle of the tent of the Testimony, and in the evening it would be over the Tabernacle like the appearance of fire until morning. ¹⁶So it would be always: the cloud would cover it and the appearance of fire at night. ¹⁷And according to when the cloud was lifted from over the tent, after that the children of Israel would travel. And in a place where the cloud would tent, the children of Israel would camp there. ¹⁸By YHWH's word the children of Israel would travel, and by YHWH's word they would camp. All the days that the cloud would tent over the Tabernacle they would camp. ¹⁹And when the cloud would extend many days over the Tabernacle, then the children of Israel kept YHWH's charge and would not travel. ²⁰And there were times that the cloud would be over the Tabernacle for a number of days: by YHWH's word they would camp, and by YHWH's word they would travel. ²¹And there were times that the cloud would be there from evening until morning, and the cloud was lifted in the morning, and then they would travel; or for a day and a night, and the cloud was lifted, and then they traveled. ²²Whether two days or a month or a year, when the cloud would extend long over the Tabernacle, to tent over it, the children of Israel would camp and would not travel, and when it was lifted they would travel. ²³By YHWH's word they would camp, and by YHWH's word they would travel. They kept YHWH's charge, by YHWH's word through Moses' hand.*

---

*With this passage the Redactor fashioned the framework for all the coming stories of Israel's travels through the wilderness. It works together with the itinerary list of Numbers 33 to set the stories in a chronological progression of episodes. It establishes that the people might stay for a long or short time at any given stop on the way, thus making it possible for a single event or a sequence of events to take place at any given location.

10

¹And YHWH spoke to Moses, saying, ²"Make two trumpets of silver. You shall make them hammered work. And you shall have them for calling the congregation and for having the camps travel. ³And when they will blow them, then all the congregation shall be gathered to you, to the entrance of the Tent of Meeting. ⁴And if they will blow with one, then the chieftains, the heads of thousands of Israel shall be gathered to you. ⁵And when you will blow a blasting sound, then the camps that are camping on the east shall travel. ⁶And when you will blow a second blasting sound, then the camps that are camping on the west shall travel. They shall blow a blasting sound for their travels. ⁷And for assembling the community you shall blow, but you shall not make a blast. ⁸And the sons of Aaron, the priests, shall blow the trumpets; and they shall be an eternal law for you through your generations. ⁹And when you will go to war in your land against a foe who afflicts you, then you shall blast the trumpets, and you will be brought to mind in front of YHWH, your God, and you will be saved from your enemies. ¹⁰And on your happy occasion and at your appointed times and on your new moons, you shall blow the trumpets over your burnt offerings and over your peace-offering sacrifices, and they shall be for a commemoration for you in front of your God. I am YHWH, your God."

¹¹And it was in the second year, in the second month, on the twentieth of the month that the cloud was lifted from over the Tabernacle of the Testimony. ¹²And the children of Israel set out on their travels from the wilderness of Sinai. And the cloud tented in the wilderness of Paran. ¹³And they traveled from the first by YHWH's word through Moses' hand.

¹⁴And the flag of the camp of the children of Judah traveled first by their armies, and over its army was Nahshon son of Amminadab. ¹⁵And over the army of the tribe of the children of Issachar was Nethanel son of Zuar. ¹⁶And over the army of the tribe of the children of Zebulun was Eliab son of Helon. ¹⁷And the Tabernacle was taken down; and the children of Gershon and the children of Merari, who carried the Tabernacle, traveled. ¹⁸And the flag of Reuben's camp by their armies traveled, and over its army was Elizur son of Shedeur. ¹⁹And over the army of the tribe of the children of Simeon was Shelumiel son of Zurishadday. ²⁰And over the army of the tribe of the children of Gad was Eliasaph son of Deuel. ²¹And the Kohathites, who carried the holy place, traveled; and they set up the Tabernacle by the time they came. ²²And the flag of the camp of the children of Ephraim by their armies traveled, and over its army was Elishama son of Ammihud. ²³And over the army of the tribe of the children of Manasseh was Gamaliel son of Pedahzur. ²⁴And

over the army of the tribe of the children of Benjamin was Abidan son of Gideoni. ²⁵And the flag of the camp of the children of Dan, the final one of all the camps, by their armies, traveled, and over its army was Ahiezer son of Ammishadday. ²⁶And over the army of the tribe of the children of Asher was Pagiel son of Ochran. ²⁷And over the army of the tribe of the children of Naphtali was Ahira son of Enan.

²⁸These were the orders of travel of the children of Israel by their armies when they traveled.

²⁹And Moses said to Hobab, the son of Reuel the Midianite, Moses' father-in-law, "We're traveling to the place that YHWH said, 'I'll give it to you.' Come with us, and we'll be good to you, because YHWH has spoken of good regarding Israel."

³⁰And he said to him, "I won't go, but rather I'll go to my land and to my birthplace."

³¹And he said, "Don't leave us, because you know the way we should camp in the wilderness, and you'll be eyes for us. ³²And it will be, when you go with us, that we'll do good for you in proportion to the good that YHWH will do for us."

³³And they traveled from the mountain of YHWH three days' journey. And the ark of the covenant of YHWH traveled in front of them three days' journey to scout a resting place for them. ³⁴And YHWH's cloud was over them by day as they traveled from the camp. ³⁵And it was, when the ark traveled, that Moses said, "Arise, YHWH, and let your enemies be scattered, and let those who hate you flee from your presence," ³⁶and when it rested, he said, "Come back, YHWH, the ten thousands of thousands of Israel."

11

¹And the people were like grumblers, bad in YHWH's ears, and YHWH heard, and His anger flared, and a fire of YHWH burned among them and consumed at the edge of the camp. ²And the people cried out to Moses, and Moses prayed to YHWH, and the fire subsided. ³And he called that place's name Taberah because a fire of YHWH burned among them.*

⁴And the gathered mass who were among them had a longing, and the children of Israel, as well, went back and cried, and they said, "Who will

---

*There is not sufficient evidence in this brief story (11:1–3) to identify it with certainty. The identification here as E is tentative.

feed us meat? ⁵We remember the fish that we would eat in Egypt for free: the cucumbers and the melons and the leek and the onions and the garlics. ⁶And now, our soul is dried up. There isn't anything—except the manna before our eyes."

⁷And the manna: it was like a seed of coriander, and its appearance was like the appearance of bdellium. ⁸The people went around and collected and ground it in mills or pounded it in a mortar and cooked it in a pot and made it into cakes. And its taste was like the taste of something creamy made with oil. ⁹And when the dew descended on the camp at night, the manna would descend on it.*

¹⁰And Moses heard the people crying by their families, each at his tent entrance, and YHWH's anger flared very much, and it was bad in Moses' eyes. ¹¹And Moses said to YHWH, "Why have you done bad to your servant, and why have I not found favor in your eyes, to set the burden of this entire people on me? ¹²Did I conceive this entire people? Did I give birth to it, that you should say to me, 'Carry it in your bosom,' the way a nurse carries a suckling, to the land that you swore to its fathers? ¹³From where do I have meat to give to this entire people, that they cry at me, saying, 'Give us meat, and let's eat'? ¹⁴I'm not able, I, by myself, to carry this entire people, because it's too heavy for me. ¹⁵And if this is how you treat me, kill me, if I've found favor in your eyes, and let me not see my suffering."**

¹⁶And YHWH said to Moses, "Gather to me seventy men from Israel's elders whom you've known because they're the people's elders and its officers, and you'll take them to the Tent of Meeting, and they'll stand up there with you. ¹⁷And I'll come down and speak And you shall say to the people, 'Consecrate yourselves for tomorrow, and you'll eat meat, because you cried in YHWH's ears saying: Who will feed us meat, because we had it good in

---

*This is a triplet of the J and P accounts of the manna that appear in Exodus 16. It contains a reference to the Tent of Meeting, which does not occur in J; and it is linked by puns to the story of Miriam's leprosy, which is E. It contains no characteristic P terms, and the story of Miriam's leprosy to which it is linked denigrates Aaron, so it cannot be P. On all these grounds, this passage must be E.

**The character development of Moses, the increasing strength in the way he speaks first to Pharaoh and then even to God, and the sympathetic treatment of his suffering are marks of E. J and P are not comparable in this respect. This is also consistent with the idea that E comes from the Mushite priesthood; that is, it is written by someone who traces his descent from Moses. Thus, here Moses makes an extraordinary, plaintive speech to God, perhaps the most audacious way that anyone speaks to God in the Hebrew Bible. See likewise Moses' last words to Pharaoh (Exod 11:4–8), his long exchange with God at the burning bush (Exodus 3–4), and his exchange with God on Mount Horeb (Exodus 32).

Egypt. And YHWH will give you meat, and you'll eat. ¹⁹You'll eat not for one day and not two days and not five days and not ten days and not twenty days. ²⁰Until a month of days! Until it will come out of your nose, and it will be a revulsion to you! Because you rejected YHWH, who was among you, and you cried in front of him, saying: Why is this that we went out from Egypt?'"

²¹And Moses said, "The people among whom I am are six hundred thousand on foot, and you've said, 'I'll give them meat, and they'll eat for a month of days!' ²²Will flock and herd be slaughtered for them, and would it provide for them? Or will all the sea's fish be gathered for them, and would it provide for them?"

²³And YHWH said to Moses, "Is YHWH's hand getting short?! Now you'll see if my word happens to you or not."

²⁴And Moses went out and spoke YHWH's words to the people. And he gathered seventy men from the people's elders, and he stood them around the tent. ²⁵And YHWH came down in a cloud and spoke to him and took some of the spirit that was on him and put it on the seventy men of the elders. And it was when the spirit rested on them: and they prophesied. Then they did not do it anymore.

²⁶And two men had been left in the camp. One's name was Eldad, and the second's name was Medad. And the spirit rested on them. And they were among the ones who were written, but they did not go out to the tent, and they prophesied in the camp. ²⁷And a boy ran and told Moses, and he said, "Eldad and Medad are prophesying in the camp!"

²⁸And Joshua, son of Nun, Moses' attendant from his chosen ones, answered, and he said, "My lord Moses, restrain them!"

²⁹And Moses said to him, "Are you jealous for me? And who would make it so that all of YHWH's people were prophets, that YHWH would put His spirit on them!" ³⁰And Moses was gathered back to the camp, he and Israel's elders.

³¹And a wind traveled from YHWH and transported quails from the sea and left them on the camp, about a day's journey in one direction and about a day's journey in the other around the camp, and about two cubits on the face of the earth. ³²And the people got up all that day and all night and all the next day and gathered the quail. The one who had the least gathered ten homers. And they spread them out, spreading around the camp. ³³And the meat was still between their teeth, not yet chewed, and YHWH's anger flared at the people, and YHWH struck at the people, a very great strike. ³⁴And he called that place's name Kibroth Hattaavah, because they buried the people who were longing there. ³⁵From Kibroth Hattaavah the people traveled to Hazeroth, and they were in Hazeroth.

12

¹And Miriam and Aaron spoke against Moses about the Cushite wife whom he had taken—because he had taken a Cushite wife. ²And they said, "Has YHWH only just spoken through Moses? Hasn't He also spoken through us?"

And YHWH heard.

³And the man Moses was very humble, more than every human who was on the face of the earth.*

⁴And YHWH said suddenly to Moses and to Aaron and to Miriam, "Go out, the three of you, to the Tent of Meeting." And the three of them went out. ⁵And YHWH came down in a column of cloud and stood at the entrance of the tent. And He called, "Aaron and Miriam." And the two of them went out. ⁶And He said, "Hear my words:

> If there will be a prophet among you,
> I, YHWH, shall be known to him in a vision;
> in a dream I shall speak through him.
> ⁷ Not so is my servant Moses;
> in all my house he is faithful.
> ⁸ Mouth to mouth I shall speak through him
> and vision and not in enigmas,
> and he will see the form of YHWH.
> And why did you not fear to speak against my servant,
> against Moses?"

⁹And YHWH's anger flared against them, and He went. ¹⁰And the cloud turned from over the tent; and, here, Miriam was leprous, like snow. And Aaron turned to Miriam, and, here, she was leprous. ¹¹And Aaron said to Moses, "In me, my lord.** Don't set a sin on us, which we did foolishly and which we sinned. ¹²Let her not be like the dead who, when he comes out of his mother's womb, half of his flesh is eaten up!"

---

*The identification of Moses as humbler than anyone on earth was one of the early matters that were raised as producing doubts that Moses was the author. It was hard to picture the humblest man on earth writing that he was the humblest man on earth.

**Only here and in the golden-calf episode does Aaron address Moses as "my lord" (Hebrew *'ădōnî.*) Both are E episodes, and both picture Aaron as doing something wrong. (And in both cases Aaron suffers no punishment, even when Miriam suffers here when she and Aaron have committed the same offense. This may be because E could not picture Israel's first high priest as suffering leprosy or any other direct punishment from God.)

¹³And Moses cried out to YHWH, saying, "Oh, God, heal her!"

¹⁴And YHWH said to Moses, "And if her father had spit in her face, wouldn't she be humiliated seven days? Let her be closed up seven days outside the camp, and after that let her be gathered back." ¹⁵And Miriam was closed up outside the camp seven days. And the people did not travel until Miriam was gathered back, and after that the people traveled from Hazeroth. And they camped in the Paran wilderness.

13

¹And YHWH spoke to Moses, saying, ²"Send men and let them scout the land of Canaan that I'm giving to the children of Israel. You shall send one man for each tribe of his fathers, every one of them a chieftain."

³And Moses sent them from the wilderness of Paran by YHWH's word. They were all men who were heads of the children of Israel. ⁴And these are their names: for the tribe of Reuben, Shammua son of Zaccur. ⁵For the tribe of Simeon, Shaphat son of Hori. ⁶For the tribe of Judah, Caleb son of Jephunneh. ⁷For the tribe of Issachar, Igal son of Joseph. ⁸For the tribe of Ephraim, Hoshea son of Nun. ⁹For the tribe of Benjamin, Palti son of Raphu. ¹⁰For the tribe of Zebulun, Gaddiel son of Sodi. ¹¹For the tribe of Joseph: of the tribe of Manasseh, Gaddi son of Susi. ¹²For the tribe of Dan, Ammiel son of Gemalli. ¹³For the tribe of Asher, Sethur son of Michael. ¹⁴For the tribe of Naphtali, Nahbi son of Vophsi. ¹⁵For the tribe of Gad, Geuel son of Machi.

¹⁶These are the names of the men whom Moses sent to scout the land. And Moses called Hoshea son of Nun Joshua. ¹⁷And Moses sent them to scout the land of Canaan.* And he said to them, "Go up there in the Negeb, and you shall go up the mountain ¹⁸and see the land, how it is; and the people who live on it, are they strong or weak, are they few or many; ¹⁹and how is the land in which they live, is it good or bad; and how are the cities in which they live, are they in camps or in fortified places; ²⁰and how is the land, is it fat or meager; does it have trees or not; and exert strength and take some fruit of the land."

---

*The J story begins without identifying who Moses sends. The original beginning of J may have been removed because it duplicated (or contradicted) the beginning of P. When the Redactor combined the two versions of the episode of the scouts, he opened with the P report that Moses sends them, and then he placed the J account of Moses' instructions to them next. Note that the phrase that comes here precisely at the juncture between the two is "And Moses sent them" (13:17). This is a verbatim repetition of the report in P a few verses earlier (13:2). Such a resumptive repetition precisely at a juncture between two sources is a frequent sign of redaction. It is also known as an epanalepsis.

And it was the days of the first grapes. ²¹And they went up and scouted the land from the wilderness of Zin to Rehob at the entrance of Hamath. ²²And they went up in the Negeb and came to Hebron. And Ahiman, Sheshai, and Talmai, the offspring of the giants, were there. (And Hebron was built seven years before Zoan of Egypt.) ²³And they came to the Wadi Eshcol, and they cut a branch and one cluster of grapes from there—and carried it on a pole by two people—and some pomegranates and some figs. ²⁴That place was called Wadi Eshcol on account of the cluster that the children of Israel cut from there. **²⁵And they came back from scouting the land at the end of forty days. ²⁶And they went and came to Moses and to Aaron and to all the congregation of the children of Israel, to the wilderness of Paran, at Kadesh; and they brought back word to them and all the congregation and showed them the land's fruit.**

²⁷And they told him and said, "We came to the land where you sent us, and also it's flowing with milk and honey, and this is its fruit. ²⁸Nonetheless: the people who live in the land are strong. And the cities are fortified, very big. And also we saw the offspring of the giants there. ²⁹Amalek lives in the land of the Negeb, and the Hittite and the Jebusite and the Amorite live in the mountains, and the Canaanite lives by the sea and along the Jordan."

³⁰And Caleb quieted the people toward Moses and said, "Let's go up, and we'll take possession of it, because we'll be able to handle it."

³¹And the men who went up with him said, "We won't be able to go up against the people, because they're stronger than we are." **³²And they brought out a report of the land that they had scouted to the children of Israel, saying, "The land through which we passed to scout it: it's a land that eats those who live in it, and all the people whom we saw in it were people of size!** ³³And we saw the Nephilim there, sons of giants from the Nephilim,* and we were like grasshoppers in our eyes, and so were we in their eyes."

14

¹And all the congregation raised and let out their voices! And the people wept that night. ²And all the children of Israel complained at Moses and at Aaron, and all the congregation said to them, "If only we had died in

---

*The Nephilim were last mentioned in a J text (Gen 6:4), which identifies them as giants, the offspring of human women and "the sons of God." Now they are found living in the land. Later (in a J text in Joshua), Joshua eliminates the giants from all the land except the city of *Gath* and two other Philistine cities (Josh 11:21–22). And later still, the famous Philistine giant Goliath comes from *Gath* (in 1 Sam 17:4, a text I identified in *The Hidden Book in the Bible* as having been written by the same author as J).

the land of Egypt! Or in this wilderness, if only we had died! ³And why is YHWH bringing us to this land to fall by the sword? Our wives and our infants will become a spoil! Isn't it better for us to go back to Egypt?" ⁴And they said, each man to his brother, "Let's appoint a chief and go back to Egypt."

⁵And Moses and Aaron fell on their faces in front of all the community of the congregation of the children of Israel.

⁶And Joshua son of Nun and Caleb son of Jephunneh, from those who had scouted the land, had torn their clothes. ⁷And they said to all the congregation of the children of Israel, saying, "The land through which we passed to scout it: the land is very, very good! ⁸If YHWH desires us, then He'll bring us to this land and give it to us, a land that flows with milk and honey! ⁹Just don't revolt against YHWH. And you, don't fear the people of the land, because they're our bread! Their protection has turned from them, while YHWH is with us. Don't fear them."

¹⁰And all the congregation said to batter them with stones.

And YHWH's glory appeared at the Tent of Meeting to all the children of Israel!

¹¹And YHWH said to Moses, "How long will this people reject me, and how long will they not trust in me, with all the signs that I've done among them? ¹²I'll strike them with an epidemic and dispossess them, and I'll make you into a bigger and more powerful nation than they are."

¹³And Moses said to YHWH, "And Egypt will hear it, for you brought this people up from among them with your power, ¹⁴and they'll say it to those who live in this land. They've heard that you, YHWH, are among this people; that you, YHWH, have appeared eye-to-eye; and your cloud stands over them; and you go in front of them in a column of cloud by day and in a column of fire by night. ¹⁵And if you kill this people as one man, then the nations that have heard about you will say it, saying, ¹⁶'Because YHWH wasn't able to bring this people to the land that He swore to them, He slaughtered them in the wilderness.' ¹⁷And now, let my Lord's power be big, as you spoke, saying, ¹⁸'YHWH is slow to anger and abounding in kindness, bearing crime and offense; though not making one innocent: reckoning fathers' crime on children, on third generations and on fourth generations.'* ¹⁹Forgive this people's crime in proportion to the magnitude of your kindness and as you've borne this people from Egypt to here."

²⁰And YHWH said, "I've forgiven according to your word. ²¹But indeed, as I live, and as YHWH's glory has filled all the earth, ²²I swear that

---

*Here in the J version of the story of the scouts, Moses quotes back to YHWH the divine formula that YHWH revealed to him at Sinai in J (Exod 34:6–7).

all of these people, who have seen my glory and my signs that I did in Egypt and in the wilderness and who have tested me ten times now and haven't listened to my voice, ²³won't see the land that I swore to their fathers, and all those who rejected me won't see it. ²⁴And my servant Caleb, because a different spirit was with him, and he went after me completely, I'll bring him to the land where he went, and his seed will possess it.* ²⁵And the Amalekite and the Canaanite live in the valley.** Turn and travel tomorrow to the wilderness by the way of the Red Sea."

²⁶And YHWH spoke to Moses and to Aaron, saying, ²⁷"How much further for this bad congregation, that they're complaining against me? I've heard the complaints of the children of Israel that they're making against me. ²⁸Say to them: As I live—word of YHWH—what you have spoken in my ears, that is what I'll do to you! ²⁹In this wilderness your carcasses will fall; and all of you who were counted, for all your number, from twenty years old and up, who complained against me, ³⁰I swear that you won't come to the land that I raised my hand to have you reside there—except Caleb son of Jephunneh and Joshua son of Nun. ³¹And your infants, whom you said would become a spoil: I'll bring them, and they will know the land that you rejected! ³²And you: your carcasses will fall in this wilderness. ³³And your children will be roving in the wilderness forty years, and they'll bear your whoring until the end of your carcasses in the wilderness. ³⁴For the number of days that you scouted the land, forty days, you shall bear your crimes a day for each year, forty years, and you shall know my frustration! ³⁵I, YHWH, have spoken: If I shall not do this to all this bad congregation who are gathered against me: in this wilderness they shall end, and they shall die there!"

³⁶And the men whom Moses sent to scout the land and came back and caused all the congregation to complain against him, bringing out a report about the land: ³⁷the men who brought out the bad report of the land died in a plague in front of YHWH. ³⁸But, out of those men who went to scout the land, Joshua son of Nun and Caleb son of Jephunneh lived.

---

*Only one scout, Caleb, opposes the scouts who give the negative report in 13:30 and 14:24 (J); but it is two scouts, both Caleb and Joshua, in 14:6–9,38 (P). The addition of Joshua in P was necessary because it had to explain why Joshua survived to arrive in the land. In E Joshua's merit is established: he is the only Israelite to be completely uninvolved in the golden-calf event, and he is the man who remains in the Tabernacle standing guard. But P cannot include these stories because in the golden-calf story Aaron is culpable for making the calf, and according to P a nonpriest such as Joshua cannot be in the Tabernacle. P therefore includes Joshua along with Caleb as the two men who survive to enter the land.

**The Amalekites live in the land in 14:25,45 (J); but they live in the wilderness in Exod 17:8–16 (E).

³⁹And Moses spoke these things to all the children of Israel, and the people mourned very much. ⁴⁰And they got up in the morning and went up to the top of the mountain, saying, "Here we are, and we'll go up to the place that YHWH said, because we've sinned."

⁴¹And Moses said, "Why are you violating YHWH's word? And it won't succeed. ⁴²Don't go up, so you won't be stricken in front of your enemies, because YHWH isn't among you. ⁴³Because the Amalekite and the Canaanite are there in front of you, and you'll fall by the sword because of the fact that you've gone back from following YHWH, and YHWH won't be with you."

⁴⁴And they acted heedlessly, going up to the top of the mountain. And the ark of the covenant of YHWH and Moses did not draw away from the camp. ⁴⁵And the Amalekite and the Canaanite who lived in that mountain came down, and they struck them and crushed them as far as Hormah.

15

¹And YHWH spoke to Moses, saying, ²"Speak to the children of Israel, and you shall say to them: When you will come to the land of your homes that I am giving to you, ³and you will make a fire offering to YHWH, a burnt offering or a sacrifice, to express a vow or as a contribution or at your appointed times,* to make a pleasant smell to YHWH from the cattle or from the flock, ⁴then the one bringing his offering to YHWH shall bring forward a grain offering, fine flour, one-tenth of a measure, mixed with a fourth of a hin of oil. ⁵And you shall make wine for a libation with the burnt offering or the sacrifice, a fourth of a hin for one lamb. ⁶Or for a ram, you shall make a grain offering, fine flour, two tenths, mixed with oil, a third of a hin, ⁷and you shall bring forward wine for a libation, a third of a hin, a pleasant smell to YHWH. ⁸And if you will make a bull a burnt offering or a sacrifice, to express a vow, or a peace offering to YHWH, ⁹then he shall

---

*Three points regarding vv. 1–31: (1) The location of this passage of law in the middle of two wilderness stories hints that it may be an insertion, especially since it has little to do with either of these stories in particular. (2) The Priestly sacrificial law was already given in Leviticus 1–7 and 17. Now this new sacrificial law comes, dealing all over again with regular sacrifices, holiday sacrifices, vow sacrifices, and individual and communal sacrifices for sinning by mistake. (3) The earlier sacrificial law repeatedly involves the Tabernacle. This second body of sacrificial law never mentions the Tabernacle. This fits with the evidence that the Tabernacle was kept in the Solomonic Temple and that P was written while the Solomonic Temple was still standing, whereas the Redactor wrote and edited in the time of the postexilic Temple, which did not contain the Tabernacle.

bring forward with the bull a grain offering, fine flour, three tenths, mixed with oil, half of a hin, [10]and you shall bring forward wine for a libation, half of a hin, an offering by fire of a pleasant smell to YHWH. [11]It shall be done this way for one ox or for one ram or for a lamb of the sheep or of the goats. [12]By the number that you will do, you shall do each one of their number this way. [13]Every citizen shall do these this way when bringing forward an offering by fire of a pleasant smell to YHWH. [14]And when an alien will reside with you—or someone who is among you—through your generations and will make an offering by fire of a pleasant smell to YHWH, as you will do so he shall do. [15]You, congregation, and the resident alien have one law, an eternal law through your generations: it will be the same for you and for the alien in front of YHWH. [16]You and the alien who resides with you shall have one instruction and one judgment."

[17]And YHWH spoke to Moses, saying, [18]"Speak to the children of Israel, and you shall say to them: When you come to the land where I'm bringing you, [19]then it will be that when you eat some of the land's bread you shall make a donation to YHWH. [20]The first of your dough: you shall make a loaf as a donation. Like a donation from the threshing floor, so you shall donate it. [21]From the first of your dough you shall give a donation to YHWH through your generations.

[22]"And when you will make a mistake and not do all of these commandments that YHWH has spoken to Moses, [23]everything that YHWH has commanded you by Moses' hand, from the day that YHWH commanded and on through your generations, [24]then it will be that, if it was done by mistake, out of the congregation's sight, then all the congregation shall do one bull of the cattle as a burnt offering for a pleasant smell to YHWH and its grain offering and its libation according to the required manner and one goat for a sin offering. [25]And the priest shall make atonement for all the congregation of the children of Israel, and it will be forgiven for them, because it was a mistake, and they brought their offering, an offering by fire to YHWH, and their sin offering in front of YHWH for their mistake. [26]And it will be forgiven for all the congregation of the children of Israel and the alien who resides among them, because it was by mistake for all the people.

[27]"And if one person will sin by mistake, then he shall bring a she-goat in its first year for a sin offering. [28]And the priest shall make atonement for the person who made the mistake, sinning by mistake, in front of YHWH to make atonement for him, and it will be forgiven for him. [29]The citizen among the children of Israel and for the alien who resides among them: you shall have one instruction for one who acts by mistake.

³⁰"But the person who will act with a high hand, a citizen or an alien, he is blaspheming YHWH, and that person will be cut off from among his people, ³¹because he disdained YHWH's word and broke His commandment. That person will be cut off. His crime is in him."

³²And the children of Israel were in the wilderness, and they found a man collecting wood on the Sabbath day. ³³And those who found him collecting wood brought him forward to Moses and to Aaron and to all the congregation. ³⁴And they left him under watch because it had not been determined what should be done to him.

³⁵And YHWH said to Moses, "The man shall be put to death! All the congregation is to batter him with stones outside the camp."

³⁶And all the congregation brought him outside the camp and battered him with stones, and he died, as YHWH commanded Moses.

³⁷And YHWH said to Moses, saying, ³⁸"Speak to the children of Israel, and you shall say to them that they shall make fringe on the corners of their clothes through their generations. And they shall put a blue string on the fringe of the corner. ³⁹And you shall have the fringe so you will see it and bring to mind all of YHWH's commandments and will do them, and you will not go around after your heart and after your eyes, because you whore after them. ⁴⁰So you will bring to mind and do all my commandments, and you will be holy to your God. ⁴¹I am YHWH, your God, who brought you out from the land of Egypt to be God to you. I am YHWH, your God."

16

¹And Korah son of Izhar son of Kohath son of Levi, and Dathan and Abiram, sons of Eliab, and On, son of Peleth, sons of Reuben, took ²[and]* got up in front of Moses—[and] two hundred fifty people from the children of Israel, chieftains of the congregation, prominent ones of the assembly, people of repute. ³And they assembled against Moses and against Aaron and said to them, "You have much! Because all of the congregation, all of them,

---

*The two occurrences of the extraneous word "and" in this verse are partly a product of the Redactor's arrangement of the combined text and partly a product of the English translation, in which a different word order from the Hebrew is necessary. Separated, the P text would read: "And Korah son of Izhar son of Kohath son of Levi took two hundred fifty people . . . ," and the J text would read: "And Dathan and Abiram, sons of Eliab, and On, son of Peleth, sons of Reuben, got up in front of Moses."

are holy, and YHWH is among them. And why do you raise yourselves up over YHWH's community?"

⁴And Moses listened, and he fell on his face. ⁵And he spoke to Korah and to all of his congregation, saying, "In the morning YHWH will make known who is His and who is holy, and He will bring him close to Him. And He will bring the one He chooses close to Him. ⁶Do this: Take incense burners, Korah and all his congregation, ⁷and put fire in them and set incense on them in front of YHWH tomorrow. And it will be that the man whom YHWH will choose, he will be the holy one. You have much, sons of Levi!" ⁸And Moses said to Korah, "Listen, sons of Levi, ⁹is it too small a thing for you that Israel's God has distinguished you from the congregation of Israel to bring you close to him, to do the work of YHWH's Tabernacle and to stand in front of the congregation to minister for them, ¹⁰and that He has brought you and all your brothers, the sons of Levi, with you close to Him? And you seek priesthood as well?! ¹¹Therefore you and all your congregation who are gathering are against YHWH! And Aaron, what is he that you complain against him?"

¹²And Moses sent to call Dathan and Abiram, sons of Eliab, and they said, "We won't come up. ¹³Is it a small thing that you brought us up from a land flowing with milk and honey to kill us in the wilderness, that you lord it over us as well? ¹⁴Besides, you haven't brought us to a land flowing with milk and honey or given us possession of field or vineyard. Will you put out those people's eyes? We won't come up."

¹⁵And Moses was very angry, and he said to YHWH, "Don't turn to their offering. Not one ass of theirs have I taken away, and I haven't wronged one of them."

¹⁶And Moses said to Korah, "You and all your congregation, be in front of YHWH—you and they and Aaron—tomorrow. ¹⁷And each man take his fire-holder, and put incense on them, and each man bring his fire-holder forward in front of YHWH, two hundred fifty fire-holders, and you and Aaron, each man his fire-holder."

¹⁸And each man took his fire-holder, and they put fire on them and set incense on them, and they stood at the entrance of the Tent of Meeting, and Moses and Aaron. ¹⁹And Korah assembled all the congregation against them, to the entrance of the Tent of Meeting. And YHWH's glory appeared to all the congregation.

²⁰And YHWH spoke to Moses and to Aaron, saying, ²¹"Separate from among this congregation, and I'll finish them in an instant!"

²²And they fell on their faces and said, "God, the God of the spirits of all flesh, will one man sin and you be angry at all the congregation?"

²³**And YHWH spoke to Moses, saying,** ²⁴**"Speak to the congregation, saying, 'Get up from around the tabernacle of Korah,** Dathan and Abiram.'"***

²⁵And Moses got up and went to Dathan and Abiram, and Israel's elders went after him. ²⁶And he spoke to the congregation, saying, "Turn away from the tents of these wicked men and don't touch anything that is theirs, or else you'll be annihilated through all their sins."

²⁷**And they got up from around the tabernacle of Korah,** Dathan and Abiram. And Dathan and Abiram came out, standing at the entrance of their tents, and their wives and their children and their infants. ²⁸And Moses said, "By this you'll know that YHWH sent me to do all these things, because it's not from my own heart. ²⁹If these die like the death of every human, and the event of every human happens to them, then YHWH hasn't sent me. ³⁰But if YHWH will create something, and the ground will open its mouth and swallow them and all that they have, and they'll go down alive to Sheol, then you'll know that these people have rejected YHWH."

³¹And it was as he was finishing speaking all these things, and the ground that was under them was broken up, ³²and the earth opened its mouth and swallowed them and their households **and all the people who were with Korah and all the property.** ³³And they went down, they and all that they had, alive to Sheol. And the earth covered them over, and they perished from among the community. ³⁴And all Israel that was around them fled at the sound of them, for they said, "Or else the earth will swallow us."

³⁵**And fire had gone out**** **from YHWH and consumed the two hundred fifty people offering the incense.**

17

¹**And YHWH spoke to Moses, saying,** ²**"Say to Eleazar son of Aaron, the priest, that he should pick up the fire-holders from the burning and disperse the fire, because they have become holy.** ³**And the fire-holders**

---

*The names Dathan and Abiram in vv. 23 and 27 appear in the Masoretic Text but not in the Greek. Either they were added by the Redactor to weave the stories together or they were added by a later scribe who, not knowing there were originally two separate stories, could not understand why the text referred only to Korah without Dathan and Abiram.

**The original text probably read "And fire went out" (*wattēṣē' 'ēš*) in the perfect tense, and the Redactor changed it to the past perfect tense, "And fire had gone out" (*wě'ēš yāṣě'āh*). This was necessary because in the combined text Korah and his company were now being pictured as going down in the earthquake with Dathan and Abiram, but they were also pictured as being burned in the fire, and so R had to clarify that they had already been burned in the fire and now were swallowed along with the live rebels in the earthquake as well.

of these who sinned at the cost of their lives: let them make them into hammered plates as plating for the altar, because they brought them forward in
front of YHWH, and they became holy, and let them become a sign to the children of Israel."

⁴And Eleazar, the priest, took the fire-holders of bronze that those who
were burned had brought forward, and they hammered them into a plating
for the altar, ⁵a commemoration for the children of Israel so that no outsider,
one who is not from Aaron's seed, will come forward to burn incense in front
of YHWH, so he will not be like Korah and like his congregation, as YHWH
spoke to him by Moses' hand.

⁶And all the congregation of the children of Israel complained the next
day against Moses and against Aaron, saying, "You killed YHWH's people!"

⁷And it was when the congregation was assembled against Moses and
against Aaron, and they turned to the Tent of Meeting; and, here, the cloud
had covered it, and YHWH's glory appeared. ⁸And Moses and Aaron came to
the front of the Tent of Meeting.

⁹And YHWH spoke to Moses, saying, ¹⁰"Move away from among this congregation, and I'll finish them in an instant!" And they fell on their faces.

¹¹And Moses said to Aaron, "Take a fire-holder and put fire from the altar
on it and set incense and carry it quickly to the congregation and make
atonement for them, because a rage has come out from in front of YHWH! The
plague has begun!"

¹²And Aaron took it as Moses had spoken, and he ran among the community. And, here, the plague had begun among the people. And he put in
incense and made atonement for the people. ¹³And he stood between the
dead and the living. And the plague was halted. ¹⁴And the dead in the plague
were fourteen thousand seven hundred, apart from the dead over the matter
of Korah. ¹⁵And Aaron went back to Moses, to the entrance of the Tent of
Meeting, when the plague had been halted.

¹⁶And YHWH spoke to Moses, saying, ¹⁷"Speak to the children of Israel
and take from them a staff for each father's house, from all their chieftains by
their fathers' house, twelve staffs. You shall write each man's name on his
staff, ¹⁸and you shall write Aaron's name on the staff of Levi, because there
shall be one staff for the head of their fathers' house. ¹⁹And you shall leave
them in the Tent of Meeting in front of the Testimony where I shall meet with
you. ²⁰And it will be that the man I shall choose: his staff will bloom. And I'll
decrease from me the complaints of the children of Israel that they're making
against you."

²¹And Moses spoke to the children of Israel, and all their chieftains gave
him a staff for each chieftain by their fathers' house, twelve staffs, and

Aaron's staff was among their staffs. ²²And Moses left the staffs in front of YHWH in the Tent of the Testimony. ²³And it was the next day, and Moses came to the Tent of the Testimony; and, here, Aaron's staff, of the house of Levi, had bloomed; and it brought out a bloom, and it made a blossom, and it produced almonds! ²⁴And Moses brought out all the staffs from in front of YHWH to the children of Israel. And they saw, and each took his staff.

²⁵And YHWH said to Moses, "Put back Aaron's staff in front of the Testimony for watching over, for a sign to rebels, and you'll end their complaints against me so they won't die!" ²⁶And Moses did it. As YHWH had commanded him, he did so.

²⁷And the children of Israel said to Moses, saying, "Here, we're expiring, we're perishing, we're all perishing! ²⁸Everyone who comes close—who comes close to YHWH's Tabernacle—will die. Have we come to the end of expiring?!"

18

¹And YHWH said to Aaron, "You and your sons and your father's house with you shall bear any crime of the holy place, and you and your sons with you shall bear any crime of your priesthood. ²And bring forward your brothers, the tribe of Levi, your father's tribe, with you as well, and they shall be connected to you and shall minister to you, and you and your sons with you shall be in front of the Tent of the Testimony. ³And they shall keep your charge, the charge of all of the tent, but they shall not come close to the equipment of the holy and to the altar, so they will not die, both they and you. ⁴And they shall be connected to you and shall keep the charge of the Tent of Meeting, for all the work of the tent, but an outsider shall not come close to you. ⁵And you shall keep the charge of the holy and the charge of the altar, so there will not be any more rage at the children of Israel. ⁶And I, here, I have taken your brothers, the Levites from among the children of Israel as a gift to you, given for YHWH, to do the work of the Tent of Meeting. ⁷And you and your sons with you shall watch over your priesthood for everything of the altar's and for inside the pavilion, and you shall serve. I give your priesthood as a gift of service. And the outsider who comes close shall be put to death."

⁸And YHWH said to Aaron, "And I, here, I have given charge of my donations to you for all the holy things of the children of Israel. I have given them to you as an anointing and to your sons as an eternal law. ⁹This shall be yours from the holy of holies, from the fire: every offering of theirs, every

grain offering of theirs and every sin offering of theirs and every guilt offering of theirs that they will pay back to me. It is holy of holies for you and for your sons. ¹⁰You shall eat it in the holy of holies. Every male shall eat it. It shall be holy to you.

¹¹"And this is yours: their gift donation, all the elevation offerings of the children of Israel. I have given them to you and to your sons and to your daughters with you as an eternal law. Everyone who is pure in your house shall eat it.

¹²"All the best of the oil and all the best of the wine and grain, the first of them that they will give to YHWH: I have given them to you. ¹³The firstfruits of everything that is in their land that they will bring to YHWH shall be yours. Everyone who is pure in your house shall eat it. ¹⁴Every devoted thing in Israel shall be yours. ¹⁵Every first birth of a womb of all flesh that they will bring forward to YHWH, human and animal, shall be yours. Just: you shall redeem the human firstborn, and you shall redeem the firstborn of an impure animal. ¹⁶And their redemption price: from one month old you shall redeem it at your appraisal, five shekels of silver by the shekel of the Holy. It is twenty gerah. ¹⁷Just: you shall not redeem a firstborn of an ox or firstborn of a sheep or firstborn of a goat. They are holy. You shall fling their blood on the altar and burn their fat to smoke, a fire offering for a pleasant smell to YHWH. ¹⁸And their meat shall be yours; like the breast of the elevation offering and the right thigh it shall be yours. ¹⁹All the donations of the holy things that the children of Israel will donate to YHWH I have given to you and to your sons and to your daughters with you as an eternal law. It is an eternal covenant of salt in front of YHWH for you and for your seed with you."

²⁰And YHWH said to Aaron, "You shall not have a legacy in their land, and you shall not have a portion among them. I am your portion and your legacy among the children of Israel. ²¹And to the children of Levi, here, I've given every tithe in Israel as a legacy in exchange for their work that they're doing, the service of the Tent of Meeting. ²²And the children of Israel shall not come near to the Tent of Meeting anymore so as to bear sin and die. ²³But he, the Levite, shall do the service of the Tent of Meeting, and they shall bear their crime. It is an eternal law through your generations. And they shall not have a legacy among the children of Israel, ²⁴because I've given to the Levites as a legacy the tithe of the children of Israel that they will give to YHWH as a donation. On account of this I've said to them: they shall not have a legacy among the children of Israel."

²⁵And YHWH spoke to Moses, saying, ²⁶"And you shall speak to the Levites and say to them: 'When you will take the tithe from the children of Israel that I have given you from them as your legacy, then you shall make a

donation for YHWH from it, a tithe of the tithe. ²⁷And it will be counted for you as your donation, like grain from the threshing floor and like the fill of the wine press. ²⁸So you shall donate, you too, a donation for YHWH from all your tithes that you will take from the children of Israel, and you shall give a donation for YHWH to Aaron, the priest, from them. ²⁹From all your gifts you shall make every donation for YHWH, from all the best of it, its holy part from it.' ³⁰And you shall say to them: 'When you donate the best of it from it, then it shall be counted to the Levites like the produce of the threshing floor and like the produce of the wine press. ³¹And you shall eat it in every place, you and your house, because it is compensation for you in exchange for your work in the Tent of Meeting. ³²And you will not bear sin over it, when you have donated its best from it, so you will not desecrate the holy things of the children of Israel, and you will not die.'"

19

¹And YHWH spoke to Moses and to Aaron, saying, ²"This is the law of the instruction that YHWH commanded, saying: Speak to the children of Israel that they should take to you an unblemished red cow that has no injury, on which a yoke has not gone. ³And you shall give it to Eleazar, the priest, and one shall bring it outside the camp and slaughter it in front of him. ⁴And Eleazar, the priest, shall take some of its blood with his finger and sprinkle some of its blood toward the front of the Tent of Meeting seven times. ⁵And one shall burn the cow before his eyes. He shall burn its skin and its meat and its blood and its dung. ⁶And the priest shall take cedarwood and hyssop and scarlet and throw them into the fire of the cow. ⁷And the priest shall wash his clothes and wash his flesh with water, and after that he shall come to the camp, and the priest shall be impure until evening. ⁸And the one who burns it shall wash his clothes with water and wash his flesh with water and be impure until evening. ⁹And a man who is pure shall gather the cow's ashes and leave them outside the camp in a pure place, and it shall be for the congregation of the children of Israel to be kept for water of impurity, for sin expiation. ¹⁰And the one who gathers the cow's ashes shall wash his clothes and be impure until evening. And it will be for the children of Israel and for the alien who resides among them as an eternal law.

¹¹"One who touches a dead body of any human being will be impure seven days. ¹²He shall do sin expiation with it on the third day, and on the seventh day he will be pure. And if he will not do sin expiation on the third day, then on the seventh day he will not be pure. ¹³Anyone who touches a

dead body of a human being who has died and does not do sin expiation has made YHWH's Tabernacle impure, and that person will be cut off from Israel. Because the water of impurity was not flung on him, he shall be impure. His impurity is still in him.

¹⁴"This is the instruction: when a human will die in a tent, anyone who comes into the tent and everything that is in the tent will be impure seven days. ¹⁵And any open container, on which there is not a fastened cover: it is impure. ¹⁶And anyone who, at an open field, will touch a corpse slain by the sword or a dead body or a human bone or a grave will be impure seven days. ¹⁷And they shall take for the one who is impure some of the ashes of the fire of sin expiation, and one shall put living water on it in a container. ¹⁸And a man who is pure shall take hyssop and dip it in the water and sprinkle it on the tent and on all the items and on the persons who were there and on the one who touched the bone or the slain corpse or the dead body or the grave. ¹⁹And the one who is pure shall sprinkle it on the impure on the third day and on the seventh day, so he shall expiate sin from him on the seventh day, and he shall wash his clothes and wash in water and be pure in the evening. ²⁰And if a man will be impure and will not do sin expiation, then that person will be cut off from among the community, because he has made YHWH's holy place impure. The water of impurity has not been flung on him: he is impure. ²¹And it will become an eternal law for them. And one who sprinkles the water of impurity shall wash his clothes, and one who touches the water of impurity will be impure until evening. ²²And whatever the impure one will touch will be impure, and the person who touches it will be impure until evening."

20

¹And the children of Israel, all the congregation, came to the wilderness of Zin in the first month, and the people stayed in Kadesh. And Miriam died there and was buried there. ²And there was no water for the congregation, and they assembled against Moses and against Aaron.* ³And the people quarreled with Moses, and they said, saying, "If only we had expired when our brothers expired in front of YHWH! ⁴And why have you brought

---

*This is a doublet of the E story of the water from the crag at Meribah (Exodus 17). This version of the story shows signs of P. It uses the terms "expire," "congregation," and "community," and refers to the Tent of Meeting. It deals with the question of who is holy, specifically in terms of a challenge to Aaron's exclusive right to the priesthood by his cousin Korah. Also, it continues from the preceding P story (see the next note).

YHWH's community to this wilderness to die there, we and our cattle? ⁵And why did you bring us up from Egypt to bring us to this bad place? It's not a place of seed and fig and vine and pomegranate, and there's no water to drink!"

⁶And Moses and Aaron came from in front of the community to the entrance of the Tent of Meeting, and they fell on their faces. And YHWH's glory appeared to them. ⁷And YHWH spoke to Moses, saying, ⁸"Take the staff and assemble the congregation, you and Aaron, your brother. And you shall speak to the rock before their eyes, and it will give its water. So you shall bring water out of the rock for them and give a drink to the congregation and their cattle."

⁹And Moses took the staff from in front of YHWH as He commanded him.* ¹⁰And Moses and Aaron assembled the community opposite the rock. And he said to them, "Listen, rebels, shall we bring water out of this rock for you?" ¹¹And Moses lifted his hand and struck the rock with his staff twice. And much water came out! And the congregation and their cattle drank.

¹²And YHWH said to Moses and to Aaron, "Because you did not trust in me, to make me holy before the eyes of the children of Israel, therefore you shall not bring this community to the land that I have given them!"

¹³They are the waters of Meribah, over which the children of Israel quarreled with YHWH, and He was made holy among them.

¹⁴And Moses sent messengers from Kadesh to the king of Edom.** "Your brother, Israel, says this: You know all the hardship that has found us: ¹⁵And our fathers went down to Egypt, and we lived in Egypt many days. And Egypt was bad to us and to our fathers, ¹⁶and we cried to YHWH, and He heard our voice and sent an angel and brought us from Egypt. And here we are in Kadesh, a city at the edge of your border. ¹⁷Let us pass through your land. We won't pass through a field or through a vineyard, and we won't drink the water of a well. We'll go by the king's road, we won't turn right or left, until we pass your border."

¹⁸And Edom said to him, "You won't pass through me, or else I'll go out to you with the sword."

---

*The staff is taken "from in front of YHWH"—which is to say: from inside the Tabernacle. That is where Aaron's staff was placed, by divine command, after it miraculously blossomed following the Korah rebellion. There God says, "Put back Aaron's staff in front of the Testimony for watching over, for a sign to rebels." And now Moses takes that staff and says, "Listen, rebels!" As usual in P, the miraculous staff is Aaron's. This is apparently why Aaron suffers the same fate as Moses: for the misuse of the staff in this episode. See W. H. Propp, "The Rod of Aaron and the Sin of Moses."

**Just as Jacob "sent messengers" to Esau in J (Gen 32:4), Moses "sent messengers" to Edom, who are the descendants of Esau.

¹⁹And the children of Israel said to him, "We'll go up by the highway, and if we drink your water, I and my cattle, then I'll pay its price. Only, it's nothing: let me pass through by foot."

²⁰And he said, "You won't pass." And Edom went out to him with a heavy mass of people and a strong hand, ²¹and Edom refused to allow Israel to pass through his border. And Israel turned away from him.

²²And they traveled from Kadesh, and the children of Israel, all the congregation, came to Mount Hor.

²³And YHWH said to Moses and to Aaron at Mount Hor, on the border of the land of Edom, saying, ²⁴"Let Aaron be gathered to his people, because he shall not come to the land that I have given to the children of Israel, because you rebelled against my word at the waters of Meribah. ²⁵Take Aaron and Eleazar, his son, and take them up Mount Hor, ²⁶and take off Aaron's clothes, and you shall put them on Eleazar, his son. And Aaron will be gathered and die there."

²⁷And Moses did as YHWH commanded him. And they went up to Mount Hor before the eyes of all the congregation. ²⁸And Moses took off Aaron's clothes and put them on Eleazar, his son. And Aaron died there on the top of the mountain. And Moses and Eleazar came down from the mountain. ²⁹And all the congregation saw that Aaron had expired, and all the house of Israel mourned Aaron thirty days.

21

¹And the Canaanite, the king of Arad, who lived in the Negeb, heard that Israel was coming by the way of Atharim, and he fought against Israel and took some of them prisoners. ²And Israel made a vow to YHWH and said, "If you will deliver this people into my hand, then I shall completely destroy their cities." ³And YHWH listened to Israel's voice and delivered the Canaanite, and they completely destroyed them and their cities. And the name of the place was called Hormah.*

⁴And they traveled from Mount Hor by way of the Red Sea road to go around the land of Edom. And the people's soul was getting short on the way. ⁵And the people spoke against God and against Moses: "Why did you

---

*The place Hormah occurs only here and in the J spies story (Num 14:45), and so this short text (Num 21:1–3) is probably J. Also, this story involves Arad, a location in the Negeb of Judah, which fits with the fact that other J stories are disproportionately focused on the southern kingdom of Judah.

bring us up from Egypt to die in the wilderness? Because there's no bread, and there's no water, and our soul is disgusted with the cursed bread."

⁶And YHWH let fiery snakes go among the people, and they bit the people, and a great many people from Israel died. ⁷And the people came to Moses, and they said, "We've sinned, because we spoke against YHWH and against you. Pray to YHWH, that He will turn the snake away from us." And Moses prayed on behalf of the people.

⁸And YHWH said to Moses, "Make a fiery one and set it on a pole, and it will be that everyone who is bitten and sees it will live." ⁹And Moses made a bronze snake and set it on a pole, and it was, if a snake bit a man, then he would look at the bronze snake and live.*

¹⁰And the children of Israel traveled, and they camped in Oboth. ¹¹And they traveled from Oboth, and they camped in Iye-abarim, in the wilderness that is toward Moab, toward the sun's rising. ¹²From there they traveled, and they camped in the Wadi Zared. ¹³From there they traveled, and they camped across the Arnon, which is in the wilderness that extends from the border of the Amorite, because Arnon is Moab's border, between Moab and the Amorite. ¹⁴On account of this it is said in the Scroll of the Wars of YHWH:

> Waheb in Suphah and the wadis of Arnon, ¹⁵and the slope of the wadis that reached to the settlement of Ar, and pressed to Moab's border.

¹⁶And from there to Beer: that is the well of which YHWH said to Moses, "Gather the people, so I may give them water." ¹⁷Then Israel sang this song:

> Spring up, well. Sing to it.
> ¹⁸ The commanders hewed the well, the people's nobles dug it, with a scepter, with their staffs.

And from the wilderness to Mattanah, ¹⁹and from Mattanah to Nahaliel, and from Nahaliel to Bamoth, ²⁰and from Bamoth in the valley, that is in the field of Moab, to the top of Pisgah, which looks toward Jeshimon.**

---

*This bronze snake, made by Moses, is later called "Nehushtan." The only prophet to allude to it is Jeremiah (Jer 8:17–22), who is associated with the same priesthood that produced E and D (the Levites of Shiloh/Anathoth). It is destroyed by King Hezekiah (2 Kgs 18:4), the king who represents the interests of the rival priesthood (the Aaronids). See *Who Wrote the Bible?* pp. 126, 210–211.

**It is difficult to identify the sources used by the Redactor in vv. 12–20, a passage composed of prose, archaic poetry, travel notices, and an explicit citation of an older source.

²¹And Israel sent messengers to Sihon, king of the Amorites, saying, ²²"Let me pass through your land. We won't turn in at a field and at a vineyard and won't drink well waters. We'll go by the king's road until we pass your border." ²³And Sihon did not allow Israel to pass within his border. And Sihon gathered all his people and went out to Israel at the wilderness and came to Jahaz and fought against Israel. ²⁴And Israel struck him by the sword and took possession of his land from Arnon to Jabbok, to the children of Ammon, because the border of the children of Ammon was strong. ²⁵And Israel took all of these cities, and Israel lived in all of the Amorite cities in Heshbon and all of its environs, ²⁶because Heshbon was the city of Sihon, the king of the Amorite, and he fought against the former king of Moab and took all of his land from his hand as far as Arnon. ²⁷On account of this they say proverbially:

> Come to Heshbon.
> Built and founded is Sihon's city.
²⁸ > For fire went out of Heshbon,
> flame from Sihon's town;
> it consumed Ar of Moab,
> the lords of the high places of Arnon.
²⁹ > Woe unto you, Moab:
> you've perished, Chemosh's people.
> He's made his sons refugees
> and his daughters captive
> to the king of the Amorite, Sihon.
³⁰ > And their fiefdom perished,
> Heshbon to Dibon,
> and we devastated up to Nophah
> which reaches to Medeba.

³¹And Israel lived in the Amorite's land. ³²And Moses sent to spy on Jazer, and they captured its environs and dispossessed the Amorite who was there. ³³And they turned and went up the road of Bashan, and Og, the king of Bashan, went out to them, he and all his people, to war at Edrei. ³⁴And YHWH said to Moses, "Don't fear him, because I've delivered him and all his people and his land into your hand, and you'll do to him as you did to Sihon, king of the Amorite, who lived in Heshbon." ³⁵And they struck him and his sons and all his people until he did not have a remnant left, and they took possession of his land.

22

¹And the children of Israel traveled, and they camped in the plains of Moab, across the Jordan from Jericho.

²And Balak, son of Zippor, saw everything that Israel had done to the Amorite.* **³And Moab was very fearful because of the people because it was numerous, and Moab felt a disgust at the children of Israel.** ⁴And Moab said** to the elders of Midian,‡ **"Now the community will lick up all of our surroundings the way an ox licks up the plants of a field!"‡‡**

And Balak, son of Zippor, was king of Moab at that time. ⁵And he sent messengers§ **to Balaam, son of Beor, at Pethor, which is on the river—the land of the children of his people—to call him, saying, "Here, a people has come out from Egypt. Here, it has covered the eye of the land.§§ And it's sitting across from me! ⁶And now, go, curse this people for me, because it's**

---

*The Balaam episode is perhaps the hardest section in the Torah in which to delineate sources. Most scholars regard this three-chapter story as a composite: first, because they think of the accounts of repeated sets of ambassadors to Balaam as a doublet; and, second, because they think there is a contradiction in the story when God tells Balaam to go with the Moabites but then is angry at him for going. I am not at all certain that these things are evidence of two sources. The several embassies to Balaam, each composed of more distinguished ambassadors, may well be the original progression of the story. And the confusion over God's sending Balaam and then being angry at him is surprising but still understandable as a single author's development, and it is not easily resolved by separating this section into two sources in any case. Evidence of language is a stronger marker of sources than these considerations. The vast majority of the terms and phrases here that are identifiable with a particular source are typical of E, while only three are typical of J. And there is a particular cluster of terms and phrases here that are also found in Exodus 10 (E). And the deity is referred to as God (Elohim) in narration here seven times. I therefore have marked the story as wholly E, except that I have marked those three J passages so that one can observe them and make of it what one will.

The first verse of the story ("And Balak, son of Zippor, saw everything that Israel had done to the Amorite") refers to the defeat of the Amorites, which had occurred only in J, not in E. This verse, therefore, either comes from J or else was added by RJE as a means of connecting the J story of the defeat of the Amorites and the E story of the defeat of the Moabites.

**"felt a disgust at the children of Israel." This is the first of a string of terms in the Balaam story that are also found in the E account of the exodus from Egypt. Cf. Exod 1:12.

‡Midian was not originally in this story. R added references to Midian (vv. 4 and 7) to reconcile a confusion in the texts that will arise later, where the J story of Baal Peor will be merged with the P story of Peor (see the note on Num 25:1). The J story is about Moab while the P story is about Midian. And later still, the P story of the Israelite defeat of Midian will refer to the death of Balaam among the Midianites.

‡‡"the plants of a field." Cf. Exod 10:15 (E).

§"and he sent messengers." Cf. Gen 32:4; Num 20:14; 21:21 (J).

§§"it has covered the eye of the land." Cf. Exod 10:5,15 (E).

more powerful than I*—maybe I'll be able: we'll strike it, and I'll drive it out from the land**—because I know that whoever you'll bless will be blessed, and whoever you'll curse will be cursed."‡

⁷And Moab's elders and Midian's elders went, and divination implements were in their hand, and they came to Balaam and spoke Balak's words to him. ⁸And he said to them, "Spend the night here tonight, and I'll bring back word to you as YHWH will speak to me." And the chiefs of Moab stayed with Balaam.

⁹And God came to Balaam and said, "Who are these people with you?"

¹⁰And Balaam said to God, "Balak, son of Zippor, king of Moab, sent to me: ¹¹'Here is a people who came out from Egypt and has covered the eye of the land.‡‡ Now go, execrate it for me. Maybe I'll be able to fight against it, and I'll drive it out.'"

¹²And God said to Balaam, "You shall not go with them. You shall not curse the people, because it is blessed."

¹³And Balaam got up in the morning and said to Balak's chiefs, "Go to your land, because YHWH refused§ to allow me to go with you."

¹⁴And the chiefs of Moab got up and came to Balak and said, "Balaam refused to go with us."

¹⁵And Balak went on again§§ to send more numerous and prestigious chiefs¶ than these. ¹⁶And they came to Balaam and said to him, "Balak, son of Zippor, said this: 'Don't be held back¶¶ from coming to me, ¹⁷because I'll honor you very much, and I'll do everything that you'll say to me.# And go, execrate this people for me.'"

¹⁸And Balaam answered, and he said to Balak's servants, "If Balak would give me a houseful of silver and gold of his I wouldn't be able to go against the mouth of YHWH, my God, to do something small or big. ¹⁹And now, stay here,## you as well, tonight, so I may know what YHWH will add to speak with me."

---

*"because it's more powerful than I." Cf. Exod 1:9 (E).

**"and I'll drive it out from the land." Cf. Exod 6:1 (E).

‡"whoever you'll bless will be blessed, and whoever you'll curse will be cursed." Somewhat similar to Gen 12:3 (J), this expression here is uncertain for source identification.

‡‡"covered the eye of the land." See the second note on 22:5.

§"refused." Cf. Exod 10:4 and five more times in E.

§§"went on again." Cf. Gen 18:29; 37:5,8; 38:26 (J), and see *The Hidden Book in the Bible*, p. 387.

¶"chiefs." (Hebrew: *śārîm*) The plural occurs in E but never in J. Cf. Exod 1:11; 18:21,25.

¶¶"held back." Cf. Gen 30:2 (E).

#"everything that you'll say to me." Cf. Gen 21:12 (E).

##"stay here" (Hebrew *šĕbû nā' bāzeh*). Cf. Exod 24:14 (E).

²⁰And God came to Balaam at night and said to him, "If these people have come to call you, get up, go with them. And just the thing that I shall speak to you—you shall do that."

²¹And Balaam got up in the morning and harnessed his ass* and went with the chiefs of Moab. ²²And God's anger flared because he was going. And an angel of YHWH stood up in the road as an adversary to him. And he was riding on his ass, and his two boys** were with him. ²³And the ass saw the angel of YHWH standing up in the road and his sword drawn in his hand, and the ass turned from the road and went into the field. And Balaam hit the ass to turn her back to the road.

²⁴And the angel of YHWH stood in the pathway of the vineyards, a fence on this side and a fence on that side. ²⁵And the ass saw the angel of YHWH, and she was pressed‡ against the wall, and she pressed Balaam's foot against the wall, and he continued hitting her.

²⁶And the angel continued passing on and stood in a narrow place where there was no way to turn right or left.‡‡ ²⁷And the ass saw the angel of YHWH, and she lay down under Balaam. And Balaam's anger flared, and he struck the ass with a stick. ²⁸And YHWH opened the ass's mouth, and she said to Balaam, "What have I done to you that you've struck me these three times?!"

²⁹And Balaam said to the ass, "Because you abused me!§ If there had been a sword in my hand§§ I would have killed you by now!"

³⁰And the ass said to Balaam, "Aren't I your ass, on whom you've ridden? From your start until this day, have I been accustomed to do like this to you?"

And he said, "No."

³¹And YHWH uncovered Balaam's eyes, and he saw the angel of YHWH standing up in the road, and his sword drawn in his hand. And he knelt and bowed to his nose. ³²And the angel of YHWH said to him, "For what have you struck¶ your ass these three times? Here, I came out as an adversary because the way was precipitous with regard to me. ³³And the ass saw me and turned in front of me these three times. If she hadn't turned from in front of me I would have killed you, too, by now and kept her alive!"

---

*"got up in the morning and harnessed his [female] ass." Cf. Gen 22:3 (E): "He got up early in the morning and harnessed his [male] ass."

**"his two boys." Cf. Gen 22:3 (E), and see the preceding note.

‡"pressed" (Hebrew *lḥṣ*, twice in this verse). Cf. Exod 3:9 (E), "oppression" (Hebrew *laḥaṣ*).

‡‡"to turn right or left." Cf. Num 20:17 (J).

§"abused." Cf. Exod 10:2 (E).

§§"a sword in my hand." Cf. Exod 5:21 (E).

¶"you struck." Cf. Exod 17:5,6 (E).

³⁴And Balaam said to the angel of YHWH, "I've sinned,* because I didn't know that you were standing up toward me in the road. And now, if it's bad in your eyes, let me go back."

³⁵And the angel of YHWH said to Balaam, "Go with the people. And nothing but the thing that I shall speak to you: that is what you shall speak." And Balaam went with Balak's chiefs.

³⁶And Balak heard that Balaam was coming, and he went out to him, to a city of Moab that was on the Arnon border, that was at the edge of the border. ³⁷And Balak said to Balaam, "Didn't I send to you, to call you? Why didn't you come to me? Am I indeed not able to honor you?!"

³⁸And Balaam said to Balak, "Here, I've come to you. Now: will I be able to speak anything? The thing that God will set in my mouth: that is what I'll speak." ³⁹And Balaam went with Balak, and they came to Kiriath Huzoth. ⁴⁰And Balak sacrificed oxen and sheep, and he let them go to Balaam and to the chiefs who were with them. ⁴¹And it was in the morning, and Balak took Balaam and brought him up to the High Places of Baal, and he saw the outer edge of the people from there.

23

¹And Balaam said to Balak, "Build seven altars for me here, and prepare seven bulls and seven rams for me here." ²And Balak did as Balaam spoke, and Balak and Balaam offered a bull and a ram on each altar. ³And Balaam said to Balak, "Stand up by your burnt offering, and let me go. Maybe YHWH will communicate to me. And whatever He'll show me, I'll tell you." And he went to a viewpoint. ⁴And God communicated to Balaam. And he said to Him, "I've arranged the seven altars and offered a bull and a ram on each altar."

⁵And YHWH put a word in Balaam's mouth, and He said, "Go back to Balak, and speak like this."

⁶And he went back to him, and here he was, standing up by his burnt offering, he and all the chiefs of Moab. ⁷And he took up his pronouncement, and he said:

> Balak led me from Aram,
> Moab's king from mountains of the East.
> "Come, curse Jacob for me!
> Come, denounce Israel!"

---

*"And he said, 'I've sinned.'" Cf. Exod 9:27; 10:16 (E).

8   How shall I execrate whom God hasn't execrated?
    And how shall I denounce whom YHWH hasn't denounced?
9   For from the top of rocks I see it,
    and from hills I view it.
    Here: a people dwelling separate
    and not reckoned among the nations.
10 Who has counted the dust of Jacob
    and the number of a fourth of Israel?
    May my soul die the death of the righteous,
    and may my future be like his!

¹¹And Balak said to Balaam, "What have you done to me?! I took you to execrate my enemies. And, here, you've blessed them!"

¹²And he answered and said, "Isn't it that whatever YHWH sets in my mouth, that is what I'll watch out to say?!"

¹³And Balak said to him, "Come on with me to another place from which you'll see it. You'll see nothing but its edge, and you won't see all of it. And execrate it for me from there." ¹⁴And he took him to the field of Zophim, to the top of Pisgah, and he built seven altars and offered a bull and a ram on each altar.

¹⁵And he said to Balak, "Stand up here by your burnt offering, and I'll be communicated with here." ¹⁶And YHWH was communicated to Balaam, and He set a word in his mouth and said, "Go back to Balak, and you shall speak this."

¹⁷And he came to him, and here he was, standing up by his burnt offering, and the chiefs of Moab were with him. And Balak said to him, "What did YHWH speak?"

¹⁸And he took up his pronouncement, and he said:

    Get up, Balak, and listen.
    Hear me, son of Zippor.
19 God is not a man, that He would lie,
    or a human being, that He would regret.
    Has He said and will not do
    or spoken and will not bring it about?
20 Here, I was taken to bless,
    and He blessed, and I won't take it back.
21 He didn't find harm in Jacob,
    and He didn't see trouble in Israel.
    YHWH, its God, is with it,
    and a shout for a king is in it.

22   God who brought them out from Egypt
      is like a wild ox's horns for it.
23   For there's no divination against Jacob
      and no enchantment against Israel.
      At this time it will be said to Jacob
      and to Israel: "What has God done?"
24   Here, a people will get up like a feline
      and like a lion will raise itself.
      It won't lie down until it has eaten prey
      and until it has drunk blood of carcasses.

²⁵And Balak said to Balaam, "Don't do either: execrate them or bless them!"

²⁶And Balaam answered, and he said to Balak, "Didn't I speak to you, saying, 'Everything that YHWH will speak, that is what I'll do'?"

²⁷And Balak said to Balaam, "Come on. I'll take you to another place. Maybe it will be right in God's eyes, and you'll execrate it for me from there." ²⁸And Balak took Balaam to the top of Peor, which looks out over Jeshimon.

²⁹And Balaam said to Balak, "Build seven altars for me here and prepare seven bulls and seven rams for me here." ³⁰And Balak did as Balaam had said, and he offered a bull and a ram on each altar.

24

¹And Balaam saw that it was good in YHWH's eyes to bless Israel, and he did not go as on previous times to divinations. And he turned his face to the wilderness, ²and Balaam raised his eyes and saw Israel, tenting according to its tribes, and God's spirit* came on him. ³And he took up his pronouncement, and he said:

      Word of Balaam, son of Beor,
      and word of the man, opened of eye;
4   word of the one who hears God's sayings,
      who sees Shadday's vision,
      falling, but with eyes uncovered.
5   How good your tents are, Jacob,
      your tabernacles, Israel.
6   They spread like palms,

---

*"God's spirit." Cf. Gen 41:38 (E). This expression also occurs in P but never in J.

> like gardens by a river,
> like aloes YHWH planted,
> like cedars by water.

7   It drips water from its branches
> and its seed in plentiful water.
> And its king will be higher than Agag,
> and its kingdom will be elevated.

8   God who brought it out from Egypt
> is like a wild ox's horns for it.
> He shall eat up nations, its foes,
> and break their bones
> and pierce with His arrows.

9   It bent, lay down, like a lion;
> and, like a feline, who will rouse it?
> Those who bless you: he's blessed.
> And those who curse you: he's cursed.

¹⁰And Balak's anger flared at Balaam, and he wrung his hands, and Balak said to Balaam, "I called you to execrate my enemies; and, here, you've blessed these three times! ¹¹And now, flee to your place! I said I would honor you; and, here, YHWH has held you back from honor!"

¹²And Balaam said to Balak, "Didn't I speak to your messengers whom you sent to me as well, saying, ¹³'If Balak would give me a houseful of silver and gold of his I wouldn't be able to go against the mouth of YHWH, to do good or bad from my own heart. Whatever YHWH speaks, that is what I'll speak.' ¹⁴And now, here, I'm going to my people. Come. I'll advise you of what this people will do to your people in the future days." ¹⁵And he took up his pronouncement, and he said:

> Word of Balaam, son of Beor,
> and word of the man whose eye is whole;

16   word of the one who hears God's sayings
> and who knows the Highest's knowledge,
> who sees Shadday's vision,
> falling, but with eyes uncovered.

17   I see it—and not now;
> I view it—and not close:
> a star has stepped from Jacob,
> and a scepter has come up from Israel
> and pierced the temples of Moab
> and the crown of all the children of Seth.

18   And Edom was a possession,

and Seir was a possession of its enemies,
and Israel was making triumph.
19 And one from Jacob dominated
and destroyed a remnant from a city.

²⁰And he saw Amalek, and he took up his pronouncement, and he said:

Amalek was foremost of nations,
and its future arrives at destruction.

²¹And he saw the Kenites, and he took up his pronouncement and said:

Your residence is strong,
and set your nest in a cliff.
22 But Cain will be for burning
How long will Asshur hold you prisoner?

²³And he took up his pronouncement, and he said:

Woe. Who will live more than what God set him?
24 And ships from the hand of Kittim:
And they degraded Asshur, and they degraded Eber.
And it, too, arrives at destruction.

²⁵And Balaam got up and went, and he went back to his place.* And Balak, too, went his way.**

25

¹And Israel lived in Shittim, and the people began to prostitute themselves to the daughters of Moab.‡ ²And they attracted the people to the sacrifices of their gods, and the people ate and bowed to their gods, ³and Israel was associated with Baal Peor. And YHWH's anger flared at Israel. ⁴And YHWH said to Moses, "Take all of the leaders of the people and hang them in front of the sun, and YHWH's flaring anger will go back from Israel."

⁵And Moses said to Israel's judges, "Each of you, kill those of his people who are associated with Baal Peor."

---

*"and went to [his] place." Cf. Gen 22:3 (E).
**"and went his way." Cf. Gen 32:2 (E).
‡The women who have sexual unions with the Israelites are Moabite in Num 25:1 (J); but they are Midianite in 25:6; 31:1–16 (P). This change is consistent with other cases of polemic in P against the Mushite priesthood. Denigrating Midianite women is a denigration of Moses' wife, who is Midianite.

⁶And, here, a man from the children of Israel came and brought forward a Midianite woman to his brothers before the eyes of Moses and before the eyes of all the congregation of the children of Israel while they were mourning at the entrance of the Tent of Meeting.* ⁷And Phinehas son of Eleazar son of Aaron, the priest, saw, and he got up from among the congregation and took a spear in his hand. ⁸And he came after the Israelite man to the enclosure** and ran the two of them through, the Israelite man and the woman, to her stomach, and the plague was halted from the children of Israel. ⁹And the dead in the plague were twenty-four thousand.‡

¹⁰And YHWH spoke to Moses, saying, ¹¹"Phinehas son of Eleazar son of Aaron, the priest, has turned back my fury from the children of Israel by his carrying out my jealousy among them, so I didn't finish the children of Israel in my jealousy. ¹²Therefore, say: Here, I'm giving him my covenant of peace, ¹³and it shall be his, and his seed's after him, a covenant of eternal priesthood, because he was jealous for his God, and he made atonement for the children of Israel."

¹⁴And the name of the stricken Israelite man, who was struck with the Midianite woman, was Zimri son of Salu, chieftain of a father's house of the Simeonites. ¹⁵And the name of the stricken Midianite woman was Cozbi daughter of Zur. He was head of the people of a father's house in Midian.

¹⁶And YHWH spoke to Moses, saying, ¹⁷"Afflict the Midianites—and you shall strike them— ¹⁸because they have been afflicting you with their conspiracies that they made against you over the matter of Peor and over the matter of Cozbi, the daughter of a chieftain of Midian, their sister who was struck on the day of the plague over the matter of Peor.

¹⁹And it was after the plague.

---

*Why are the people mourning? The last verse of P before this was Num 20:29, the conclusion of the account of Aaron's death. It says "all the congregation saw that Aaron had expired, and all the house of Israel mourned Aaron thirty days." After a four-chapter hiatus, P now continues where it left off: "all the congregation of the children of Israel were mourning."

**The enclosure (Hebrew *qubbâ*) refers to the inner sanctum of the Tent of Meeting. That is why it must be a priest who goes in after them, and that is why he can execute them on the spot, with no trial: this is what is done to a nonpriest who enters the Tent of Meeting. This also explains why there is a plague that has seemingly come from nowhere. P says earlier that a plague came if the people came too close to the holy zone of the Tent of Meeting: "so there will not be a plague in the children of Israel when the children of Israel would come near to the Holy" (Num 8:19).

‡Besides the plague, the Tent of Meeting, and the central role of the priest Phinehas, who is Aaron's grandson, the Priestly terms "brought forward" and "congregation" also identify this narrative as P.

26

¹And YHWH said to Moses and to Eleazar son of Aaron, the priest, saying, ²"Add up the heads of all of the congregation of Israel from twenty years old and up, by their fathers' house, everyone going out to Israel's army."

³And Moses and Eleazar, the priest, spoke with them in the plains of Moab by the Jordan toward Jericho, saying, ⁴"From twenty years old and up," as YHWH commanded Moses and the children of Israel who had gone out from the land of Egypt.

⁵Reuben, Israel's firstborn; the children of Reuben:

Hanoch: the family of the Hanochites. Of Pallu: the family of the Palluites. ⁶Of Hezron: the family of the Hezronites. Of Carmi: the family of the Carmites. ⁷These are the families of the Reubenites, and their counts were forty-three thousand seven hundred thirty. ⁸And Pallu's sons: Eliab. ⁹And Eliab's sons: Nemuel and Dathan and Abiram. That is the Dathan and Abiram, prominent ones of the congregation, who fought against Moses and against Aaron in Korah's congregation when they fought against YHWH, ¹⁰and the earth opened its mouth and swallowed them and Korah when the congregation died, when the fire consumed the two hundred fifty men, and they became a sign. ¹¹But Korah's sons did not die.*

¹²The children of Simeon by their families:

Of Nemuel: the family of the Nemuelites. Of Jamin: the family of the Jaminites. Of Jachin: the family of the Jachinites. ¹³Of Zerah: the family of the Zerahites. Of Saul: the family of the Saulites. ¹⁴These are the families of the Simeonites: twenty-two thousand two hundred.

¹⁵The children of Gad by their families:

Of Zephon: the family of the Zephonites. Of Haggi: the family of the Haggites. Of Shuni: the family of the Shunites. ¹⁶Of Ozni: the family of the Oznites. Of Eri: the family of the Erites. ¹⁷Of Arod: the family of the Arodites. Of Areli: the family of the Arelites. ¹⁸These are the families of the children of Gad by their counts: forty thousand five hundred.

---

*This note (vv. 8–11) breaks the pattern of the genealogical list in which it appears. Each tribe is listed by its families, and then its total number of members is given. But here, following the conclusion of the genealogy of the tribe of Reuben, the text stops to identify Dathan and Abiram and connect them with Korah. R apparently added it to support his merger of the Korah episode with the Dathan-Abiram episode in Numbers 16. The structure "That is Dathan and Abiram . . . who . . ." occurs only here and in another passage that is identified with R on other grounds as well: "That is Aaron and Moses who . . ." (Exod 6:26).

¹⁹Judah's sons were Er and Onan, but Er and Onan died in the land of Canaan. ²⁰Then the children of Judah by their families were:

Of Shelah: the family of the Shelanites. Of Perez: the family of the Perezites. Of Zerah: the family of the Zerahites. ²¹And the children of Perez were: Of Hezron: the family of the Hezronites. Of Hamul: the family of the Hamulites. ²²These are the families of Judah by their counts: seventy-six thousand five hundred.

²³The children of Issachar by their families:

Of Tola: the family of the Tolaites. Of Puwah: the family of the Punites. ²⁴Of Jashub: the family of the Jashubites. Of Shimron: the family of the Shimronites. ²⁵These are the families of Issachar by their counts: sixty-four thousand three hundred.

²⁶The children of Zebulun by their families:

Of Sered: the family of the Seredites. Of Elon: the family of the Elonites. Of Jahleel: the family of the Jahleelites. ²⁷These are the families of the Zebulunites by their counts: sixty thousand five hundred.

²⁸The children of Joseph by their families were Manasseh and Ephraim.

²⁹Of the children of Manasseh: Of Machir: the family of the Machirites. And Machir fathered Gilead. Of Gilead: the family of the Gileadites. ³⁰These are the children of Gilead: Of Iezer: the family of the Iezerites. Of Helek: the family of the Helekites. ³¹And Asriel: the family of the Asrielites. And Shechem: the family of the Shechemites. ³²And Shemida: the family of the Shemidaites. And Hepher: the family of the Hepherites. ³³And Zelophehad son of Hepher had no sons, just daughters, and the names of Zelophehad's daughters were Mahlah and Noah, Hoglah, Milcah, and Tirzah. ³⁴These are the families of Manasseh; and their counts: fifty-two thousand seven hundred.

³⁵These are the children of Ephraim by their families:

Of Shuthelah: the family of the Shuthelahites. Of Becher: the family of the Becherites. Of Tahan: the family of the Tahanites. ³⁶And these are the children of Shuthelah: Of Eran: the family of the Eranites. ³⁷These are the families of the children of Ephraim by their counts: thirty-two thousand five hundred. These are the sons of Joseph after their families.

³⁸The children of Benjamin by their families:

Of Bela: the family of the Belaites. Of Ashbel: the family of the Ashbelites. Of Ahiram: the family of the Ahiramites. ³⁹Of Shephupham: the family of the Shuphamites. Of Hupham: the family of the Huphamites. ⁴⁰And the children of Bela were Ard and Naaman: The family of the Ardites. Of Naaman: the family of the Naamites. ⁴¹These are the children of Benjamin by their families; and their counts: forty-five thousand six hundred.

⁴²These are the children of Dan by their families:

Of Shuham: the family of the Shuhamites. These are the families of Dan after their families. ⁴³All the families of the Shuhamites by their counts: sixty-four thousand four hundred.

⁴⁴The children of Asher by their families:

Of Imnah: the family of Imnah. Of Ishvi: the family of the Ishvites. Of Beriah: the family of the Beriites. ⁴⁵Of the children of Beriah: Of Heber: the family of the Heberites. Of Malchiel: the family of the Malchielites. ⁴⁶And Asher's daughter's name was Serah. ⁴⁷These are the families of the children of Asher by their counts: fifty-three thousand four hundred.

⁴⁸The children of Naphtali by their families:

Of Jahzeel: the family of the Jahzeelites. Of Guni: the family of the Gunites. ⁴⁹Of Jezer: the family of the Jezerites. Of Shillem: the family of the Shillemites. ⁵⁰These are the families of Naphtali by their families, and their counts: forty-five thousand four hundred.

⁵¹These are the counts of the children of Israel: six hundred one thousand seven hundred thirty.

⁵²And YHWH spoke to Moses, saying, ⁵³"The land shall be distributed to these as a legacy with the number of names. ⁵⁴For the large you shall make its legacy larger, and for the small you shall make its legacy smaller. Each man will be given his legacy according to his counts. ⁵⁵Just: the land shall be distributed by lot. They shall have a legacy by the names of their fathers' tribes. ⁵⁶Its legacy shall be distributed according to the lot, whether large or small."

⁵⁷And these are the counts of the Levites by their families:

Of Gershon: the family of the Gershonites. Of Kohath: the family of the Kohathites. Of Merari: the family of the Merarites. ⁵⁸These are the families of the Levites: the family of the Libnites, the family of the Hebronites, the family of the Mahlites, the family of the Mushites, the family of the Korahites.

And Kohath fathered Amram. ⁵⁹And the name of Amram's wife was Jochebed, a daughter of Levi, who was born to Levi in Egypt. And she gave birth for Amram to Aaron and Moses and Miriam, their sister. ⁶⁰And Nadab and Abihu, Eleazar and Ithamar were born to Aaron. ⁶¹And Nadab and Abihu died when they brought forward unfitting fire in front of YHWH.

⁶²And their counts were twenty-three thousand, every male from a month old and up, because they were not counted among the children of Israel because a legacy was not given to them among the children of Israel.

⁶³These are the counts of Moses and Eleazar, the priest, who counted the children of Israel in the plains of Moab by the Jordan toward Jericho; ⁶⁴and there was not a man among these from the counts of Moses and Aaron,

the priest, who counted the children of Israel in the wilderness of Sinai, [65]because YHWH said of them, "They shall die in the wilderness," and not a man was left of them except Caleb son of Jephunneh and Joshua son of Nun.

27

[1]And the daughters of Zelophehad son of Hepher son of Gilead son of Machir son of Manasseh, of the families of Manasseh son of Joseph, came forward. And these are his daughters' names: Mahlah, Noah, and Hoglah and Milcah and Tirzah. [2]And they stood in front of Moses and in front of Eleazar, the priest, and in front of the chieftains and all the congregation at the entrance of the Tent of Meeting, saying, [3]"Our father died in the wilderness. And he wasn't among the congregation who were gathered against YHWH: in Korah's congregation. Rather, he died through his own sin. And he had no sons. [4]Why should our father's name be subtracted from among his family because he didn't have a son? Give us a possession among our father's brothers."

[5]And Moses brought their case forward in front of YHWH.

[6]And YHWH said to Moses, saying, [7]"Zelophehad's daughters speak right. You shall give them a possession for a legacy among their father's brothers, and you shall pass their father's legacy to them. [8]And you shall speak to the children of Israel, saying, 'A man who will die and not have a son: you shall pass his legacy to his daughter. [9]And if he does not have a daughter, then you shall give his legacy to his brothers. [10]And if he does not have brothers, then you shall give his legacy to his father's brothers. [11]And if there are no brothers of his father, then you shall give his legacy to his relative who is closest to him of his family, and he shall possess it.' And it shall become a law of judgment for the children of Israel, as YHWH commanded Moses."

[12]And YHWH said to Moses, "Go up to this mountain of Abarim and see the land that I've given to the children of Israel. [13]And you'll see it, and then you'll be gathered to your people, you as well, as Aaron, your brother, was gathered, [14]because you rebelled against my word in the wilderness of Zin in the congregation's quarrel to make me holy with water before their eyes. That is the water of Meribah of Kadesh at the wilderness of Zin."

[15]And Moses spoke to YHWH, saying, [16]"Let YHWH, God of the spirits of all flesh, appoint a man over the congregation [17]who will go out in front of them and who will come in in front of them and who will bring them out and who will bring them in, so YHWH's congregation won't be like sheep that don't have a shepherd."

¹⁸And YHWH said to Moses, "Take Joshua son of Nun, a man with spirit in him, and lay your hand on him. ¹⁹And you shall stand him in front of Eleazar, the priest, and in front of all the congregation, and you shall command him before their eyes. ²⁰And you shall put some of your eminence on him so that all the congregation of the children of Israel will hear. ²¹And he shall stand in front of Eleazar, the priest; and he shall ask him in judgment of the Urim in front of YHWH. By his word they shall go out, and by his word they shall come in, he and all the children of Israel with him and all the congregation."

²²And Moses did as YHWH commanded him, and he took Joshua and stood him in front of Eleazar, the priest, and in front of all the congregation. ²³And he laid his hands on him and commanded him, as YHWH had spoken by Moses' hand.

28

¹And YHWH spoke to Moses, saying, ²"Command the children of Israel, and you shall say to them: You shall observe to bring forward my sacrifice to me, my bread, for my offering by fire, my pleasant smell, at its appointed time.

³"And you shall say to them: This is the offering by fire that you shall bring forward to YHWH: two unblemished one-year-old lambs per day as a continual burnt offering. ⁴You shall do one lamb in the morning, and you shall do the second lamb 'between the two evenings.' ⁵And a tenth of an ephah of fine flour for a grain offering, mixed with a fourth of a hin of pressed oil, ⁶the continual burnt offering that was done at Mount Sinai for a pleasant smell, an offering by fire to YHWH. ⁷And its libation shall be a fourth of a hin for one lamb. Pour a libation of beer in the holy place for YHWH. ⁸And you shall do the second lamb 'between the two evenings,' and you shall do it like the morning grain offering and like its libation, an offering by fire of a pleasant smell to YHWH.

⁹"And on the Sabbath day two unblemished one-year-old lambs and two tenths of fine flour, a grain offering, mixed with oil, and its libation: ¹⁰the burnt offering of each Sabbath in its week, beside the continual burnt offering and its libation.

¹¹"And at the beginning of your months you shall bring forward a burnt offering to YHWH: two bulls of the cattle and one ram, seven unblemished one-year-old lambs, ¹²with three tenths of fine flour, a grain offering, mixed with oil for one bull and two tenths of fine flour mixed with oil for the one ram, ¹³and one tenth of fine flour, a grain offering, mixed with oil for each lamb, a burnt offering as a pleasant smell, an offering by fire to YHWH.

¹⁴And their libations: half a hin will be for a bull and a third of a hin for a ram and a fourth of a hin for a lamb—wine. This is the burnt offering of each new month in its month for the months of the year. ¹⁵And one goat for a sin offering to YHWH shall be done, beside the continual burnt offering and its libation.

¹⁶"And in the first month on the fourteenth day of the month is a Passover to YHWH. ¹⁷And on the fifteenth day of this month is a holiday. For seven days unleavened bread shall be eaten. ¹⁸On the first day is a holy assembly. You shall not do any act of work. ¹⁹And you shall bring forward an offering by fire, a burnt offering to YHWH. You shall have two bulls of the cattle and one ram and seven unblemished one-year-old lambs. ²⁰And their grain offering shall be fine flour mixed with oil. You shall do three tenths for a bull and two tenths for a ram. ²¹And you shall do one tenth for each lamb, for the seven lambs. ²²And one goat for a sin offering to make atonement over you. ²³You shall do these aside from the morning burnt offering that is for the continual burnt offering. ²⁴You shall do food as a fire offering, a pleasant smell to YHWH, like these daily for seven days. It shall be done beside the continual burnt offering and its libation. ²⁵And on the seventh day you shall have a holy assembly. You shall not do any act of work.

²⁶"And on the Day of Firstfruits, when you bring a new grain offering to YHWH on your Feast of Weeks, you shall have a holy assembly. You shall not do any act of work. ²⁷And you shall bring forward a burnt offering for a pleasant smell to YHWH: two bulls of the cattle, one ram, seven one-year-old lambs ²⁸and their grain offering, fine flour mixed with oil, three tenths for one bull, two tenths for one ram, ²⁹one tenth for each lamb, for the seven lambs, ³⁰one goat to make atonement over you. ³¹You shall do it aside from the continual burnt offering and its grain offering—they shall be unblemished for you—and their libations.

29

¹"And in the seventh month on the first of the month you shall have a holy assembly. You shall not do any act of work. You shall have a day of horn-blasting. ²And you shall do a burnt offering for a pleasant smell for YHWH: one bull of the cattle, one ram, seven unblemished one-year-old lambs, ³and their grain offering, fine flour mixed with oil, three tenths for a bull, two tenths for a ram, ⁴and one tenth for each lamb, for the seven lambs, ⁵and one goat for a sin offering to make atonement over you, ⁶aside from the burnt offering of the new month and its grain offering and the

continual burnt offering and its grain offering and their libations as required, for a pleasant smell, an offering by fire to YHWH.

⁷"And on the tenth of this seventh month you shall have a holy assembly. And you shall degrade yourselves. You shall not do any act of work. ⁸And you shall bring forward a burnt offering to YHWH for a pleasant smell: you shall have one bull of the cattle, one ram, seven unblemished one-year-old lambs, ⁹and their grain offering, fine flour mixed with oil, three tenths for a bull, two tenths for one ram, ¹⁰one tenth for each lamb, for the seven lambs, ¹¹one goat for a sin offering, aside from the sin offering of atonement and the continual burnt offering and its grain offering and their libations.

¹²"And on the fifteenth day of the seventh month you shall have a holy assembly. You shall not do any act of work. And you shall celebrate a holiday for YHWH for seven days. ¹³And you shall bring forward a burnt offering, an offering by fire for a pleasant smell to YHWH: thirteen bulls of the cattle, two rams, fourteen one-year-old lambs. They shall be unblemished. ¹⁴And their grain offering shall be fine flour mixed with oil, three tenths for each bull, for thirteen bulls, two tenths for each ram, for two rams, ¹⁵and one tenth for each lamb, for fourteen lambs, ¹⁶and one goat for a sin offering, aside from the continual burnt offering, its grain offering, and its libation.

¹⁷"And on the second day: twelve bulls of the cattle, two rams, fourteen unblemished one-year-old lambs ¹⁸and their grain offering and their libations for the bulls, for the rams, and for the lambs by their number as required, ¹⁹and one goat for a sin offering, aside from the continual burnt offering and its grain offering and their libations.

²⁰"And on the third day: eleven bulls, two rams, fourteen unblemished one-year-old lambs ²¹and their grain offering and their libations for the bulls, for the rams, and for the lambs by their number as required, ²²and one goat for a sin offering, aside from the continual burnt offering and its grain offering and its libation.

²³"And on the fourth day: ten bulls, two rams, fourteen unblemished one-year-old lambs, ²⁴their grain offering and their libations for the bulls, for the rams, and for the lambs by their number as required, ²⁵and one goat for a sin offering, aside from the continual burnt offering, its grain offering, and its libation.

²⁶"And on the fifth day: nine bulls, two rams, fourteen unblemished one-year-old lambs ²⁷and their grain offering and their libations for the bulls, for the rams, and for the lambs by their number as required, ²⁸and one goat for a sin offering, aside from the continual burnt offering and its grain offering and its libation.

²⁹"And on the sixth day: eight bulls, two rams, fourteen unblemished one-year-old lambs ³⁰and their grain offering and their libations for the bulls, for the rams, and for the lambs by their number as required, ³¹and one goat for a sin offering, aside from the continual burnt offering, its grain offering, and its libations.

³²"And on the seventh day: seven bulls, two rams, fourteen unblemished one-year-old lambs ³³and their grain offering and their libations for the bulls, for the rams, and for the lambs by their number according to their requirement, ³⁴and one goat for a sin offering, aside from the continual burnt offering, its grain offering, and its libation.

³⁵"On the eighth day you shall have a convocation. You shall not do any act of work. ³⁶And you shall bring forward a burnt offering, and offering by fire, a pleasant smell to YHWH: one bull, one ram, seven unblemished one-year-old lambs, ³⁷their grain offering and their libations for the bull, for the ram, and for the lambs by their number as required, ³⁸and one goat for a sin offering, aside from the continual burnt offering and its grain offering and its libation.

³⁹"You shall do these for YHWH at your appointed times, aside from your vows and your contributions for your burnt offerings and for your grain offerings and for your libations and for your peace offerings."

30

¹And Moses said it to the children of Israel, according to everything that YHWH commanded Moses.*

---

*Numbers 28–29 is a body of laws of sacrifice. The laws of grain offerings and libations were introduced in Numbers 15, but here they are assumed to exist along with the meat offerings. This passage therefore appears to come from the same source as Numbers 15 and to continue it (or it may be a later addition, but it is not earlier than Numbers 15). It is therefore identified as R, just as Numbers 15 is. This is further confirmed by the absence of any reference to the Tabernacle in this passage, just as there is none in Numbers 15 or in any passage identified as R—because R comes from the time of the post-exilic Temple, which did not contain the Tabernacle. (See the Collection of Evidence, pp. 22–23, and the comment on Exod 26:1.)

Also, in P *the law is given at Sinai.* Hardly any law is given in P after the departure from Sinai unless it has something to do with a story. (For example, the priestly and Levitical matters in Numbers 18 follow on what has just happened in the Korah rebellion and its aftermath.) The one possible exception is the matter of the red heifer. If these two long chapters (Numbers 28–29) are P, then they are anomalous, the only long independent body of law in P that is not revealed at Sinai.

This two-chapter section is the fulcrum of the view of Israel Knohl that there was a "Holiness School" (H) that came later than P and was responsible for the redaction of P. But for Knohl this section must be P, a view that he never defends. He rather starts with

²And Moses spoke to the heads of the tribes of the children of Israel, saying, "This is the thing that YHWH commanded:* ³A man who will make a vow to YHWH or has sworn an oath to make a restriction on himself shall not desecrate his word. He shall do it according to everything that comes out of his mouth.

⁴"And a woman who will make a vow to YHWH and made a restriction in her father's house in her youth, ⁵and her father hears her vow and her restriction that she made on herself, and her father keeps quiet to her, then all her vows shall stand, and every restriction that she made on herself shall stand. ⁶But if her father held her back on the day he heard all her vows and her restrictions that she made on herself, it will not stand. And YHWH will forgive her because her father held her back.

⁷"And if she will have a husband while her vows or the thing she let out of her lips with which she restricted herself are on her, ⁸and her husband hears and keeps quiet on the day he heard it, then her vows will stand, and her restrictions that she made on herself will stand. ⁹But if, on the day her husband hears it, he will hold her back and will break her vow that is on her and what was let out of her lips by which she restricted herself, then YHWH will forgive her.

¹⁰"And a widow's or divorced woman's vow, everything by which she has restricted herself, shall stand regarding her.

¹¹"And if she vowed or made a restriction on herself by an oath at her husband's house, ¹²and her husband heard it and kept quiet to her—he did not hold her back—then all her vows shall stand, and every restriction that she made on herself shall stand. ¹³But if her husband broke them on the day he heard all that came out of her lips for her vows and for restricting herself, it shall not stand. Her husband had broken them, and YHWH will forgive her. ¹⁴Every vow and every oath of restriction to degrade oneself: her husband shall make it stand, and her husband shall break it. ¹⁵And if her husband will keep quiet in regard to her from that day to the next, then he has made all her vows and all her restrictions that are on her stand. He has made them

---

the statement "Scholars generally agree that Numbers 28–29 is wholly P" (*The Sanctuary of Silence*, p. 9). But neither Noth nor I identified it as P. Although Milgrom holds a similar view to Knohl's, he notes cautiously, "All arguments from Numbers are precarious" (*Leviticus 1–16*, Anchor Bible 3, p. 13). Moreover, Milgrom lists thirteen terms that are marks of pre-exilic P language in Numbers, and none of them appears here in Numbers 28–29. Knohl and Milgrom may be right that H was composed later than P, and they may or may not be right that H played a role in the redaction of the Torah. But those things should not be based on this text in Numbers 28–29.

*It is difficult to determine whether this section (30:2–17) is P or R. The identification as P here is tentative.

stand because he kept quiet to her on the day he heard it. ¹⁶And if he will break them after he has heard them, then he shall bear her crime."

¹⁷These are the laws that YHWH commanded Moses between a man and his wife, between a father and his daughter in her youth at her father's house.

31

¹And YHWH spoke to Moses, saying, ²"Get revenge for the children of Israel from the Midianites. After that you'll be gathered to your people."

³And Moses spoke to the people, saying, "Let people from you be equipped for the army, so they'll be against Midian to put YHWH's revenge in Midian. ⁴You shall send a thousand per tribe, a thousand per tribe, for all Israel's tribes, to the army."

⁵And, from Israel's thousands, a thousand per tribe were delivered, twelve thousand equipped for the army. ⁶And Moses sent them, a thousand per tribe, to the army; them and Phinehas son of Eleazar, the priest, to the army, with the equipment of the Holy and the trumpets for blasting in his hand. ⁷And they made war on Midian as YHWH had commanded Moses. And they killed every male. ⁸And they killed the kings of Midian—Evi and Rekem and Zur and Hur and Reba, the five kings of Midian—over their corpses. And they killed Balaam son of Beor by the sword. ⁹And the children of Israel took the women of Midian and their infants prisoner, and they despoiled all their animals and all their livestock and all their wealth. ¹⁰And they burned all their cities with their homes and all their encampments in fire. ¹¹And they took all the spoil and all the prey, human and animal. ¹²And they brought the prisoners and the prey and the spoil to Moses and to Eleazar, the priest, and to the congregation of the children of Israel, to the camp, to the plains of Moab, which is by the Jordan toward Jericho.

¹³And Moses and Eleazar, the priest, and all the congregation's chieftains went out to them, outside the camp. ¹⁴And Moses was angry at the officers of the army, the chiefs of thousands and the chiefs of hundreds who were coming from the army of the war. ¹⁵And Moses said to them, "Did you keep every female alive?!* ¹⁶Here, they came to bring about a breach against

---

*Moses is pictured here in P as angry that the Israelites have not killed the Midianite women, who, he says, caused the breach at Peor. Thus, in P, Moses denounces his wife's people, the Midianites, and he orders all nonvirgin Midianite women to be killed. This might or might not include his own wife, but either way it denigrates Moses' connection to Midian through his wife, and it possibly denigrates the Mushite priesthood, who are descended from Moses and that Midianite woman. (It is interesting that P never says whether this demand by Moses to kill the Midianite women is carried out.)

YHWH by the children of Israel, at Balaam's word, over the matter of Peor, so there was the plague in YHWH's congregation! ¹⁷So now, kill every male among the infants, and kill every woman who has known a man for male intercourse. ¹⁸But all infants among the women who have not known a male's intercourse: keep alive. ¹⁹And you, camp outside the camp for seven days: everyone who killed a life and everyone who touched a corpse, do sin expiation on the third day and on the seventh day, you and your prisoners. ²⁰And for every piece of clothing and every leather item and everything made from goats and every wood item you shall do expiation."

²¹And Eleazar, the priest, said to the men of the army who had come to the war, "This is the law of the instruction that YHWH commanded Moses: ²²Just the gold and the silver, the bronze, the iron, the tin, and the lead, ²³every thing that will go in fire, you shall pass through fire and purify. It shall be expiated from sin just in water of impurity. And everything that will not go in fire, you shall pass through water. ²⁴And you shall wash your clothes on the seventh day, and you will be pure, and after that you shall come to the camp."

²⁵And YHWH said to Moses, saying, ²⁶"Add up the heads of the prey, the prisoners, human and animal, you and Eleazar, the priest, and the heads of the fathers of the congregation. ²⁷And you shall split the prey between the warriors who went out to the army and all the congregation. ²⁸And you shall levy a tax for YHWH from the men of war who went out to the army, one individual out of five hundred, from humans and from cattle and from asses and from sheep. ²⁹You shall take from their half and you shall give to Eleazar, the priest, YHWH's donation. ³⁰From the half of the children of Israel you shall take one share out of fifty, from humans, from cattle, from asses, and from sheep, from all the animals, and you shall give them to the Levites, who keep the watch of YHWH's Tabernacle."

³¹And Moses and Eleazar, the priest, did as YHWH commanded Moses. ³²And the prey, over and above the spoil that the people of the army had taken, was: six hundred seventy-five thousand sheep ³³and seventy-two thousand cattle ³⁴and sixty-one thousand asses ³⁵and human beings—from the women who had not known male intercourse—all the persons were thirty-two thousand. ³⁶So the half, the portion of those who went out in the army was: the number of sheep was three hundred thirty-seven thousand five hundred. ³⁷And the tax for YHWH from the sheep was six hundred seventy-five. ³⁸And the cattle were thirty-six thousand, and their tax for YHWH was seventy-two. ³⁹And asses were thirty thousand five hundred, and their tax for YHWH was sixty-one. ⁴⁰And human beings were sixteen thousand, and their tax for YHWH was thirty-two persons. ⁴¹And Moses gave the tax, a donation for YHWH, to Eleazar, the priest, as YHWH commanded

Moses. ⁴²And of the half for the children of Israel, which Moses had split from the people who were serving in the army: ⁴³and the congregation's half of the sheep was three hundred thirty-seven thousand five hundred. ⁴⁴And the cattle were thirty-six thousand. ⁴⁵And asses were thirty thousand five hundred. ⁴⁶And human beings were sixteen thousand. ⁴⁷And Moses took from the half of the children of Israel one share out of fifty, from humans and from animals, and gave them to the Levites, who kept the watch of YHWH's Tabernacle, as YHWH commanded Moses.

⁴⁸And the officers who were over the thousands of the army came forward to Moses, the chiefs of the thousands and the chiefs of the hundreds. ⁴⁹And they said to Moses, "Your servants have added up the heads of the men of war who are in our hands, and not a man of them is lacking. ⁵⁰And we have made an offering for YHWH—whatever each man found: an item of gold, an armlet or bracelet, a ring, an earring, or an ornament—to make atonement for ourselves in front of YHWH." ⁵¹And Moses and Eleazar, the priest, took the gold from them, every item of handiwork. ⁵²And all the gold of the donation that they donated to YHWH was sixteen thousand seven hundred fifty shekels, from the chiefs of the thousands and from the chiefs of the hundreds. ⁵³The men of the army each had kept as spoil what was his. ⁵⁴And Moses and Eleazar, the priest, took the gold from the chiefs of the thousands and the hundreds and brought it to the Tent of Meeting, a commemoration for the children of Israel in front of YHWH.

32

¹And the children of Reuben and the children of Gad had a great amount of livestock, very substantial.* And they saw the land of Jazer and the land of Gilead; and, here, the place was a place for livestock. **²And the children of Gad and the children of Reuben came and said to Moses and to Eleazar, the priest, and to the chieftains of the congregation, saying,** ³Ataroth and Dibon and Jazer and Nimrah and Heshbon and Elealeh and Sebam

---

*This chapter appears to be composed of material from both J and P, but it is difficult to separate and identify which verses are from which source. The division here is tentative. It is based on (1) distinguishing sources in light of characteristic terminology of J and P, (2) the presence of Aaron's son Eleazar in P, and (3) determining if it is possible to identify two complete, consistent accounts in light of the fact that the Redactor's method elsewhere is visibly to retain both the P and the JE accounts in their entirety whenever possible.

and Nebo and Beon, **⁴"the land that YHWH struck in front of the congregation of Israel: it's livestock land, and your servants have livestock."** ⁵And they said, "If we've found favor in your eyes, **let this land be given to your servants for a possession;*** don't have us cross the Jordan."

⁶**And Moses said** to the children of Gad and to the children of Reuben, "Will your brothers go to war while you sit here?!** ⁷And why do you hold back the heart of the children of Israel from crossing to the land that YHWH has given them? ⁸That's what your fathers did when I sent them from Kadesh-barnea to see the land. ⁹And they went up to the Wadi Eshcol and saw the land,‡ but they held back the heart of the children of Israel so as not to go to the land that YHWH had given them. ¹⁰And YHWH's anger flared on that day, and he swore saying, ¹¹"The people who came up from Egypt, from twenty years old and up, won't see the land that I swore to Abraham, to Isaac, and to Jacob,‡‡ because they didn't go after me completely, ¹²except Caleb son of Jephunneh, the Kenizzite, and Joshua son of Nun§ because they went after YHWH completely.' ¹³**And YHWH's anger flared at Israel, and he made them roam in the wilderness forty years, until the end of all the generation§§** who were doing bad in YHWH's eyes. ¹⁴**And, here, you've gotten up in your fathers' place, a group of sinning people, to add more onto YHWH's flaring anger at Israel.** ¹⁵**If you go back from behind Him, then He'll add more to leave them in the wilderness, and you'll have destroyed all of this people!"**

¹⁶**And they came over to him and said, "We'll build walls for our livestock here, and cities for our infants.** ¹⁷**And we shall be equipped, ready in front of the children of Israel until we've brought them to their place, and our infants will live in fortified cities because of the residents of the land.** ¹⁸**We won't go back to our houses until the children of Israel take possession, each of his legacy.** ¹⁹**Because we won't have a possession with them from the farther**

The term "possession" ('ăhuzzāh*) is characteristic of P.

**The words of Moses that follow are a combination of J and P dialogue. Presumably the words "And Moses said" preceded each source's dialogue, but there was no need for the Redactor to retain such a repetition.

‡"to the Wadi Eshcol"; cf. Num 13:23 (J). "see the land"; cf. Num 13:18 (J).

‡‡"the land that I swore to Abraham, Isaac, and Jacob." Cf. "the land that I swore to their fathers," Num 14:23 (J).

§This same report occurs in Num 14:24 (J) and in Josh 14:14, but there only Caleb "went after YHWH completely." Joshua is not mentioned. It appears that Joshua was added here by the Redactor because he was merging both J and P texts, and in P Joshua had been added alongside Caleb in the scouts story. See the note on Num 14:24.

§§"in the wilderness forty years until the end." Cf. Num 14:33 (P). Also, this verse begins with a repetition of the words "And YHWH's anger flared at Israel" (cf. v. 10).

side of the Jordan, because our possession has come to us from the east-ward side of the Jordan."

²⁰And Moses said to them, "If you'll do this thing: if you'll get equipped for war in front of YHWH, ²¹and everyone of you will cross the Jordan equipped in front of YHWH until He dispossesses his enemies in front of him, ²²and the land will be subdued in front of YHWH, then, after that, you'll go back, and, from YHWH and from Israel, you'll be free, and this land will become yours for a possession in front of YHWH. ²³But if you won't do this, here, you've sinned to YHWH, and know that your sin will find you. ²⁴Build cities for your infants and fences for your flocks, and do what has come out of your mouths."

²⁵And the children of Gad and the children of Reuben said to Moses, saying, "Your servants will do as my lord commands. ²⁶Our infants, our women, our livestock, and all our animals will be there in the cities of Gilead. ²⁷And your servants will cross, everyone equipped for the army, in front of YHWH for war as my lord speaks."

²⁸And Moses commanded Eleazar, the priest, and Joshua son of Nun and the heads of the fathers of the tribes of the children of Israel for them. ²⁹And Moses said to them, "If the children of Gad and the children of Reuben will cross the Jordan with you, everyone equipped for war, in front of YHWH, and the land will be subdued in front of you, then you shall give them the land of Gilead for a possession. ³⁰But if they will not cross equipped with you, then they will have possessions among you in the land of Canaan."

³¹And the children of Gad and the children of Reuben answered, saying, "What YHWH has spoken to your servants: we shall do so. ³²We'll cross equipped in front of YHWH to the land of Canaan while we'll have our legacy possession across the Jordan."

³³And Moses gave them, the children of Gad and the children of Reuben and half of the tribe of Manasseh son of Joseph, the kingdom of Sihon, king of the Amorites, and the kingdom of Og, king of Bashan, the land with its cities, with the borders of the land's cities all around. ³⁴And the children of Gad built Dibon and Ataroth and Aroer ³⁵and Atroth-shophan and Jazer and Jogbehah ³⁶and Beth-Nimrah and Beth-Haran, fortified cities and fences for flocks. ³⁷And the children of Reuben built Heshbon and Elealeh and Kiriathaim ³⁸and Nebo and Baal-meon—with changes of name—and Sibmah, and they called the names of the cities that they built by new names. ³⁹And the children of Machir son of Manasseh went to Gilead and captured it and dispossessed the Amorite who was in it. ⁴⁰And Moses gave Gilead to Machir son of Manasseh, and they lived in it. ⁴¹And Jair son of Manasseh went and captured their villages, and he called them

Havvoth-Jair. ⁴²And Nobah went and captured Kenath and its towns, and he called it Nobah after his own name.

33

¹*These are the travels of the children of Israel who went out from the land of Egypt by their armies* by the hand of Moses and Aaron.* ²And Moses wrote their stops for their travels by YHWH's word, and these are their travels and their stops.

³*And they traveled from Rameses in the first month on the fifteenth day of the first month. On the day after the Passover, the children of Israel went out with a high hand before the eyes of all Egypt.* ⁴*And the Egyptians were burying those whom YHWH had struck among them: every firstborn. And YHWH had made judgments on their gods.*

⁵*And the children of Israel traveled from Rameses and camped in Succoth.* ⁶*And they traveled from Succoth and camped in Etham, which is at the edge of the wilderness.* ⁷*And they traveled from Etham and turned back toward Pi-hahiroth, which is in front of Baal-Zephon: and they camped in front of Migdol.* ⁸*And they traveled from before Pi-hahiroth and passed through the sea to the wilderness. And they went three days' journey in the wilderness of Etham and camped in Marah.* ⁹*And they traveled from Marah and came to Elim. And in Elim were twelve springs of water and seventy palm trees. And they camped there.* ¹⁰*And they traveled from Elim and camped by the Red Sea.* ¹¹*And they traveled from the Red Sea and camped in the wilderness of Sin.* ¹²*And they traveled from the wilderness of Sin and camped in Dophkah.* ¹³*And they traveled from Dophkah and camped in Alush.* ¹⁴*And they traveled from Alush and camped at Rephidim. And there was no water there for the people to drink.* ¹⁵*And they traveled from Rephidim and camped in the wilderness of Sinai.* ¹⁶*And they traveled from the wilderness of Sinai and camped at Kibroth Hattaavah.* ¹⁷*And they traveled from Kibroth Hattaavah and camped at Hazeroth.* ¹⁸*And they traveled from Hazeroth and camped in Rithmah.* ¹⁹*And they traveled from Rithmah and camped at Rimmon-parez.* ²⁰*And they traveled from Rimmon-parez and camped in Libnah.* ²¹*And they traveled from Libnah and camped at Rissah.* ²²*And they traveled from Rissah and camped in Kehelathah.* ²³*And they traveled from Kehelathah and camped at Mount Shapher.* ²⁴*And they traveled from Mount Shapher and camped in Haradah.* ²⁵*And they traveled from Haradah*

---

*This is the itinerary list of Israel's travels that R used in order to organize the wilderness episodes chronologically. See the note on Num 9:23.

and camped in Makheloth. ²⁶And they traveled from Makheloth and camped at Tahath. ²⁷And they traveled from Tahath and camped at Tarah. ²⁸And they traveled from Tarah and camped in Mithkah. ²⁹And they went from Mithkah and camped in Hashmonah. ³⁰And they traveled from Hashmonah and camped at Moseroth. ³¹And they traveled from Moseroth and camped in Bene-jaakan. ³²And they traveled from Bene-jaakan and camped at Hor-haggidgad. ³³And they went from Hor-haggidgad and camped in Jotbathah. ³⁴And they traveled from Jotbathah and camped at Ebronah. ³⁵And they traveled from Ebronah and camped at Ezion-geber. ³⁶And they traveled from Ezion-geber and camped in the wilderness of Zin. That is Kadesh. ³⁷And they traveled from Kadesh and camped in Mount Hor, at the edge of the land of Edom.

³⁸And Aaron, the priest, went up into Mount Hor at the word of YHWH and died there in the fortieth year after the children of Israel came out of the land of Egypt, in the fifth month, on the first day of the month. ³⁹And Aaron was a hundred twenty-three years old when he died in Mount Hor.

⁴⁰And the Canaanite, the king of Arad, who lived in the Negeb in the land of Canaan, heard of the coming of the children of Israel. ⁴¹And they traveled from Mount Hor and camped in Zalmonah. ⁴²And they traveled from Zalmonah and camped in Punon. ⁴³And they traveled from Punon and camped in Oboth. ⁴⁴And they traveled from Oboth and camped in Iyye-abarim, in the border of Moab. ⁴⁵And they traveled from Iyyim and camped in Dibon-gad. ⁴⁶And they traveled from Dibon-gad and camped in Almon-diblathaim. ⁴⁷And they traveled from Almon-diblathaim and camped in the mountains of Abarim in front of Nebo. ⁴⁸And they traveled from the mountains of Abarim and camped in the plains of Moab by the Jordan toward Jericho. ⁴⁹And they camped by the Jordan from Beth-jeshimoth to Abel-shittim in the plains of Moab.

⁵⁰And YHWH spoke to Moses in the plains of Moab by the Jordan toward Jericho, saying, ⁵¹"Speak to the children of Israel, and you shall say to them: When you cross the Jordan to the land of Canaan, ⁵²you shall dispossess all the residents of the land in front of you, and destroy all their carved figures, and you shall destroy all their molten images and demolish all their high places. ⁵³And you shall take possession of the land and live in it, because I've given the land to you to possess it. ⁵⁴And you shall give legacies of the land by lot, by your families: for the large you shall make its legacy larger, and for the small you shall make its legacy smaller. Wherever the lot indicates for it shall belong to it. You shall give legacies to the tribes of your fathers. ⁵⁵And if you don't dispossess the residents of the land in front of you, then those whom you leave of them will become sticks in your eyes and thorns in your sides, and they'll afflict you on the land in which you're living. ⁵⁶And it will be that, as I meant to do to them, I'll do to you!"

34

¹And YHWH spoke to Moses, saying, ²"Command the children of Israel, and you shall say to them: When you come to the land of Canaan, this is the land that will fall to you as a legacy, the land of Canaan by its borders: ³And the southern side for you shall be from the wilderness of Zin next to Edom, and the southern border for you shall be from the edge of the Dead Sea to the east. ⁴And the border for you shall turn from the south to the ascent of Akrabim and will pass to Zin, and its extent shall be from the south to Kadesh-barnea, and it shall go out to Hazar-addar and pass to Azmon. ⁵And the border shall turn from Azmon to the Wadi of Egypt, and its extent shall be to the sea. ⁶And the western border: and the big sea shall be a border for you. This shall be the western border for you. ⁷And this shall be the northern border for you: you shall mark from the big sea to Mount Hor, ⁸from Mount Hor you shall mark to the entrance of Hamath, and the border's extent shall be to Zedad, ⁹and the border shall go out to Ziphron, and its extent shall be to Hazar-enan. This shall be the northern border for you. ¹⁰And you shall mark for the border to the east from Hazar-enan to Shepham, ¹¹and the border shall go down from Shepham to Riblah at the east of Ain, and the border shall go down and rub on the shoulder of the Sea of Kinneret on the east, ¹²and the border shall go down to the Jordan, and its extent will be to the Dead Sea. This shall be the land for you by its borders all around."

¹³And Moses commanded the children of Israel, saying, "This is the land that you shall give as legacies by lot, which YHWH commanded to give to the nine tribes and the half of a tribe." ¹⁴Because the tribe of the children of the Reubenites by their fathers' house and the tribe of the children of the Gadites by their fathers' house had taken and half of the tribe of Manasseh had taken their legacy. ¹⁵The two tribes and the half of a tribe had taken their legacy from across the Jordan toward Jericho on the east side—to the east.

¹⁶And YHWH spoke to Moses, saying, ¹⁷"These are the names of the people who will give the land as legacies to you: Eleazar, the priest, and Joshua son of Nun; ¹⁸and you shall take one chieftain for each tribe to give the land as legacies. ¹⁹And these are the people's names: For the tribe of Judah, Caleb son of Jephunneh. ²⁰And for the tribe of the children of Simeon, Samuel son of Ammihud. ²¹For the tribe of Benjamin, Elidad son of Chislon. ²²And for the tribe of the children of Dan, a chieftain, Bukki son of Jogli. ²³For the children of Joseph: for the tribe of the children of Manasseh, a chieftain, Hanniel son of Ephod; ²⁴and for the tribe of the children of Ephraim, a chieftain, Kemuel son of Shiphtan. ²⁵And for the tribe of the children of Zebulun, a chieftain, Elizaphan son of Parnach. ²⁶And for the tribe of the children of

Issachar, a chieftain, Paltiel son of Azzan. ²⁷And for the tribe of the children of Asher, a chieftain, Ahihud son of Shelomi. ²⁸And for the tribe of the children of Naphtali, a chieftain, Pedahel son of Ammihud."

²⁹These are the ones whom YHWH commanded to give the children of Israel legacies in the land of Canaan.

35

¹And YHWH spoke to Moses in the plains of Moab by the Jordan toward Jericho, saying, ²"Command the children of Israel that, from the legacy of their possession, they shall give the Levites cities in which to live, and you shall give the Levites surrounding land for the cities all around them. ³And the cities shall be theirs to live in, and their surrounding lands shall be for their cattle and for their property and for their animals. ⁴And the surrounding lands of the cities that you shall give to the Levites: from the city wall outward, a thousand cubits all around. ⁵And you shall measure outside the city: on the eastern side two thousand in cubits, and on the southern side two thousand in cubits, and on the western side two thousand in cubits, and on the northern side two thousand in cubits, and the city in the middle. This shall be the surrounding lands of the cities for them. ⁶And the cities that you shall give to the Levites: six cities of refuge that you shall give for the manslayer to flee there, and you shall give in addition to them forty-two cities. ⁷All the cities that you shall give to the Levites: forty-eight cities, them and their surrounding lands. ⁸And the cities that you shall give from the possession of the children of Israel: from the larger you shall give more, and from the smaller you shall give fewer. Each shall give some of his cities to the Levites according to his legacy that they will give."

⁹And YHWH spoke to Moses, saying, ¹⁰"Speak to the children of Israel, and you shall say to them: When you cross the Jordan to the land of Canaan, ¹¹you shall establish cities; they shall be cities of refuge for you, and a manslayer who strikes a life by mistake shall flee there. ¹²And you shall have the cities for refuge from an avenger so the manslayer will not die until he stands in front of the congregation for judgment. ¹³And the cities that you shall give: You shall have six cities of refuge. ¹⁴You shall put three of the cities across the Jordan, and you shall put three of the cities in the land of Canaan. They shall be cities of refuge.

¹⁵"These six cities shall be for refuge for the children of Israel and for the alien and for the visitor among them, for anyone who strikes a life by mistake to flee there. ¹⁶But if he struck him with an iron item so that he died, he is a murderer. The murderer shall be put to death. ¹⁷And if he struck him with a

stone in the hand by which one could die, so that he died, he is a murderer. The murderer shall be put to death. [18]Or if he struck him with a wooden object in the hand by which one could die, so that he died, he is a murderer. The murderer shall be put to death. [19]The blood avenger, he shall kill the murderer. When he comes upon him, he shall kill him. [20]And if he pushed him in hatred or threw something on him through scheming so that he died, [21]or if he struck him with his hand in enmity so that he died, the one who struck shall be put to death. He is a murderer. The blood avenger shall kill the murderer when he comes upon him. [22]But if by chance, not in enmity, he pushed him or threw any object on him not through scheming, [23]or with any stone by which one could die, without seeing, so that he dropped it on him so that he died, and he was not an enemy to him and was not seeking to harm him, [24]then the congregation shall judge between the one who struck and the blood avenger on the basis of these judgments. [25]And the congregation shall rescue the manslayer from the blood avenger's hand, and the congregation shall bring him back to his city of refuge to which he fled, and he shall live in it until the death of the high priest whom one anointed with the holy oil. [26]But if the murderer will go out the border of his city of refuge to which he will flee, [27]and the blood avenger will find him outside the border of his city of refuge, and the blood avenger will murder the murderer, he does not have blood, [28]because he shall live in his city of refuge until the high priest's death, and after the high priest's death the murderer shall go back to the land of his possession.

[29]"And these shall become a law of judgment for you through your generations in all your homes. [30]Anyone who strikes a life, the murderer shall be murdered by the mouth of witnesses. And one witness shall not testify against a person so as to die. [31]And you shall not take a ransom for a murderer's life, because he did wrong so as to die, but he shall be put to death. [32]And you shall not take a ransom to flee to his city of refuge, to go back to live in the land until the priest's death. [33]So you shall not pollute the land in which you are. Because blood: it will pollute the land, and the land will not have expiation for blood that is spilled in it except by the blood of the one who spilled it! [34]And you shall not make the land impure in which you are living, in which I tent, because I, YHWH, tent among the children of Israel."

36

[1]And the heads of the fathers of the family of the children of Gilead son of Machir son of Manasseh, from the families of the children of Joseph, came forward and spoke in front of Moses and in front of the

chieftains, heads of fathers of the children of Israel. ²And they said, "YHWH commanded my lord to give the land as legacy by lot to the children of Israel, and my lord was commanded by YHWH to give the legacy of Zelophehad, our brother, to his daughters. ³If they will become wives to one of the sons of the tribes of the children of Israel, then their legacy will be subtracted from our fathers' legacy and added onto the legacy of the tribe to whom they will belong, and it will be subtracted from our legacy by the lot. ⁴And if the children of Israel will have the jubilee, then their legacy will be added onto the legacy of the tribe to whom they will belong, and their legacy will be subtracted from the legacy of our fathers' tribe."

⁵And Moses commanded the children of Israel by YHWH's word, saying, "The tribe of the children of Joseph speak right. ⁶This is the thing that YHWH has commanded Zelophehad's daughters, saying: They shall become wives for any in whose eyes it is good, except: they shall become wives to the family of their father's tribe. ⁷So a legacy of the children of Israel will not turn from tribe to tribe, but the children of Israel shall each cling to the legacy of his fathers' tribe. ⁸And any daughter who inherits a legacy from the tribes of the children of Israel shall become a wife to someone from a family of her father's tribe, so that the children of Israel will each inherit his fathers' legacy, ⁹and a legacy will not turn from a tribe to another tribe, but the tribes of the children of Israel shall each cling to its legacy."

¹⁰As YHWH commanded Moses, so Zelophehad's daughters did. ¹¹And Mahlah, Tirzah, and Hoglah and Milcah and Noah, Zelophehad's daughters, became wives to their uncles' sons. ¹²They became wives within the families of the children of Manasseh son of Joseph, and their legacy was on the tribe of their father's family.

¹³These are the commandments and the judgments that YHWH commanded by Moses' hand to the children of Israel in the plains of Moab by the Jordan toward Jericho.

DEUTERONOMY

1 ¹These are the words that Moses spoke to all of Israel* across the Jordan** in the wilderness, in the plain opposite Suph between Paran and Tophel and Laban and Hazeroth and Di-zahab, ²eleven days from Horeb‡ by way of Mount Seir up to Kadesh-barnea. ³And it was in the fortieth year, in the eleventh month, on the first of the month, Moses spoke to the children of Israel of everything that YHWH commanded him to them. ⁴After

---

*The opening verses, composed by the Deuteronomistic historian for the original edition of the history (Dtr1), cast the words that follow as the farewell speech of Moses before his death. This speech then takes up thirty chapters: all of Deuteronomy 1–30. This presentation as a farewell address enabled the historian to address broad matters of history and covenant (chapters 1–11) and to introduce a lengthy code of laws (Dtn, chapters 12–26) that now fit into a context of history.

**The narrator pictures Moses speaking "across the Jordan" many times in Deuteronomy. This was one of the early signs that led people to question whether Moses himself was the author of the Torah. These words reflect the perspective of an author who is in Israel. The author thus refers to Moses' location in Moab as "across the Jordan." This would not be the perspective of an author who is in Moab at the time. See also the note on Deut 3:20.

‡The name Horeb here is part of a group of elements that E and D have in common, as opposed to J and P. E and D both refer to the mountain as Horeb, whereas J and P refer to it as Sinai. E and D both downgrade Aaron; both include the golden-calf incident and the incident of Miriam's leprosy; J and P do not mention these incidents. E and D both use the expression "the place where YHWH will put His name" (or "tent His name" or "commemorate my name"). J and P do not. E and D both develop Moses' character and importance to a degree far beyond that of J and P. E and D both emphasize the role of prophets. In contrast, P uses the word "prophet" only once (figuratively) and J never uses it at all. E and D both endorse the Levites, regard them as priests, and provide for their maintenance, while in P the Levites are not regarded as priests and are rather lower than the priests, and in J the Levites are condemned to be dispersed as retribution for the acts of their ancestor, Levi (Gen 49:5–7). This association of E and D on these elements is consistent with the notion that these two sources derive from the same community, the Levites of Shiloh/Anathoth, sometimes known as Mushite.

309

he struck Sihon, king of the Amorites, who lived in Heshbon, and Og, king of Bashan, who lived in Ashtaroth at Edrei, [5]across the Jordan in the land of Moab, Moses undertook to make this instruction clear, saying, [6]"YHWH our God spoke to us in Horeb, saying, 'You've had enough of staying at this mountain. [7]Turn and travel and come to the Amorite hill country and to all its neighboring places, in the plain, in the hill country, and in the lowland and in the Negeb and by the seashore, the land of the Canaanite and Lebanon as far as the big river, the Euphrates River. [8]See: I've put the land in front of you. Come and possess the land that YHWH swore to your fathers, to Abraham, to Isaac, and to Jacob, to give to them and to their seed after them.'

[9]"And I said to you at that time, saying, 'I'm not able to carry you by myself. [10]YHWH, your God, has made you multiply, and here today you're like the stars of the skies for multitude. [11](May YHWH, your fathers' God, add on to you a thousand times more like you! And may He bless you as He spoke to you.) [12]How shall I carry your stress and your burden and your quarrels by myself? [13]Get wise and understanding and knowledgeable people for your tribes, and I'll set them among your heads.'

[14]"And you answered me, and you said, 'The thing that you've spoken is good to do.'

[15]"And I took heads of your tribes, wise and knowledgeable people, and I set them as heads over you, chiefs of thousands and chiefs of hundreds and chiefs of fifties and chiefs of tens and officers for your tribes. [16]And I commanded your judges at that time, saying, 'Hear between your brothers, and you shall judge with justice between a man and his brother or between him and his alien. [17]You shall not recognize a face in judgment: you shall hear the same for small and for big. Don't be fearful in front of a man— because justice is God's. And a matter that will be too hard for you, you shall bring forward to me, and I'll hear it.' [18]And I commanded you at that time all the things that you should do.

[19]"And we traveled from Horeb and went through all that big and fearful wilderness that you've seen by way of the Amorite hill country as YHWH, our God, commanded us, and we came to Kadesh-barnea. [20]And I said to you, 'You've come to the Amorite hill country that YHWH, our God, is giving us. [21]See: YHWH, our God, has put the land in front of you. Go up, possess it as YHWH, your fathers' God, spoke to you. Don't be afraid and don't be dismayed.'

[22]"And you came forward to me, all of you, and said, 'Let's send men ahead of us, and let them explore the land for us and bring us back word of the way by which we'll go up and of the cities to which we'll come.' [23]And the thing was good in my eyes, and I took twelve men from you, one man

per tribe. ²⁴And they turned and went up to the hill country and came to the Wadi Eshcol and spied it out. ²⁵And they took some of the land's fruit in their hand and brought it down to us, and they brought us back word and said, the land that YHWH, our God, is giving us is good. ²⁶But you weren't willing to go up, and you rebelled against the word of YHWH, your God, ²⁷and you grumbled in your tents and said, 'Because of YHWH's hatred for us He brought us out from the land of Egypt, to put us in the Amorite's hand to destroy us! ²⁸To where are we going up? Our brothers have melted our heart, saying, "We saw a bigger and taller people than we are, big cities and fortified to the skies, and also giants!"'

²⁹"And I said to you, 'Don't be scared and don't be afraid of them. ³⁰YHWH, your God, who is going in front of you, He will fight for you—like everything that He did with you in Egypt before your eyes ³¹and in the wilderness, as you've seen that YHWH, your God, carried you the way a man would carry his child through all the way that you've gone until you came to this place. ³²And in this thing, don't you trust in YHWH, your God, ³³who was going in front of you on the way to scout a camping place for you, in fire at night to let you see the way in which you would go, and in a cloud by day?!'

³⁴"And YHWH heard the sound of your words and was angry and swore, saying, ³⁵'Not a man of these people, this bad generation, will see the good land that I swore to give to your fathers; ³⁶just Caleb son of Jephunneh: he will see it, and I shall give the land on which he went to him and to his children because he went after YHWH fully.' ³⁷(YHWH was incensed at me, too, because of you, saying, 'You, too, shall not come there. ³⁸Joshua son of Nun, who is standing in front of you: he shall come there. Strengthen him, because he shall get Israel its legacy.') ³⁹'And your infants whom you said would become a spoil,* and your children today who haven't known good and bad, they will come there, and I'll give it to them, and they will possess it. ⁴⁰But you: turn and travel to the wilderness by way of the Red Sea.'

⁴¹"And you answered and said to me, 'We've sinned against YHWH. We'll go up! And we'll fight, according to everything that YHWH, our God, commanded us.' And you each put on his weapons of war, and you were willing to go up to the hill country.

⁴²"And YHWH said to me, 'Say to them: You shall not go up, and you shall not fight, because I am not among you, so you won't be stricken

---

*This is a direct quotation of the words in the episode of the scouts in P: "your infants whom you said would become a spoil!" (Num 14:31). It may be further evidence that P preceded D, as P is quoted here in Dtr1; but we must be cautious because this phrase appears here in Deut 1:39 in the Hebrew (Masoretic) text and in the Qumran (Dead Sea Scrolls) text, but it does not appear in the Greek (Septuagint) text.

before your enemies.' ⁴³And I spoke to you, but you didn't listen, and you rebelled against YHWH's word and acted presumptuously and went up to the hill country. ⁴⁴And the Amorite who lives in that hill country came out at you and pursued you the way bees do, and they crushed you in Seir as far as Hormah. ⁴⁵And you came back and wept in front of YHWH, but YHWH didn't listen to your voices and didn't hear you!

⁴⁶"So you lived in Kadesh many days—as many days as you lived there.

2 ¹"And we turned and traveled to the wilderness by way of the Red Sea as YHWH spoke to me, and we stayed around Mount Seir many days.

²"And YHWH said to me, saying, ³'You've had enough of staying around this mountain. Turn north. ⁴And command the people, saying: You're crossing the border of your brothers, the children of Esau, who live in Seir. And they'll be afraid of you, so be very watchful. ⁵Don't get agitated at them, because I won't give you any of their land, even as much as a footstep, because I've given Mount Seir to Esau as a possession. ⁶Food: you shall buy from them with money, and then you'll eat. And water, too: you shall purchase from them with money, and then you'll drink. ⁷Because YHWH, your God, has blessed you in all your hand's work. He has known your walking in this big wilderness. These forty years, YHWH, your God, has been with you. You haven't lacked a thing.' ⁸So we passed by our brothers, the children of Esau, who live in Seir, from the way of the plain, from Eilat, and from Ezion-geber, and we turned and passed by way of the wilderness of Moab.

⁹"And YHWH said to me, 'Don't oppose Moab and don't agitate them with war, because I won't give you a possession from its land, because I've given Ar as a possession to the children of Lot. ¹⁰The Emim had lived there before, a people that was big and numerous and tall as giants. ¹¹They were also thought to be Rephaim, like the giants, but the Moabites call them Emim. ¹²And the Horites lived in Seir before, but the children of Esau dispossessed them and destroyed them in front of them and lived in their place, as Israel did to the land of its possession that YHWH gave them. ¹³Now get up and cross the Wadi Zered.' And we crossed the Wadi Zered. ¹⁴And the days that we went from Kadesh-barnea until we crossed the Wadi Zered were thirty-eight years, until the end of all the generation, the men of war, from among the camp, as YHWH swore to them. ¹⁵And YHWH's hand was against them, to eliminate them from among the camp until their end.

¹⁶"And it was when all the men of war had ended, dying from among the people, ¹⁷and YHWH spoke to me, saying, ¹⁸'You're crossing the border

of Moab, Ar, today. ¹⁹And when you come close opposite the children of Ammon, don't oppose them and don't get agitated at them, because I won't give you a possession from the land of the children of Ammon, because I've given it as a possession to the children of Lot.' ²⁰(It, too, was thought to be a land of Rephaim: Rephaim had lived there before, and the Ammonites call them Zamzummim, ²¹a people that was big and numerous and tall as giants, but YHWH destroyed them in front of them, and they dispossessed them and lived in their place, ²²as He did for the children of Esau, who live in Seir, in that He destroyed the Horite in front of them, and they dispossessed them and have lived in their place to this day. ²³So the Avvim, who lived in villages as far as Gaza: the Caphtorites who left Caphtor destroyed them, and they dwelled in their place.) ²⁴"Get up, travel, and cross the Wadi Arnon. See: I've put Sihon, king of Heshbon, the Amorite, and his land in your hand. Begin. Dispossess! And you shall agitate him with war. ²⁵This day I'll begin to put an awe of you and a fear of you on the faces of the peoples under all the skies so that when they'll hear the news of you they'll tremble and writhe in front of you.'

²⁶"And I sent messengers from the wilderness of Kedemoth to Sihon, king of Heshbon, words of peace, saying, ²⁷'Let me pass through your land. I'll go on the road, on the road! I won't turn right or left. ²⁸Food: you'll sell me for money, and I'll eat. And water: you'll give me for money, and I'll drink. Only let me pass on my feet ²⁹as the children of Esau, who live in Seir, and the Moabites who live in Ar did for me, until I'll cross the Jordan to the land that YHWH, our God, is giving us.' ³⁰But Sihon, king of Heshbon, was not willing to let us pass through it, because YHWH, your God, had hardened his spirit and made his heart bold in order to put him in your hand—as it is this day.

³¹"And YHWH said to me, 'See: I've begun to put Sihon and his land before you. Begin. Dispossess, so as to possess his land.'

³²"And Sihon came out at us, he and all his people, for war at Jahaz. ³³And YHWH, our God, put him before us, and we struck him and his sons and all his people. ³⁴And we captured all his cities at that time, and we put every city to complete destruction: men and women and infants. We didn't leave a remnant. ³⁵Only the animals we despoiled for ourselves, and the spoil of the cities that we captured. ³⁶From Aroer, which is on the edge of the Wadi Arnon and the city that is in the wadi, to Gilead, there wasn't a town that was too high for us. YHWH, our God, put it all before us. ³⁷Only to the land of the children of Ammon did you not come close, all along the Wadi Jabbok, and the cities of the hill country, and whatever YHWH, our God, commanded.

3

[1]"And we turned and went up the way to Bashan. And Og, king of Bashan, came out at us, he and all his people, for war at Edrei. [2]And YHWH said to me, 'Don't be afraid of him, because I've put him and all his people and his land in your hand, and you shall do to him as you did to Sihon, king of the Amorites, who lived in Heshbon.' [3]And YHWH, our God, put Og, king of Bashan, and all his people in our hand as well, and we struck him until he did not have a remnant left. [4]And we captured all his cities at that time. There wasn't a town that we didn't take from them: sixty cities—all the region of Argob, Og's kingdom in Bashan. [5]All of these were fortified cities—a high wall, double gates, and a bar—aside from a great many unwalled cities. [6]And we completely destroyed them as we did to Sihon, king of Heshbon, completely destroying every city: men, women, and infants. [7]And we despoiled all the animals and the spoil of the cities for ourselves. [8]And at that time we took the land from the hand of the two kings of the Amorites that was across the Jordan, from the Wadi Arnon to Mount Hermon [9](Sidonians call Hermon Sirion, and the Amorites call it Senir), [10]all the cities of the plain and all of Gilead and all of Bashan as far as Salcah and Edrei, cities of Og's kingdom in Bashan. [11]Because only Og, king of Bashan, was left from the rest of the Rephaim. Here, his bedstead was a bedstead of iron. Isn't it in Rabbah of the children of Ammon? Its length is nine cubits and its width is four cubits by a man's cubit. [12]And we took possession of this land at that time. I gave the Reubenites and the Gadites from Aroer, which is on the Wadi Arnon, and half of the hill country of Gilead and its cities. [13]And I gave the rest of Gilead and all of Bashan, Og's kingdom, to half of the tribe of Manasseh. All the region of Argob: all of that Bashan is called 'the land of the Rephaim.' [14]Jair son of Manasseh had taken all the region of Argob as far as the border of the Geshurites and the Maachathites, and he called them, the Bashan, by his name, Havvoth-Jair, to this day. [15]And I gave Gilead to Machir. [16]And I gave the Reubenites and the Gadites from Gilead to the Wadi Arnon, the middle of the wadi being the border, and to the Wadi Jabbok, the border of the children of Ammon, [17]and the plain, with the Jordan being the border, from the Kinneret to the sea of the plain, the Dead Sea, below the slopes of Pisgah eastward.

[18]"And I commanded you at that time, saying, 'YHWH, your God, has given you this land to take possession of it. You shall pass equipped, all the warriors, in front of your brothers, the children of Israel. [19]Only your wives and your infants and your livestock (I knew that you have a great amount of livestock) shall stay in your cities that I've given you [20]until YHWH will give

your brothers rest like you, and they, too, will get possession of the land that YHWH, your God, is giving them across the Jordan.* Then you shall go back, each to his possession that I've given you.' ²¹And I commanded Joshua at that time, saying, 'Your eyes, that have seen everything that YHWH, your God, has done to these two kings: so may YHWH do to all the kingdoms to which you're crossing. ²²You shall not fear them, because YHWH, your God: He is the one fighting for you.'

²³"And I implored YHWH at that time, saying, ²⁴'My Lord, YHWH, you've begun to show your servant your greatness and your strong hand, for who is a god in the skies and in the earth who can do anything like your acts and like your victories?! ²⁵Let me cross and see the good land that's across the Jordan, this good hill country and the Lebanon.'

²⁶"But YHWH was cross at me for your sakes, and He would not listen to me. And YHWH said to me, 'You have much. Don't go on speaking to me anymore of this thing. ²⁷Go up to the top of Pisgah and raise your eyes west and north and south and east and see it with your eyes, because you won't cross this Jordan. ²⁸And command Joshua and strengthen him and make him bold, because he will cross in front of this people, and he will get them the land that you'll see as a legacy.'

²⁹"And we stayed in the valley opposite Beth-peor.

4

¹"And now, Israel, listen to the laws and to the judgments that I'm teaching you to do, so that you'll live, and you'll come and take possession of the land that YHWH, your fathers' God, is giving you. ²You shall not add onto the thing that I command you, and you shall not subtract from it: observing the commandments of YHWH, your God, that I command you. ³It's your eyes that saw what YHWH did at Baal Peor, that every man who went after Baal Peor: YHWH, your God, destroyed him from among you. ⁴But you who were clinging to YHWH, your God: you're all alive today! ⁵See: I've taught you laws and judgments as YHWH, my God, commanded

---

*As noted above on Deut 1:1, the references to Moses being "across the Jordan" suggest that the text was not by Moses but by someone located in Israel, referring to Moses' location in Moab as being "across the Jordan." One might argue that Moses could still have written these words because he was addressing his message to a future audience who would be reading it in Israel. Note, though, that when Moses is *quoted* in the text he refers to the land of *Israel* as being across the Jordan, but when the narrator speaks he refers to *Moses* as being across the Jordan. The distinction between the perspective of the narrator and the perspective of Moses is maintained consistently.

me, to do so within the land to which you're coming to take possession of it. ⁶And you shall observe and do them because it's your wisdom and your understanding before the eyes of the peoples, in that they will hear all these laws and will say, 'Only a wise and understanding people is this great nation.' ⁷Because who is a great nation that has gods close to it like YHWH, our God, in all our calling to him? ⁸And who is a great nation that has just laws and judgments like all this instruction that I'm putting in front of you today?

⁹"Only be watchful, and watch yourself very much, in case you'll forget the things that your eyes have seen and in case they'll turn away from your heart, all the days of your life. But you shall make them known to your children and to your children's children: ¹⁰the day that you stood in front of YHWH, your God, at Horeb, when YHWH said to me, 'Assemble the people to me, and I'll make them hear my words so that they'll learn to fear me all the days that they're living on the land, and they'll teach their children.' ¹¹And you came forward and stood below the mountain, and the mountain was burning in fire to the heart of the skies: darkness, cloud, and nimbus. ¹²And YHWH spoke to you from inside the fire. You were hearing the sound of words, but you weren't seeing a form, just sound. ¹³And He told you His covenant that He commanded you to do, the Ten Commandments, and He wrote them on two tablets of stones. ¹⁴And YHWH commanded me at that time to teach you laws and judgments, for you to do them in the land to which you're crossing to take possession of it. ¹⁵And you shall be very watchful of yourselves—because you didn't see any form in the day that YHWH spoke to you at Horeb from inside the fire— ¹⁶in case you'll be corrupted, and you'll make a statue, a form of any figure, a design of a male or a female, ¹⁷a design of any animal that's in the earth, a design of any winged bird that flies in the skies, ¹⁸a design of anything that creeps on the ground, a design of any fish that's in the water under the earth, ¹⁹and in case you'll raise your eyes to the skies, and you'll see the sun and the moon and the stars, all the array of the skies, and you'll be moved so that you'll bow to them and serve them, when YHWH, your God, has allocated them to all the peoples under all the skies. ²⁰But YHWH has taken you, and He has brought you out from the iron furnace, from Egypt, to become a legacy people for him, as it is this day.

²¹"And YHWH had been incensed at me over your matters, and He swore that I would not cross the Jordan and not come to the good land that YHWH, your God, is giving you as a legacy. ²²So I am dying in this land. I'm not crossing the Jordan. But you are crossing, and you shall possess this good land. ²³Watch yourselves, in case you'll forget the covenant of

YHWH, your God, that He made with you, and you'll make a statue of any form about which YHWH, your God, has commanded you, ²⁴because YHWH, your God: He is a consuming fire, a jealous God.

²⁵**"When you'll produce children and grandchildren and will have been in the land long, and you'll be corrupt and make a statue of any form and do what is bad in the eyes of YHWH, your God, to provoke Him, ²⁶I call the skies and the earth to witness regarding you today that you'll perish quickly from the land to which you're crossing the Jordan to take possession of it. You won't extend days on it, but you'll be destroyed! ²⁷And YHWH will scatter you among the peoples, and you'll be left few in number among the nations where YHWH will drive you. ²⁸And you'll serve gods, the work of human hands, wood and stone, there, that don't see and don't hear and don't eat and don't smell.**

²⁹**"But if you'll seek YHWH, your God, from there, then you'll find Him, when you'll inquire of Him with all your heart and all your soul. ³⁰When you have trouble, and all these things have found you, in the future days, if you'll go back to YHWH, your God, and listen to His voice, ³¹He won't let you down, and he won't destroy you, because YHWH, your God, is a merciful God, and He won't forget your fathers' covenant that He swore to them.*** ³²Because ask of the earliest days that were before you, from the day that God created a human on the earth, and from one end of the skies to the other end of the skies: has there been anything like this great thing? or has anything like it been heard of? ³³Has a people heard God's voice speaking from inside a fire the way you heard—and lived? ³⁴Or has God put it to the test, to come to take for Himself a people from among

---

*Deuteronomy 4 divides into three visible thematic units: verses 1–24, 25–31, and 32–40. The middle unit is a Dtr2 addition. The grounds for this identification are: (1) Verses 32ff. continue sensibly from v. 24. (2) There are repeated references to fire in the first and third units (4:11,12,15,24,33,36 twice). (3) More specifically, God is pictured as a burning fire and as an *'ēl qannā'* (jealous God) in these units, but then in the middle unit, breaking the image of the divine consuming fire, comes a different picture of the deity: a promise that even in exile the people can seek God and find Him, a God who "won't let you down" and "won't destroy you." And instead of an *'ēl qannā'* He is an *'ēl raḥûm* (merciful God). (4) In the middle unit Moses summons the skies and earth as witnesses. This is an element of a passage attributed to Dtr2 in Deuteronomy 31. See the note on Deut 31:30. (5) The references in the middle unit to the "future days" and to the fact that troubles will "find" the people without God's protection also occur in the Dtr2 sections of Deuteronomy 31. (6) The idea that God will scatter Israel among the peoples also occurs only in passages in the Deuteronomistic history that are identified as Dtr2 on other grounds. (7) The themes of the middle unit are apostasy leading to exile, after which a return to God can lead to restoration. (8) The wording of the middle unit is strikingly similar to a letter that Jeremiah sends to the exiles in Babylon (Deut 4:29; cf. Jer 29:13).

another people with tests, with signs, and with wonders and with war and with a strong hand and with an outstretched arm and with great fears like everything that YHWH, your God, has done for you in Egypt before your eyes? ³⁵You have been shown in order to know that YHWH: He is God. There is no other outside of Him. ³⁶From the skies He had you hear His voice in order to discipline you, and on the earth He showed you His great fire, and you heard His words from inside the fire. ³⁷And because He loved your fathers He chose their seed after them, so He brought you out in front of Him from Egypt by His great power, ³⁸to dispossess bigger and more powerful nations than you in front of you, to bring you, to give you their land as a legacy as it is today. ³⁹And you shall know today and store it in your heart that YHWH: He is God in the skies above and on the earth below. There isn't another. ⁴⁰And you shall observe His laws and His commandments that I command you today so it will be good for you and for your children after you, and so that you'll extend days on the land that YHWH, your God, is giving you forever."

⁴¹Then Moses distinguished three cities across the Jordan toward the sun's rising, ⁴²for the manslayer who would slay his neighbor without knowing—and he had not hated him from the day before yesterday—to flee there, so he would flee to one of these cities and would live: ⁴³Bezer in the wilderness of the plain for the Reubenites, and Ramoth in Gilead for the Gadites, and Golan in Bashan for the Manassites.

⁴⁴And this is the instruction that Moses set before the children of Israel. ⁴⁵These are the testimonies and the laws and the judgments that Moses spoke to the children of Israel when they went out from Egypt, ⁴⁶across the Jordan in the valley opposite Beth-peor, in the land of Sihon, king of the Amorites, who lived in Heshbon, whom Moses and the children of Israel struck when they came out from the land of Egypt. ⁴⁷And they took possession of his land, and of the land of Og, king of Bashan, the two kings of the Amorites who were across the Jordan at the sun's rising, ⁴⁸from Aroer, which is on the edge of the Wadi Arnon, to Mount Sion—that is Hermon— ⁴⁹and all the plain across the Jordan eastward to the sea of the plain below the slopes of Pisgah.

5

¹And Moses called all of Israel and said to them, "Listen, Israel, to the laws and the judgments that I'm speaking in your ears today. And you shall learn them and be watchful to do them. ²YHWH, our God, had made a covenant with us at Horeb. ³YHWH did not make this covenant with our

fathers, but with us! We! These! Here! Today! All of us! Living! [4]Face-to-face, YHWH spoke with you at the mountain from inside the fire [5](I was standing between YHWH and you at that time to tell you YHWH's word because you were afraid on account of the fire, and you didn't go up in the mountain), saying:

[6]I am YHWH, your God, who brought you out from the land of Egypt, from a house of slaves.

[7]You shall not have other gods before my face.

[8]You shall not make a statue, any form that is in the skies above or that is in the earth below or that is in the water below the earth. [9]You shall not bow to them, and you shall not serve them. Because I, YHWH, your God, am a jealous God, counting parents' crime on children and on the third generation and on the fourth generation of those who hate me, [10]but practicing kindness to thousands for those who love me and for those who observe my commandments.

[11]You shall not bring up the name of YHWH, your God, for a falsehood, because YHWH will not make one innocent who will bring up His name for a falsehood.

[12]Observe the Sabbath day, to make it holy, as YHWH, your God, commanded you. [13]Six days you shall labor and do all your work, [14]and the seventh day is a Sabbath to YHWH, your God. You shall not do any work: you and your son and your daughter and your servant and your maid and your ox and your ass or any animal and your alien who is in your gates—in order that your servant and your maid will rest like you, [15]and you shall remember that you were a slave in the land of Egypt and YHWH, your God, brought you out from there with a strong hand and an outstretched arm. On account of this, YHWH, your God, has commanded you to do the Sabbath day.*

[16]Honor your father and your mother, as YHWH, your God, commanded you, so that your days will be extended and so that it will be good for you on the land that YHWH, your God, is giving you.

[17]You shall not murder.

---

*Dtr1 gives a reason here for the Sabbath commandment that differs from the reason found in the Exodus 20 text of the Decalogue. In Exodus, the reason is that God created the world in seven days and then rested, which is based on the words of Genesis 1. But here the reason is that "you were a slave in the land of Egypt," which is a repeated premise in D (Deut 15:15; 16:12; 24:18,22).

And you shall not commit adultery.

And you shall not steal.

And you shall not testify against your neighbor as a false witness.

¹⁸And you shall not covet your neighbor's wife, and you shall not long for your neighbor's house, his field, or his servant or his maid, his ox or his ass or anything that your neighbor has.

¹⁹"YHWH spoke these words to your entire community at the mountain from inside the fire, the cloud, and the nimbus, a powerful voice.* And He did not add. And He wrote them on two tablets of stones and gave them to me.

²⁰"And it was when you heard the voice from inside the darkness, as the mountain was burning in fire, that you came forward to me, all the heads of your tribes and your elders, ²¹and you said, 'Here, YHWH, our God, has shown us His glory and His greatness, and we've heard His voice from inside the fire. This day we've seen that God may speak to a human and he lives. ²²So now why should we die? Because this big fire will consume us. If we go on hearing the voice of YHWH, our God, anymore, then we'll die. ²³Because who, of all flesh, is there who has heard the voice of the living God speaking from inside fire as we have and lived? ²⁴You go forward and listen to everything that YHWH, our God, will say, and you'll speak to us everything that YHWH, our God, will speak to you, and we'll listen, and we'll do it.'

²⁵"And YHWH listened to your words' voice when you were speaking to me, and YHWH said to me, 'I've listened to the voice of this people's words that they spoke to you. They've been good in everything that they've spoken. ²⁶Who would make it so, that they would have such a heart, to fear me and observe all my commandments every day, so it would be good for them and for their children forever! ²⁷Go say to them, "Go back to your tents." ²⁸And you, stand here with me so I may speak to you all the commandment and the laws and the judgments that you shall teach them so they'll do them in the land that I'm giving them to take possession of it. ²⁹And you shall be watchful to do as YHWH, your God, has commanded you. You shall not turn right or left. ³⁰You shall go in all the way that YHWH, your God, has commanded you, so that you'll live, and it will be good for you, and you'll extend days in the land that you'll possess.'

---

*Moses says that he is stating here the words that God spoke at Horeb, but there are a number of large and small differences between the text here and the Horeb text (Exodus 20).

6

[1]"And this is the commandment, the laws, and the judgments that YHWH, your God, commanded to teach you to do in the land to which you're crossing to take possession of it, [2]so that you'll fear YHWH, your God, to observe all His laws and His commandments that I'm commanding you: you and your child and your child's child, all the days of your life, and so that your days will be extended. [3]And you shall listen, Israel, and be watchful to do it, that it will be good for you and that you'll multiply very much, as YHWH, your fathers' God, spoke to you: a land flowing with milk and honey.

[4]"Listen, Israel: YHWH is our God. YHWH is one. [5]And you shall love YHWH, your God, with all your heart and with all your soul and with all your might. [6]And these words that I command you today shall be on your heart. [7]And you shall impart them to your children, and you shall speak about them when you sit in your house and when you go in the road and when you lie down and when you get up. [8]And you shall bind them for a sign on your hand, and they shall become bands between your eyes. [9]And you shall write them on the doorposts of your house and in your gates.

[10]"And it will be when YHWH, your God, will bring you to the land that He swore to your fathers, to Abraham, to Isaac, and to Jacob, to give you big and good cities that you didn't build, [11]and houses filled with everything good that you didn't fill, and cisterns hewed that you didn't hew, vineyards and olives that you didn't plant, and you'll eat and be satisfied, [12]watch yourself in case you'll forget YHWH, who brought you out from the land of Egypt, from a house of slaves. [13]It's YHWH, your God, whom you'll fear, and it's He whom you'll serve, and it's in His name that you'll swear. [14]You shall not go after other gods, from the gods of the peoples who are around you, [15]because YHWH, your God, is a jealous God among you, in case the anger of YHWH, your God, will flare at you, and He'll destroy you from the face of the earth. [16]You shall not test YHWH, your God, as you tested at Massah. [17]You shall observe the commandments of YHWH, your God, and His testimonies and His laws that He commanded you. [18]And you shall do what is right and good in YHWH's eyes so it will be good for you, and you'll come and take possession of the good land that YHWH swore to your fathers, [19]to push all your enemies from in front of you, as YHWH has spoken.

[20]"When your child will ask you tomorrow, saying, 'What are the testimonies and the laws and the judgments that YHWH, our God, commanded you?' [21]then you shall say to your child, 'We were slaves to Pharaoh in Egypt, and YHWH brought us out from Egypt with a strong hand. [22]And

YHWH put great and harsh signs and wonders in Egypt at Pharaoh and at all of his household before our eyes. [23]And He brought us out from there in order to bring us to give us the land that He swore to our fathers. [24]And YHWH commanded us to do all these laws, to fear YHWH, our God, for our good every day, to keep us alive as we are this day. [25]And we'll have virtue when we are watchful to do all of this commandment in front of YHWH, our God, as He commanded us.'

7

[1]"When YHWH, your God, will bring you to the land to which you're coming to take possession of it and will eject numerous nations from in front of you—the Hittite and the Girgashite and the Amorite and the Canaanite and the Perizzite and the Hivite and the Jebusite—seven nations more numerous and powerful than you, [2]and YHWH, your God, will put them in front of you, and you'll strike them: you shall completely destroy them! You shall not make a covenant with them, and you shall not show grace to them. [3]And you shall not marry with them. You shall not give your daughter to his son, and you shall not take his daughter for your son, [4]because he'll turn your son from after me, and they'll serve other gods, and YHWH's anger will flare at you, and He'll destroy you quickly. [5]But this is what you shall do to them: you shall demolish their altars and shatter their pillars and cut down their Asherahs and burn their statues in fire. [6]Because you are a holy people to YHWH, your God. YHWH, your God, chose you to become a treasured people to Him out of all the peoples who are on the face of the earth. [7]It wasn't because of your being more numerous than all the peoples that YHWH was attracted to you so that He chose you, because you're the smallest of all the peoples. [8]But because of YHWH's loving you and because of His keeping the oath that He swore to your fathers, YHWH brought you out with a strong hand and redeemed you from a house of slaves, from the hand of Pharaoh, king of Egypt. [9]Therefore you shall know that YHWH, your God, He is God, the faithful God, keeping the covenant and kindness for those who love Him and who observe His commandments to the thousandth generation [10]and paying back to those who hate Him to their faces to destroy them. He won't delay toward one who hates Him. He'll pay him back to his face. [11]So you shall observe the commandment and the laws and the judgments that I command you today, to do them.

[12]"And it will be because you'll listen to these judgments and observe and do them that YHWH, your God, will keep the covenant and kindness for you that he swore to your fathers. [13]And He'll love you and bless you and

multiply you and bless the fruit of your womb and the fruit of your land: your grain and your wine and your oil, your cattle's offspring and your flock's young, on the land that He swore to your fathers to give to you. [14]You'll be more blessed than all the peoples. There won't be an infertile male or female among you or among your animals. [15]And YHWH will turn away from you every illness. And all the bad diseases of Egypt that you knew: He won't set them among you but will put them among all who hate you. [16]And you shall eat up all the peoples that YHWH, your God, is giving you. Your eye shall not pity them. And you shall not serve their gods, because that's a trap for you.

[17]"If you say in your heart, 'These nations are more numerous than I; how shall I be able to dispossess them?' [18]you shall not fear them. You shall remember what YHWH, your God, did to Pharaoh and to all Egypt: [19]the big tests that your eyes saw and the signs and the wonders and the strong hand and the outstretched arm by which YHWH, your God, brought you out. So YHWH, your God, will do to the peoples before whom you fear! [20]And YHWH, your God, will send the hornet against them as well until those who remain and those who are hidden perish from in front of you. [21]Don't be scared in front of them, because YHWH, your God, is among you, a great and fearful God. [22]And YHWH, your God, will eject these nations from in front of you little by little. You won't be able to finish them quickly, or else the animal of the field will become many at you. [23]And YHWH, your God, will put them in front of you and put them into a big tumult until they're destroyed. [24]And He'll put their kings in your hand, and you'll destroy their name from under the skies. Not a man will stand in front of you, until you've destroyed them. [25]You shall burn the statues of their gods in fire. You shall not covet the silver and gold on them and take them for yourself, in case you'll be trapped through it, because that is an offensive thing to YHWH, your God, [26]and you shall not bring an offensive thing to your house, so that you'll be a thing to be completely destroyed like it. You shall detest it and find it abhorrent, because it is a thing to be completely destroyed.

8

[1]"All of the commandment that I command you today you shall be watchful to do, so that you'll live, and you'll multiply, and you'll come and take possession of the land that YHWH swore to your fathers. [2]And you shall remember all the way that YHWH, your God, had you go these forty years in the wilderness in order to degrade you, to test you, to know what

was in your heart: would you observe His commandments or not. ³So He degraded you and made you hunger and then fed you the manna, which you had not known and your fathers had not known, to let you know that a human doesn't live by bread alone, but a human lives by every product of YHWH's mouth. ⁴Your garment didn't wear out on you, and your foot didn't swell these forty years. ⁵So you shall know in your heart that, the way a man disciplines his child, so YHWH, your God, disciplines you. ⁶And you shall observe the commandments of YHWH, your God, to go in His ways and to fear Him. ⁷Because YHWH, your God, is bringing you to a good land, a land of wadis of water, springs, and deeps coming out in valleys and in hills, ⁸a land of wheat and barley and vine and fig and pomegranate, a land of olive, oil, and honey, ⁹a land in which you won't eat bread in scarcity, in which you won't lack anything, a land whose stones are iron and from whose hills you'll hew bronze. ¹⁰And you'll eat and be full and bless YHWH, your God, for the good land that He has given you.

¹¹"Watch yourself in case you'll forget YHWH, your God, so as not to observe His commandments and His judgments and His laws that I command you today, ¹²in case you'll eat, and you'll be full, and you'll build good houses, and you'll live there, ¹³and your oxen and your flock will multiply, and silver and gold will multiply for you, and everything that you'll have will multiply, ¹⁴and your heart will be lifted, and you'll forget YHWH, your God, who brought you out from the land of Egypt, from a house of slaves, ¹⁵who led you in the big and fearful wilderness of fiery snake and scorpion and thirst, where there isn't water, who brought out water for you from the flint rock, ¹⁶who fed you manna in the wilderness, which your fathers had not known, in order to degrade you and in order to test you to be good to you in your future; ¹⁷and you'll say in your heart: 'My power and my hand's strength made this wealth for me.' ¹⁸Then you shall remember YHWH, your God, because He is the one who gave you power to make wealth so as to uphold His covenant that He swore to your fathers—as it is this day.

¹⁹"And it will be, if you'll forget YHWH, your God, and you'll go after other gods and serve them and bow to them, I call witness regarding you today that you'll perish! ²⁰Like the nations that YHWH is making to perish in front of you, so will you perish, because you wouldn't listen to the voice of YHWH, your God.*

---

*8:19–20 is Dtr2. The infinitival emphatic *'ābōd tō'bēdûn* here occurs in two other passages that are identified as Dtr2 (4:26; 30:18), and it occurs nowhere else. The expression "I call to witness" also occurs only here and in other passages that are identified as Dtr2. And the subject is the people's perishing from the land because of going after other gods, which is a common exilic, Dtr2 theme.

9

¹"Listen, Israel: you're crossing the Jordan today to come to dispossess nations bigger and stronger than you, big cities and fortified to the skies, ²a people big and tall, giants, of whom you have known, and of whom you have heard it said: 'Who can stand in front of the giants?!' ³So you shall know today that YHWH, your God: He is the one who is crossing in front of you, a consuming fire. He will destroy them, and He will subdue them in front of you, so you'll dispossess them and destroy them quickly as YHWH has spoken to you.

⁴"Don't say in your heart when YHWH pushes them from in front of you, saying, 'Because of my virtue YHWH has brought me to take possession of this land,' when it is because of these nations' wickedness that YHWH dispossesses them from before you. ⁵It's not because of your virtue and your heart's integrity that you're coming to take possession of their land, but it is because of these nations' wickedness that YHWH, your God, dispossesses them from before you, and in order to uphold the thing that YHWH swore to your fathers, to Abraham, to Isaac, and to Jacob. ⁶So you shall know that it is not because of your virtue that YHWH, your God, gives you this good land to take possession of it, because you're a hard-necked people. ⁷Remember—don't forget!—that you made YHWH, your God, angry in the wilderness. From the day that you went out from the land of Egypt until you came to this place, you've been rebellious toward YHWH. ⁸And you made YHWH angry at Horeb, and YHWH was so incensed at you as to destroy you. ⁹When I went up to the mountain to get the tablets of stones, the tablets of the covenant that YHWH made with you, and I stayed in the mountain forty days and forty nights, I didn't eat bread and didn't drink water. ¹⁰And YHWH gave me the two tablets of stones, written by the finger of God,* and on them were all the words that YHWH had spoken with you at the mountain from inside the fire in the day of the assembly. ¹¹And it was: at the end of forty days and forty nights YHWH gave me the two tablets of stones, the tablets of the covenant.

¹²"And YHWH said to me, 'Get up. Go down quickly from here, because your people whom you brought out from Egypt has become corrupt. They've turned quickly from the way that I commanded them. They've

---

*The notation that God gave Moses tablets of stone written with the finger of God is a reference to P (Exod 31:18). The phrase "finger of God" has occurred only in P (Exod 8:15; 31:18). This is one of the signs that D (in this case Dtr1) was written later than P and that the Deuteronomist was familiar with P.

made themselves a molten thing.' ¹³And YHWH said to me, saying, 'I've seen this people; and, here, it's a hard-necked people. ¹⁴Hold back from me, and I'll destroy them and wipe out their name from under the skies, and I'll make you into a more powerful and numerous people than they.'

¹⁵"And I turned and went down from the mountain—and the mountain was burning in fire—and the two tablets of the covenant were on my two hands. ¹⁶And I saw! And, here, you'd sinned against YHWH, your God. You'd made yourselves a molten calf. You'd turned quickly from the way that YHWH had commanded you. ¹⁷And I grasped the two tablets and threw them from on my two hands and shattered them before your eyes.

¹⁸"And I prostrated myself in front of YHWH like the first time, forty days and forty nights—I didn't eat bread and didn't drink water—over all your sin that you did, to do what was bad in YHWH's eyes, to provoke Him, ¹⁹because I was dreading on account of the anger and the fury, that YHWH was so angry at you as to destroy you. But YHWH listened to me that time as well. ²⁰And YHWH was very incensed at Aaron so as to destroy him,* and I prayed for Aaron at that time as well. ²¹And your sin that you made, the calf: I took it and burned it in fire and crushed it, grinding it well until it was thin as dust, and I threw its dust into the wadi that comes down from the mountain.

²²"And at Taberah and at Massah and at Kibroth Hattaavah you were making YHWH angry. ²³And when YHWH sent you from Kadesh-barnea, saying, 'Go up and take possession of the land that I've given you,' then you rebelled at the word of YHWH, your God, and you didn't trust Him and didn't listen to His voice. ²⁴You've been rebelling toward YHWH from the day I knew you.

²⁵"So I prostrated myself in front of YHWH for the forty days and forty nights that I had fallen down because YHWH had said He would destroy you, ²⁶and I prayed to YHWH and said, 'My Lord YHWH, don't destroy your people and your legacy whom you redeemed by your greatness, whom you brought out from Egypt with a strong hand. ²⁷Remember your servants Abraham, Isaac, and Jacob. Don't look to this people's hardness and to its wickedness and to its sin, ²⁸or else the land from which you brought us out will say: Because YHWH wasn't able to bring them to the land of which He spoke to them, and because He hated them, He brought them out to kill

---

*Aaron is mentioned in 109 verses in Exodus, 77 in Leviticus, and 97 in Numbers. But here in Deuteronomy, when Moses recounts those forty years, he mentions Aaron only to say that he made the golden calf and that he died. This is not only a striking difference in D; it is consistent with the notion that D is a Mushite source and P is plainly an Aaronid source.

them in the wilderness! ²⁹And they're your people and your legacy, whom you brought out by your great power and by your outstretched arm.'

10

¹"At that time YHWH said to me, 'Carve two tablets of stones like the first ones, and come up to me at the mountain. And you shall make an ark of wood. ²And I'll write on the tablets the words that were on the first tablets, which you shattered, and you shall set them in the ark.'

³"And I made an ark of acacia wood, and I carved two tablets of stones like the first ones, and I went up the mountain with the two tablets in my hands. ⁴And He wrote on the tablets like the first writing: the Ten Commandments that YHWH spoke to you at the mountain from inside the fire in the day of the assembly, and YHWH gave them to me. ⁵And I turned and went down from the mountain, and I set the tablets in the ark that I had made, and they have been there, as YHWH commanded me.

⁶"And the children of Israel had traveled from Beeroth-bene-Jaakan to Moserah. There Aaron died, and he was buried there; and Eleazar, his son, functioned as priest in his place. ⁷From there they traveled to Gudgod, and from Gudgod to Jotbah, a land of wadis of water. ⁸At that time YHWH distinguished the tribe of Levi to carry the ark of YHWH's covenant, to stand in front of YHWH to serve Him, and to bless in His name to this day. ⁹Therefore Levi has not had a portion and a legacy with its brothers. YHWH: He is its legacy, as YHWH, your God, spoke to it.

¹⁰"And I: I stood in the mountain as in the first days: forty days and forty nights. And YHWH listened to me that time as well. YHWH was not willing to destroy you. ¹¹And YHWH said to me, 'Get up. Set out on the journey in front of the people, and they'll come and take possession of the land that I swore to their fathers to give to them.'

¹²"And now, Israel, what is YHWH, your God, asking from you except to fear YHWH, your God, to go in all His ways, and to love Him and to serve YHWH, your God, with all your heart and all your soul, ¹³to observe YHWH's commandments and His laws that I command you today to be good for you. ¹⁴Here, YHWH, your God, has the skies—and the skies of the skies!—the earth and everything that's in it. ¹⁵Only, YHWH was attracted to your fathers, to love them, and He chose their seed after them: you, out of all the peoples, as it is this day. ¹⁶So you shall circumcise the foreskin of your heart, and you shall not harden your necks anymore. ¹⁷Because YHWH, your God: He is the God of gods and the Lord of lords, the great, the mighty, and the awesome God, who won't be partial and won't take a bribe, ¹⁸doing judgment for an orphan and a widow and loving an alien, to

give him bread and a garment. [19]So you shall love the alien, because you were aliens in the land of Egypt. [20]You shall fear YHWH, your God, you shall serve Him, and you shall cling to Him, and you shall swear by His name. [21]He is your splendor, and He is your God, who did these great and awesome things for you that your eyes have seen. Your fathers went down to Egypt with seventy persons, and now YHWH, your God, has made you like the stars of the skies for multitude.

11

[1]"And you shall love YHWH, your God, and keep His charge and His laws and His judgments and His commandments every day. [2]And you shall know today that it's not with your children, who didn't know and who didn't see the discipline of YHWH, your God, His greatness and His strong hand and His outstretched arm [3]and His signs and His deeds that He did in Egypt to Pharaoh, king of Egypt, and to all his land, [4]and what He did to Egypt's army and to his horses and his chariots, that He flowed the waters of the Red Sea over their faces when they pursued you so YHWH destroyed them to this day, [5]and what He did for you in the wilderness until you came to this place, [6]and what He did to Dathan and to Abiram,* sons of Eliab son of Reuben, that the earth opened its mouth and swallowed them and their households and their tents and all the substance that was at their feet among the children of Israel— [7]but it's your eyes, that saw every great deed of YHWH's that He did. [8]And you shall observe all of the commandment that I command you today so that you'll be strong and you'll come and take possession of the land that you're crossing there to take possession of it, [9]and so that you'll extend days on the land that YHWH swore to your fathers to give to them and to their seed, a land flowing with milk and honey.

[10]"Because the land to which you're coming to take possession of it: it's not like the land of Egypt from which you've come out, where you plant your seed and water it at your feet like a garden of plants. [11]But the land to which you're crossing to take possession of it is a land of hills and valleys. It drinks water by the skies' showers. [12]A land that YHWH, your God, cares about; YHWH's eyes are always on it, from the year's beginning to year's end. [13]So

---

*Deuteronomy refers back to the rebellion of Korah, Dathan, and Abiram (Numbers 16), but it mentions only Dathan and Abiram, who are the rebels in the J portion of the story. It never mentions Korah and his assembly, who are the rebels in the P portion of the story.

it will be, if you'll listen to my commandments that I command you today, to love YHWH, your God, and to serve Him with all your heart and with all your soul, ¹⁴then I'll give your land's showers at their time, early rain and late rain, and you'll gather your grain and your wine and your oil. ¹⁵And I'll give vegetation in your field for your animals, and you'll eat and be full.

¹⁶"Watch yourselves in case your heart will be deceived so you'll turn and serve other gods and bow to them, ¹⁷and YHWH's anger will flare at you, and He'll hold back the skies, and there won't be showers, and the earth won't give its crop, and you'll perish quickly from the good land that YHWH is giving you. ¹⁸So you shall set these words of mine on your heart and on your soul, and you shall bind them for a sign on your hand, and they shall become bands between your eyes, ¹⁹and you shall teach them to your children, to speak about them when you sit in your house and when you go in the road and when you lie down and when you get up, ²⁰and you shall write them on the doorposts of your house and in your gates, ²¹so that your days and your children's days will be many on the land that YHWH swore to your fathers to give them, like the days of the skies over the earth. ²²Because, if you will observe all of this commandment that I command you, to do it, to love YHWH, your God, to go in all His ways and to cling to Him, ²³then YHWH will dispossess all these nations in front of you, and you'll dispossess bigger and more powerful nations than you. ²⁴Every place in which your foot will step shall be yours, from the wilderness and Lebanon, from the river, the Euphrates River, to the far sea shall be your border. ²⁵Not a man will stand up in front of you. YHWH, your God, will put awe of you and fear of you on the face of all the land on which you'll step, as He spoke to you.

²⁶"See: I'm putting in front of you today a blessing and a curse: ²⁷the blessing when you'll listen to the commandments of YHWH, your God, that I command you today, ²⁸and the curse if you won't listen to the commandments of YHWH, your God, and you'll turn from the way that I command you today, to go after other gods, whom you haven't known. ²⁹And it shall be, when YHWH, your God, will bring you to the land to which you're coming to take possession of it, that you shall put the blessing on Mount Gerizim and the curse on Mount Ebal. ³⁰Aren't they across the Jordan, beyond the way of the sun's setting, in the land of the Canaanite who lives in the plain, opposite Gilgal, near the oaks of Moreh? ³¹Because you're crossing the Jordan to come to take possession of the land that YHWH, your God, is giving you; and you shall take possession of it and live in it ³²and be watchful to do all the laws and the judgments that I'm putting in front of you today.

12

¹"These are the laws and the judgments that you shall be watchful to do in the land that YHWH, your fathers' God, has given you to take possession of it, every day that you're living on the land:*

²"You shall destroy all the places where the nations that you're dispossessing worshiped their gods there: on the high mountains and on the hills and under every lush tree. ³And you shall demolish their altars and shatter their pillars and burn their Asherahs in fire and cut down the statues of their gods in fire and destroy their name from that place.

⁴"You shall not do that for YHWH, your God. ⁵But, rather, you shall inquire at the place that YHWH, your God, will choose from all your tribes to set His name there, to tent it. And you shall come there, ⁶and bring there your burnt offerings and your sacrifices and your tithes and your hand's donation and your vows and your contributions and the firstborn of your herd and your flock. ⁷And you shall eat there in front of YHWH, your God. And you shall rejoice about everything your hand has taken on, you and your households, in that YHWH, your God, has blessed you. ⁸You shall not do it like everything that we're doing here today, each one, everything that's right in his own eyes, ⁹because up to now you haven't come to the resting place and to the legacy that YHWH, your God, is giving you. ¹⁰But when you'll cross the Jordan and live in the land that YHWH, your God, is giving you as a legacy, and He'll give you rest from all your enemies all around, and you'll live securely, ¹¹then it shall be, the place that YHWH, your God, will choose to tent His name there: there you shall bring everything that I command you, your burnt offerings and your sacrifices, your tithes and your hand's donation and every choice one of your vows that you'll make to YHWH. ¹²And you shall rejoice in front of YHWH, your God: you and your sons and your daughters and your servants and your maids and the Levite who is in your gates because he doesn't have a portion or a legacy with you.

¹³"Watch yourself in case you would make your burnt offerings in any place that you'll see. ¹⁴But, rather, in the place that YHWH will choose in one of your tribes: there you shall make your burnt offerings, and there you shall do everything that I command you. ¹⁵Only, as much as your soul desires you may slaughter and may eat meat according to the blessing of YHWH, your God, that He has given you in all your gates. The impure and the pure may eat it: like a gazelle,

---

*Deuteronomy 12–26 is a corpus of law known as the Deuteronomic law code. It is identified by the symbol Dtn. It is an old, independent document that was used by the Deuteronomistic historian in the Dtr1 edition of the work. There are passages in which the Deuteronomistic historian may have expanded on the text, but it is now difficult to separate such expansions from the core text of laws.

like a deer. ¹⁶*Only, you shall not eat the blood. You shall spill it like water on the earth.* ¹⁷*You may not eat within your gates the tithe of your grain or your wine or your oil or the firstborn of your herd or your flock or all your vows that you'll make or your contributions or your hand's donation.* ¹⁸*But, rather, you shall eat them in front of YHWH, your God, in the place that YHWH, your God, will choose: you and your son and your daughter and your servant and your maid and the Levite who is in your gates. And you shall rejoice in front of YHWH, your God, about everything your hand has taken on.* ¹⁹*Watch yourself in case you would leave the Levite, all your days in your land.*

²⁰*"When YHWH, your God, will widen your border as He spoke to you, and you'll say, 'Let me eat meat,' because your soul will desire to eat meat, you may eat meat as much as your soul desires.* ²¹*When the place that YHWH, your God, will choose to put His name there will be far from you, then you shall slaughter from your herd and from your flock that YHWH has given you as I've commanded you, and you may eat within your gates as much as your soul desires.* ²²*Just: as a gazelle and a deer are eaten, so you shall eat it. The impure and the pure may eat it together.* ²³*Only, be strong not to eat the blood, because the blood: it's the life; and you shall not eat the life with the meat.* ²⁴*You shall not eat it. You shall spill it like water on the earth.* ²⁵*You shall not eat it, so it will be good for you and for your children after you when you do what is right in YHWH's eyes.*

²⁶*"Only, you shall carry your holy things that you'll have and your vows and shall come to the place that YHWH will choose.* ²⁷*And you shall do your burnt offerings, the meat and the blood, on the altar of YHWH, your God. And the blood of your sacrifices shall be spilled on the altar of YHWH, your God, and you shall eat the meat.* ²⁸*Be watchful that you listen to all these things that I command you so that it will be good for you and for your children after you forever when you'll do what is good and right in the eyes of YHWH, your God.*

²⁹*"When YHWH, your God, will cut off the nations that you're coming there to dispossess from in front of you, and you'll dispossess them and live in their land,* ³⁰*watch yourself in case you'll be trapped after them, after their destruction from in front of you, and in case you'll inquire about their gods, saying, 'How did these nations serve their gods? And I'll do that—I, too.'* ³¹*You shall not do this for YHWH, your God, because they did every offensive thing of YHWH that He hates for their gods, because they would also burn their sons and their daughters in fire to their gods!*

13

¹*"Everything that I command you: you shall be watchful to do it. You shall not add onto it, and you shall not subtract from it.*

²"When a prophet or one who has a dream will get up among you and will give you a sign or a wonder, ³and the sign or the wonder of which he spoke to you—saying, 'Let's go after other gods,' whom you haven't known, 'and let's serve them' —will come to pass, ⁴you shall not listen to that prophet's words or to that one who has the dream, because YHWH, your God, is testing you, to know whether you are loving YHWH, your God, with all your heart and with all your soul. ⁵You shall go after YHWH, your God, and you shall fear Him, and you shall observe His commandments and listen to His voice and serve Him and cling to Him. ⁶And that prophet or that one who has the dream shall be put to death, because he spoke a misrepresentation about YHWH, your God, who brought you out from the land of Egypt and who redeemed you from a house of slaves, to drive you from the way in which YHWH, your God, commanded you to go. So you shall burn away what is bad from among you.

⁷"When your brother, your mother's son or your father's son, or the wife of your bosom, or your friend who is as your own self will entice you in secret, saying, 'Let's go and serve other gods,' whom you haven't known, you and your fathers, ⁸from the gods of the peoples who are all around you, those close to you or those far from you, from one end of the earth to the other end of the earth, ⁹you shall not consent to him, and you shall not listen to him, and your eye shall not pity him, and you shall not have compassion and shall not cover it up for him. ¹⁰But you shall kill him. Your hand shall be on him first to put him to death, and all the people's hand thereafter. ¹¹And you shall stone him with stones so he dies because he sought to drive you away from YHWH, your God, who brought you out from the land of Egypt, from a house of slaves. ¹²And all Israel will hear and fear and won't continue to do a bad thing like this among you.

¹³"When you'll hear in one of your cities that YHWH, your God, is giving you to live there, saying, ¹⁴'Good-for-nothing people have gone out from among you and driven away their city's residents, saying: "Let's go and serve other gods,"' whom you haven't known,' ¹⁵and you'll inquire and investigate and ask well, and, here, the thing is true—this offensive thing was done among you— ¹⁶you shall strike that city's residents by the sword, completely destroying it and everything in it and its animals with the sword. ¹⁷And you shall gather all its spoil into the middle of its square, and you shall burn the city and all its spoil in fire entirely to YHWH, your God, and it shall be a tell eternally. It shall not be rebuilt again. ¹⁸And let nothing from the complete destruction cling in your hand, so that YHWH will turn back from His flaring anger and will give you mercy. And He'll be merciful to you and multiply you as He swore to your fathers ¹⁹when you'll listen to the voice of YHWH, your God, to observe all His commandments that I command you today, to do what is right in the eyes of YHWH, your God.

14

¹"You are children of YHWH, your God. You shall not cut yourselves and shall not make a bald place between your eyes for the dead. ²Because you are a holy people to YHWH, your God, and YHWH has chosen you to become a treasured people to Him out of all the peoples who are on the face of the earth.

³"You shall not eat any offensive thing. ⁴This is the animal that you shall eat: ox, lamb of sheep, and lamb of goats, ⁵deer and gazelle and roebuck and wild goat and bison and antelope and mountain sheep ⁶and every animal that has a hoof and that has a split of hooves in two, that regurgitates cud, among animals, you shall eat it. ⁷Except you shall not eat this out of those that regurgitate the cud and out of those that have a hoof: the camel and the rock-badger and the hare, because they regurgitate cud and do not have a hoof; they are impure to you. ⁸And the pig, because it has a hoof but no cud; it is impure to you. You shall not eat from their meat, and you shall not touch their carcass.

⁹"You shall eat this out of all that are in the water: you shall eat every one that has fins and scales. ¹⁰And you shall not eat any one that does not have fins and scales; it is impure to you.

¹¹"And you shall eat any pure bird. ¹²And this is what you shall not eat from them: the eagle and the vulture and the black vulture ¹³and the kite and the falcon by its kind ¹⁴and every raven by its kind ¹⁵and the eagle owl and the nighthawk and the sea gull and the hawk by its kind, ¹⁶the little owl and the great owl and the white owl ¹⁷and the pelican and the fish hawk and the cormorant ¹⁸and the stork and the heron by its kind and the hoopoe and the bat.

¹⁹"And every swarming thing of flying creatures; it is impure to you. It shall not be eaten. ²⁰You shall eat every pure bird.

²¹"You shall not eat any carcass. You shall give it to the alien who is in your gates, and he will eat it, or sell to a foreigner. Because you are a holy people to YHWH, your God.

"You shall not cook a kid in its mother's milk.

²²"You shall tithe all of your seed's produce that comes out of the field year by year. ²³And you shall eat the tithe of your grain, your wine, and your oil and the firstborn of your herd and your flock in front of YHWH, your God, in the place that He will choose to tent His name there, so that you'll learn to fear YHWH, your God, all the days. ²⁴And if the way will be too long for you because you won't be able to carry it because the place that YHWH, your God, will choose to set His name there will be far from you, because YHWH, your God, will bless you, ²⁵then you shall give it by money. And you shall enclose the money in your hand and go to the place that YHWH, your God, will choose. ²⁶And you shall spend the money for anything that your soul will desire: for herd and for flock

and for wine and for beer and for anything that your soul will ask of you. And you shall eat there in front of YHWH, your God, and you shall rejoice, you and your household. ²⁷And the Levite who is in your gates: you shall not leave him, because he doesn't have a portion and legacy with you.

²⁸"At the end of three years you shall bring out all the tithe of your produce in that year and leave it within your gates, ²⁹and the Levite will come, because he doesn't have a portion and legacy with you, and the alien and the orphan and the widow who are in your gates, and they shall eat and be full, so that YHWH, your God, will bless you in all your hand's work that you'll do.

15

¹"At the end of seven years you shall make a remission. ²And this is the matter of the remission: every holder of a loan is to remit what he has lent his neighbor. He shall not demand it of his neighbor and his brother, because a remission for YHWH has been called. ³You may demand it of a foreigner, but your hand shall remit whatever of yours is with your brother. ⁴Nonetheless, there won't be an indigent one among you, because YHWH will bless you in the land that YHWH, your God, is giving you as a legacy, to take possession of it— ⁵only if you'll listen to the voice of YHWH, your God, to be watchful to do all of this commandment that I command you today. ⁶When YHWH, your God, will have blessed you as He spoke to you, then you'll lend to many nations, but you won't borrow; and you'll dominate many nations, but they won't dominate you.

⁷"When there will be an indigent one among you from one of your brothers within one of your gates in your land that YHWH, your God, is giving you, you shall not fortify your heart and shall not shut your hand from your brother who is indigent. ⁸But you shall open your hand to him and shall lend to him, enough for his shortage that he has. ⁹Watch yourself in case there will be something good-for-nothing in your heart, saying, 'The seventh year, the remission year, is getting close,' and your eye will be bad toward your brother who is indigent, and you won't give to him; and he'll call to YHWH about you, and it will be a sin in you. ¹⁰You shall give to him, and your heart shall not be bad when you're giving to him, because on account of this thing YHWH, your God, will bless you in everything you do and in everything your hand has taken on. ¹¹Because there won't stop being an indigent in the land. On account of this I command you, saying: you shall open your hand to your brother, to your poor, and to your indigent in your land.

¹²"When your Hebrew brother or sister will be sold to you, then he shall work for you six years, and in the seventh year you shall let him go liberated from you. ¹³And when you let him go liberated from you, you shall not let him go

empty-handed. ¹⁴*You shall provide him from your flock and from your threshing floor and from your wine press; as YHWH, your God, has blessed you, you shall give to him. ¹⁵And you shall remember that you were a slave in the land of Egypt, and YHWH, your God, redeemed you. On account of this, I command you this thing today.*

¹⁶*"And it will be, if he'll say to you, 'I won't go out from you' because he loves you and your house, because it is good for him with you, ¹⁷then you shall take an awl and put it in his ear and in the door, and he shall be a slave forever to you. And you shall also do this to your maid. ¹⁸It shall not be hard in your eyes when you let him go liberated from you, because he served you six years at twice the value of an employee, and YHWH, your God, will bless you in everything that you'll do.*

¹⁹*"Every male firstborn that will be born in your herd and in your flock you shall consecrate to YHWH, your God. You shall not work with your ox's firstborn, and you shall not shear your sheep's firstborn. ²⁰You shall eat it in front of YHWH, your God, year by year in the place that YHWH will choose—you and your household. ²¹And if there will be an injury in it—crippled or blind, any bad injury—you shall not sacrifice it to YHWH, your God. ²²You shall eat it within your gates—the impure and the pure together, like a gazelle and like a deer. ²³Only: you shall not eat its blood. You shall spill it like water on the ground.*

16

¹*"Observe the month of Abib, and you shall make Passover for YHWH, your God, because in the month of Abib YHWH, your God, brought you out from Egypt at night. ²And you shall make a Passover sacrifice to YHWH, your God, of the flock and herd, in the place that YHWH will choose to tent His name there. ³You shall not eat leavened bread with it. Seven days you shall eat unleavened bread, the bread of degradation, with it, because you went out from the land of Egypt in haste—so that you will remember the day you went out from the land of Egypt all the days of your life. ⁴And you shall not have leaven appear within all your borders for seven days, and none of the meat that you will sacrifice in the evening on the first day shall remain until the morning. ⁵You may not make the Passover sacrifice within one of your gates that YHWH, your God, is giving you. ⁶But, rather, to the place that YHWH, your God, will choose to tent His name: there you shall make the Passover sacrifice in the evening at sunset, the time when you went out from Egypt. ⁷And you shall cook and eat it in the place that YHWH, your God, will choose; and you shall turn in the morning and go to your tents. ⁸Six days you shall eat unleavened bread, and on the seventh day shall be a convocation to YHWH, your God. You shall not do work.*

⁹"You shall count seven weeks. From when the sickle begins to be in the standing grain you shall begin to count seven weeks. ¹⁰And you shall make a Festival of Weeks for YHWH, your God, the full amount of your hand's contribution that you can give insofar as YHWH, your God, will bless you. ¹¹And you shall rejoice in front of YHWH, your God—you and your son and your daughter and your servant and your maid and the Levite who is within your gates and the alien and the orphan and the widow who are among you—in the place that YHWH, your God, will choose to tent His name there. ¹²And you shall remember that you were a slave in Egypt, and you shall be watchful and do these laws.

¹³"You shall make a Festival of Booths seven days, when you gather from your threshing floor and from your wine press. ¹⁴And you shall rejoice on your festival—you and your son and your daughter and your servant and your maid and the Levite and the alien and the orphan and the widow who are within your gates. ¹⁵Seven days you shall celebrate for YHWH, your God, in the place that YHWH will choose, because YHWH, your God, will bless you in all your produce and all your hands' work, and you shall just be happy.

¹⁶"Three times in the year every male of yours shall appear in front of YHWH, your God, in the place that He will choose: on the Festival of Unleavened Bread and on the Festival of Weeks and on the Festival of Booths. And he shall not appear in front of YHWH empty-handed: ¹⁷each according to what his hand can give, according to the blessing of YHWH, your God, that He has given you.

¹⁸"You shall put judges and officers in all your gates that YHWH, your God, is giving you, for your tribes, and they shall judge the people: judgment with justice. ¹⁹You shall not bend judgment, you shall not recognize a face, and you shall not take a bribe, because bribery will blind the eyes of the wise and undermine the words of the virtuous. ²⁰Justice, justice you shall pursue, so that you'll live, and you'll take possession of the land that YHWH, your God, is giving you.

²¹"You shall not plant an Asherah of any wood near the altar of YHWH, your God, that you will make. ²²And you shall not set up a pillar, which YHWH, your God, hates.

17

¹"You shall not sacrifice to YHWH, your God, a bull or a sheep in which will be any injury, any bad thing, because that is an offensive thing of YHWH, your God.

²"If there will be found among you, in one of your gates that YHWH, your God, is giving you, a man or woman who will do what is bad in the eyes of YHWH, your God, to violate His covenant, ³and will go and serve other gods and

bow to them and to the sun or to the moon or to any of the array of the skies, which I did not command, ⁴and it will be told to you and you will hear it, and you will inquire well, and, here, it is true, the thing is right, this offensive thing has been done in Israel, ⁵then you shall bring that man or that woman who did this bad thing out to your gates, the man or the woman, and you shall stone them with stones so they die.

⁶"On the word of two witnesses or three witnesses shall the one who is to die be put to death. One shall not be put to death on the word of one witness. ⁷The witnesses' hand shall be on him first to put him to death, and all the people's hand after that. So you shall burn away what is bad from among you.

⁸"If a matter for judgment will be too daunting for you, between blood and blood, between law and law, and between injury and injury, matters of disputes in your gates, then you shall get up and go up to the place that YHWH, your God, will choose. ⁹And you shall come to the Levite priests and to the judge who will be in those days, and you shall inquire, and they will tell you the matter of judgment. ¹⁰And you shall do according to the word on the matter that they will tell you from that place that YHWH will choose, and you shall be watchful to do according to everything that they will instruct you. ¹¹You shall do it according to the word of the instruction that they will give you and according to the judgment that they will say to you. You shall not turn from the thing that they will tell you, right or left. ¹²And the man who will act presumptuously, not listening to the priest who is standing to serve YHWH, your God, there, or to the judge: that man shall die. So you shall burn away what is bad from Israel. ¹³And all the people will listen and fear and won't act presumptuously anymore.

¹⁴"When you'll come to the land that YHWH, your God, is giving you, and you'll take possession of it and live in it, and you'll say, 'Let me set a king over me like all the nations that are around me,' ¹⁵you shall set a king over you whom YHWH, your God, will choose! You shall set a king from among your brothers over you. You may not put a foreign man, who is not your brother, over you. ¹⁶Only he shall not get himself many horses, and he shall not bring the people back to Egypt in order to get many horses, when YHWH has said to you, 'You shall not go back this way ever again.' ¹⁷And he shall not get himself many wives, so his heart will not turn away. And he shall not get himself very much silver and gold. ¹⁸And it will be, when he sits on his kingdom's throne, that he shall write himself a copy of this instruction on a scroll from in front of the Levite priests. ¹⁹And it shall be with him, and he shall read it all the days of his life, so that he will learn to fear YHWH, his God, to observe all the words of this instruction and these laws, to do them, ²⁰so his heart will not be elevated above his brothers, and so he will not turn from the commandment,

*right or left, and so he will extend days over his kingdom, he and his sons, within Israel.**

18

¹*"The Levite priests, all the tribe of Levi, shall not have a portion and legacy with Israel. They shall eat YHWH's offerings by fire and His legacy. ²But he shall not have a legacy among his brothers. YHWH: He is his legacy, as He spoke to him. ³And this shall be the rule for the priests from the people, from those who make a sacrifice, whether an ox or a sheep: he shall give the shoulder, the cheeks, and the stomach. ⁴You shall give him the first of your grain, your wine, and your oil, and the first shearing of your sheep. ⁵Because YHWH, your God, has chosen him from all your tribes to stand to serve in YHWH's name, he and his sons, for all time.*

⁶*"And when a Levite will come from one of your gates, from all of Israel, where he lives, then he shall come as much as his soul desires to the place that YHWH will choose ⁷and serve in the name of YHWH, his God, like all of his Levite brothers who are standing there in front of YHWH. ⁸They shall eat, portion for portion, aside from his sales of patrimony.*

⁹*"When you come to the land that YHWH, your God, is giving you, you shall not learn to do like the offensive things of those nations. ¹⁰There shall not be found among you someone who passes his son or his daughter through fire, one who practices enchantment, a soothsayer or a diviner or a sorcerer ¹¹or one who casts spells or who asks of a ghost or of a spirit of an acquaintance or inquires of the dead, ¹²because everyone who does these is an offensive thing of YHWH, and because of these offensive things YHWH, your God, is dispossessing them from in front of you. ¹³You shall be unblemished with YHWH, your God, ¹⁴because these nations whom you are dispossessing listen to soothsayers and enchanters, but you: YHWH, your God, has not permitted such for you. ¹⁵YHWH, your God, will raise up for you a prophet from among you, from your brothers, like me. You shall listen to him— ¹⁶in accordance with everything that you asked from YHWH, your God, at Horeb in the day of the assembly, saying, 'Let me not continue to hear the voice of YHWH, my God, and let me not see this big fire anymore, so I won't die!'*

¹⁷*"And YHWH said to me, 'They've been good in what they've spoken. ¹⁸I'll raise up a prophet for them from among their brothers, like you, and I'll put my*

---

*On the origin of the Deuteronomic Law of the King as deriving from the time of the inauguration of the first king of Israel, see Baruch Halpern, *The Constitution of Monarchy in Israel* (Atlanta: Scholars Press, 1981).

words in his mouth, and he'll speak to them everything that I'll command him. [19]And it will be: the man who won't listen to my words that he'll speak in my name, I shall require it from him! [20]Just: the prophet who will presume to speak a thing in my name that I didn't command him to speak, and who will speak in the name of other gods—that prophet shall die.'

[21]"And if you'll say in your heart, 'How shall we know the thing, that YHWH didn't speak it?!' — [22]when the prophet will speak in YHWH's name, and the thing won't be and won't come to pass: that is the thing that YHWH did not say. The prophet spoke it presumptuously. You shall not be fearful of him.

19

[1]"When YHWH, your God, will cut off the nations whose land YHWH, your God, is giving you, and you'll dispossess them and live in their cities and in their houses, [2]you shall distinguish three cities within your land that YHWH, your God, is giving you to take possession of it. [3]You shall prepare the way and divide the border of your land that YHWH, your God, will give you as a legacy into three sections, and it will be for any murderer to flee there. [4]And this is the case of the manslayer who will flee there and live: one who will strike his neighbor without knowing, when he did not hate him from the day before yesterday; [5]and one who will come with his neighbor into the forest to cut down trees, and his hand will be moved with the axe to cut down the tree, and the axe head will come off the wood and find his neighbor, and he dies. He shall flee to one of these cities and live. [6]In case an avenger of blood will pursue the manslayer when his heart will be hot and will catch up to him because the way will be long, and he'll strike him mortally though he does not have a sentence of death, because he did not hate him from the day before yesterday, [7]on account of this I command you, saying, 'You shall distinguish three cities.' [8]And if YHWH, your God, will widen your border as He swore to your fathers and will give you all the land that He spoke to give to your fathers, [9]when you'll observe all of this commandment to do it, that which I command you today, to love YHWH, your God, and to go in His ways every day, then you shall add three more cities to these three. [10]So innocent blood will not be spilled within your land that YHWH, your God, is giving you as a legacy, and blood would be on you.

[11]"But if there will be a man who hates his neighbor and will lie in wait for him and get up against him and strike him mortally, and he dies, and he will flee to one of these cities, [12]then his city's elders shall send and take him from there and put him in the hand of the avenger of blood, so he will die. [13]Your eye shall not pity him. And you shall burn away the innocent blood from Israel, and it will be well with you.

¹⁴*"You shall not move your neighbor's landmark that the first ones set, in your legacy that you will have in the land that YHWH, your God, is giving you to take possession of it.*

¹⁵*"One witness shall not get up against a man for any crime or for any sin, in any sin that one will commit. On the word of two witnesses or on the word of three witnesses a case shall stand up.* ¹⁶*If a malicious witness will get up against a man to testify a misrepresentation against him,* ¹⁷*and the two people who have the dispute shall stand in front of YHWH, in front of the priests and the judges who will be in those days,* ¹⁸*and the judges will inquire well, and, here, the witness is a lying witness, he testified a lie against his brother,* ¹⁹*then you shall do to him as he schemed to do to his brother. So you shall burn away what is bad from among you.* ²⁰*And those who remain will listen and fear and won't continue to do anything like this bad thing anymore among you.* ²¹*And your eye shall not pity: life for life, eye for eye, tooth for tooth, hand for hand, foot for foot.*

20

¹*"When you'll go out to war against your enemies,** *and you'll see horses and chariots, a people more numerous than you, you shall not fear them, because YHWH, your God, is with you, who brought you up from the land of Egypt.* ²*And it will be, when you approach the war, that the priest shall go over and speak to the people.* ³*And he shall say to them, 'Listen, Israel, you're approaching war against your enemies today. Let your heart not be weak. Don't be afraid and don't panic and don't be scared in front of them,* ⁴*because YHWH, your God, is the one going with you to fight for you with your enemies, to save you.'*

⁵*"And the officers shall speak to the people, saying, 'Who is a man who has built a new house and has not dedicated it? Let him go, and let him go back to his house, in case he would die in the war and another man would dedicate it.* ⁶*And who is a man who has planted a vineyard and has not desanctified it? Let him go, and let him go back to his house, in case he would die in the war and*

---

*The laws of war in Deuteronomy 20 and 21 appear to be directed to the entire people who have been mustered for military service, not to a professional army. Professional armies are claimed for biblical Israel only in the era of the monarchy. These laws therefore (1) do not appear to derive from the court and (2) appear to derive from the period before the monarchy. Thus, even if we trace the Deuteronomistic history to the period of Josiah (and a second edition in the Babylonian exile), portions of these laws in Dtn may come from much earlier sources. (See *Who Wrote the Bible?* pp. 119–122.)

another man would desanctify it. ⁷And who is a man who has betrothed a woman and has not taken her? Let him go, and let him go back to his house, in case he would die in the war and another man would take her.' ⁸And the officers shall continue to speak to the people and shall say, 'Who is a man who is afraid and weakhearted? Let him go, and go back to his house, so he won't melt his brothers' heart like his heart.' ⁹And it will be, when the officers finish speaking to the people, that they shall appoint officers of the armies at the head of the people.

¹⁰"When you'll approach a city to fight against it, then you shall call to it for peace. ¹¹And it will be, if it will answer you with peace and open up to you, then it will be that all the people who are found in it shall become yours for a work-company and shall serve you. ¹²And if it will not make peace with you, but it will make war with you, then you shall besiege it. ¹³And YHWH, your God, will put it in your hand, and you shall strike all its males by the sword. ¹⁴Only, you shall take as spoil the women and the infants and the animals and everything that will be in the city, all its spoil, and you shall eat your enemies' spoil that YHWH, your God, has given you. ¹⁵That is what you shall do to all the cities that are very distant from you, those that are not from these nations' cities. ¹⁶Only from these peoples' cities that YHWH, your God, is giving you as a legacy shall you not let any soul live. ¹⁷But you shall completely destroy them—the Hittite and the Amorite, the Canaanite and the Perizzite, the Hivite and the Jebusite—as YHWH, your God, has commanded you, ¹⁸so they won't teach you to do things like all their offensive things that they did for their gods, and you'll sin to YHWH, your God.

¹⁹"When you'll besiege a city many days, fighting against it to capture it, you shall not destroy a tree of it, moving an axe at it, because you'll eat from it, so you shall not cut it down; because is a tree of the field a human, to go from in front of you in a siege?! ²⁰Only a tree that you'll know that it isn't a tree for eating: that one you may destroy and cut down so you may build a siege-work against the city that is making war with you until its fall.

21

¹"If a corpse will be found in the land that YHWH, your God, is giving you to take possession of it, fallen in the field, unknown who struck him, ²then your elders and your judges shall go out and measure to the cities that are around the corpse. ³And it will be, the closest city to the corpse: that city's elders shall take a heifer that has not been worked with, that has not pulled in a yoke. ⁴And that city's elders shall take the heifer down to a strongly flowing wadi that would not be worked with and would not be seeded, and they shall

break the heifer's neck there in the wadi. ⁵And the priests, sons of Levi, shall go over, because YHWH, your God, chose them to serve Him and to bless in YHWH's name, and every dispute and every injury shall be by their word. ⁶And all of that city's elders, who are close to the corpse, shall wash their hands over the heifer whose neck was broken in the wadi. ⁷And they shall testify, and they shall say, 'Our hands did not spill this blood, and our eyes did not see it. ⁸Grant atonement for your people Israel, whom you redeemed, YHWH, and don't impute innocent blood among your people Israel.' And for them the blood will be atoned for. ⁹So you shall burn away the innocent blood from among you when you will do what is right in YHWH's eyes.

¹⁰"When you'll go out to war against your enemies, and YHWH, your God, will put him in your hand, and you'll take prisoners from him, ¹¹and you'll see among the prisoners a woman with a beautiful figure, and you'll be attracted to her and take her for yourself as a wife, ¹²then you shall bring her into your house, and she shall shave her head and do her nails ¹³and take away her prisoner's garment from on her. And she shall live in your house and shall mourn her father and her mother a month of days. And after that you may come to her and marry her, and she shall become your wife. ¹⁴And it will be, if you don't desire her then you shall let her go on her own, and you shall not sell her for money. You shall not get profit through her, because you degraded her.

¹⁵"When a man will have two wives, one loved and one hated, and they'll give birth to children for him, the loved and the hated, and the hated will have the firstborn son, ¹⁶then it will be, on the day that he gives what he has as a legacy to his children, he shall not be able to give a son of the loved one the birthright before the firstborn son of the hated one. ¹⁷But he shall recognize the firstborn son of the hated one, to give him a double portion of all that he has, because he is the beginning of his might. The legal due of the firstborn is his.

¹⁸"When a man will have a stubborn and rebellious son, not listening to his father's voice and his mother's voice, and they will discipline him, but he will not listen to them, ¹⁹then his father and his mother shall take hold of him and bring him out to his city's elders and to the gate of his place. ²⁰And they shall say to his city's elders, 'This son of ours is stubborn and rebellious, he doesn't listen to our voice, a glutton, and a drunk.' ²¹And all his city's people shall batter him with stones so he dies. So you shall burn away what is bad from among you. And all Israel will listen and fear.

²²"And if there will be a sin bringing a sentence of death on a man, and he will be put to death, and you will hang him on a tree, ²³you shall not leave his corpse on the tree, but you shall bury him on that day, because a hanged person is an offense to God, and you shall not make impure your land that YHWH, your God, is giving you as a legacy.

22

¹"You shall not see your brother's ox or his sheep driven off, and you hide yourself from them. You shall bring them back to your brother. ²And if your brother is not close to you, and you don't know him, then you shall gather it into your house, and it shall be with you until your brother inquires about it, and you shall give it back to him. ³And you shall do that with his ass, and you shall do that with his garment, and you shall do that with any lost thing of your brother's that will be lost by him and you find it. You may not hide yourself. ⁴You shall not see your brother's ass or his ox falling in the road, and you hide yourself from them. You shall lift it up with him.

⁵"There shall not be a man's item on a woman, and a man shall not wear a woman's garment, because everyone who does these is an offensive thing of YHWH, your God.

⁶"When a bird's nest will happen to be in front of you on the road in any tree or on the ground—chicks or eggs—and the mother is sitting over the chicks or over the eggs, you shall not take the mother along with the children. ⁷You shall let the mother go, and you may take the children for you, so that it will be good for you, and you will extend days.

⁸"When you'll build a new house, you shall make a railing for your roof, so you won't set blood in your house when someone will fall from it.

⁹"You shall not seed your vineyard with two kinds, or else the whole of the seed that you'll sow and the vineyard's produce will become holy. ¹⁰You shall not plow with an ox and an ass together. ¹¹You shall not wear sha'atnez: wool and linen together.

¹²"You shall make braided threads on the four corners of your apparel with which you cover yourself.

¹³"When a man will take a wife and come to her and then hate her, ¹⁴and he'll assert words of abuse toward her and bring out a bad name on her and say, 'I took this woman, and I came close to her, and I didn't find signs of virginity for her,' ¹⁵then the young woman's father and her mother shall take and bring out the signs of the young woman's virginity to the city's elders at the gate.

¹⁶"And the young woman's father shall say to the elders, 'I gave my daughter to this man for a wife, and he hated her. ¹⁷And, here, he has asserted words of abuse, saying: "I didn't find signs of virginity for your daughter." But these are the signs of my daughter's virginity!' And they shall spread out the garment in front of the city's elders.

¹⁸"And that city's elders shall take the man and discipline him. ¹⁹And they shall fine him a hundred weights of silver and give it to the young woman's

father because he brought out a bad name on a virgin of Israel. And she shall be his for a wife: he shall not be able to let her go, all his days.

²⁰"But if this thing was true—signs of virginity for the young woman were not found— ²¹then they shall take the young woman out to the entrance of her father's house, and the people of her city shall stone her with stones so she dies, because she did a foolhardy thing in Israel, to whore at her father's house. So you shall burn away what is bad from among you.

²²"If a man will be found lying with a woman who is a husband's wife, then the two of them shall die: the man who lay with the woman, and the woman. So you shall burn away what is bad from Israel.

²³"If it will be that a virgin young woman will be betrothed to a man, and a man will find her in the city and lie with her, ²⁴then you shall take the two of them to that city's gate and stone them with stones so they die: the young woman on account of the fact that she did not cry out in the city, and the man on account of the fact that he degraded his neighbor's wife. So you shall burn away what is bad from among you. ²⁵But if the man will find the betrothed young woman in the field, and the man will take hold of her and lie with her, then only the man who lay with her shall die, ²⁶but you shall not do a thing to the young woman. The young woman does not have a sin deserving death, because, just as a man would get up against his neighbor and murder him: this case is like that; ²⁷because he found her in the field, the betrothed young woman cried out, and there was no one to save her.

²⁸"If a man will find a virgin young woman who is not betrothed, and he'll grasp her and lie with her, and they'll be found, ²⁹then the man who lay with her shall give the young woman's father fifty weights of silver, and she shall be his for a wife. Because he degraded her, he shall not be able to let her go, all his days.

23

¹"A man shall not take his father's wife, so he will not expose his father's hem. ²One who is wounded by crushing or whose organ is cut off shall not come into YHWH's community. ³A bastard shall not come into YHWH's community; even in the tenth generation one shall not come into YHWH's community. ⁴An Ammonite and a Moabite shall not come into YHWH's community; even in the tenth generation they shall not come into YHWH's community, forever, ⁵on account of the fact that they did not meet you with bread and with water on the way when you came out from Egypt, and the fact that it hired Balaam son of Beor from Pethor of Aram Naharaim against you to curse you. ⁶But YHWH, your

God, was not willing to listen to Balaam, and YHWH, your God, turned the curse into a blessing for you because YHWH, your God, loved you. [7]You shall not seek their well-being or their good, all your days, forever.

[8]"You shall not abhor an Edomite, because he is your brother. You shall not abhor an Egyptian, because you were an alien in his land. [9]Third-generation children who will be born to them may come into YHWH's community.

[10]"When you'll go out encamped against your enemies, you shall be watchful against any bad thing. [11]If there will be among you a man who will not be pure by a night occurrence, then he shall go outside the camp. He shall not come inside the camp. [12]And it shall be: toward evening he shall wash in water, and when the sun sets he shall come inside the camp. [13]And you shall have a location outside the camp, and you shall go out there, outside; [14]and you shall have a spade among your equipment, and it shall be, when you sit outside, that you shall dig with it, and you shall go back and cover what comes out of you. [15]Because YHWH, your God, is going within your camp, to rescue you and to put your enemies in front of you, so your camp shall be holy, so He won't see an exposure of something in you and turn back from you.

[16]"You shall not turn over to his master a slave who will seek deliverance with you from his master. [17]He shall live with you, among you, in the place that he will choose in one of your gates, where it is good for him. You shall not persecute him.

[18]"There shall not be a sacred prostitute from the daughters of Israel, and there shall not be a sacred prostitute from the sons of Israel. [19]You shall not bring the price of a prostitute or the cost of a dog to the house of YHWH, your God, for any vow, because the two of them are both an offensive thing of YHWH.

[20]"You shall not require interest for your brother: interest of money, interest of food, interest of anything that one might charge. [21]For a foreigner you may require it, but for your brother you shall not require it, so that YHWH, your God, will bless you in everything your hand has taken on, on the land to which you're coming to take possession of it.

[22]"When you'll make a vow to YHWH, your God, you shall not delay to fulfill it, because YHWH, your God, will require it from you, and it will be a sin in you. [23]But if you desist from vowing, that will not be a sin in you. [24]You shall watch what comes out of your lips and do as you vowed to YHWH, your God, the contribution that you spoke with your mouth.

[25]"When you'll come into your neighbor's vineyard, then you may eat grapes as you wish, your fill; but you shall not put any into your container. [26]When you'll come into your neighbor's standing grain, then you may pluck ears with your hand; but you shall not lift a sickle at your neighbor's grain.

24

¹"When a man will take a woman and marry her, and it will be that, if she does not find favor in his eyes because he has found an exposure of something in her, and he will write a document of cutting-off for her and put it in her hand and let her go from his house, ²and she will go out from his house and go and become another man's, ³and the latter man will hate her and write a document of cutting-off for her and put it in her hand and let her go from his house, or if the latter man who took her to him for a wife will die: ⁴her first husband who let her go shall not be able to come back to take her to be his for a wife since she has been made impure, because that is an offensive thing in front of YHWH, and you shall not bring sin on the land that YHWH, your God, is giving you as a legacy.

⁵"When a man will take a new wife, he shall not go out in the army and not go along with it for any matter. He shall be free at his house for one year and shall make his wife whom he has taken happy. ⁶One shall not take a mill or an upper millstone as security, because he is taking one's life as security.

⁷"When a man will be found stealing a person from among his brothers, from the children of Israel, so he will get profit through him and sell him, then that thief shall die. So you shall burn away what is bad from among you.

⁸"Be watchful with the plague of leprosy, to be very watchful and to do according to everything that the Levite priests will instruct you. You shall be watchful to do according to what I commanded them. ⁹Remember what YHWH, your God, did to Miriam on the way when you were coming out from Egypt.

¹⁰"When you'll make a loan of anything to your neighbor, you shall not come into his house to get his pledge. ¹¹You shall stand outside, and the man to whom you're lending shall bring the pledge outside to you. ¹²And if he is a poor man, you shall not lie down with his pledge. ¹³You shall give back the pledge to him as the sun sets, and he'll lie down with his clothing, and he'll bless you, and you'll have virtue in front of YHWH, your God.

¹⁴"You shall not exploit a poor or an indigent employee, from your brothers or from your aliens who are in your land, in your gates. ¹⁵You shall give his pay in his day, and the sun shall not set on it—because he is poor, and he maintains his life by it—so he won't call against you to YHWH, and it will be a sin in you.

¹⁶"Fathers shall not be put to death for sons, and sons shall not be put to death for fathers. They shall each be put to death through his own sin.

¹⁷"You shall not bend judgment of an alien or an orphan, and you shall not take a widow's clothing as security. ¹⁸And you shall remember that you were a slave in Egypt, and YHWH, your God, redeemed you from there. On account of this I command you to do this thing. ¹⁹When you'll reap your harvest in your

field, and you'll forget a sheaf in the field, you shall not go back to take it. It shall be the alien's and the orphan's and the widow's, so that YHWH, your God, will bless you in all your hands' work. ²⁰When you'll beat your olive trees, you shall not do a bough afterward. It shall be the alien's and the orphan's and the widow's. ²¹When you'll cut off grapes of your vineyard, you shall not glean afterward. It shall be the alien's and the orphan's and the widow's. ²²And you shall remember that you were a slave in the land of Egypt. On account of this I command you to do this thing.

25

¹*"When there will be a dispute between people, and they will go over to judgment, and they will judge them, then they shall find in favor of the one who is in the right and find against the one who is in the wrong. ²And it will be, if the one who is in the wrong is to be struck, that the judge shall have him laid down and have him struck in front of him, according to his wrongdoing in number. ³They shall strike him forty times. He shall not add, in case he would add onto these to strike him a great amount, and your brother would be treated as inconsequential before your eyes.*

⁴*"You shall not muzzle an ox when it is threshing.*

⁵*"When brothers will live together, and one of them will die, and he had no son, the dead man's wife shall not be an unrelated man's, outside. Her brother-in-law shall come to her and take her to him for a wife and shall do the brother-in-law's duty for her. ⁶And the firstborn to whom she will give birth shall be signified by the name of his brother who died, so his name will not be wiped out from Israel. ⁷And if the man won't desire to take his sister-in-law, then his sister-in-law shall go up at the gate to the elders and say, 'My brother-in-law refuses to preserve a name for his brother in Israel. He was not willing to do the brother-in-law's duty for me.' ⁸And his city's elders shall call him and speak to him, and if he'll stand and say, 'I don't desire to take her,' ⁹then his sister-in-law shall go over to him before the elders' eyes and take off his shoe from his foot and spit in front of him. And she shall answer and say, 'Thus shall be done to the man who will not build up his brother's house.' ¹⁰And his name shall be called in Israel 'the house of the one whose shoe was taken off.'*

¹¹*"If people will fight together, a man and his brother, and the wife of one will come close to rescue her husband from the hand of the one striking him, and she'll put out her hand and take hold of his private parts, ¹²then you shall cut off her hand. Your eye shall not pity.*

¹³*"You shall not have in your bag multiple stones, a big and a small. ¹⁴You shall not have in your house multiple ephah measures, a big and a small. ¹⁵You*

shall have a whole and honest stone; you shall have a whole and honest ephah measure, so your days will be extended on the land that YHWH, your God, is giving you. ¹⁶*Because everyone who does these is an offensive thing of YHWH, everyone who does injustice.*

¹⁷*"Remember what Amalek did to you on the way when you came out from Egypt,* ¹⁸*how he fell upon you on the way and cut off all the weak ones at your rear, when you were exhausted and tired, and he didn't fear God.* ¹⁹*So it shall be, when YHWH, your God, will give you rest from all your enemies all around in the land that YHWH, your God, is giving you as a legacy to take possession of it, you shall wipe out the memory of Amalek from under the skies. You shall not forget.*

26

¹*"And it shall be, when you'll come to the land that YHWH, your God, is giving you as a legacy, and you'll take possession of it and live in it,* ²*that you shall take from the first of all the land's fruit that you'll bring in from your land that YHWH, your God, is giving you, and set it in a basket and go to the place that YHWH, your God, will choose to tent His name there.* ³*And you shall come to the priest who will be in those days and say to him:*

> *I declare today to YHWH, your God, that I've come to the land that YHWH swore to our fathers to give to us.*

⁴*And the priest shall take the basket from your hand and set it down in front of the altar of YHWH, your God.* ⁵*And you shall answer and say in front of YHWH, your God:*

> *My father was a perishing Aramean, so he went down to Egypt and resided there with few persons and became a big, powerful, and numerous nation there.* ⁶*And the Egyptians were bad to us and degraded us and imposed hard work on us.* ⁷*And we cried out to YHWH, our fathers' God, and YHWH listened to our voice and saw our degradation and our trouble and our oppression.* ⁸*And YHWH brought us out from Egypt with a strong hand and an outstretched arm and with great fear and with signs and with wonders.* ⁹*And He brought us to this place and gave us this land, a land flowing with milk and honey.* ¹⁰*And now, here, I've brought the first of the fruit of the land that you've given me, YHWH.*

And you shall set it down in front of YHWH, your God, and bow in front of YHWH, your God. ¹¹*And you shall rejoice in all the good that YHWH, your God, has given to you and to your house, you and the Levite and the alien who is among you.*

¹²"When you'll finish doing all the tithe of your produce in the third year, the year of the tithe, and you'll give it to the Levite, to the alien, to the orphan, and to the widow, and they'll eat in your gates and be full, ¹³then you shall say in front of YHWH, your God:

I have taken away what was holy from the house, and I have also given it to the Levite and to the alien, to the orphan, and to the widow according to all your commandment that you've commanded me. I have not violated and have not forgotten any of your commandments. ¹⁴I have not eaten any of it while I was mourning, and I have not taken any of it away while impure, and I have not given any of it to the dead. I have listened to the voice of YHWH, my God. I have done according to everything that you commanded me. ¹⁵Gaze from your holy abode, from the skies, and bless your people, Israel, and the land that you've given us as you swore to our fathers, a land flowing with milk and honey.

¹⁶"This day YHWH, your God, commands you to do these laws and judgments. And you shall be watchful and do them with all your heart and all your soul. ¹⁷You have proclaimed YHWH today to be God to you, and to go in His ways and to observe His laws and His commandments and His judgments and to listen to His voice. ¹⁸And YHWH proclaimed you today to be a treasured people to Him as He spoke to you—and to observe all His commandments— ¹⁹and to set you high above all the nations that He has made in praise and name and beauty, and for you to be a holy people to YHWH, your God, as He spoke."

27

¹And Moses and Israel's elders commanded the people, saying, "Observe all the commandment that I command you today. ²And it shall be, in the day that you'll cross the Jordan to the land that YHWH, your God, is giving you, that you shall set up big stones and cover them with plaster. ³And you shall write on them all the words of this instruction when you cross so that you'll come to the land that YHWH, your God, is giving you, a land flowing with milk and honey, as YHWH, your fathers' God, spoke to you. ⁴And it shall be, when you cross the Jordan, that you shall set up these stones that I command you today in Mount Ebal and cover them with plaster. ⁵And you shall build an altar to YHWH, your God, there, an altar of stones. You shall not lift iron over them. ⁶You shall build the altar of YHWH, your God, of whole stones, and you shall offer burnt offerings on it

to YHWH, your God. ⁷And you shall sacrifice peace offerings and eat there and rejoice in front of YHWH, your God. ⁸And you shall write on the stones all the words of this instruction very clearly."

⁹And Moses and the Levite priests spoke to all Israel, saying, "Be silent, and listen, Israel: this day you have become a people to YHWH, your God. ¹⁰And you shall listen to the voice of YHWH, your God, and do His commandments and His laws that I command you today."

¹¹And Moses commanded the people on that day, saying, ¹²"These shall stand to bless the people on Mount Gerizim when you cross the Jordan: Simeon and Levi and Judah and Issachar and Joseph and Benjamin. ¹³And these shall stand for the curse on Mount Ebal: Reuben, Gad, and Asher and Zebulun, Dan, and Naphtali. ¹⁴And the Levites shall answer, and they shall say in a loud voice to every man of Israel:

> ¹⁵'Cursed be the man who will make a statue or molten thing, an offensive thing of YHWH, a stone engraver's work, and set it up in secret.'
>
> And all the people shall answer, and they shall say: 'Amen.'
> ¹⁶'Cursed be one who disrespects one's father and his mother.'
> And all the people shall say: 'Amen.'
> ¹⁷'Cursed be one who moves his neighbor's landmark.'
> And all the people shall say: 'Amen.'
> ¹⁸'Cursed be one who misleads a blind person on the way.'
> And all the people shall say: 'Amen.'
> ¹⁹'Cursed be one who bends the judgment of an alien, an orphan, or a widow.'
> And all the people shall say: 'Amen.'
> ²⁰'Cursed be one who lies with his father's wife, because he has exposed his father's hem.'
> And all the people shall say: 'Amen.'
> ²¹'Cursed be one who lies with any animal.'
> And all the people shall say: 'Amen.'
> ²²'Cursed be one who lies with his sister—his father's daughter or his mother's daughter.'
> And all the people shall say: 'Amen.'
> ²³'Cursed be one who lies with his mother-in-law.'
> And all the people shall say: 'Amen.'
> ²⁴'Cursed be one who strikes his neighbor in secret.'
> And all the people shall say: 'Amen.'

²⁵'Cursed be one who takes a bribe to strike a person—innocent blood.'

And all the people shall say: 'Amen.'

²⁶'Cursed be one who will not uphold the words of this instruction, to do them.'

And all the people shall say: 'Amen.'

28

¹"And it will be, if you'll listen to the voice of YHWH, your God, to be watchful to do all His commandments that I command you today, that YHWH, your God, will set you high above all the nations of the earth. ²And all these blessings will come on you and catch up with you when you'll listen to the voice of YHWH, your God: ³You'll be blessed in the city, and you'll be blessed in the field. ⁴The fruit of your womb and the fruit of your land and the fruit of your animals, your cattle's offspring and your flock's young, will be blessed. ⁵Your basket and your bowl will be blessed. ⁶You'll be blessed when you come in, and you'll be blessed when you go out. ⁷YHWH will make your enemies who come up against you stricken in front of you. By one road they'll come out at you, and by seven roads they'll flee in front of you. ⁸YHWH will command the blessing for you in your storehouses and in everything your hand takes on and will bless you in the land that YHWH, your God, is giving you. ⁹YHWH will establish you for him as a holy people as He swore to you if you'll keep the commandments of YHWH, your God, and go in His ways. ¹⁰And all the peoples of the earth will see that YHWH's name is called on you, and they'll be afraid of you. ¹¹And YHWH will give you a surplus of good in the fruit of your womb and in the fruit of your animals and in the fruit of your land, on the land that YHWH swore to your fathers to give you. ¹²YHWH will open His good treasure, the skies, to you, to give your land's showers at their time and to bless all your hand's work. And you'll lend to many nations, and you won't borrow; ¹³and YHWH will put you at the head and not at the tail; and you'll only be above, and you won't be below—if you'll listen to the commandments of YHWH, your God, that I command you today, to observe and to do, ¹⁴and you won't turn from all the things that I command you today, right or left, to go after other gods, to serve them.

¹⁵"And it will be, if you won't listen to the voice of YHWH, your God, to be watchful to do all His commandments and His laws that I command you today, that all these curses will come on you and catch up with you:

¹⁶You'll be cursed in the city, and you'll be cursed in the field. ¹⁷Your basket and your bowl will be cursed. ¹⁸The fruit of your womb and the fruit of your land, your cattle's offspring and your flock's young, will be cursed. ¹⁹You'll be cursed when you come in, and you'll be cursed when you go out. ²⁰YHWH will send curse and tumult and annoyance at you in everything your hand takes on that you'll do, until you're destroyed and until you perish quickly because of your bad practices, in that you left me. ²¹YHWH will make an epidemic cling to you until He finishes you from the land to which you're coming to take possession of it. ²²YHWH will strike you with consumption and with fever and with inflammation and with burning and with the sword and with blight and with mildew. And they'll pursue you until you perish. ²³And your skies that are over your head will be bronze, and the land that is under you iron. ²⁴YHWH will make your land's showers powder and dust; it will fall on you from the skies until you're destroyed. ²⁵YHWH will make you stricken in front of your enemies. By one road you'll go out at him, and by seven roads you'll flee in front of him. And you'll be a horrifying thing to all the earth's kingdoms. ²⁶And your carcass will become food for every bird of the skies and for the animals of the earth, with no one making them afraid. ²⁷YHWH will strike you with the boils of Egypt and with hemorrhoids and with scabs and with itches, from which you won't be able to be healed. ²⁸YHWH will strike you with madness and with blindness and with amazement of heart. ²⁹And you'll be feeling around at noon the way the blind would feel around, in the dark. And you won't make your ways successful, but you'll just be exploited and robbed every day, and there will be no one to save you. ³⁰You'll betroth a woman, and another man will ravish her. You'll build a house, and you won't live in it. You'll plant a vineyard, and you won't desanctify it. ³¹Your ox slaughtered before your eyes—and you won't eat any of it. Your ass stolen from in front of you—and it won't come back to you. Your sheep given to your enemies—and you'll have no one to save you. ³²Your sons and your daughters given to another people—while your eyes are looking for them all day and giving out, and there's no God at your hand. ³³A people whom you haven't known will eat your land's fruit and all the product of your exhaustion, and you'll only be exploited and crushed every day. ³⁴And you'll be driven mad from the sight before your eyes that you'll see. ³⁵YHWH will strike you with bad boils on the knees and on the thighs from which you won't be able to be healed, from your foot to the top of your head. **³⁶YHWH will drive you and your king whom you'll set up over you to a nation whom you haven't known, you and your fathers, and you'll serve other gods, wood and stone, there. ³⁷And you'll become an astonishment, a proverb, and an**

expression among all the peoples to which YHWH will drive you.* ³⁸You'll take out much seed to the field, but you'll gather little, because locusts will finish it off. ³⁹You'll plant vineyards and work them, but you won't drink wine or gather grapes, because worms will eat it. ⁴⁰You'll have olives within all your border, but you won't anoint with oil, because your olive will drop off. ⁴¹You'll give birth to sons and daughters, but you won't have them, because they'll go into captivity. ⁴²Crickets will take possession of all your trees and your land's fruit. ⁴³The alien who is among you will go up above you higher and higher, and you will go down lower and lower. ⁴⁴He will lend to you, but you won't lend to him. He will become a head, and you will become a tail.

⁴⁵"And all these curses will come over you and pursue you and catch up with you until you're destroyed because you didn't listen to the voice of YHWH, your God, to observe His commandments and His laws that He commanded you. ⁴⁶And they'll be a sign and a wonder in you and in your seed forever. ⁴⁷Because you didn't serve YHWH, your God, with joy and with good feeling from the abundance of everything, ⁴⁸so you'll serve your enemies whom YHWH will send at you in hunger and in thirst and in nakedness and in lack of everything. And He'll put an iron yoke on your neck until He has destroyed you. ⁴⁹YHWH will fetch a nation from far, from the end of the earth, over you the way an eagle soars, a nation whose language you won't understand, ⁵⁰a fierce-faced nation who won't be partial to the old and won't show grace to the young— ⁵¹and it will eat the fruit of your animals and the fruit of your land until you are destroyed—who won't leave you grain, wine, and oil, your cattle's offspring and your flock's young until it has made you perish. ⁵²And it will close you in, in all your gates, until your high and fortified walls in which you trust come down in all your land; and it will close you in, in all your gates, in all your land that YHWH, your God, has given you. ⁵³And you'll eat the fruit of your womb, the flesh of your sons and your daughters whom YHWH, your God, has given you, in the siege and in the constraint that your enemy will put on you. ⁵⁴The tenderest man among you and the very delicate: his eye will look with evil intent at his brother and the wife of his bosom and the rest of his children that he'll have left ⁵⁵from giving to one of them any of the flesh of his children that he'll eat, because nothing will be left to him in the siege and in the constraint that

*28:36–37 is Dtr2. The context concerns curses that affect the body and the land. But then these two verses intrude with references to exile of the people and its king. And immediately after this threat of exile, the curses are still referring to things that take place while the people are in their land.

your enemy will put on you in all your gates. ⁵⁶The tenderest and the most delicate woman among you, who wouldn't risk setting her foot on the ground out of delicacy and tenderness: her eye will look with evil intent at the man of her bosom and her son and her daughter ⁵⁷and her afterbirth that comes out from between her legs and her children to whom she'll give birth, because she'll eat them in secret due to the lack of everything in the siege and in the constraint that your enemy will put on you in your gates. ⁵⁸If you won't be watchful to do the words of this instruction that are written in this scroll, to fear this honored and awesome name: YHWH, your God, ⁵⁹then YHWH will make your plagues and your seed's plagues astonishing, great and enduring plagues, and great and enduring illnesses. ⁶⁰And He'll bring back among you every disease of Egypt, which you were dreading, and they'll cling to you. ⁶¹YHWH will bring over you every illness and every plague that is not written in this scroll of instruction, as well, until you are destroyed. ⁶²And you'll be left with few persons when you had been like the stars of the skies for multitude, because you didn't listen to the voice of YHWH, your God. **⁶³And it will be: as YHWH had satisfaction over you to do good to you and to multiply you, so YHWH will have satisfaction over you to make you perish and to destroy you, and you'll be torn away from the land to which you're coming to take possession of it. ⁶⁴And YHWH will scatter you among all the peoples from one end of the earth to the other end of the earth. And you'll serve other gods, whom you haven't known, you and your fathers, there, wood and stone. ⁶⁵And among those nations you won't have a respite, and there won't be a resting place for your foot, and YHWH will give you there a trembling heart and a failing of eyes and a fainting of soul. ⁶⁶And your life will be hanging opposite you, and you'll fear night and day, and you won't trust in your life. ⁶⁷In the morning you'll say, 'Who would make it evening,' and in the evening you'll say, 'Who would make it morning,' because of your heart's fear that you'll have and because of the sight before your eyes that you'll see. ⁶⁸And YHWH will bring you back to Egypt in boats, by the way that I said to you: 'You won't go on to see it anymore.' And you'll sell yourselves there to your enemies as slaves and as maids, and none will buy!"** *

---

*This last section of the curse list (1) shifts from simply listing the curses to describing God's emotions toward the people's behavior ("He will have satisfaction over you to destroy you . . ."); (2) refers to "scattering" with a term (Hebrew *hēpîṣ*) that occurs in two other passages that appear to be Dtr2 on other grounds as well; (3) concerns exile; (4) ends with a curse that Israel will one day return to Egypt, which comes to pass at the very end of the Deuteronomistic history: "And all the people, from youngest to oldest, rose and came to Egypt" (2 Kgs 25:26), which is the Dtr2 conclusion of the work. The last curse of the list thus is fulfilled in the last line of the history.

⁶⁹These are the words of the covenant that YHWH commanded Moses to make with the children of Israel in the land of Moab, aside from the covenant that He made with them at Horeb.

29

¹And Moses called all of Israel and said to them, "You've seen everything that YHWH did before your eyes in the land of Egypt to Pharaoh and to all his servants and to all his land, ²the great tests that your eyes saw, those great signs and wonders. ³But YHWH did not give you a heart to know and eyes to see and ears to hear until this day. ⁴As I led you forty years in the wilderness, your clothing did not become worn on you, and your shoe did not become worn on your foot, ⁵you didn't eat bread, and you didn't drink wine and beer, so you would know that 'I am YHWH your God.' ⁶And you came to this place. (And Sihon, king of Heshbon, and Og, king of Bashan, came out at us for war, and we struck them. ⁷And we took their land and gave it as a legacy to the Reubenite and to the Gadite and to half of the Manassite tribe.) ⁸And you shall observe the words of this covenant and do them so that you'll understand all that you'll do.

⁹"You're standing today, all of you, in front of YHWH, your God—your heads, your tribes, your elders, and your officers, every man of Israel, ¹⁰your infants, your women, and your alien who is in your camps, from one who cuts your wood to one who draws your water— ¹¹for you to enter into the covenant of YHWH, your God, and into His oath, which YHWH, your God, is making with you today, ¹²in order to establish you today for Him as a people, and He will be a God to you, as He spoke to you and as He swore to your fathers: to Abraham, to Isaac, and to Jacob. ¹³And I am not making this covenant and this oath with you alone, ¹⁴but with the one who is here standing with us today in front of YHWH, our God, and with the one who isn't here with us today. ¹⁵Because you know that we lived in the land of Egypt and that we passed among the nations that you passed. ¹⁶And you've seen their disgraces and their idols, wood and stone, silver and gold, that were with them. ¹⁷In case there will be among you a man or woman or family or tribe whose heart is turning today from YHWH, our God, to go to serve those nations' gods; in case there is among you a root bearing poison and wormwood, ¹⁸and it will be when he hears the words of this oath that he'll feel himself blessed in his heart, saying, 'I'll have peace, though I'll go on in my heart's obstinacy,' so as to annihilate the wet with the dry: ¹⁹YHWH will not be willing to forgive him, because YHWH's anger and His jealousy will then smoke against that man, and every curse that is written in this scroll

will weigh on him, and YHWH will wipe out his name from under the skies. ²⁰And YHWH will separate him from all of Israel's tribes for bad, according to all the curses of the covenant that is written in this scroll of instruction.

²¹"And a later generation will say—your children who will come up after you, and the foreigner who will come from a far land, when they'll see that land's plagues and its illnesses that YHWH put in it, ²²brimstone and salt, all the land a burning, it won't be seeded and won't grow, and not any vegetation will come up in it, like the overturning of Sodom and Gomorrah, Admah and Zeboiim, which YHWH overturned in His anger and His fury— ²³and all the nations will say, 'For what did YHWH do something like this to this land? What is this big flaring of anger?'

²⁴"And they'll say, 'For the fact that they left the covenant of YHWH, their fathers' God, which He made with them when He brought them out from the land of Egypt. ²⁵And they went and served other gods and bowed to them, gods whom they hadn't known and He hadn't allocated to them. ²⁶And YHWH's anger flared at that land, to bring over it every curse that was written in this scroll. ²⁷And YHWH plucked them from their land in anger and in fury and in great rage, and He threw them into another land, as it is this day.'*

²⁸"The hidden things belong to YHWH, our God, and the revealed things belong to us and to our children forever, to do all the words of this instruction.

30

¹And it will be, when all these things, the blessing and the curse that I've put in front of you, will come upon you, and you'll store it in your heart among the nations to which YHWH, your God, has driven you, ²and you'll come back to YHWH, your God, and listen to His voice, according to everything that I command you today, you and your children, with all your heart and with all your soul, ³that YHWH, your God, will bring back your captivity and be merciful to you. And He'll come back and gather you from all the peoples to which YHWH, your God, has scattered you. ⁴If you'll be driven to the end of the skies, YHWH, your God, will gather you from

---

*Deut 29:21–27 is Dtr2. The signs of this are: (1) In the preceding verses the subject is what would happen to an individual who would turn to foreign gods, but suddenly in v. 21 it is as if the entire people had been the subject. (2) The fate of the entire people in this section is to be cast into a different land. (3) The wording of vv. 23–25 is nearly identical to 1 Kgs 9:8–9, which is another section of the Deuteronomistic history that is identified as Dtr2 on other grounds.

there, and He'll take you from there. [5]And YHWH, your God, will bring you to the land that your fathers possessed, and you'll take possession of it, and He'll be good to you and multiply you more than your fathers. [6]And YHWH, your God, will circumcise your heart and your seed's heart so as to love YHWH, your God, with all your heart and with all your soul so that you'll live. [7]And YHWH, your God, will put all these curses on your enemies and on those who hate you who have pursued you. [8]And you'll come back and listen to YHWH's voice and do all His commandments that I command you today. [9]And YHWH, your God, will give you extra of all your hand's work, of the fruit of your womb and of the fruit of your animals and the fruit of your land for good. Because YHWH will come back to have satisfaction over you for good as He had satisfaction over your fathers, [10]when you'll listen to the voice of YHWH, your God, to observe His commandments and His laws, written in this scroll of instruction, when you'll come back to YHWH, your God, with all your heart and with all your soul.

[11]"Because this commandment that I command you today: it's not too wondrous for you, and it's not too far. [12]It's not in the skies, that one would say, 'Who will go up for us to the skies and get it for us and enable us to hear it so we'll do it?' [13]And it's not across the sea, that one would say, 'Who will cross for us, across the sea, and get it for us and enable us to hear it so we'll do it?' [14]But the thing is very close to you, in your mouth, and in your heart, to do it.*

[15]"See: I've put in front of you today life and good, and death and bad, [16]in that I command you today to love YHWH, your God, to go in His ways and to observe His commandments and His laws and His judgments so you'll live and multiply, and YHWH, your God, will bless you in the land to which you're coming to take possession of it. [17]But if your heart will turn away, and you won't listen, and you'll be driven so that you'll bow to other gods and serve them, [18]I've told you today that you'll perish. You won't extend days on the land to which you're crossing the Jordan to come to take possession of it. [19]I call the skies and the earth to witness regarding you today: I've put life and death in front of you, blessing and curse. And you shall choose life, so you'll live, you and your seed, [20]to love YHWH, your

---

*Deut 30:11–4. This section connects back to 29:28, which is where Dtr1 left off. When reconnected, this is a continuous unit that compares the hidden things, which belong to YHWH, to the commandment, which "is very close to you, in your mouth, and in your heart, to do it." The text that now breaks in between this unit is Dtr2 (30:1–10). It uses the term for scattering, *hēpîṣ*, that occurs in two other passages identified as Dtr2 on other grounds (Deut 4:27; 28:64). Thematically, it addresses an exiled people: it urges them to come back to God and assures them that God is merciful, and it says that restoration to their land is possible.

God, to listen to His voice and to cling to Him, because He is your life and the extension of your days to reside on the land that YHWH swore to your fathers, to Abraham, to Isaac, and to Jacob, to give to them."*

31

¹And Moses went and spoke these things to all Israel. ²And he said to them, "I'm a hundred twenty years old today. I'm not able to go out and come in anymore. And YHWH said to me, 'You shall not cross this Jordan.' ³YHWH, your God: He is crossing in front of you. He'll destroy these nations in front of you, and you'll dispossess them. Joshua: he is crossing in front of you, as YHWH has spoken. ⁴And YHWH will do to them as He did to Sihon and to Og, the kings of the Amorites, and to their land, that He destroyed them. ⁵And YHWH will put them in front of you, and you shall do to them according to all of the commandment that I've commanded you. ⁶Be strong and be bold. Don't be afraid and don't be scared in front of them, because YHWH, your God: He is the one going with you. He won't let you down and won't leave you."

⁷And Moses called Joshua and said to him before the eyes of all Israel, "Be strong and be bold, because you will come with this people to the land that YHWH swore to their fathers to give to them, and you will get it for them as a legacy. ⁸And YHWH: He is the one who is going in front of you. He will be with you. He won't let you down and won't leave you. You shall not fear, and you shall not be dismayed."

⁹And Moses wrote this instruction and gave it to the priests, sons of Levi, who were carrying the ark of YHWH's covenant, and to all of Israel's elders. ¹⁰And Moses commanded them, saying, "At the end of seven years, at the appointed time of the year of the remission, on the Festival of Booths, ¹¹when all Israel comes to appear before YHWH, your God, in the place that He will choose, you shall read this instruction in front of all Israel in their ears. ¹²Assemble the people—the men and the women and the infants and your alien who is in your gates—so they will listen and so they will learn and will fear YHWH, your God, and they will be watchful to do all the words of this instruction. ¹³And their children who have not known will listen and learn to fear YHWH, your God, all the days that you're living on the land to which you're crossing the Jordan to take possession of it."

---

*Deut 30:15–20. This section continues the Dtr2 addition. In it Moses summons the skies and earth as witnesses, as in two other Dtr2 passages (4:26; 31:28; cf. 32:1); Moses uses the infinitival emphatic *'ābōd tō'bēdûn*, which also appears in one of the skies-and-earth passages (4:26); and the subject of the passage is an exilic, Dtr2 theme: extending or losing residence on the land.

¹⁴And YHWH said to Moses, "Here, your days to die have come close. Call Joshua, and stand up in the Tent of Meeting, and I'll command him." And Moses and Joshua went and stood up in the Tent of Meeting. ¹⁵And YHWH appeared in the tent in a column of cloud, and the column of cloud stood at the entrance of the tent.

¹⁶And YHWH said to Moses, "Here, when you're lying with your fathers, this people will get up and whore after foreign gods of the land into which it is coming, and it will leave me and break my covenant that I've made with it. ¹⁷And my anger will flare at it on that day, and I'll leave them, and I'll hide my face from them, and it will become prey, and many bad things and troubles will find it. And it will say on that day, 'Isn't it because my God is not present in me that these evils have found me?' ¹⁸But I: I'll hide my face on that day over all the bad that it has done, because it turned to other gods. ¹⁹So now write this song and teach it to the children of Israel. Set it in their mouths, so this song will become a witness for me among the children of Israel. ²⁰When I'll bring it to the land that I swore to its fathers, flowing with milk and honey, and it will eat and be full and get fat and turn to other gods, and they will serve them and reject me, and it will break my covenant, ²¹then it will be, when many bad things and troubles will find it, that this song will testify as a witness in front of it, because it won't be forgotten from its seed's mouth. Because I know its inclination that it is doing today even before I bring it to the land that I swore."

²²And Moses wrote this song on that day, and he taught it to the children of Israel.

²³And He commanded Joshua, son of Nun, and said, "Be strong and bold, because you will bring the children of Israel to the land that I swore to them, and I shall be with you."

²⁴And it was when Moses finished writing the words of this instruction on a scroll to their end, ²⁵and Moses commanded the Levites, who carried the ark of the covenant of YHWH, saying, ²⁶"Take this scroll of instruction and set it at the side of the ark of the covenant of YHWH, your God, and it will be there for you as a witness. ²⁷Because I know your rebellion and your hard neck. Here, while I'm still alive with you today, you've been rebelling at YHWH, so how much more after my death!* ²⁸Assemble all the elders of your tribes and your officers to me so I may speak these things in their ears

---

*31:9–13 and 24–27. These two sections of this chapter refer to the Scroll of Instruction (*sēper hattôrāh*) that Moses writes and directs the Levites to keep as a witness for future times. This scroll then is found and read in the time of Josiah (2 Kgs 22:8–13). The scroll is the witness in Dtr1. The text of the Song of Moses is then added as an additional witness in Dtr2. See the next note.

and call the skies and the earth to witness regarding them, [29]because I know, after my death, that you'll be corrupted, and you'll turn from the way that I've commanded you. And the bad thing will happen to you in the future days when you'll do what is bad in YHWH's eyes to provoke Him with your hands' work."

[30]And Moses spoke in the ears of all the community of Israel the words of this song to their end:*

32

[1] Listen, skies, so I may speak,
and let the earth hear what my mouth says.
[2]   Let my teaching come down like showers;
let my saying emerge like dew,
like raindrops on plants
and like rainfalls on herbs.
[3]   When I call YHWH's name,
avow our God's greatness.
[4]   The Rock: His work is unblemished,
for all His ways are judgment.
A God of trust, and without injustice,
He's virtuous and right.
[5]   It corrupted at Him—not His children, their flaw—
a crooked and twisted generation.
[6]   Is it to YHWH that you repay like this?!
Foolish people and unwise!
Isn't He your father, who created you,

---

*The long poem that takes up Deuteronomy 32, known as the Song of Moses, is an independent poem that was inserted by the Deuteronomistic historian in the Dtr2 edition of the work. The Dtr2 sections of this chapter (31:16–22,28–30) refer to the song and derive some of their wording directly from it: the first section refers to the hiding of the face (v. 18) and to "rejecting" God (v. 20), which derive from the words of the song (32:1–20). The second section refers to Moses' calling the skies and earth as witnesses (v. 28), which corresponds to the opening words of the song: "Listen skies, so I may speak, and let the earth hear what my mouth says," and it uses the term "corrupted" (v. 29), which comes from the song (32:5), and the word for provoking God's anger (v. 29), which also occurs in the song (32:21). These sections also refer to God's leaving the people, and to the people's becoming a prey to other nations; and these things are stated not as a threat but as a prophecy of an actual situation, which corresponds to the exile rather than to the time of Josiah.

He who made you and reared you?
7　Remember the days of old.
Grasp the years through generations.
Ask your father, and he'll tell you,
your elders, and they'll say to you:
8　When the Highest gave nations legacies,
when He dispersed humankind,
He set the peoples' borders
to the number of the children of Israel.
9　For YHWH's portion is His people.
Jacob is the share of His legacy.
10　He found it in a wilderness land
and in a formless place, a howling desert.
He surrounded it. He attended to it.
He guarded it, like the pupil of his eye.
11　As an eagle stirs its nest,
hovers over its young,
spreads its wings, takes it,
lifts it on its pinion,
12　YHWH, alone, led it,
and no foreign god with Him.
13　He had it ride over earth's high places
and fed it the field's bounties
and had it suck honey from a rock
and oil from a flint rock
14　and curds of cattle and milk of the flock
and fat of lambs
and Bashan rams and he-goats
with fat of innards of wheat
—and from grape's blood you drank wine.
15　And Jeshurun got fat and kicked
—you got fat, you got wide, you got stuffed!—
and it left God who made it
and took its saving rock for granted.
16　They made Him jealous with outsiders.
With offensive things they made him angry.
17　They sacrificed to demons, a non-god,
gods they hadn't known;
new ones, they came of late;
your fathers hadn't been acquainted with them.

¹⁸   The rock that fathered you, you ignored,
and you forgot God who bore you.

¹⁹   And YHWH saw and rejected
from His sons' and His daughters' angering.

²⁰   And He said, "Let me hide my face from them;
I'll see what their end will be.
For they're a generation of overthrows,
children with no trust in them.

²¹   They made me jealous with no-god.
They provoked me with their nothings.
And I: I'll make them jealous with no-people.
I'll make them angry with a foolish nation.

²²   For fire has ignited in my anger
and burned to Sheol at bottom
and consumed land and its crop
and set the mountains' foundations ablaze.

²³   I'll mass bad things over them.
I'll exhaust my arrows on them,

²⁴   sapped by hunger and devoured by flame.
And bitter destruction
and animals' teeth I'll let loose at them
with venom of serpents of the dust.

²⁵   Outside: a sword will bereave,
and inside: terror,
both young man and virgin,
suckling with aged man.

²⁶   I'd say, 'I'll erase them.
I'll make their memory cease from mankind,'

²⁷   if I didn't fear the enemy's anger,
in case their foes would misread,
in case they'd say, 'Our hand was high,
and it wasn't YHWH who did all this!'

²⁸   For they're a nation void of counsel,
and there's no understanding in them.

²⁹   If they were wise they'd comprehend this;
they'd grasp their future.

³⁰   How could one pursue a thousand
and two chase ten thousand
if not that their rock had sold them,
that YHWH had turned them over?"

³¹ For their rock is not like our rock,
though our enemies are the judges.

³² For their vine is from Sodom's vine
and from Gomorrah's fields.
Their grapes are poison grapes.
They have bitter clusters.

³³ Their wine is serpents' venom
and cruel poison of cobras.

³⁴ "Isn't it stored with me,
sealed in my treasuries?

³⁵ Vengeance and recompense are mine,
for the time their foot will slip;
for the day of their ordeal is close
and comes fast: things prepared for them."

³⁶ For YHWH will judge His people
and regret about his servants
when He'll see that their strength is gone
and there's none: held back or left alone.

³⁷ And He'll say, "Where are their gods,
the rock in whom they sought refuge,

³⁸ who would eat the fat of their sacrifices,
would drink the wine of their libations?
Let them get up and help you!
Let that be a shelter over you.

³⁹ See now that I, I am He,
and there is no god with me.
I cause death and give life.
I've pierced, and I'll heal.
And there's no deliverer from my hand,

⁴⁰ when I raise my hand to the skies,
and I say, 'As I live forever,

⁴¹ if I whet the lightning of my sword,
and my hand takes hold of judgment,
I'll give back vengeance to my foes
and pay back those who hate me.

⁴² I'll make my arrows drunk with blood,
and my sword will eat flesh
from the blood of the slain and captured,
from the head of loose hair of the enemy.'"

⁴³ Nations: cheer His people!

> For He'll requite His servants' blood
> and give back vengeance to His foes
> and make atonement for His land, His people.

[44]And Moses came and spoke all the words of this song in the people's ears, he and Hoshea son of Nun.

[45]And Moses finished speaking all these things to all of Israel. [46]And he said to them, "Pay attention to all the things that I testify regarding you today, that you'll command them to your children, to observe and to do all the words of this instruction. [47]Because it's not an empty thing for you, because it's your life. And through this thing you'll extend days on the land to which you're crossing the Jordan to take possession of it."

[48]And YHWH spoke to Moses in this very day, saying, [49]"Go up to this mountain of Abarim, Mount Nebo, which is in the land of Moab, which is facing Jericho, and see the land of Canaan, which I'm giving to the children of Israel for a possession. [50]And die in the mountain to which you're going up, and be gathered to your people, as Aaron, your brother, died in Mount Hor and was gathered to his people, [51]because you made a breach with me among the children of Israel at the waters of Meribah of Kadesh at the wilderness of Zin, because you didn't make me holy among the children of Israel. [52]Because you'll see the land from opposite, but you shall not come there, to the land that I'm giving to the children of Israel.*

33

[1]And this is the blessing with which Moses, the man of God, blessed the children of Israel before his death. [2]And he said:**

> YHWH came from Sinai
> and rose from Seir for them.
> He shone from Mount Paran
> and came from ten thousands of the holy,
> slopes at His right, for them.

---

*This section (32:48–52) repeats the divine command to Moses to ascend Abarim that appears in P in Num 27:12–14. The Redactor thus folds the words and events of Deuteronomy into the context that had been established at the end of Numbers.

**The long poem that takes up Deuteronomy 33, known as the Blessing of Moses, is an old, separate source that was inserted at the end of Moses' address, probably by the Deuteronomistic historian in the Dtr1 edition of the work.

3   Also loving peoples,
     all holy ones are in your hand.
     And they knelt at your feet;
     they bore your words.
4   Moses commanded us instruction,
     a possession, community of Jacob.
5   And He was king in Jeshurun
     when the people's heads were gathered:
     Israel's tribes together.
6 Let Reuben live and not die,
     but his men will be few in number.
7 And this for Judah—and he said:
     Hear, YHWH, Judah's voice,
     and bring him to his people.
     With his hands he strove for himself,
     and you'll be a help from its foes.
8 And for Levi he said:
     Your Thummim and your Urim are your faithful man's,
     whom you tested at Massah,
     disputed with him over Meribah's water.
9   Who said of his father and his mother:
     "I haven't seen him,"
     and didn't recognize his brothers
     and didn't know his children,
     for they observed what you said
     and kept your covenant.
10   They'll teach your judgments to Jacob
     and your instruction to Israel.
     They'll set incense at your nose,
     entirely burnt on your altar.
11   Bless, YHWH, his wealth
     and accept his hands' work.
     Pierce his adversaries' hips,
     and those who hate him, so they won't get up.
12 For Benjamin he said:
     Beloved of YHWH,
     he'll dwell in security by Him.
     He shelters over him all day
     as he dwells between his shoulders.

¹³ And for Joseph he said:
  Blessed of YHWH is his land,
  from the skies' abundance, from dew,
  and from the deep, crouching below,
¹⁴   and from the abundance of the sun's produce
  and from the abundance of the moon's output
¹⁵   and from the top of the ancient mountains
  and from the abundance of the hills of antiquity
¹⁶   and from the abundance of earth and what fills it
  and the favor of the one who dwelt in the bush.
  May it be on Joseph's head,
  on the top of the head of the one separate from his brothers.
¹⁷   His firstborn bull: it has majesty.
  And its horns are a wild ox's horns.
  It will gore peoples with them,
  together, the ends of the earth.
  And they're Ephraim's ten thousands,
  And they're Manasseh's thousands.
¹⁸ And for Zebulun he said:
  Rejoice, Zebulun, when you go out,
  and Issachar in your tents.
¹⁹   They'll call peoples to the mountain.
  There they'll offer the sacrifices of virtue.
  For they'll suck the seas' bounty
  and the sand's hidden treasures.
²⁰ And for Gad he said:
  Blessed is one who enlarges Gad.
  Like a feline, abiding
  and tearing an arm and the top of a head,
²¹   so he saw the foremost for himself,
  for a ruler's share was kept there.
  And the heads of the people came.
  And he did YHWH's justice
  and His laws with Israel.
²² And for Dan he said:
  Dan is a lion's whelp
  that leapt from Bashan.
²³ And for Naphtali he said:
  Naphtali is full of favor
  and filled with YHWH's blessing.
  He'll possess west and south.

²⁴ And for Asher he said:
>> Blessed out of the sons is Asher.
>> Let him be favored by his brothers
>> and dipping his foot in oil.
²⁵ >> Your lock is iron and bronze,
>> and your strength is as much as your days.
²⁶ There's none like the God of Jeshurun,
> riding skies to help you
> and clouds in His majesty.
²⁷ The ancient God is a refuge;
> and below: the arms of the eternal.
> And He drove out an enemy before you
> and said, "Destroy!"
²⁸ And Israel will dwell secure,
> Jacob dwells alone.
> To a land of grain and wine;
> and its skies drop dew.
²⁹ Happy are you, Israel!
> Who is like you,
> a people saved by YHWH,
> your strong shield
> who is your majestic sword?!
> And your enemies will fawn to you.
> And you: you'll step on their high places.

34

¹And Moses went up from the plains of Moab to Mount Nebo, the top of Pisgah, which is facing Jericho. And YHWH showed him all of the land, Gilead to Dan, ²and all of Naphtali and the land of Ephraim and Manasseh and all the land of Judah to the far sea ³and the Negeb and the plain, the valley of Jericho, city of the palms, to Zoar.

⁴And YHWH said to him, "This is the land that I swore to Abraham, to Isaac, and to Jacob, saying, 'I'll give it to your seed.' I've caused you to see it with your eyes, but you won't cross there."*

⁵And Moses, YHWH's servant, died there in the land of Moab by YHWH's mouth, ⁶and He buried him in the valley in the land of Moab

---

*The first four verses of this chapter refer back to God's command to Moses to go up Mount Pisgah and not cross into the land in Deut 3:27 (Dtr1).

opposite Beth-peor. And no man knows his burial place to this day. ⁷And Moses was a hundred twenty years old at his death. His eye was not dim, and his vitality had not fled.*

⁸And the children of Israel mourned Moses in the plains of Moab thirty days. And the days of weeping, the mourning of Moses, ended. ⁹And Joshua son of Nun was full of the spirit of wisdom because Moses had laid his hands on him, and the children of Israel listened to him. And they did as YHWH commanded Moses.**

¹⁰And a prophet did not rise again in Israel like Moses, whom YHWH knew face-to-face, ¹¹with all the signs and the wonders that YHWH sent him to do in the land of Egypt to Pharaoh and to all his servants and to all his land, ¹²and with all the strong hand and with all the great fear that Moses made before the eyes of all Israel.‡

---

*This section is J. It notes that Moses lives to be one hundred twenty years old, which is the limit that YHWH sets on human life in J (Gen 6:3). It notes that his eye was not dim; and the expression that it uses for the dimming of the eye occurs only here and in Isaac's blessing of Jacob in Gen 27:1, which is J, and in the report of Eli's dim eyes in 1 Sam 3:2 (which, I have argued elsewhere, comes from the same author; see *The Hidden Book in the Bible*).

**This section is P. It notes a thirty-day mourning period for Moses, which is the same that is given for Aaron in P (Num 20:29). And it refers to Moses' laying hands on Joshua, and also to Joshua's having spirit in him, which occur in P as well (Num 27:15–23).

‡This final section is Dtr1. It uses the expression "did not rise like him," which is applied to only two persons in scripture: to Moses here and to King Josiah in the Dtr1 description of that king. It is part of a series of parallels between Moses and Josiah in Dtr1. (See the Collection of Evidence, pp. 24–26.)

BIBLIOGRAPHY

WORKS BY RICHARD ELLIOTT FRIEDMAN RELATING TO THE COMPOSITION OF THE BIBLE

Books

The Exile and Biblical Narrative. Harvard Semitic Monographs 22. Atlanta: Scholars Press, 1981.

Who Wrote the Bible? New York: Summit/Simon & Schuster, 1987 (first edition). San Francisco: HarperSanFrancisco, 1996 (second edition).

The Hidden Book in the Bible. San Francisco: HarperSanFrancisco, 1998.

Articles

"The Tabernacle in the Temple." *Biblical Archaeologist* 43 (1980): 241–248.

"Sacred History and Theology: The Redaction of Torah." In *The Creation of Sacred Literature,* edited by Richard Elliott Friedman, pp. 25–34. Berkeley: University of California Press, 1981.

"From Egypt to Egypt: Dtr1 and Dtr2." In *Traditions in Transformation: Turning-Points in Biblical Faith,* Festschrift honoring Frank Moore Cross, edited by B. Halpern and J. Levenson, pp. 167–192. Winona Lake, IN: Eisenbrauns, 1981.

"The Recession of Biblical Source Criticism." In *The Future of Biblical Studies: The Hebrew Scriptures,* edited by Richard Elliott Friedman and H. G. M. Williamson, pp. 81–101. Atlanta: Scholars Press, 1987.

"Is Everybody an Expert on the Bible?" *Bible Review* 7:2 (1991): 16–18, 50–51.

"Scholar, Heal Thyself." *The Iowa Review* 21 (1991): 33–47.

"Tabernacle." *The Anchor Bible Dictionary*, vol. 6, pp. 292–300. New York: Doubleday, 1992.

"Torah." *The Anchor Bible Dictionary*, vol. 6, pp. 605–622. New York: Doubleday, 1992.

"Late for a Very Important Date." *Bible Review* 9:6 (1993): 12–16.

"The Deuteronomistic School." In *Fortunate the Eyes That See: Essays in Honor of David Noel Freedman in Celebration of His Seventieth Birthday*, edited by Astrid Beck et al., pp. 70–80. Grand Rapids, MI: Eerdmans, 1995.

"Some Recent Non-arguments Concerning the Documentary Hypothesis." In *Texts, Temples, and Traditions: A Tribute to Menahem Haran*, edited by Michael Fox et al., pp. 87–101. Winona Lake, IN: Eisenbrauns, 1996.

"Solomon and the Great Histories." In *Jerusalem in Bible and Archaeology— The First Temple Period*, edited by Ann Killebrew and Andrew Vaughn. Atlanta: Society of Biblical Literature, 2003.

"An Essay on Method." In *Le-David Maskil*, edited by Richard Elliott Friedman and William Henry Propp. Biblical and Judaic Studies from the University of California, San Diego. Winona Lake, IN: Eisenbrauns, 2003.

GENERAL BIBLIOGRAPHY

Addis, W. E. *Documents of the Hexateuch*. London, 1892.

Aharoni, Y., "The Solomonic Temple, the Tabernacle, and the Arad Sanctuary." In *Orient and Occident: Essays Presented to Cyrus H. Gordon on the Occasion of His Sixty-fifth Birthday*, edited by H. A. Hoffner Jr. Neukirchen: Neukirchener, 1973.

Astruc, Jean. *Conjectures sur les mémoires originaux dont ilparait que Moyse s'est servi, pour composer le livre de la Genese*. 1753.

Blenkinsopp, Joseph, *The Pentateuch*. New York: Doubleday, 1992.

———. "Theme and Motif in the Succession History (2 Sam xi 2ff) and the Yahwist Corpus." In *Volume du Congrès: Genève 1965*, edited by

G. W. Anderson et al. Supplements to *Vetus Testamentum* 15. Leiden: Brill, 1966.

Blum, Erhard. *Die Komposition der Vätergeschichte*. WMANT 57. Neukirchen-Vluynx: Neukirchener Verlag, 1984.

———. *Studien zur Komposition des Pentateuch*. BZAW 189. Berlin: W. de Gruyter, 1990.

Boadt, Lawrence. *Reading the OT: An Introduction*. New York: Paulist Press, 1984.

Bright, John, "Modern Study of Old Testament Literature." In *The Bible and the Ancient Near East: Essays in Honor of William Foxwell Albright*, edited by G. Ernest Wright. New York: Doubleday, 1961.

Campbell, Antony, and O'Brien, Mark. *Sources of the Pentateuch: Texts, Introductions, Annotations*. Philadelphia: Fortress, 1993.

Carpenter, J. E., and Harford-Battersby, G. *The Hexateuch*. 2 vols. London: Longmans, Green, 1902.

Carr, David M. "Controversy and Convergence in Recent Studies of the Formation of the Pentateuch." *Religious Studies Review* 23 (1997): 22–31.

———. *Reading the Fractures of Genesis: Historical and Literary Approaches*. Louisville, KY: Westminster/John Knox Press, 1996.

Cassuto, Umberto. *A Commentary on the Book of Exodus*. Jerusalem: Magnes. Hebrew edition 1951, English edition 1979.

———. *From Adam to Noah: A Commentary on the Book of Genesis I–VI*. Jerusalem: Magnes. Hebrew edition 1944, English edition 1978.

———. *From Noah to Abraham: A Commentary on the Book of Genesis VI–XI*. Jerusalem: Magnes. Hebrew edition 1959, English edition 1984.

Clements, Ronald. *Abraham and David*. London: SCM Press, 1967.

Cogan, Mordecai. "Israel in Exile—The View of a Josianic Historian." *Journal of Biblical Literature* 97 (1978): 40–44.

Coote, Robert. *In Defense of Revolution: The Elohist History*. Philadelphia: Fortress, 1991.

Coote, Robert, and Ord, David Robert. *The Bible's First History*. Philadelphia: Fortress, 1989.

Cross, Frank Moore. *Canaanite Myth and Hebrew Epic*. Cambridge: Harvard University Press, 1973.

———. *From Epic to Canon*. Baltimore: Johns Hopkins University Press, 1998.

———. "The Priestly Tabernacle." *Biblical Archaeologist* 10 (1947): 45–68. Reprinted in *Biblical Archaeologist Reader* I (1961), pp. 201–228.

Cross, Frank Moore, and Freedman, David Noel. *Studies in Ancient Yahwistic Poetry*. Grand Rapids, MI: Eerdmans, 1975.

Dozeman, Thomas B. "The Institutional Setting of the Late Formation of the Pentateuch in the Work of John Van Seters." In *Society of Biblical Literature: 1991 Seminar Papers*, pp. 253–264.

Driver, S. R. *Introduction to the Literature of the Old Testament*. 9th ed. Edinburgh: T. & T. Clark, 1913.

Duff, Archibald. *History of Old Testament Criticism*. London: Watts, 1910.

Eissfeldt, Otto. *The Old Testament: An Introduction*. 3d ed. Translated from German by P. Ackroyd. New York: Harper & Row, 1934.

Ellis, Peter. *The Yahwist: The Bible's First Theologian*. Notre Dame, IN: Fides, 1968.

Emerton, J. A. "An Examination of a Recent Structuralist Interpretation of Genesis XXXVIII." *Vetus Testamentum* 26 (1976).

———. "An Examination of Some Attempts to Defend the Unity of the Flood Narrative in Genesis." *Vetus Testamentum* 37 (1987): 401–420 and 38 (1988): 1–21.

———. "The Origin of the Promises to the Patriarchs in the Older Sources of the Book of Genesis." *Vetus Testamentum* 32 (1982): 14–32.

———. "Some Problems in Genesis XXXVIII." *Vetus Testamentum* 25 (1975).

Engnell, Ivan. *A Rigid Scrutiny*. Nashville:Vanderbilt University Press, 1969.

Fohrer, Georg. *Introduction to the Old Testament*. Nashville: Abingdon, 1968.

Freedman, David Noel. *Divine Commitment and Human Obligation*. 2 vols. Grand Rapids, MI: Eerdmans, 1997.

————. "Pentateuch." *Interpreter's Dictionary of the Bible* (1962), vol. 3, pp. 711–727.

————. *Pottery, Poetry, and Prophecy.* Winona Lake, IN: Eisenbrauns, 1980.

Gnuse, Robert K. "Redefining the Elohist?" *Journal of Biblical Literature* 119 (2000): 201–220.

Gray, Edward M. *Old Testament Criticism.* New York, 1923.

Habel, Norman. *Literary Criticism of the Old Testament.* Philadelphia: Fortress, 1971.

Hacket, Jo Ann. "Balaam." *The Anchor Bible Dictionary,* vol. 1, pp. 569–572.

————. *The Balaam Text from Deir 'Alla.* Harvard Semitic Monographs 31. Atlanta: Scholars Press, 1984.

Hahn, E. *The Old Testament in Modern Research.* Philadelphia: Fortress, 1966.

Halpern, Baruch. *The Constitution of Monarchy in Israel.* Harvard Semitic Monographs. Atlanta: Scholars Press, 1981.

————. *The First Historians.* San Francisco: Harper, 1988.

————. "Sacred History and Ideology: Chronicles' Thematic Structure—Indications of an Earlier Source." In *The Creation of Sacred Literature,* edited by R. E. Friedman, pp. 35–54. Berkeley: University of California Press, 1981.

Haran, Menahem. "The Priestly Image of the Tabernacle." *Hebrew Union College Annual* 36 (1965): 191–226.

————. "Shiloh and Jerusalem: The Origin of the Priestly Tradition in the Pentateuch." *Journal of Biblical Literature* 81 (1962): 14–24.

————. *Temples and Temple Service in Ancient Israel.* New York: Oxford University Press, 1978.

Hendel, Ronald. "'Begetting' and 'Being Born' in the Pentateuch: Notes on Historical Linguistics and Source Criticism." *Vetus Testamentum* 50 (2000): 38–46.

Hobbes, Thomas. *Leviathan.* Part 3, Chapter 33. 1651.

Homan, Michael M. *To Your Tents, O Israel! The Terminology, Function, Form, and Symbolism of Tents in the Hebrew Bible and the Ancient Near East.* Leiden: Brill, 2002.

Hurvitz, Avi. "Continuity and Innovation in Biblical Hebrew—The Case of 'Semantic Change' in Post-Exilic Writings." In *Studies in Ancient Hebrew Semantics,* edited by T. Muraoka, pp. 1–10. Abr-Nahrain Supplement Series 4. Leuven: Peeters, 1995.

———. "The Evidence of Language in Dating the Priestly Code." *Revue Biblique* 81 (1974): 24–56.

———. "The Historical Quest for 'Ancient Israel' and the Linguistic Evidence of the Hebrew Bible: Some Methodological Observations." *Vetus Testamentum* 47 (1997): 301–315.

———. *A Linguistic Study of the Relationship Between the Priestly Source and the Book of Ezekiel.* Cahiers de la Revue Biblique. Paris: Gabalda, 1982.

———. "The Relevance of Biblical Linguistics for the Historical Study of Ancient Israel." In *Proceedings of the Twelfth World Congress of Jewish Studies,* pp. 21–33. Jerusalem: World Union of Jewish Studies, 1999.

———. "The Usage of שׁשׁ and בוץ in the Bible and Its Implication for the Date of P." *Harvard Theological Review* 60 (1967): 117–121.

Jenks, Alan. *The Elohist and North Israelite Traditions.* Atlanta: Scholars Press, 1977.

Kapelrud, A. S. "The Date of the Priestly Code." *Annual of the Swedish Theological Institute* 3 (1964): 58–64.

Kaufmann, Yehezkel. *The Religion of Israel.* Translated and edited by Moshe Greenberg. Chicago: University of Chicago Press, 1960. Abridged from the Hebrew edition, 1937.

Kennedy, A. R. S. "Tabernacle." *Hastings Dictionary of the Bible,* vol. 4, pp. 653–668.

Kikkawada, I. M., and Quinn, A. *Before Abraham Was: The Unity of Genesis 1–11.* Nashville: Abingdon, 1985.

Knohl, Israel. *The Sanctuary of Silence: The Priestly Torah and the Holiness School.* Minneapolis: Fortress, 1995.

Levenson, Jon. "Who Inserted the Book of the Torah?" *Harvard Theological Review* 68 (1975): 203–233.

Levine, Baruch. *Numbers.* 2 vols. Anchor Bible 4. New York: Doubleday, 1993 and 2000.

Levitt-Kohn, Risa. *A New Heart and a New Soul: Ezekiel, the Exile, and the Torah.* JSOT Supplement Series. Sheffield: Sheffield Academic Press, 2002.

Liver, Jacob. "Korah, Dathan, and Abiram." *Scripta Hierosolymitana* 8. Jerusalem: Hebrew University, 1961.

Lohfink, Norbert. "Auslegung deuteronomischer Texte, IV." *Bibel und Leben* 5 (1964).

Lundbom, Jack R. "Jeremiah, Book of." *The Anchor Bible Dictionary*, vol. 3, pp. 706–721.

McBride, S. Dean. "The Deuteronomic Name Theology." Ph.D. dissertation, Harvard University, 1969.

McEvenue, Sean. *The Narrative Style of the Priestly Writer.* Rome: Pontifical Biblical Institute, 1971.

McKenzie, Steven L. *The Chronicler's Use of the Deuteronomistic History.* Harvard Semitic Monographs 33. Atlanta: Scholars Press, 1984.

———. *The Trouble with Kings: The Composition of the Book of Kings in the Deuteronomistic History.* Supplements to *Vetus Testamentum* 42. Leiden: Brill, 1991.

Milgrom, Jacob. *Cult and Conscience.* Leiden: Brill, 1976.

———. *Leviticus.* 3 vols. Anchor Bible 3. New York: Doubleday, 1991–2001.

———. "Numbers, Book of." *The Anchor Bible Dictionary*, vol. 4, pp. 1146–1155.

———. *Studies in Levitical Terminology,* I. Berkeley: University of California Press, 1970.

Moran, William A. "The Literary Connection Between Lev. 11:13–19 and Deut. 14:12–28." *Catholic Biblical Quarterly* 28 (1966): 271–277.

Mowinckel, Sigmund. *Erwägungen zur Pentateuch Quellenfrage.* Trondheim: Universitetsforlaget, 1964.

———. *Prophecy and Tradition.* Oslo, 1946.

———. *Zur Komposition des Buches Jeremia.* Oslo, 1914.

Nelson, Richard. *The Double Redaction of the Deuteronomistic History.* JSOT Supplement Series. Sheffield: Sheffield Academic Press, 1981.

Nicholson, Ernest W. *Deuteronomy and Tradition.* Philadelphia: Fortress, 1967.

———. "The Pentateuch in Recent Research: A Time for Caution." In *Congress Volume: Leuven, 1989*, edited by J. A. Emerton, pp. 10–21. Supplements to *Vetus Testamentus* 43. Leiden: Brill, 1991.

———. *The Pentateuch in the Twentieth Century*. Oxford: Clarendon, 1998.

North, Robert. "Can Geography Save J from Rendtorff?" *Biblica* 63 (1982): 47–55.

Noth, Martin. *The Deuteronomistic History*. Translated by J. Doull. JSOT Supplement Series. Sheffield: Sheffield Academic Press, 1981. (Original German edition, *Überlieferungsgeschichtliche Studien*. Tübingen, Max Niemeyer, 1943.)

———. *Exodus*. Philadelphia: Westminster, 1962.

———. *A History of Pentateuchal Traditions*. Translated from German by B. Anderson. Englewood Cliffs, NJ: Prentice-Hall, 1948.

———. *The Laws in the Pentateuch*. Edinburgh: Oliver and Boyd, 1966.

———. *Leviticus*. Philadelphia: Westminster, 1965.

———. *Numbers*. Philadelphia: Westminster, 1968.

Perdue, L. G., and Kovacs, B. W., eds. *A Prophet to the Nations: Essays in Jeremiah Studies*. Winona Lake, IN: Eisenbrauns, 1984.

Polzin, Robert M. *Late Biblical Hebrew: Toward an Historical Typology of Biblical Hebrew Prose*. Harvard Semitic Monographs. Decatur, GA: Scholars Press, 1976.

Propp, William H. C. *Exodus 1–18*. Anchor Bible 2. New York: Doubleday, 1998.

———. "The Rod of Aaron and the Sin of Moses." *Journal of Biblical Literature* 107 (1988): 19–26.

———. "The Skin of Moses' Face—Transfigured or Disfigured?" *Catholic Biblical Quarterly* 49 (1987): 375–86.

———. *Water in the Wilderness*. Harvard Semitic Monographs 40. Atlanta: Scholars Press, 1987.

Propp, William H. C.; Halpern, Baruch; and Freedman, David Noel, eds. *The Hebrew Bible and Its Interpreters*. Biblical and Judaic Studies from the University of California, San Diego, 1. Winona Lake, IN: Eisenbrauns, 1990.

Provan, Iain. *Hezekiah and the Books of Kings: A Contribution to the Debate About the Composition of the Deuteronomistc History.* BZAW 172. Berlin: W. de Gruyter, 1988.

Pury, Albert de. "Yahwist ('J') Source." *The Anchor Bible Dictionary,* vol. 6, pp. 1016–1020.

Rabe, Virgil. "The Identity of the Priestly Tabernacle." *Journal of Near Eastern Studies* 25 (1966): 132–134.

Rad, Gerhard von. *Deuteronomy: A Commentary.* London: SCM Press, 1966.

———. *Genesis.* Philadelphia: Westminster, 1961.

———. *The Problem of the Hexateuch.* Translated by E. W. T. Dicken. New York: McGraw-Hill, 1958.

———. *Studies in Deuteronomy.* Studies in Biblical Theology 9. London: SCM Press, 1953.

Rendsburg, Gary. "David and His Circle in Genesis 38." *Vetus Testamentum* 36 (1986): 438–446.

———. "Late Biblical Hebrew and the Date of P." *Journal of the Ancient Near East Society* 12 (1980): 65–80.

Rendtorff, Rolf. *The Problem of the Process of Transmission in the Pentateuch.* Translated by J. Scullion. Sheffield: JSOT, 1990. (Original German edition: *Das überlieferungsgeschichtliche Problem des Pentateuch.* BZAW 147. Berlin: W. de Gruyter, 1977.)

Rogerson, John. *Old Testament Criticism in the Nineteenth Century: England and Germany.* London: SPCK, 1984.

Rose, M. *Deuteronomist und Yahwist, Berührungspunkte beider Literatur-werke.* ATANT 67. Zurich, 1981.

Rowley, H. H. *The Old Testament and Modern Study.* New York: Oxford University Press, 1951.

Schmid, H. H. *Der sogenannte Jahwist.* Zurich: Theologischer Verlag, 1976.

Schmidt, Werner H. "A Theologian of the Solomonic Era? A Plea for the Yahwist." In *Studies in the Period of David and Solomon and Other Essays,* edited by Tomoo Ishida, pp. 55–73. Winona Lake, IN: Eisenbrauns, 1982.

Speiser, E. A. *Genesis.* Anchor Bible 1. Garden City, NY: Doubleday, 1964.

Spinoza, Benedict. *Tractatus theologico-politicus.* 1670.

Stulman, Louis. *The Prose Sermons of the Book of Jeremiah.* SBL Dissertation Series 83. Atlanta: Scholars Press, 1986.

Thompson, R. J. *Moses and the Law in a Century of Criticism Since Graf.* Supplements to *Vetus Testamentum* 19. Leiden: Brill, 1970.

Tigay, Jeffrey H., ed. *Empirical Models for Biblical Criticism.* Philadelphia: University of Pennsylvania Press, 1985.

Tillesse, G. Minette de. "Sections 'tu' et sections 'vous' dans le Deutéronome." *Vetus Testamentum* 12 (1962): 29–87.

Van Seters, John. *Abraham in History and Tradition.* New Haven: Yale University Press, 1975.

———. *The Life of Moses: The Yahwist as Historian in Exodus–Numbers.* Louisville, KY: Westminster/John Knox Press, 1994.

———. *The Pentateuch.* Sheffield: Sheffield Academic Press, 1999.

———. *Prologue to History: The Yahwist as Historian in Genesis.* Louisville, KY: Westminster/John Knox Press, 1992.

———. "Scholars Face Off Over Age of Biblical Stories." *Bible Review* 10:4 (1994): 40–44, 54.

———. *In Search of History.* New Haven: Yale University Press, 1983.

Weinfeld, Moshe. "Deuteronomy." *The Anchor Bible Dictionary,* vol. 2, pp. 168–183.

———. *Deuteronomy and the Deuteronomic School.* London: Oxford University Press, 1972.

———. *Deuteronomy 1–11.* Anchor Bible 5. New York: Doubleday, 1991.

———. "Getting at the Roots of Wellhausen's Understanding of the Law of Israel on the 100th Anniversary of the *Prolegomena*." Report No. 14/79. Jerusalem: Institute for Advanced Studies, Hebrew University, 1979.

Wellhausen, Julius. *Prolegomena to the History of Ancient Israel.* Translated by J. S. Black and A. Menzies. Edinburgh, 1885. German edition, 1883.

Wette, W. M. L. de. *Dissertatio Critica qua a prioribus Deuteronomium Pentateuchi libris diversam, alius cuiusdam recentioris auctoris opus esse monstratur.* 1805. Reprinted in Berlin by Opuscula Theologica, 1830.

Whybray, R. N. *The Making of the Pentateuch.* JSOT Supplement Series 53. Sheffield: Sheffield Academic Press, 1987.

Wolff, Hans Walter. "Das Kerygma des deuteronomistischen Geschichts-werks." *Zeitschrift für die alttestamentliche Wissenschaft* 73 (1961): 171–186.

Wright, George Ernest. "The Book of Deuteronomy." *The Interpreter's Bible,* vol. 2, pp. 311–537. New York: Abingdon, 1953.

————. "The Lawsuit of God: A Form-Critical Study of Deuteronomy 32." In *Israel's Prophetic Heritage,* edited by B. Anderson and W. Harrelson. New York: Harper, 1962.

Zevit, Ziony. "Converging Lines of Evidence Bearing on the Date of P." *Zeitschrift für die alttestamentliche Wissenschaft* 94 (1982): 502–509.

————. "The Priestly Redaction and Interpretation of the Plague Narrative in Exodus." *Jewish Quarterly Review* 66 (1976): 193–211.

ACKNOWLEDGMENTS

I owe many teachers and colleagues a debt of gratitude for what I learned from them as my studies in this subject went on. They are:

My teachers on the Hebrew Bible faculty at Harvard University, especially Professors Ernest Wright, of blessed memory, and Frank Moore Cross.

My teachers on the Hebrew Bible faculty at the Jewish Theological Seminary, especially Professor Yohanan Muffs.

My teacher at the University of Miami, Professor Ronald Veenker.

My hosts and colleagues at the University of Cambridge, where I was a Visiting Fellow at Clare Hall, especially Professors John Emerton and H. G. M. Williamson (now Regius Professor of Hebrew at Oxford).

My hosts and colleagues at Oxford University, where I was a Visiting Scholar at the Oxford Centre for Hebrew Studies, especially Professor Ernest Nicholson.

My colleagues on the faculty of the University of California, San Diego, Professors David Noel Freedman, David Goodblatt, Thomas Levy, and William Propp, and our distinguished Visiting Faculty in Hebrew Bible and Archaeology, especially Professors Alan Cooper, Baruch Halpern, Menahem Haran, Avi Hurvitz, Jack Lundbom, Shalom Paul, Yigal Shiloh, of blessed memory, Moshe Weinfeld, and Ziony Zevit.

My colleagues in the Biblical Colloquium and in the Biblical Colloquium West.

I owe a different sort of debt of gratitude to the persons who made it possible to produce this book:

My agent, Elaine Markson, without whom there would not be any of my books.

My publisher, Stephen Hanselman, and the other fine people at HarperSanFrancisco, a division of HarperCollins, especially Sam Barry,

Margery Buchanan, Jeff Hobbs, Terri Leonard, Michael Maudlin, Ann Moru, Julia Roller, Mark Tauber, Cindy DiTiberio, Jim Warner, and Liz Winer.

And, as always, I am grateful to my wife, Randy Linda, and our daughters, Jesse and Alexa, without whom not much of anything happens.